Freedom in the World

Political Rights and Civil Liberties
1979

Freedom in the World

Political Rights and Civil Liberties
1979

RAYMOND D. GASTIL

With papers by

Bohdan R. Bociurkiw

Herbert J. Ellison

Lewis S. Feuer

Teresa Rakowska-Harmstone

A
FREEDOM
HOUSE
BOOK

Published by Freedom House in cooperation with G. K. Hall & Co.

G.K.HALL&CO.
70 LINCOLN STREET, BOSTON, MASS.

FREEDOM HOUSE
20 WEST 40 STREET, NEW YORK, N.Y.

International Standard Book Number: 0–932088–01–5
Freedom House, 20 West 40th Street, New York, N.Y. 10018

International Standard Book Number: 0–8161–8387–2
G. K. Hall & Co., 70 Lincoln Street, Boston, Mass. 02111

Library of Congress Cataloging in Publication Data

Gastil, Raymond D
    Freedom in the world.

    Includes bibliographical references and index.
    1. Civil rights.   I.   Bociurkiw, Bohdan R.,
joint author.   II.   Title.
JC571.G336   1980   323.4   79–87596

Contents

PREFACE ix

PART I: THE SURVEY IN 1978

The Comparative Survey of Freedom: Nature and Purposes 3

Survey Ratings and Tables for 1978 15

PART II: FREEDOM, EQUALITY, AND CULTURE

Freedom and Equality 63

National Cultures and Universal Democracy 75

PART III: SUPPORTING LIBERALIZATION IN
THE SOVIET UNION

Supporting Liberalization in the Soviet Union 85

The Struggle for National Self-Assertion and
Liberalization in the Soviet Union 100
Teresa Rakowska-Harmstone

Comments and Discussion 111

Religious Dissent in the Soviet Union: Status,
Interrelationships, and Future Potential 115
Bohdan R. Bociurkiw

Comments and Discussion 133

Reform and Repression in the USSR: The Western
Influence, Herbert J. Ellison 137

Comments and Discussion 152

American Activists and Soviet Power 161
  Lewis S. Feuer

Comments and Discussion:
Strategy and Tactics for Liberalizing the USSR 173

Summary and Conclusions 194

PART IV: COUNTRY SUMMARIES

Introduction 201

Summaries 205

INDEX 311

Map and Tables

The Map of Freedom   26–27

Tables

1. Independent Nations: Comparative Measures of Freedom   16
2. Related Territories: Comparative Measures of Freedom   20
3. Ranking of Nations by Political Rights   22
4. Ranking of Nations by Civil Liberties   23
5. National Elections and Referenda   32
6. Estimated Levels of Political Terror   38
7. Political-Economic Systems   40
8. Major Peoples Without a Nation-State   46
9. Major Peoples Separated from Existing Nation-States   50

Preface

Not only ratings of public figures rise and fall in the polls. Vital human affairs are treated as transiently. Freedom and human rights are a current example.

The year 1977, as this yearbook noted in its previous edition, was regarded as the Year of Human Rights. The subject of this second yearbook, covering 1978, was, if anyone bothered to name it, the Year of Disaffection. This despite indicators showing there were significant gains for freedom around the world. Yet, human rights, particularly as observed from the United States, were seen—excuse the inapt analogy—as a two-edged sword. We, it is said, persuaded the Shah to rush modernization and expand human rights; and what happened? We "lost" Iran. That could give human freedom a bad name!

Indeed, those who long questioned America's role in Iran must view with concern the new authoritarianism. For the estimate of the Comparative Survey of Freedom—the centerpiece of this, as of the first *Freedom in the World*—is that the freedoms of the citizens of Iran, on an objective scale, are only slightly improved.

The Carter administration nevertheless declares human rights to be the "genuine historic inevitability of our times." Those who strive to raise the universal level of political rights and civil liberties devoutly hope so.

Whether they use governmental or nongovernmental efforts to enlarge human freedoms, citizens thus engaged will recognize as one of their major obstacles the fickleness of the public's agenda-setters (in and out of government and the independent communications media).

This volume argues for turning away from "supporting freedom by exception"—only when it suits national military or economic policy—to "adopt a personal and public policy of supporting freedom with *consistency.*" That is not to suggest an automatic priority of freedom issues over any other. It does call for recognition that in today's world it is often in our longer-term interest that our military and economic policies should be *early* on the side of the *earnest* freedom advocates abroad.

ix

The prescient essay, "The Case of Iran," by Richard W. Cottam in last year's *Freedom in the World*, made that point months before it became clear that the Shah's regime could not survive. Cottam detailed the intricate policy choices facing the United States: the unhappy case history of millenial-old traditions cum modern authoritarianism, both confronted by the "historic inevitability" of the human rights issue. It is now said that in Iran our intelligence services failed to inform the president, and the news media misinformed the public. Yet, independent American scholars who knew the area were aware of the likely denouement—as Dr. Cottam in last year's yearbook demonstrated with precision *before* the revolution.

This year's edition again conveys in the Survey (Part I) and the Country Summaries (Part IV) the information and judgments that may be useful to communicators, scholars, officials, and human rights activists in formulating present and future attitudes and actions. We are pleased to observe after eight years that the Comparative Survey of Freedom has become a staple resource—even during times when human rights are not an "in" subject.

The favorable reception of our first yearbook is additionally gratifying. Perhaps the most important contribution made by the Survey and *Freedom in the World* is their year-round focusing on political rights and civil liberties as a fundamental, worldwide aspect of human society, and, indeed, international affairs. We expect, in years to come, that this yearbook will be increasingly useful, not only for the annual judgments and correlations, but for the special attention given each year to particular aspects of freedom. The 1978 edition examined human rights, East and West, and the aforementioned case of Iran. It also discussed the definitions and distinctions of freedom and democracy and the relation of alternate political-economic systems to freedom, and included analyses of the "democratic role" and democracy as a polyarchy, and an essay on self-determination, subnationalities, and freedom.

The special sections in this 1979 edition are Freedom, Equality, and Culture (Part II) and Supporting Liberalization in the Soviet Union (Part III). Andrei Amalrik, the Soviet writer now living abroad, sees "the only real solution" to many domestic and foreign problems generated by the government of the Soviet Union as the *future* "liberalization of the Soviet system." The distinguished Soviet philosopher, now exiled, Alexander Zinoviev, believes the USSR's "liberal" period is *behind* it—in the "Khrushchev era and the first years of the Brezhnev government."

A similarly broad spectrum of views appeared at the Freedom House conference on Soviet liberalization reported and discussed in this volume. As the editor properly notes, "consensus is a valuable but by no means necessary result" of a conference. "Significant disagreement" was apparent, though most of the scholars agreed that the Soviet Union persistently pursues the "ideological goal of bringing the world under both Soviet and communist domination." Many different modes of response are considered, as is the role and impact of Soviet dissenters. Private individuals and organizations, it was agreed, could make a contribution to Soviet liberalization—provided the American government and the American public understand and share similar goals. That suggests an assignment for the journalist, an objective for the educator, and a responsibility for the government official. All need to illuminate far more realistically the complex interactions between the United States and the Soviet Union. We hope this volume may contribute to a wiser appraisal of those realities.

*   *   *

Once again, we are grateful for the assistance provided by the Advisory Panel for the Comparative Survey, consisting of Robert J. Alexander, Professor of Economics, Rutgers University; Richard W. Cottam, Professor of Political Science, University of Pittsburgh; Herbert J. Ellison, Professor of History, University of Washington; Seymour Martin Lipset, Senior Fellow, the Hoover Institution; Lucian Pye, Professor of Political Science, Massachusetts Institute of Technology; Leslie Rubin, lawyer, professor, and African specialist; Giovanni Sartori, Professor of Political Science, Stanford University; Robert Scalapino and Paul Seabury, Professors of Political Science, University of California, Berkeley.

We acknowledge the extensive contributions to *Freedom in the World, 1979* and to our Freedom House conference, "Supporting Liberalization in the Soviet Union," made by the participants: Drs. Alexander, Cottam, Ellison, Lipset, and Rubin among the advisors mentioned above; Bohdan R. Bociurkiw, Professor of Political Science, Carleton University, Ottawa; John B. Dunlop, Hoover Institution on War, Revolution, and Peace, Stanford; Lewis S. Feuer, Professor of Sociology, University of Virginia; Teresa Rakowska-Harmstone, Professor of Political Science, Carleton University; William R. Kintner, President, Foreign Policy Research Institute, Philadelphia; C. Grant Pendill, Jr.; Howland H. Sargeant, of the Freedom House Executive Committee; and Leonard R. Sussman and William C. Thoma of the organization's staff. Raymond D. Gastil organized the conference.

We are grateful for the continuing support provided by several foundations. Without their assistance, the Survey and these yearbooks could not have moved from conception to publication. We thank the J. Howard Pew Freedom Trust, the Earhart Foundation, the Charles Stewart Mott Foundation, and the John M. Olin Foundation.

LEONARD R. SUSSMAN
EXECUTIVE DIRECTOR, FREEDOM HOUSE

PART I

The Survey in 1978

The Comparative Survey of Freedom: Nature and Purposes

Since 1972 Freedom House has rated the level of freedom in each country in the world by means of a Comparative Survey of political and civil rights.[1] The Surveys provide an objective reference for judging political and civil rights within the maelstrom of emerging governments and changing standards.

Aside from its intrinsic interest, there are several reasons for such an objective reference. First, a recurrent American policy has been to go to the aid of other countries because their governments represented democratic systems similar to our own, or were struggling against forces hostile to democracy. But the policy can hardly be implemented if we cannot distinguish convincingly the more free from the less free states, particularly in the Third World.[2] Secondly, opinion leaders in the developed democracies need a basis for a more balanced appraisal of the imperfections in freedom that they discover in their own societies. It is always important to protect democracies; like all systems they will continually fall away from their ideals. But it is equally necessary to maintain perspective on these imperfections, to remember the vast difference between societies that have means to discover, publicize, and often correct abuses of the rights of men and those that do not. Careless, fashionable pessimism about the level of freedom in imperfect free societies destroys the morale of their peoples; it encourages and nourishes the propaganda of those who truly hold their peoples in chains.

In the 1960's it was fashionable among political analysts to avoid the issue of freedom by judging political systems primarily in economic and organizational terms. Such an analysis might see President Nixon as a poor manager of internal party affairs, or judge that Haile Selassie was overthrown because he failed to solve his nation's economic problems. Freedom in this analysis became an alternative means to administrative ends or the product of a certain stage of material and political progress. Such a view of freedom is a natural consequence of the materialistic, technocratic, "value-free" ethos of our

3

time. This approach also appeals to the analyst because freedom is hard to measure. It is easier to know if wheat production is higher this year than last, or if there are fewer beggars in the streets. However, those whose memories extend back as far as the thirties can never accept the claim that freedom inevitably accompanies economic or organizational progress, or that people who achieve material progress but are denied freedom necessarily prefer bread to liberty. Many questions go begging: How can we know what people think or want unless certain basic freedoms exist? Why is there so little evolution toward freedom in the Soviet Union, despite its advances in organization and technology? If freedom comes from material progress, why do so many Americans worry about the impact of further technological and organizational change upon freedom?

There is more to political organization than efficiency. By its simple existence the Freedom House Survey suggests that freedom is a goal that must be pursued separately from modernization. It inclines leaders of the new nations to notice that material results are not all that count. It suggests to citizens of developed democracies that the freedoms for which so many have struggled in the past will not inevitably triumph in the future. At the same time, a survey of freedom encourages people everywhere to reassess what they mean by freedom, its variations and its degrees, and to distinguish freedom more clearly from other desirable features in political systems.

Reassessment might also lead world leaders to a more acceptable understanding of modernization. Certainly the most dramatic revolution of 1978 was the revolt of the Iranian people against the Shah. Although led by conservative religious forces the revolt was inspired by years of political and social oppression.[3] The mistake of the Shah was not that he modernized the country too rapidly but that his efforts were unbalanced. Highly advanced technology in a few fields and the largest body of overseas students of any country in the world simply did not go with suppression of the media, political imprisonment, the suppression of religious leaders, and dependence on the United States. Our leaders and the leaders of the Third World cannot afford to forget that modernization in the image of the West and freedom cannot long be divorced.

In the Survey freedom is defined in terms of those *political rights* that allow people to participate freely and effectively in choosing their leaders or in voting directly on legislation, and those *civil liberties* that guarantee freedoms such as speech, privacy, and a fair trial. Of special importance for freedom in this sense are civil liberties making it possible to criticize the political, economic, and religious systems under which people live. This definition does not include the libertarian conception of liberty that denies majorities the power to regulate the nonpolitical public behavior of people in communities, nor does it include welfare interests, as in the rhetorical extensions "freedom from fear" or "freedom from want." In this definition independence may contribute to political freedom, but an independent state is not thereby "free." Whether the laws are codified or not, the freedoms of interest to the Survey must be guaranteed by a sense of law, by a regularized understanding of the forms and limits of government. Freedoms cannot be secure if they are continually threatened by the whims of personalities or even of majorities.

After placing a nation on scales for political rights and civil liberties we determine whether to label a state as free, partly free, or not free. The rating for political freedom is determined by factors such as the existence of two or more competing political parties or the independence of opposition candidates from government control. For a nation to achieve a high rating in the Survey, elections and legislatures have to demonstrate a significant opposition, and those elected have to be given real power. Civil freedoms include freedom of the press, the openness of public discussion, the existence of organizations separate from the government, an independent judiciary, and the absence of political imprisonment. Everything is in comparative terms. All nations fall short of perfection; on the other hand, perfect despotism would be hard to create or maintain. The sense of *degrees* of freedom that this approach produces is an important lesson in itself.

At the beginning of 1979 there were fifty-five independent nations in the world classified *not free*, forty-seven classified as *free*, and another fifty-six as *partly free*. In population terms this means that roughly forty percent of the world was considered not free, thirty-five percent free, and the remaining twenty-five percent fell somewhere in between. To be sure, hundreds of millions classified as free are just marginally so, and almost as many classified as partly free could, with slight shifts of arbitrary category boundaries, be considered not free.

The free states include those in Western Europe, the United Kingdom, and most overseas English-speaking nations, including the United States. The category also includes states such as Japan, Venezuela, India, and Fiji. Characteristic of all these states are a free press, an open political process, and a judiciary that often decides against the government. Among the partly free states are Mexico, Morocco, Nigeria, or South Korea. Characteristic of such states are the maintenance of organized opposition groups and publicly expressed opposition. In these states there is repression of some important opposition groups; here elections are a means of registering dissent rather than a way to seriously threaten the ruling group.

Among not free states are Uruguay, Zaire, Haiti, Tanzania, and most Communist states. These are characterized by lack of significant public expression of opposition within either the electoral process or the legislature. Some criticism of policy implementation, of cultural tendencies, and of low-ranking officials may be allowed.

Critics have objected that the Survey's definition of freedom reflects nothing more than a generalization of the values of Western constitutional democracies. They see no reason why these values are necessarily of importance to the rest of the world, or why Americans should feel called upon to promote such standards for people in other countries.[4] The first reply to these objections is that the traditional world cultures that preceded Westernization play little role in any imporant political system today. For example, while cultural tones differ, the modern political systems of Japan and China are modeled on those of Western Europe and the Soviet Union respectively. One can understand more about the organization of Vietnam today by studying comparative communist administration than by studying a thousand years of pre-French Vietnamese history.

The second reply to the accusation of cultural ethnocentrism is that unless there are democratic freedoms, observers simply do not have any idea what a people wants. To outsiders populations often seem most satisfied when they are most hopelessly oppressed. Before Sihanouk was overthrown in Cambodia, we were assured by the media that, for all his faults, the Cambodian people loved him—he fit their style. After his downfall, reporters suddenly found no one in Phnom Penh with a good word for Sihanouk. The communists who conquered Cambodia ruled until January 1979 in a style neither media nor area experts prepared us for. Similarly, in India no one could imagine the strength of opposition to Mrs. Gandhi's oppressions before she put her rule to a vote. Most peoples accept tyrannies passively, either because tyrannies are all they have known, or they see no way of combining to overthrow tyrannies. When a people learns of alternatives to tyranny, and sees a chance of overthrowing it, they will grasp at the chance. Today the alternative they hope for is usually a version of Western democracy.

The survey is often accused of being right-wing: certainly communist and one-party socialist regimes fare poorly. However, the Survey's only ideology is the importance of political and personal freedom. For this reason it should not be surprising that Chile was rated "free" under Allende, but "not free" since. The Chilean case illustrates the Survey's attempt to reflect the best information on current conditions, rather than reflecting what opposition groups report is "actually happening" in a country. It may be that Allende was trying to set up a

left-wing dictatorship in 1973, but up to his ouster he had not succeeded, and the nation remained free. His successors set up a dictatorship. In the eyes of the military their actions may have been necessary;
we note only that some military interventions under similar conditions
elsewhere have been far less drastic, and have appeared to achieve
all legitimate purposes.

The experience of the Survey suggests that it is difficult to maintain
a high level of political rights alongside a low level of civil liberties;
if the opposition cannot present its case, the right to vote is not very
meaningful. On the other hand, people with strong civil liberties will
soon clamor for more political rights. Increasing political rights is an
obvious issue to raise, where it can be raised, by aspiring leaders outside
the system. If their demands are widely supported, incumbent leaders
are forced either to increase political rights or to reduce civil liberies
in order to cut off the discussion. Thus, ever since the peoples of the
world became aware of the freedoms achieved in the West, developments toward or away from freedom have had an internal logic of their
own. Once movement starts toward or away from freedom, it tends
to continue inexorably through a process that might be described as
the rectification of recurrent imbalances between civil and political
freedoms. This is a primary reason communist regimes have been so
fearful of even hesitant steps toward liberalization.

These last observations point up many issues related to the Survey
that have not been carefully examined. Should independence itself
be taken more seriously by the Survey? It may be said that the blacks
in Tanzania "feel free" in a sense that blacks in South Africa cannot.
This is very difficult to judge. One reason to doubt such a generalization
is that most new states are made up of a variety of peoples, only
some of which have access to rule. Secession may merely move the
problem to a different plane. This was one of the paradoxes of the
Ibo revolt in Nigeria, for within the rebel Ibo state of Biafra there
were other smaller tribes that felt endangered in turn by the Ibos. This
is nearly always the case. It is not at all clear that a Peruvian Indian
or a Zairian pygmy feels happy to have a supposed norte-americano
or European yoke replaced by the yoke of a native ethnic group. What
we call a "people" from our distant vantage point frequently dis-
solves into many peoples when viewed up close.[5]

Similar questions arise when we try to define a "colony." The Soviet
Union and China rule over a number of areas that are not populated
by Russians or Chinese, and yet these areas are not normally considered colonies. If we consider Soviet Tadzhikistan a colony, would
not Northern Ireland also be a colony? In any event, in Northern
Ireland people have had a fair chance to vote on the issue of what

nation they belong in. In how many, even democratic, countries is this the case?

Socialist critics believe we underrate the importance of economic equality in the definition of freedom.[6] They think it ridiculous to call India a free country in view of its great economic disparities, hunger, and illiteracy. There is justice in the objection. Yet socioeconomic equality cannot in itself be necessary for democracy: even the most advanced democracies are oligarchies. Apparently competing party organizations operate throughout India, people vote relatively freely, and the results of their votes have a guiding power comparable to that in richer, more egalitarian states.[7] Interest in freedom is not a reflection of prosperity. Indeed, a recent study of Turkey shows that the poorest peasants are those most likely to vote; in India polls show the poor are the most attached to democratic institutions.[8] Capitalist critics of the Survey have perhaps an equally good case in arguing that we should "take off points" for socialism or centralized planning. Government control to the extent required by these systems reduces civil liberties. Increasing the number of people directly dependent on government inevitably restricts the population's ability to vote incumbents out of office.

More fundamentally, communism challenges our definitions of freedom both as they relate to internal and external policy. In communist ideology, or Marxist "science," political power is always expressed in favor of the interests of the dominant group in a society and against the interests of everyone else. It follows that freedoms in any society can only be meaningful for the dominant and are essentially nonexistent for others. The only difference between communist and noncommunist society becomes, then, the difference in who is oppressed. Communists describe the dominant group in noncommunist societies as those with control over the means of production, and the dominant group in communist (technically "socialist") societies as the workers and peasants. Since workers and peasants make up a larger percentage of almost every society than holders of productive property, it follows that there must be more freedom in communist societies.[9]

The problem with this communist picture of reality is twofold. First, while property is a significant form of power, and capitalists or large landholders exert more than their share of power in noncommunist states, property holders have only limited power in noncommunist states. The increasing tax load borne by the wealthy in all noncommunist states is certainly an example of this limitation of control. It is also a mistake to assume that adherence to principle and moral suasion cannot play a part in political life. The freedoms of the politically powerless, such as their rights to self-expression, choice of education, religious affiliation, or change of residence, are recognized most of the time in democracies today. The laws and principles of democracies, accepted in part as the basis for compromise among a number of conflicting groups fearful of one another's power, tend to be institutionalized in ways that redound to the benefit of all.

The first error of the communist analysis, then, comes from an underevaluation both of the significance for freedom of the conflicts within capitalist societies and of the importance of idealism. The second error of communist analysis comes from an overevaluation of communist idealism and a dogmatic identification of majority interests with communist party interests in communist societies, whether viewed hypothetically or empirically. There is no reason in communist ideology or human experience to imagine that a ruling group, especially when unchecked by regularly contested elections, will not twist the ruling ideology to its own interests rather than the interests of the people it serves. While revolutionary fervor may lead to moments of high idealism, communists in the long run cannot be expected to act unselfishly—and generally they do not. Communist ideologists have also allowed ideology to rule their social science by imagining that majorities of any people belong to an undifferentiated workers or peasants class that for more than the briefest moments has a unified set of interests and goals that can be expressed by an ideologically rigorous party platform. Even less is it likely that a party that does not provide itself with competitive and critical media is likely to know what the interests of the majority are. The communist theoretician's answer is that the party alone knows what the people essentially want, for they alone know what must be.[10] In ideological terms, communists believe that only when a people does what it must is it truly free.[11] A swimmer is free only if he knows how to swim.

But this turns the definition of freedom on its head; Marxist "science" has robbed it of the essential kernel of meaning with which the discussion began.[12] For in civic life freedom must mean the right to be wrong, express foolish opinions, vote for poor candidates.

It appears that communist analysis offers a useful reminder of the imperfections, necessary as well as remediable, in the freedoms of noncommunist societies. But it offers no sensible alternative. In an imperfect world it offers only a utopian mirage full of disappointment.

Whatever its faults, the Survey has become a monitoring facility by which people may become more responsibly concerned with the progress of freedom in their own and other countries. Since the Survey was initiated, several countries have lost freedom while others have gained it. Greece, Spain, and Portugal have given us hope, while Chile and the Philippines have been disappointments. The communist world has expanded in these years; freedom in the noncommunist world has also advanced. There is more freedom today in India, Sri Lanka, the Dominican Republic, Rhodesia, Iran, and many other countries than there was two or three years ago. And within the communist world, in Poland, China, and Hungary, freedom has also made gains.

Experience with the Survey suggests that people everywhere prefer freedom to tyranny in whatever form. But whether a country attains or sustains freedom depends on the willingness of elites to be satisfied with the limited power and compromise democracy requires. The Survey also suggests the degree to which the political trends of neighboring states, or of closely related states, are often copied. Elites will choose systems that are successful or fashionable and serve their interests.[13] Authoritarian military regimes look for legitimation, means of control, and international support to similar regimes, particularly in Latin America. Some elites find communism the best road to absolute power, as in Cuba or Cambodia. In many developing countries the one-party socialist model, taken originally from communist countries, has become a popular official form (although the content given to socialism varies widely). This model is especially important for legitimating antidemocratic governments in Africa. During the period of the Survey Sierra Leone has moved away from freedom through imitation of Guinea; earlier Zambia had taken the same road, apparently in imitation of Tanzania. However, because of the inherent attractiveness of democracy to common people, the people with residual power in all societies, there repeatedly arise leaders in every society that look to the models of Western democratic institutions. Most recently we see these in Thailand and India, Nigeria and Ghana, even in Egypt and Iran. These are the people, often educated in the West, that we cannot afford to fail.

These observations suggest the importance of the ideological and informational warfare that ceaselessly goes on around us. It also suggests how the real world impinges on this struggle. If *one* free system fails competitively to perform as well as a nonfree, this failure hurts all free systems. If *one* relatively free society fails to maintain itself militarily this hurts all free societies. Therefore, the first requirement for the victory of free societies is military and economic success. And today we find economic weaknesses in free societies; and we find military weaknesses, particularly because of the growing strategic strength of the USSR, its recently developed ability to project its power overseas, and the unwillingness of the United States after Vietnam to project its countervailing power.[14]

The second requirement for the success of freedom is ideological: democratic institutions must capture the imagination and allegiance of the educated elites of the world. This involves economic and military strength, but it also involves much more. It involves the identification of the liberal democracies with the idealistic longings of mankind, particularly in the area of human rights.

Pursuing military, economic, and idealistic strategies for protecting and expanding the arena of freedom in the world presents the publics and governments of free nations such as the United States or Japan with many dilemmas. The USSR is both a market for our goods and a danger to our existence. It punishes dissidents, and sometimes our protests seem only to make this punishment more severe. In 1978 an authoritarian Nicaraguan president found it harder than ever to get U.S. support for suppressing revolutionaries that may have a hard core of communist support. In Iran an oppressive Shah long identified with U.S. interests struggled to retain his power against revolutionaries who were simultaneously reactionary and radical, anti-American and anti-Israeli. We had to ask ourselves repeatedly: What should our policy be? Where should the pressure of public opinion be applied?

In the past the tendency of Western leaders and "responsible" publics has been to emphasize short-term material and military interests, and to resolutely stand up for freedom only when there is little conflict with these interests. This is commitment to freedom by exception. However, to win the ideological struggle and ultimately therefore the struggle for freedom everywhere we need to reverse these priorities and stand up for freedom regularly. With this priority we would ignore freedom only when this is demonstrably in our long- as well as short-run interest.

The strength of free institutions everywhere is weakened when we as citizens or governments fail to criticize the Pinochet regime of Chile, General Somoza in Nicaragua, the Shah in Iran, the whites in South Africa, just as it is weakened when we ignore the recent inhumanities in Indochina or Uganda, or the suppression of intellectual dissent by the cruel fabrications of Soviet courts. Consistency is justice, it builds, one case upon another, toward an international consensus that by its nature leaves totalitarianism out in the cold. Inconsistency makes all our actions, idealistic or Machiavellian, appear insincere, to be merely the manipulation of the pain of others for short-term advantage. For this reason a strategy for freedom must employ inconsistency most sparingly.

We have had many examples of the results of idealism by exception. In the early 60's the king of Afghanistan attempted to establish a constitutional monarchy. In ten years the experiment had progressed, the media were freer, political activity was more open, the country had held its freest elections in history. Then Prince Daud staged a coup with the aid of the army and reestablished an authoritarian system. Neither official spokesman nor private citizens raised an alarm in the West. A government struggling to copy free institutions was swept under, and the Western public was told it was all just as well, it was not really democracy anyhow.[15] In 1978 one of the parties nourished by that democratic experiment, driven underground, rose to take over the state and turn it into a fair copy of a totalitarian Soviet dictatorship.

In Greece the military suppressed democratic institutions for years, and too many Americans cheered them on. Yet the generals failed either to gain the support of their people or to achieve stability, and ended up precipitating the Turkish invasion of Cyprus. The Greeks managed in the aftermath to establish a democracy in spite of this legacy, but the ghost of America's role still haunts Grecian democracy.

In Ethiopia Western democracies supported a system that brooked no opposition, allowed little growth of free institutions, and maintained gross feudal inequities. When the revolution came, as we should have known it would, the free world was automatically the established enemy of the new order. The freest countries in the world were seen as the champions of oppression. The United States went along with the Portuguese dictatorship, viewed as the agent of stability. When the dictatorship collapsed, we almost lost Portugal to communism. We did lose all the African colonies—Angola, Mozambique, Guinea-Bissau, Cape Verde Islands, Sao Tome and Principe—to communist or quasi-communist systems. To the peoples of these colonies, who had no experience with democracy, and to whom the West was the oppressor, there seemed no other choice.

By early 1979 the Shah of Iran had gone into exile. His opposition had been in part a democratic, constitutionalist opposition, in part traditionalist and religious; the opposition of the Shah and the constitution, of king against mullah and bazaari is an old one in Iran. But in 1978-79 the opposition was also bitterly anti-American. It remembered the military and police support we had given the Shah and his legions, his spies, his military courts and regal pretensions over so many years. We hope the eventual government may be moderate and democratic, but we will be very lucky if Iran does not become a barren ground for growth of a truly democratic society dedicated to Western liberties.

The point of these examples is that the policy of human rights by exception fails too often to maintain or achieve freedoms. It leads to failure in the struggle of systems materially, on the basis of who wins, and on the basis of "the system that rules next door." *And* this policy leads to failure in the worldwide ideological struggle because too often it suggests to the idealists who legitimize ideologies that the free world does not really care about extending its values to others, that the Western democracies are willing to let others suffer the inequities of tyranny as long as Westerners can enjoy the freedoms of our societies at home.

In many countries, and especially many developed democracies, political terror has become a part of political life. Of course, there will always be irrational, crazy, misguided persons for whom violence and idealism are an indigestible but addictive diet. Yet may it not be that the survival and growth of terrorist groups within Western societies is facilitated and sustained by the much larger penumbra of persons convinced that true respect for the freedoms of people, especially stateless peoples and people in the Third World, is not to be found in the Western democracies?

In conclusion, experience shows that there are important strengths in the world of free nations. Peoples repeatedly choose freedom when given a choice by the elites that guide them. The progress of freedom is menaced, however, by certain dangers. There are the well-known military and economic problems. Equally important is the ideological problem of changing the balance of impressions of opinion-forming elites everywhere on the relative merits of liberal and authoritarian solutions to human problems, including the problem of individual freedom itself. Allegiance to Western democracies and their ideals must be shown to make a difference everywhere. The struggle for freedom will be won only when we turn away from supporting freedom by exception and adopt a personal and public policy of supporting freedom with consistency.

NOTES

1. The first edition of the Survey was R. D. Gastil, "The New Criteria of Freedom," *Freedom at Issue*, no. 17 (January-February 1973). It has been published at least in every succeeding January-February edition of *Freedom at Issue*, and in the first Freedom House annual, *Freedom in the World 1978* (New York and Boston: Freedom House and G. K. Hall, 1978).

2. The other two reports used for making these distinctions are the Amnesty International Annual reports (latest: *Amnesty International Report 1978* [London: Amnesty International, 1979]) and the annual reports of the U. S. State Department to Congress on human rights (latest: "Report on Human Rights Practices in Countries Receiving U. S. Aid" [Washington: Department of State, February 8, 1979]). The purposes of these are complementary and supplementary to that of the Comparative Survey. Unlike the Survey both of these are less complete in their coverage of nations. The topics of primary interest to Amnesty are political imprisonment, torture, and capital punishment. Table 6 (below) addresses Amnesty's special area of interest. Amnesty specifically abjures making comparisons among nations. Whenever it hears of an offense against its standards, Amnesty attempts by publicity to bring pressure. Therefore, where

there is a great deal of information and its pressure seems likely to be productive Amnesty turns its spotlight. On the other hand, Department of State reports look at a broader group of factors than freedom, including efforts in areas such as employment or health services. With some notable exceptions State Department reports are forced by political considerations to avoid direct comparisons and to give as good a complexion to the human rights performances of other countries as possible. State Department reports would, for example, be most loath to bring up many self-determination questions. Profiting greatly from both of these sources, the Comparative Survey goes considerably further in attempting to judge relative conditions or performance.

3. See Richard Cottam, "The Case of Iran," *Freedom in the World 1978*, pp. 88–108.

4. This issue is examined more theoretically below, pp. 75–82.

5. For an extended discussion of these issues see *Freedom in the World 1978*, pp. 180–215.

6. For more extended discussions of this issue see *Freedom in the World 1978*, pp. 163–179, and the present volume below, pp. 63–74.

7. See Ram Joshi and Kirtidev Desai, "Toward a More Competitive Party System in India," *Asian Survey*, XVIII, no. 11 (November 1978), 1091–1116.

8. Ergun Özbudun, *Social Change and Political Participation in Turkey* (Princeton: Princeton University Press, 1976), pp. 56–161; and Samuel Huntington and Joan Nelson, *No Easy Choice* (Cambridge: Harvard University Press, 1976), pp. 82–83.

9. For this discussion compare Herbert Aptheker, *The Nature of Democracy and Freedom* (New York: International Publishers, 1967), especially pp. 60–74.

10. C. B. Macpherson, *The Real World of Democracy* (New York: Oxford University Press, 1966).

11. Aptheker, *The Nature of Democracy and Freedom*, pp. 71–73.

12. For our definition of freedom see *Freedom in the World 1978*, pp. 111–26.

13. This analysis is developed in *Freedom in the World 1978*, pp. 147–62.

14. See International Institute for Strategic Studies, *The Military Balance 1978–79* (London, 1978), especially pp. 112–18.

15. For a discussion of this affair see *Freedom in the World 1978*, pp. 156–59.

Survey Ratings and Tables For 1978

Progress toward greater freedom that began with the help of President Carter in 1977 continued in 1978. The gains were seldom of major proportions, often not widely known, and frequently so glacial that their ascription to 1978 is arbitrary. The gains were frequently accompanied by violence or unresolved political questions severe enough to place their future in question; this was most dramatically the case in Iran. Because of the magnitude of the population involved, and the fact that it occurred within a communist state, the most hopeful of all changes was the rising crescendo of dissent at year's end in mainland China, and the government's promises of a legal structure and social freedoms. By mid-January dissent had gone beyond moderate communism to questioning communism itself and, on the other hand, to the involvement of poor Chinese in populist demonstrations for more food. Clearly in 1979 the momentum of dissent would have to be halted by a reinstitutionalization of tyranny or China would take a decisive step toward freedom.

THE TABULATED RATINGS

The accompanying Table of Independent Nations and Table of Related Territories rate each state or territory on seven-point scales for political and civil freedoms, and then provide an overall judgment of each as "free," "partly free," or "not free." In each scale, a rating of (1) is freest and (7) least free. Instead of using absolute standards, standards are comparative—that is, most observers would be likely to judge states rated (1) as freer than those rated (2), and so on. No state, of course, is absolutely free or unfree, but the degree of freedom does make a difference in the quality of life.[1]

In *political rights*, states rated (1) have a fully competitive electoral process and those elected clearly rule. Most West European democracies belong here. Relatively free states may receive a (2) because although the electoral process works and the elected rule, there are

15

Table 1
Independent Nations:
Comparative Measures of Freedom

	Political Rights[1]	Civil Liberties[1]	Status of Freedom[2]	Outlook[3]
Afghanistan	7-	7-	NF	0
Albania	7	7	NF	0
Algeria	6	6	NF	0
Angola	7	7	NF	0
Argentina	6	5+	NF	0
Australia	1	1	F	0
Austria	1	1	F	0
Bahamas	1	2	F	0
Bahrain	6	4	PF	0
Bangladesh	4+	4	PF	+
Barbados	1	1	F	0
Belgium	1	1	F	0
Benin	7	7	NF	0
Bhutan	5●	5●	PF	0
Bolivia	5+	3+	PF	+
Botswana	2	3	F	0
Brazil	4	4+	PF	+
Bulgaria	7	7	NF	0
Burma	7	6	NF	0
Burundi	7	7●	NF	0
Cameroon	6	6●	NF	0
Canada	1	1	F	0
Cape Verde Islands	6	6	NF	0
Central African Emp.	7	7	NF	0
Chad	6+	6	NF	0
Chile	6+	5	NF	0
China (Mainland)	6	6	NF	+
China (Taiwan)	5	5-	PF	0
Colombia	2	3	F	0
Comoro Islands	5-	4	PF	+
Congo	7	7●	NF	0
Costa Rica	1	1	F	0
Cuba	6	6	NF	0
Cyprus	3	4	PF	0
Czechoslovakia	7	6	NF	0
Denmark	1	1	F	0

Notes to the Table

1. The scales use the numbers 1-7, with 1 comparatively offering the highest level of political or civil rights, and 7 the lowest. A plus or minus following a rating indicates an improvement or decline in 1978. A rating marked with a period (●) has been changed since the 1978 yearbook due to reevaluation by the author. This does not imply any change in the country.

2. A free state is designated by F, a partly free state by PF, and a not-free state by NF.

3. A positive outlook for freedom is indicated by a plus sign, a negative outlook, by a minus, and relative stability of ratings by a zero. The outlook for freedom is based on the problems the country is facing, the way the government and people are reacting to these problems, and the longer run political traditions of the society. A judgment of outlook may also reflect an imminent change, such as the expected adoption of a meaningful new constitution.

4. Current official name of Cambodia.

5. Became independent in 1978.

	Political Rights[1]	Civil Liberties[1]	Status of Freedom[2]	Outlook[3]
Djibouti	3	4	PF	0
Dominica[5]	2	3	F	0
Dominican Republic	2+	2	F+	0
Ecuador	5+	4	PF	+
Egypt	5	5-	PF	0
El Salvador	5- •	5- •	PF	0
Equatorial Guinea	7	7	NF	0
Ethiopia	7	7	NF	0
Fiji	2	2	F	0
Finland	2	2	F	0
France	1	2	F	0
Gabon	6	6	NF	0
Gambia	2	2	F	0
Germany (E)	7	6+•	NF	0
Germany (W)	1	2	F	0
Ghana	5+	4+	PF	+
Greece	2	2	F	0
Grenada	2	3	F	0
Guatemala	3	4	PF	0
Guinea	7	7	NF	0
Guinea-Bissau	6	6	NF	0
Guyana	4-	4- •	PF	-
Haiti	7	6	NF	0
Honduras	6	3	PF	0
Hungary	6	5	NF	0
Iceland	1	1	F	0
India	2	2	F	0
Indonesia	5	5	PF	0
Iran	5+	5	PF+	+
Iraq	7	6•	NF	0
Ireland	1	1	F	0
Israel	2	2	F	0
Italy	2	2	F	0
Ivory Coast	6	5	PF+•	0
Jamaica	2	3	F	0
Japan	2	1	F	0
Jordan	6	6	NF	0
Kampuchea[4]	7	7	NF	0
Kenya	5	4+	PF	0
Korea (N)	7	7	NF	0
Korea (S)	4+	5	PF	0
Kuwait	6	4	PF	0
Laos	7	7	NF	0
Lebanon	4	4	PF	0
Lesotho	5	5•	PF	0
Liberia	6	5•	PF	0
Libya	6	6	NF	0
Luxembourg	1	1	F	0
Madagascar	6- •	6- •	NF- •	0
Malawi	6+	7•	NF	0
Malaysia	3	4	PF	0
Maldives	5•	5•	PF	+
Mali	7	6+•	NF	0
Malta	2	2	F	0

17

Table 1 —Continued

	Political Rights[1]	Civil Liberties[1]	Status of Freedom[2]	Outlook[3]
Mauritania	6	6	NF	+
Mauritius	2	4-	PF-	0
Mexico	4	4•	PF	0
Mongolia	7	7	NF	0
Morocco	3	4	PF	0
Mozambique	7	7	NF	0
Nauru	2	2	F	0
Nepal	6	5	PF	+
Netherlands	1	1	F	0
New Zealand	1	1	F	0
Nicaragua	5	5	PF	0
Niger	7	6	NF	0
Nigeria	5	3+	PF	+
Norway	1	1	F	0
Oman	6	6	NF	0
Pakistan	6	5-	PF	0
Panama	5+	5	PF+	0
Papua New Guinea	2	2	F	0
Paraguay	5	5+	PF+	0
Peru	5+	4	PF	+
Philippines	5	5	PF	0
Poland	6	5	PF+•	0
Portugal	2	2	F	0
Qatar	5	5	PF	0
Rhodesia	5+	5	PF+	+
Rumania	7	6	NF	0
Rwanda	6•+	6•	NF	0
Sao Tome and Principe	6	6•	NF	0
Saudi Arabia	6	6	NF	0
Senegal	4+	3	PF	+
Seychelles	6	5•	PF	0
Sierra Leone	5	5	PF	0
Singapore	5	5	PF	0
Solomon Islands[5]	2	2	F	0
Somalia	7	7	NF	0
South Africa	5	6	PF	0
Spain	2	2+•	F	0
Sri Lanka	2	3•	F	0
Sudan	5+	5	PF+	0
Surinam	2	2	F	0
Swaziland	5•	5•	PF	0
Sweden	1	1	F	0
Switzerland	1	1	F	0
Syria	5	6	PF	0
Tanzania	6	6	NF	0
Thailand	5+	4+	PF+	+
Togo	7	6	NF	0
Tonga	5	3	PF	0
Transkei	5+	5	PF+	0
Trinidad & Tobago	2	2	F	0
Tunisia	6	5	PF+•	0
Turkey	2	3	F	0
Tuvalu[5]	2	2	F	0

	Political Rights[1]	Civil Liberties[1]	Status of Freedom[2]	Outlook[3]
Uganda	7	7	NF	0
USSR	6•	6	NF	0
United Arab Emirates	5	5	PF	0
United Kingdom	1	1	F	0
United States	1	1	F	0
Upper Volta	2+	3+	F+	0
Uruguay	6	6	NF	0
Venezuela	1	2	F	0
Vietnam	7	7	NF	0
Western Samoa	4	2	PF	0
Yemen (N)	6	5	NF	0
Yemen (S)	6+	7	NF	0
Yugoslavia	6	5	NF	0
Zaire	6	6	NF	0
Zambia	5	5	PF	0

factors which cause us to lower our rating of the effective equality of the process. These factors may include extreme economic inequality, illiteracy, or intimidating violence. They also include the weakening of effective competition that is implied by the absence of periodic shifts in rule from one group or party to another.

Below this level, political ratings of (3) through (5) represent successively less effective implementation of democratic processes. Mexico, for example, has periodic elections and limited opposition, but for many years its governments have been selected outside the public view by the leaders of factions within the dominant Mexican party. Governments of states rated (5) sometimes have no effective voting processes at all, but strive for consensus among a variety of groups in society in ways weakly analogous to those of the democracies. States at (6) do not allow competitive electoral processes that would give the people a chance to voice their desire for a new ruling party or for a change in policy. The rulers of states at this level assume that one person or a small group has the right to decide what is best for the nation, and that no one should be allowed to challenge that right. Such rulers do respond, however, to popular desire in some areas, or respect (and therefore are constrained by) belief systems (for example, Islam) that are the general property of the society as a whole. At (7) the political despots at the top appear by their actions to feel little constraint from either public opinion or popular tradition.

Turning to the scale for *civil liberties,* in countries rated (1) publi-

Table 2
Related Territories:
Comparative Measures of Freedom

	Political Rights[1]	Civil Liberties[1]	Status of Freedom[2]	Outlook[3]
Australia				
Christmas Island (in Indian Ocean)	4	2	PF	0
Cocos Islands	4	2	PF	+
Norfolk Island	4	2	PF	+
Chile				
Easter Island	7	6	NF	0
Denmark				
Faroe Islands	2	1	F	0
Greenland	4	1	PF	+
France				
French Guiana	3	2	PF	0
French Polynesia	3	2	PF	0
Guadeloupe	3	2	PF	0
Martinique	3	2	PF	0
Mayotte	2	2	F	0
Monaco[4]	4	2●	PF	0
New Caledonia	4	3	PF	0
Reunion	3	2	PF	0
Saint Pierre & Miquelon	3	2	PF	0
Wallis and Futuna	4	3	PF	0
Israel				
Occupied Territories	5	4	PF	0
Italy				
San Marino[4]	2	1	F	0
Netherlands				
Neth. Antilles	2	1	F	0
New Zealand				
Cook Islands	3-	2	F	0
Niue	2	2	F	0
Tokelau Islands	4	2	PF	0
Portugal				
Azores	2	2	F	0
Macao	3	3	PF	0
Madeira	2	2	F	0
South Africa				
Bophuthatswana[5]	6	6	NF	0
South West Africa (Namibia)	5+	5	PF+	0
Spain				
Canary Islands	2	2	F	0
Places of Sovereignty in North Africa	2	2	F	0

Notes to the Table

1., 2., 3. See Notes, Table 1.

4. These states are not listed as independent because all have explicit legal forms of dependence on a particular country (or, in the case of Andorra, countries) in the spheres of foreign affairs, defense, etc.

5. This homeland became officially independent in 1977. Its geography and history cause us to continue to consider it a dependency.

6. West Indies Associated States.

	Political Rights[1]	Civil Liberties[1]	Status of Freedom[2]	Outlook[3]
Switzerland				
Liechtenstein[4]	4	1	PF	0
United Kingdom				
Anguilla	2	2	F	0
Antigua and Barbuda[6]	2	2	F	0
Belize	1	2	F	0
Bermuda	2	1	F	0
Brit. Virgin Islands	3	2	PF	0
Brunei[4]	6	5	NF	0
Cayman Islands	2	2	F	0
Channel Islands	2	1	F	0
Falkland Islands	2	2	F	0
Gibraltar	1	2	F	0
Gilbert Islands	2	2	F	0
Hong Kong	3	2	PF	0
Isle of Man	2	1	F	0
Montserrat	3	2	F	0
St. Helena	2	2	F	0
St. Kitts and Nevis[6]	2	3	F	0
St. Lucia[6]	2	3	F	0
St. Vincent[6]	2	2	F	0
Turks and Caicos	3	2	PF	0
United States				
American Samoa	3	2	PF	0
Canal Zone	5	3	PF	-
Guam	3	2	PF	0
Micronesia	4	2	PF	+
Northern Marianas	2	2	F	0
Puerto Rico	2	1	F	0
Virgin Islands	3	2	PF	+
France-Spain Condominium				
Andorra[4]	4	3	PF	0
France-United Kingdom Condominium				
New Hebrides	3	3	PF	+

cations are not closed because of the expression of rational political opinion, especially when the intent of the expression is to affect the legitimate political process. No major media are simply conduits for government propaganda. The courts protect the individual; persons are not imprisoned for their opinions; private rights and desires in education, occupation, religion, residence, and so on, are generally respected; law-abiding persons do not fear for their lives because of their rational political activities. States at this level include most traditional democracies. There are, of course, flaws in the liberties of all these states, and these flaws are significant when measured against the standards these states set for themselves.

Movement down from (2) to (7) represents a steady loss of the civil freedoms we have detailed. Compared to (1), the police and courts of states at (2) have more authoritarian traditions. Some states at (2) simply have a less institutionalized or secure set of liberties, such as Portugal or Greece. Those rated (3) or below may have

Table 3
Ranking of Nations by Political Rights

Most Free 1	2	3	4	5	6	Least Free 7
Australia	Botswana	Cyprus	Bangladesh	Bhutan	Algeria	Afghanistan
Austria	Colombia	Djibouti	Brazil	Bolivia	Argentina	Albania
Bahamas	Dominica	Guatemala	Guyana	China (Taiwan)	Bahrain	Angola
Barbados	Dominican Republic	Malaysia	Korea (S)	Comoro Is.	Cameroon	Benin
Belgium	Fiji	Morocco	Lebanon	Ecuador	Cape Verde Is.	Bulgaria
Canada	Finland		Mexico	Egypt	Chad	Burma
Costa Rica	Gambia		Senegal	El Salvador	Chile	Burundi
Denmark	Greece		Western Samoa	Ghana	China (Mainland)	Central African Emp.
France	Grenada			Indonesia	Cuba	Congo
Germany (W)	India			Iran	Gabon	Czechoslovakia
Iceland	Israel			Kenya	Guinea-Bissau	Equatorial Guinea
Ireland	Italy			Lesotho	Honduras	Ethiopia
Luxembourg	Jamaica			Maldives	Hungary	Germany (E)
Netherlands	Japan			Nicaragua	Ivory Coast	Guinea
New Zealand	Malta			Nigeria	Jordan	Haiti
Norway	Mauritius			Panama	Kuwait	Iraq
Sweden	Nauru			Paraguay	Liberia	Kampuchea
Switzerland	Papua New Guinea			Peru	Libya	Korea (N)
United Kingdom	Portugal			Philippines	Madagascar	Laos
United States	Solomon Is.			Qatar	Malawi	Mali
Venezuela	Spain			Rhodesia	Mauritania	Mongolia
	Sri Lanka			Sierra Leone	Nepal	Mozambique
	Surinam			Singapore	Oman	Niger
	Trinidad & Tobago			South Africa	Pakistan	Rumania
	Turkey			Sudan	Poland	Somalia
	Tuvalu			Swaziland	Rwanda	Togo
	Upper Volta			Syria	Sao Tome & Principe	Uganda
				Thailand	Saudi Arabia	Vietnam
				Tonga	Seychelles	Uruguay
				Transkei	Tanzania	Yemen (N)
				United Arab Emirates	Tunisia	Yemen (S)
				Zambia	USSR	Yugoslavia
						Zaire

22

Table 4
Ranking of Nations by Civil Liberties

Most Free						Least Free
1	2	3	4	5	6	7
Australia	Bahamas	Bolivia	Bahrain	Argentina	Algeria	Afghanistan
Austria	Dominican Republic	Botswana	Bangladesh	Bhutan	Burma	Albania
Barbados	Fiji	Colombia	Brazil	Chile	Cameroon	Angola
Belgium	Finland	Dominica	Comoro Is.	China (Taiwan)	Cape Verde Is.	Benin
Canada	France	Dominica	Cyprus	Egypt	Chad	Bulgaria
Costa Rica	Gambia	Grenada	Djibouti	El Salvador	China (Mainland)	Burundi
Denmark	Germany (W)	Honduras	Ecuador	Hungary	Cuba	Central African Emp.
Iceland	Greece	Jamaica	Ghana	Indonesia	Czechoslovakia	Congo
Ireland	India	Nigeria	Guatemala	Iran	Gabon	Equatorial Guinea
Japan	Israel	Senegal	Guyana	Ivory Coast	Germany (E)	Ethiopia
Luxembourg	Italy	Sri Lanka	Kenya	Korea (S)	Guinea-Bissau	Guinea
Netherlands	Malta	Tonga	Kuwait	Lesotho	Haiti	Kampuchea
New Zealand	Nauru	Turkey	Lebanon	Liberia	Iraq	Korea (N)
Norway	Papua New Guinea	Upper Volta	Malaysia	Maldives	Jordan	Laos
Sweden	Portugal		Mauritius	Nepal	Libya	Malawi
Switzerland	Solomon Is.		Mexico	Nicaragua	Madagascar	Mongolia
United Kingdom	Spain		Morocco	Pakistan	Mali	Mozambique
United States	Surinam		Peru	Panama	Mauritania	Somalia
	Trinidad & Tobago		Thailand	Paraguay	Niger	Uganda
	Tuvalu			Philippines	Oman	Vietnam
	Venezuela			Poland	Rumania	Yemen (S)
	Western Samoa			Qatar	Rwanda	
				Rhodesia	Sao Tome & Principe	
				Seychelles	Saudi Arabia	
				Sierra Leone	South Africa	
				Singapore	Syria	
				Sudan	Tanzania	
				Swaziland	Togo	
				Transkei	USSR	
				Tunisia	Uruguay	
				United Arab Emirates	Zaire	
				Yemen (N)		
				Yugoslavia		
				Zambia		

23

political prisoners and generally varying forms of censorship. Too often their security services practice torture. States rated (6) almost always have political prisoners; usually the legitimate media are completely under government supervision; there is no right of assembly; and, often, travel, residence, and occupation are narrowly restricted. However, at (6) there still may be relative freedom in private conversation, especially in the home; illegal demonstrations do take place; underground literature is published; and so on. At (7) there is pervading fear, little independent expression takes place in private, almost no expressions of opposition emerge in the police-state environment, and execution is often swift and sure.

A cumulative judgment of "free," "partly free," or "not free" is made on the basis of the foregoing seven-point ratings, and an understanding of how they were derived. Generally, states rated (1) and (2) will be "free"; those at (3), (4), and (5), "partly free"; and those at (6) and (7), "not free." When the ratings for political rights and civil liberties differ, the status of freedom must be decided by rough averaging. It must be remembered, however, that the ratings represent categories on arbitrary scales rather than arithmetical units. There are, of course, marginal cases. A (6) and a (5) may lead either to a rating of "not free" or "partly free," depending on whether the (5) or (6) are a high (5) or low (5), a high (6) or low (6). In addition, political rights are given slightly more weight in marginal cases.

The tables also include an entry for *outlook*. Since we are not in a position to adequately judge the futures of all the societies under review, this column reports many fewer trends than a more detailed study would discover. Primarily, we include cases where a forthcoming election appears likely to improve the freedoms of a country, or a downward trend is in prospect because a retrogressive process underway at the time of the Survey has not yet actually reached fruition. By the nature of the signals we use, more pluses are likely to appear under *outlook* than minuses.

DECLINES IN FREEDOM

The year 1978 saw few serious declines. In *Afghanistan,* a new, apparently communist, regime imposed a harsh totalitarian police state on what had been an authoritarian but traditionalist country. A coup in the *Comoro Islands* and resulting elections led to a decline in the rating. The *Egyptian* government effectively destroyed the legitimation it briefly granted to a meaningful opposition, and curtailed the opposition press. The ninety-eight percent support received in a plebiscite suggested at least a highly controlled political discussion. In *El Sal-*

vador, pressure on the media increased, as did political violence by both opposition and government, especially as directed against peasants. Elections were held, but in an atmosphere of intimidation and with unreliable procedures that led the main opposition party to abstain. Although there were many ups and downs during the year, by year's end *China (Taiwan)* had imposed a more rigorous censorship and a major opposition paper had been forced into progovernment hands. A constitutional referendum receiving a ninety-seven percent favorable vote in *Guyana,* in spite of vigorous opposition, suggests growing repression. In *Madagascar* the parliament seems to have played very little role in 1978, while control over media and public discussion was further tightened. The arrest of leading members of the opposition party in *Mauritius* for taking part in an illegal demonstration caused that nation to decline to "partly free" in the ratings. Civil liberties declined in *Pakistan,* with additional pressures against the press and journalists and the jailing of many leaders of the opposition.

ADVANCES IN FREEDOM

Advances in 1978 were substantial in a number of countries, although seldom dramatic. In several of these cases the advances are recorded in spite of great turmoil, often including brutal repression and a very doubtful longevity for recent reforms.

Press freedom improved in *Argentina*; at least for a time, imprisonment and disappearances lessened. Although open to some question, the presidential election in *Bangladesh* signified an advance. By conventional measures, the annulment of the election in *Bolivia* should make it a failure, yet subsequent coups were based, respectively, on the election results and on the urgency of planning and carrying through a more valid election. More than ever, Bolivia is ruled by an armed compromise between the army and a variety of popular forces. Censorship ended in *Brazil,* union activity increased, political imprisonment became less common and severe. On the political side, successful parliamentary elections confirmed the country's continuing progress. In *Chad,* representatives of the rebellious north were included in a new government. In *Chile,* the plebiscite that opened the year was handled unfairly; yet it demonstrated a willingness to allow a public expression of opposition. Subsequently the state of siege was ended and a general amnesty declared. (This hardly helps those who have "disappeared," but the Survey judges only current conditions.)

The greatest advance in Latin America was registered in the *Dominican Republic,* where the presidential election brought the opposition to power. At first, the compromises required to achieve military acqui-

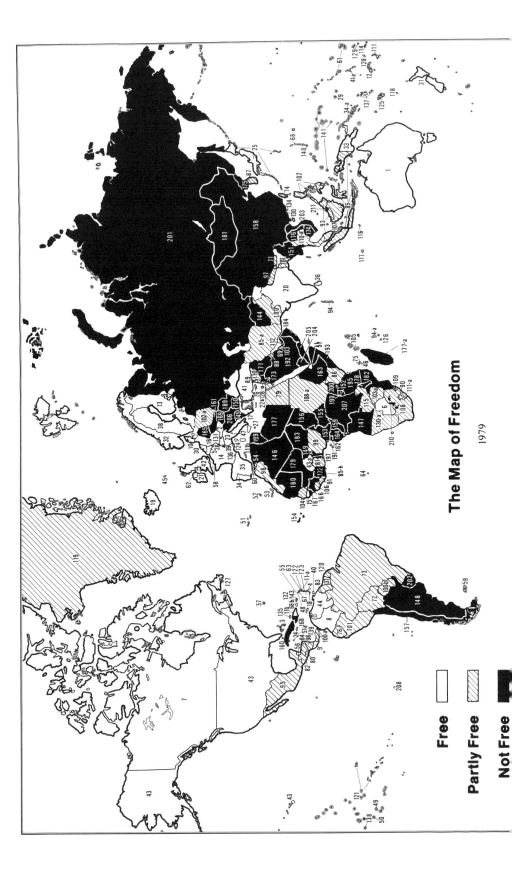

The Map of Freedom

1979

Free

Partly Free

Not Free

Free Nations

1 Australia
2 Austria
3 Bahamas
4 Barbados
5 Belgium
6 Botswana
7 Canada
8 Colombia
9 Costa Rica
10 Denmark
11a Dominica
11b Dominican Republic
12 Fiji
13 Finland
14 France
15 Gambia
16 Germany (W)
17 Greece
18 Grenada
19 Iceland
20 India
21 Ireland
22 Israel
23 Italy
24 Jamaica
25 Japan
26 Luxembourg
27 Malta
28 Nauru
29 Netherlands
30 New Zealand
31 Norway
32 Papua New Guinea
33 Portugal
34 Solomon Islands
35 Spain
36 Sri Lanka
37 Surinam
38 Sweden
39 Switzerland
40 Trinidad & Tobago
41 Turkey
41a Tuvalu
42 United Kingdom
43 United States
43a Upper Volta
44 Venezuela

Related Territories

Denmark:
45 Faroe Islands
France:
46 Mayotte
Italy:
47 San Marino
Netherlands:
48 Antilles
New Zealand:
49 Cook Islands
50 Niue
Portugal:
51 Azores
52 Madeira
Spain:
53 Canary Islands
54 Places of Sov. in No. Africa
United Kingdom:
55 Anguilla
56 Belize
57 Bermuda
57a Cayman Islands
58 Channel Islands
59 Falkland Islands
60 Gibraltar
61 Gilbert Islands
62 Isle of Man
63 Montserrat
64 St. Helena
67 West Indies Ass. States
United States:
68a Northern Marianas
68b Puerto Rico

Partly Free Nations

69 Bahrain
70 Bangladesh
71 Bhutan
72 Bolivia
73 Brazil
74 China (Taiwan)
75 Comoro Islands
76 Cyprus
77 Djibouti
78 Ecuador
79 Egypt
80 El Salvador
81 Ghana
82 Guatemala
83 Guyana
84 Honduras
85 Indonesia
85a Iran
85b Ivory Coast
86 Kenya
87 Korea (S)
88 Kuwait
89 Lebanon
90 Lesotho
91 Liberia
93 Malaysia
94 Maldives
94a Mauritius
95 Mexico
96 Morocco
97 Nepal
98 Nicaragua
99 Nigeria
100 Pakistan
100a Panama
100b Paraguay
101 Peru
102 Philippines
102a Poland
103 Qatar
103a Rhodesia
104 Senegal
105 Seychelles
106 Sierra Leone
107 Singapore
108 South Africa
108a Sudan
109 Swaziland
110 Syria
110a Thailand
111 Tonga
111a Transkei
111b Tunisia
112 United Arab Emirates
114 Western Samoa
115 Zambia

Related Territories

Australia:
116 Christmas Island
117 Cocos Islands
118 Norfolk Island
Denmark:
119 Greenland
France:
120 French Guiana
121 French Polynesia
122 Guadeloupe
123 Martinique
124 Monaco
125 New Caledonia
126 Reunion
127 St. Pierre & Miquelon
128 Wallis & Futuna
Israel:
128a Occupied Territories
New Zealand:
129 Tokelau Islands
Portugal:
130 Macao
South Africa:
130a South West Africa (Namibia)
Switzerland:
131 Liechtenstein
United Kingdom:
132 British Virgin Islands
134 Hong Kong
135 Turks & Caicos Islands
France-Spain Condominium:
136 Andorra
France-U.K. Condominium:
137 New Hebrides
United States:
138 American Samoa
139 Canal Zone
140 Guam
141 Micronesia
143 Virgin Islands

Not Free Nations

144 Afghanistan
145 Albania
146 Algeria
147 Angola
148 Argentina
149 Benin
150 Bulgaria
151 Burma
152 Burundi
153 Cameroon
154 Cape Verde Islands
155 Central African Empire
156 Chad
157 Chile
158 China (Mainland)
159 Congo
160 Cuba
161 Czechoslovakia
162 Equatorial Guinea
163 Ethiopia
164 Gabon
165 Germany (E)
166 Guinea
167 Guinea-Bissau
168 Haiti
169 Hungary
171 Iraq
173 Jordan
174 Kampuchea
175 Korea (N)
176 Laos
177 Libya
177a Madagascar
178 Malawi
179 Mali
180 Mauritania
181 Mongolia
182 Mozambique
183 Niger
184 Oman
189 Rumania
190 Rwanda
191 Sao Tome and Principe
192 Saudi Arabia
193 Somalia
195 Tanzania
197 Togo
200 Uganda
201 USSR
202 Uruguay
203 Vietnam
204 Yemen (N)
205 Yemen (S)
206 Yugoslavia
207 Zaire

Related Territories

Chile:
208 Easter Island
South Africa:
210a Bophuthatswana
United Kingdom:
211 Brunei

escence in the result cast doubt on the reality of the transfer of power, yet the new government has proved to be surprisingly independent. Elections in *Ecuador* and the campaigns that accompanied them demonstrated considerable advance in freedom. In *East Germany*, opposition of several kinds was apparent, especially the organized opposition of the church to compulsory military training in secondary schools. In *Ghana*, a constitutional referendum was poorly handled. But in the period before the vote, and after the coup that followed the vote, freedom of expression registered a gain over previous years; civilian political leaders again began to play a de facto role in politics. Although elections in *Guatemala* were accompanied by violence and results were contested, they marked an improvement over previous performance.

During most of 1978, *Iran* experienced an improvement in freedom, marked by the elimination of censorship, the legalizing of party formation, and the release of political prisoners. However, increasingly violent demonstrations and strikes, combined with the intransigence produced by years of repression, led to a military clampdown in November that reversed some of the year's gains. The newspapers remained closed until year's end by their own choice (and opened in January only when official censorship was removed). Most opposition leaders remained free and the people expressed their opinions freely in demonstrations and conversation in the face of intermittent repression. This gain over the outward acceptance of the regime a year ago justified a change of rating from "not free" to "partly free."

In *Kenya* the written media became freer and all well-known prisoners of conscience were released toward the end of the year. In *South Korea* the opposition was allowed to win a plurality in assembly elections. This was a gain even though little formal power was attained by this success. *Malawi* continued a very cautious advance with the first election that allowed a modicum of choice. In *Nigeria*, the year's record was very mixed, but the lifting of the long-standing state of emergency and the permission of political activity marked advances. Political parties took no part, but elections in *Panama* were freer and were accompanied by a more vocal opposition than in the recent past. The situation was comparable to that in the Philippines. In *Paraguay*, 1978 saw a strengthening of dissident activity and the release of most prisoners of conscience. In *Peru*, the election of a constituent assembly with the full participation of the parties marked an important forward step, although the assembly has no official part in government for the time being. The incorporation of important black leaders in the *Rhodesian* government marked an important gain for freedom. Unfortunately, the equalization of civil rights in a number of areas of political and social life was largely nullified by the extension of battle area conditions to much of the country.

Although all major parties could not participate, elections in *Senegal* marked an important forward step, as did new opposition publications and the subsequent chartering of an additional opposition party. While still a one-party state, the *Sudan* allowed members of former opposition parties de facto participation and considerable success in its parliamentary elections. Its policy of national reconciliation included a free election and a restructured government in the Negro Southern Region. Civil liberties were expanded in *Thailand* as political prisoners were freed and restrictions on the press moderated. The process of constitutional development signaled the gradual return of civilian leaders to political influence (as in Peru, Nigeria, and Ghana). The opposition increased its strength within the *Transkei* assembly, and the government demonstrated more independence than ever from South Africa. In spite of repressions and violence, 1978 saw a strengthening of opposition forces in *Tunisia*, particularly through the publication of opposition papers. *Upper Volta* returned to freedom with both legislative and presidential elections. Although there were allegations that the elections were fraudulent, the results were consistent with a reasonably fair process. Subsequently the three major parties were included in the government. *South Yemen* held a parliamentary election offering a very small range of choice.

FURTHER COMMENT ON CHANGES IN FREEDOM

The three new island states that came into existence this year were transferred from Table 2 (Related Territories) to Table 1 (Independent Nations). They were the *Solomon Islands* and *Tuvalu* in the Pacific, and *Dominica* in the Caribbean. The ratings stayed the same; it was felt that their effective level of freedom was only slightly raised over what they had already enjoyed under British control.

Elsewhere political ferment and rapid change characterize a number of polities, but in most cases the implications of this ferment for freedom are not yet clear. *Mainland China* continued to move away from revolutionary populism toward a more traditionalist, bureaucratic, and pragmatic system. By the end of the year new bursts of popular expression were occurring, but the permanence and further development of these blooms were still unpredictable.

Poland is reclassified in the Table of Independent Nations as "partly free" because of a combination of recent trends and a general reevaluation of its situation. Poland should be set apart from other Eastern European states. While it shares with Hungary or Yugoslavia positive characteristics such as a large private sector, particularly in agriculture, and relatively open travel and religious activity, in the communist world only Poland allows an organized and powerful opposition movement. This social, if not political, opposition includes an intellectual movement relatively stronger than that in the USSR (with even an "underground university") and a powerful church hierarchy willing and able to enter into social and quasi-political controversy. This hierarchy supports legal Catholic publications that directly oppose Marxist theory. Nevertheless, a highly refined censorship remains an important part of Polish life, particularly with regard to materials reaching the general public.

Several reclassifications of less significance may also be noticed in Table 1. Although there was some additional institutionalization of freedoms during the year, raising the ratings of *Ivory Coast, Mali, Rwanda,* and *Spain* was mainly due to comparative reevaluation. Reconsideration of evidence led to a slight reduction in *Sri Lanka's* rating.

Coups occurring in *Honduras* and *Mauritania* did not immediately affect the ratings, although they may eventually lead to democratic change. *Sierra Leone* saw the final steps taken in the imposition of one-party rule, with the explicit affirmation that an opposition does not have the right to exist. The suspiciously high ninety-seven percent majority attained in a referendum for one-party government compares unfavorably with the widely disparaged election processes this year in Chile or the Philippines. The freeing of some political prisoners by the *Cubans* in 1978 is to be welcomed, but seemed to be more a means of getting rid of undesirables than evidence of a change in the level of oppression. Similarly, prisoner release in *Indonesia* demonstrates relatively little change in civil liberties. Some improvements in freedom early in the year, as in *Haiti,* were followed by declines to the level of previous years; elsewhere, declines, as in *Indonesia,* early in the year were followed by advances toward previous levels.

Violence in *Nicaragua* was caused by persistent attempts to raise the level of freedom (as well as to change the holders of power) coming into conflict with the attempt of the government to maintain its present level of repression, or at least to liberalize at a very slow pace. In spite of the reported atrocities accompanying insurrection or civil war, for most of the year opposition media and movements operated with surprising freedom.

The attentive reader will note some minor adjustments in Table 2 (Related Territories) in addition to the deletion of the three territories that became independent. Most important of these changes was the improvement in the status of *South West Africa (Namibia).* This territory is now undergoing rapid change, including a greater equalization of rights and more respect for local political forces. While December elections were carried out under pressure and boycotted by important parties, they represented an advance. Paradoxically, in this colony of South Africa the black majority now has more of a role in the government than in South Africa itself. As in Rhodesia, the fate of these changes in 1979 under international and revolutionary pressure is very much in doubt. It should also be noted that in *Micronesia* a successful constitutional referendum represented an important step toward greater self-determination (although not as a unified federation).

ELECTIONS AND REFERENDA

Evidence for political freedom is primarily found in the occurrence and nature of elections or referenda. Therefore, as a supplement to our ratings we have attempted in the accompanying Table 5 to summarize those national elections that occurred in independent countries in 1978. Indirect elections are included only in the more important cases. The reader should assume that the electoral process appeared comparatively open and competitive unless our remarks suggest otherwise; extremely one-sided outcomes imply an unacceptable electoral process. Voter participation figures are often not comparable, even when available. Many states compel their citizens to vote, in others it is unclear whether participation is a percentage of those registered or of those of voting age.

INHUMANITY: LEVELS OF POLITICAL TERROR

Contributing to the judgment of the level of civil liberties in a country is the degree to which its citizens are subject to political terror, either from its government or from other groups within the society. Political terror, in turn, includes a variety of different aspects. Murder, torture, beating, imprisonment (especially without fair trials or just laws), exile, passport restriction, denial of vocation, ubiquitous presence of police controls, threats against relatives, all contribute to the fear that is labeled political terror.

In Table 6 five levels of political terror are distinguished. Countries on *Level A* live under a secure rule of law, people are not imprisoned for their views, and torture is rare or exceptional (though police and prison brutality may occur). Political murders are extremely rare. There is no detention without trial, and laws protect individual and group rights. On *Level B* there is a limited amount of imprisonment for nonviolent political activity. However, few persons are affected, torture and beating are exceptional, and psychiatric institutions are not

Table 5
National Elections and Referenda

Nation and Date	Type of Election	Percentage Voting	Results and Remarks
Albania 11/12/78	parliamentary	99.9%	single list
Bangladesh 6/3/78	presidential	52%	president received 75-77%; plausible in spite of irregularities
Belgium 12/17/78	general	87% valid	little change; conservatives and communists gain; voting obligatory
Bolivia 7/9/78	general	unknown	numerous irregularities led to annulment
Brazil 10/15/78	presidential	indirect	government candidate wins: 355-226
11/15/78	general	unknown	opposition received 56% of Senate vote, but resulting distribution favors government ca. 228-192 (House) and 47-20 (Senate)
Burma 1/2/78-1/15/78	parliamentary	unknown	"vast majority" said to vote for approved list
Cameroon 5/28/78	legislative	99%	highly controlled; no choice
Chile 1/4/78	referendum	91%	75% support government; phrasing hard for a patriot to reject; opposition publicity curtailed but not absent
China (Mainland) 11/77-2/78	general	unknown	indirect; no choice, but some individuals rejected by communities
Colombia 2/26/78	legislative	30%	ruling liberals 55%; conservatives 36%; others 9%
6/4/78	presidential	40%	liberal candidate narrowly wins with 51% of vote

32

Comoro Islands			
10/1/78	referendum	99.3%	99.3% approve constitution
10/22/78	presidential	98.8%	99.9% approve (no choice); majority support probable
12/8 & 12/15/78	parliamentary	unknown	nonparty election; run-off elections required
Costa Rica			
2/5/78	general	81%	opposition party wins presidency (48.8%) and plurality in legislature
Denmark			
9/19/78	referendum	80% (?)	approved lowering voting age to 18; 5/4 majority
Dominican Republic			
5/16/78	general	74%	opposition wins presidency with 50% vote; attains majority in lower house; compromise gives control of Senate to former ruling party
Ecuador			
1/15/78	referendum	90%	43% approve new constitution; 32% support revision of old; 23% blank or spoiled ballots—voting obligatory
7/16/78	presidential	80%	two candidates selected for run-off in 1979; many irregularities and delays in recount; results generally accepted
Egypt			
5/21/78	referendum	85.4%	98.3% reportedly approve proposal to curtail opposition parties and control media criticism; opposition to referendum severely restricted
El Salvador			
3/12/78	legislative	40-50%	government wins 50 of 54 seats; principle opposition party boycotts; very limited campaign
Finland			
1/15-16/78	presidential	69%	incumbent wins with 82% of vote; all major parties support; support of USSR determines outcome
France			
3/12 and 3/19/78	legislative	82-85%	parties supporting government win by narrow margin (50.5% of vote)
Ghana			
3/30/78	referendum	43%	constitutional proposal; returns indicating acceptance disputed; later events nullify result
Guatemala			
3/5/78	general	34%	narrow victory in three-way contest; exclusion of fourth candidate led to 1/3 of ballots being deliberately spoiled; many parties attain congressional seats

33

Table 5 — Continued

Nation and Date	Type of Election	Percentage Voting	Results and Remarks
Guyana 7/10/78	referendum	70% (?)	97% supported proposal to eliminate future need to bring constitutional revisions to referendum; with good cause opposition protested campaign tactics and claimed very low voter participation
Iceland 6/25/78	general	89%	ruling coalition loses many seats; new coalition to the left
Italy 6/11-12/78	referendum	81%	voters reject liberalizing public order laws and public support of political parties (77% and 56% majorities)
6/29-7/8/78	presidential	indirect	electoral college including both houses and others; 16 ballots before president chosen
Kenya 10/6, 10/28/78	party and presidential	indirect	by party congress and parliament
Korea (S) 5/78	electoral college	78%	contested but controlled; followed by near unanimous indirect re-election of president in July
12/12/78	legislative	77%	opposition wins 33% of votes to 31% for governing party (the remainder to other parties and independents); government retains majority because of appointed seats and electoral system
Malawi 6/29/78	legislative	unknown	voters given some choice among approved party candidates; no campaigning or party opposition
Malaysia 7/9/78	general	70%	governing front wins 131 of 154 seats, with 55% of vote (60% in 1974); restriction of opposition campaign
Maldives 7/28/78	presidential	unknown	nominated by parliament; 90% approve
New Zealand 11/25/78	parliamentary	unknown	government loses ground but retains majority of seats

Country / Date	Type	Participation	Notes
Panama 8/6/78	legislative	80% (?)	505 individual seats; elected mostly government supporters; very disproportionate districts; no parties allowed
10/11/78	presidential	indirect	selected government candidate elected 452-53 by legislature
Paraguay 2/12/78	general	82%	president and party win 90% of vote; voting compulsory
Peru 6/18/78	constituent	unknown	winners divided among many parties; one major party abstained, plurality to its rival; fair vote and campaign
Philippines 4/7/78	parliamentary	80-90%	government wins all but a few regional seats; traditional opposition boycotts; campaigning closely controlled; legitimate doubt of tabulation
Rwanda 12/17/78	referendum	unknown	90% accept one-party constitution
12/24/78	presidential	unknown	99% endorse unopposed incumbent
Senegal 2/26/78	general	50-63%	president and his party win 82% of vote and 83% of seats; a major opposition party not allowed participation
Sierra Leone 6/25/78	referendum	96% (?)	97% endorse one-party constitution; campaign slight and quick; credible doubt of extent of participation
Spain 12/6/78	referendum	67%	88% approve new constitution; fair vote and campaign
Sudan 2/2/78	legislative	unknown	one-party approval of all candidates; however, elected represent a broad spectrum of former parties, and local dignitaries were often elected
Swaziland 10/27/78	parliamentary	55%	no campaigning; apparently choice; electors chosen to select parliament
Switzerland 2/26/78	referendum	unknown	reject lowering retirement age and restricting highway construction
5/28/78	referendum	unknown	reject carless Sunday, daylight saving, and abortion compromise
9/24/78	referendum	41.5%	82.3% approve formation of new canton

Table 5 — *Continued*

Nation and Date	Type of Election	Percentage Voting	Results and Remarks
Switzerland (cont'd) 12/3/78	referendum	ca.43%	55% reject national police force
Syria 2/8/78	presidential	97%	99.6% approve single candidate; cause for doubt
United States 11/7/78	legislative	40%	results show little trend; slight Republican gain
Upper Volta 4/30/78	legislative	30-40%	plurality won by largest party in independence period; several other parties win seats
5/14/78 and 5/28/78	presidential	30-44%	incumbent re-elected; from largest party
Venezuela 12/3/78	presidential	87%	opposition candidate wins with 46% of the vote; voting obligatory
Yemen (S) 12/16-18/78	parliamentary	91%	limited choice among authorized candidates
Yugoslavia 4-5/78	general	indirect	election of approved candidates; two tiers before parliament is selected
Zambia 12/12/78	general	66%	80% approval; no choice, negative votes allowed

36

used to silence political opponents. Political murder is rare, or if present, characteristic of small terrorist organizations. On *Level C* there is extensive political imprisonment, or a recent history of such imprisonment. Executions or other political murders and brutality are often common and go largely unpunished. Security police tend to be ubiquitous. Unlimited detention, with or without trial, for political views is accepted. Incarceration in mental hospitals and the involuntary use of strong drugs may supplement imprisonment. On *Level D* the practices of Level C are generally expanded to larger numbers. Murders, disappearances, and torture are a common part of life in some societies at this level. In others there is large-scale incarceration of ideological opponents in labor camps or reeducation centers. In still others the terror may stem primarily from the arbitrary and capricious manner in which opponents are punished. In spite of its generality, on this level terror affects primarily those who interest themselves in politics or ideas. On *Level E* the terrors of D have been extended to the whole population, and may result from religious, ethnic, or ideological fanaticism. The leaders of these societies place no limits on the means or thoroughness with which they pursue personal or ideological goals. The worst periods of Nazi Germany or Stalinist Russia characterize countries on Level E.

This table measures the crimes against humanity of greatest interest to organizations such as Amnesty International. In doing so it fills a gap in the explanation of how the Comparative Survey of Freedom relates to other human rights concerns and perceptions. Some critics have felt that there was a need to separate out those countries that follow particularly evil practices from those that simply deny freedom at the 7, 7 levels of the ratings for political and civil freedoms. Others have wondered how the Survey could continue to rate countries such as Nicaragua, that have a high level of terror and violence, as highly as it does on the scales of political and civil freedoms.

Table 6 establishes the point that in some cases fairly free institutions coexist with egregious violations of humanity. Comparison of this table with others will suggest that while levels of freedom are obviously related to levels of terror, the correlation is not as high as might be imagined. It has been a surprising finding of the Survey that some societies—for example several in Central America—exhibit a remarkable level of freedom in the face of widespread political violence, both governmental and nongovernmental. In part this is due to the unorganized, anarchic nature of violence in such countries, in part to the unwillingness of many of their citizens to be terrorized by others.

The categorization in Table 6 is obviously very rough. It is based

Table 6
Estimated Levels of Political Terror

Level A		Level B		Level C	
Australia	F	Gabon[5]	NF	Algeria	NF
Austria	F	Grenada	F	Bahrain	PF
Bahamas[1]	F	Guyana	PF	Bangladesh	PF
Barbados	F	Hungary	NF	Benin[5]	NF
Belgium	F	India	F	Bolivia	PF
Botswana[1]	F	Italy[6]	F	Brazil[3]	PF
Canada	F	Ivory Coast	PF	Burma	NF
Costa Rica	F	Kenya[2]	PF	Burundi[5]	NF
Denmark	F	Kuwait[5]	PF	Cameroon	NF
Dominica[1]	F	Liberia	PF	Chad	NF
Dominican		Mauritius	PF	China	
Republic[1]	F	Nigeria	PF	(Mainland)[2]	NF
Fiji	F	Panama[2]	PF	China	
Finland	F	Peru[2]	PF	(Taiwan)	PF
France[1]	F	Poland	PF	Colombia	F
Gambia	F	Saudi Arabia	NF	Cuba	NF
Germany (W)[1]	F	Senegal[2]	PF	Cyprus	PF
Greece[1]	F	Spain[6]	F	Czechoslovakia	NF
Iceland	F	Sri Lanka	F	Djibouti[5]	PF
Ireland	F	Sudan[2]	PF	Ecuador	PF
Israel[1/4]	F	Thailand[5]	PF	Egypt	PF
Japan[1]	F	Transkei	PF	Germany (E)	NF
Luxembourg	F	Trinidad &		Ghana[3]	PF
Malta	F	Tobago	F	Guinea-Bissau	NF
Nauru	F	Venezuela	F	Honduras[5]	PF
Netherlands	F	Zambia[5]	PF	Iran[5]	PF
New Zealand	F			Jamaica	F
Norway	F			Jordan	NF
Papua New				Korea(S)	PF
Guinea[1]	F			Lesotho[5]	PF
Portugal[1]	F			Libya	NF
Surinam[1]	F			Madagascar[5]	NF
Sweden	F			Malaysia	PF
Switzerland	F			Mali	NF
United				Mauritania	NF
Kingdom[1]	F			Mexico	PF
United				Morocco	PF
States[1]	F			Nepal	PF

on very incomplete knowledge in some cases, and it is confused by the attempt to integrate very different types of terror in the same scheme of judgment. As in the other tables, the degree of accuracy we strive for is to be never more than a category off for any country. For example, a B state should perhaps be placed on levels A or C, but we are quite sure it does not belong on level D. The reader should also remember that while in most states the government is principally to blame for the level of terror, in some the government is simply too weak to control the terror. Since this table is an experiment this year, the levels of terror are not included in the country summaries in the back, nor are all countries listed in Table 6.

		Level D		Level E	
Niger	NF	Afghanistan[5]	NF	Albania[5]	NF
Oman[5]	NF	Angola	NF	Equatorial Guinea	NF
Pakistan[5]	PF	Argentina[3]	NF	Ethiopia[3]	NF
Philippines	PF	Bulgaria	NF	Kampuchea	NF
Rumania	NF	Central African Empire	NF	Uganda	NF
Sierra Leone[5]	PF	Chile[3]	NF		
Singapore	PF	Congo[5]	NF		
South Africa	PF	El Salvador	PF		
Swaziland	PF	Guatemala	PF		
Syria	PF	Guinea	NF		
Tanzania	NF	Haiti[5]	NF		
Togo[5]	NF	Indonesia[3]	PF		
Tunisia	PF	Iraq	NF		
Turkey	F	Korea(N)	NF		
USSR	NF	Laos	NF		
Yemen(N)	NF	Lebanon[3/6]	PF		
Yugoslavia	NF	Malawi[3]	NF		
		Mozambique[5]	NF		
		Nicaragua	PF		
		Paraguay	PF		
		Rhodesia[6]	PF		
		Somalia	NF		
		Uruguay	NF		
		Vietnam	NF		
		Yemen(S)	NF		
		Zaire	NF		

Notes to the Table

Countries for which information is insufficient to include in this table are: Bhutan, Cape Verde Islands, Comoro Islands, Maldives, Mongolia, Qatar, Rwanda, Sao Tome and Principe, Seychelles, Solomon Islands, Tonga, Tuvalu, United Arab Emirates, Upper Volta, and Western Samoa.

1. Special situations, cases of terror in the recent past, or general political environment cast doubt on this rating.
2. Recent improvements have moved the country up to this level.
3. Recent improvements may have raised the country above this level.
4. Does not include occupied territories.
5. The current situation is very unclear.
6. This rating is primarily due to anti-government terrorism or civil war.

THE RELATION OF POLITICAL-ECONOMIC SYSTEMS TO FREEDOM

The accompanying Table of Political-Economic Systems (Table 7) fills two needs. It offers the reader additional information about the countries we have rated. For example, those with libertarian views may wish to raise the relative ratings of capitalist countries, while those who place more value on redistributive systems may wish to raise the ratings of countries toward the socialist end of the spectrum. The table also makes possible an analysis of the relation between political and economic forms and the freedom ratings of the Survey. Perusal of the table will show that freedom is directly related to the existence of multi-

Table 7 Political-

POLITICAL ►	Multiparty		Dominant-Party
	Centralized	Decentralized	
ECONOMIC — Capitalist — Inclusive	Bahamas F Ireland F Barbados F Italy³ F Colombia⁴ F Japan F Costa Rica F Luxembourg F Djibouti PF Mauritius PF Dominica⁴ F New Zealand³ F Dominican Spain F Republic⁴ F Surinam F France³ F Trinidad & Greece F Tobago F Grenada F Upper Volta³ F Iceland F	Australia F Belgium F Canada F Cyprus PF Germany (W)³ F Lebanon PF Switzerland F United States F	El Salvador¹ PF Korea (S) PF Malaysia PF
Capitalist — Noninclusive	Fiji⁴ F Gambia⁴ F Guatemala PF Lesotho PF Morocco PF Papua New Guinea³ F Solomon Islands² F	Botswana F	Nicaragua 1/4 PF Transkei⁵ PF
Capitalist-Statist — Inclusive	Malta F South Africa PF Sri Lanka F Turkey⁴ F Venezuela F	Brazil 1/3 4 PF	China (Taiwan) PF Mexico PF Singapore PF
Capitalist-Statist — Non-inclusive	Bangladesh¹ PF Rhodesia⁴ PF	India F	Indonesia 1/4 PF Paraguay 1/3/4 PF
Capitalist-Socialist — Inclusive	Austria F Jamaica F Denmark F Netherlands F Finland F Norway F Guyana PF Portugal F Israel F Sweden F United Kingdom F		Egypt 3/4 PF Senegal 3/4 PF Syria 1/4 PF
Capitalist-Socialist — Non-inclusive			
Socialist — Inclusive			
Socialist — Noninclusive			Iraq 1/3/4 NF

Notes

1. Military dominated.

2. Party relationships analogous to this category.

3. Close decision on capitalist-to-socialist dimension.

4. Close decision on inclusive/noninclusive dimension.

5. Over 50 percent of income from remittances of persons working in South Africa.

40

Economic Systems

<table>
<thead>
<tr><th colspan="3">One-Party</th><th colspan="2">Nonparty</th></tr>
<tr><th>Socialist</th><th>Communist</th><th>Nationalist</th><th>Military</th><th>Traditional</th></tr>
</thead>
<tbody>
<tr>
<td></td><td></td><td></td>
<td>Chile $^{1/3}$ NF</td>
<td>Jordan^1 NF</td>
</tr>
<tr>
<td>ierra Leone PF</td>
<td></td>
<td>Cameroon^3 NF
Central Afr. Emp.^{1} NF
Gabon NF
Haiti NF
Ivory Coast^4 PF
Kenya PF
Liberia PF
Malawi NF
Philippines $^{2/3/4}$ PF</td>
<td>Chad^1 NF
Ecuador^1 PF
Honduras $^{1/4}$ PF
Niger^1 NF
Thailand $^{1/3}$ PF
Uganda^1 NF
Yemen (N) $^{1/3}$ NF</td>
<td>Bhutan^3 PF
Comoro Islands PF
Maldives PF
Nepal^3 PF
Swaziland PF
Tonga PF
Tuvalu F
Western Samoa PF</td>
</tr>
<tr>
<td>ibya $^{1/3}$ NF</td>
<td></td>
<td></td>
<td>Argentina^1 NF
Ghana $^{1/4}$ PF
Panama $^{1/3}$ PF</td>
<td>Bahrain PF
Iran^4 PF
Kuwait PF
Nauru F
Qatar PF
Saudi Arabia NF
United Arab Ems. PF</td>
</tr>
<tr>
<td></td>
<td></td>
<td>Zaire^1 NF</td>
<td>Mauritania^1 NF
Nigeria $^{1/3/4}$ PF
Pakistan^1 PF</td>
<td>Oman NF</td>
</tr>
<tr>
<td>unisia^4 PF</td>
<td>Poland^3 PF
Yugoslavia^3 NF</td>
<td>Seychelles^3 PF</td>
<td>Uruguay^1 NF</td>
<td></td>
</tr>
<tr>
<td>fghanistan^3 NF
urma^1 NF
urundi^3 NF
ongo $^{1/3}$ NF
omalia $^{1/3}$ NF
ambia^3 PF</td>
<td></td>
<td>Madagascar $^{1/3}$ NF
Mali^1 NF
Rwanda $^{1/3}$ NF
Sudan^1 PF
Togo^1 NF</td>
<td>Bolivia^1 PF
Peru $^{1/4}$ PF</td>
<td></td>
</tr>
<tr>
<td>lgeria NF</td>
<td>Albania NF
Bulgaria NF
China(Mainland) NF
Cuba NF
Czechoslovakia NF
Germany (E) NF
Hungary NF
Kampuchea NF
Korea (N) NF
Mongolia NF
Rumania NF
USSR NF
Vietnam NF</td>
<td></td>
<td></td>
<td></td>
</tr>
<tr>
<td>ngola NF
nin $^{1/3}$ NF
pe Verde Is. $^{3/4}$ NF
quatorial Guinea^4 NF
uinea NF
uinea-Bissau^3 NF
ozambique NF
o Tome and
rincipe^3 NF
nzania NF
emen (S) NF</td>
<td>Laos NF</td>
<td></td>
<td></td>
<td>Ethiopia $^{1/3}$ NF</td>
</tr>
</tbody>
</table>

party systems: the further a country is from such systems, the less freedom it is likely to have. This could be considered a trivial result, since a publicly competitive political system is one of the criteria of freedom, and political parties are considered evidence for such competition. However, the result is not simply determined by our definitions: we searched for evidence of authentic public competition in countries without competitive parties, and seldom found the search rewarded. Both theoretical and empirical studies indicate the difficulty of effective public political opposition in one-party systems.[2]

The relation between economic systems and freedom is more complicated and, because of our lack of emphasis on economic systems in devising our ratings of freedom, is not predetermined by our methods. Historically, the table suggests that there are three types of societies competing for acceptance in the world. The first, or *traditional* type, is marginal and in retreat, but its adherents have borrowed political and economic bits and pieces from both of the other types. The second and third, the *Euro-American* and *Sino-Soviet* types, are strongest near their points of origin, but have spread by diffusion and active propagation all over the world. The Leninist-socialist style of political organization was exported along with a socialist concept of economic organization, just as constitutional democracy had been exported along with capitalist economic concepts. In this interpretation, the relation of economic systems to freedom found in the table may be an expression of historical chance rather than necessary relationships. Clearly, capitalism does not cause nations to be politically free, nor does socialism cause them to be politically unfree. Still, socialists must be concerned by the empirical relationship between the rating of "not free" and socialism that is found in tables such as this.

In the table, economies are roughly grouped in categories from "capitalist" to "socialist." Labeling economies as capitalist or socialist has a fairly clear significance in the developed world, but it may be doubted that it is very useful to label the mostly poor and largely agrarian societies of the Third World in this manner. Raymond Aron, for example, casts doubt on the legitimacy of calling any Third World, noncommunist society "socialist," regardless of what it may call itself.[3] However, Third World states with dual economies, that is, with a modern sector and a preindustrial sector, have economic policies or goals that can be placed along the continuum from socialist to capitalist. A socialist Third World state has usually nationalized all of the modern sector—except possibly some foreign investment—and claims central government jurisdiction over the land and its products, with only temporary assignment of land to individuals or cooperatives. The capitalist Third World state has a capitalist modern sector and a traditionalist agricultural sector, combined in some cases with new agricultural projects either on family farm or agribusiness models. Third World economies that fall between capitalist and socialist do not have the high taxes of their industrialized equivalents, but they have major nationalized industries (for example, oil) in the modern sector and their agricultural world may include emphasis on cooperatives or large-scale land reform, as well as more traditional forms.

States with *inclusive capitalist* forms are generally developed states that rely on the operation of the market and on private provision for industrial welfare. Taxes may be high, but they are not confiscatory, while government interference is generally limited to subsidy and regulation. States classified as *noninclusive capitalist*, such as Liberia or Thailand, have not over fifty percent of the population included in a capitalist modern economy, with the remainder of the population still living traditionally. In such states the traditional economy may be individual, communal, or feudal, but the direction of change as development proceeds is capitalistic.

Capitalist states grade over into capitalist-statist or capitalist-socialist nations. *Capitalist-statist* nations are those such as Brazil, Turkey, or Saudi Arabia, that have very large government productive enterprises, either because of an elitist development philosophy or major dependence on a key resource such as oil. Government interferes in the economy in a major way in such states, but not primarily because of egalitarian motives. *Capitalist-socialist* systems, such as those in Israel, the Netherlands, or Sweden, provide social services on a large scale through governmental or other nonprofit institutions, with the result that private control over property is sacrificed to egalitarian purposes. These nations still see capitalism as legitimate, but its legitimacy is accepted grudgingly by many in government. Governments of other states grouped here, such as Egypt or Poland, proclaim themselves to be socialist, but in fact allow rather large portions of the economy to remain in the private domain. Both variants have *noninclusive* versions, such as India or Madagascar.

Socialist economies, on the other hand, strive programmatically to place an entire national economy under direct or indirect government control. States such as the USSR or Cuba may allow some modest private productive property, but this is only by exception, and right to such property can be revoked at any time. The leaders of *noninclusive socialist* states have the same goals as the leaders of inclusive socialist states, but their relatively primitive economies or peoples have not yet been effectively included in the socialist system. Such states generally have a small socialized modern economy and a large preindustrial economy in which the organization of production and trade is still largely traditional. It should be understood that the characterizations in the table are impressionistic; the continuum between capitalist and socialist economies is necessarily cut arbitrarily into categories for this presentation.

Political systems range from democratic multiparty to absolutist one-party systems. Theoretically, the most democratic countries should be those with *decentralized multiparty systems*, for here important powers are held by the people at two or more levels of the political system, and dissent is legitimated and mobilized by opposition parties. More common are *centralized multiparty systems*, such as France or Japan, in which the central government organizes lower levels of government primarily for reasons of efficiency. *Dominant-party* systems allow the forms of democracy, but structure the political process so that opposition groups do not have a realistic chance of achieving power. Such limitations may be through vote fraud, imprisonment of opposition leaders, or other devices.

The now classical form of one-party rule is that in *one-party* states such as the USSR or Vietnam that proclaim themselves to be *communist*. The slightly larger group of *socialist one-party* states are ruled by elites that use Marxist-Leninist rhetoric, organize ruling parties very much along communist lines, but either do not have the disciplined organization of communist states or have explicitly rejected one or another aspect of communism. A final group of *nationalist one-party* states adopt the political form popularized by the communists (and the fascists in the last generation), but the leaders generally reject the revolutionary ideologies of socialist or communist states and fail to develop the totalitarian controls that characterize these states. There are several borderline states that might be switched beween socialist and nationalist categories (for example, Libya or Syria). It should also be noted that "socialist" is used here to designate a political rather than economic system. A socialist "vanguard party" established along Marxist-Leninist lines will almost surely develop a socialist economy, but a state with a socialist economy need not be ruled by a vanguard party. It should be pointed out that the totalitarian-libertarian continuum is not directly reflected by this categorization.

Nonparty systems can be democratic, as in the small island of Nauru, but generally they are not. Such systems may be *traditional nonparty* systems ranging from Tonga to Saudi Arabia. Much more important are the many *military nonparty systems*, such as those in Argentina or Uganda.

SELF-DETERMINATION

In a world in which national self-determination is considered to be a fundamental political right, it is necessary for a survey of freedom to consider the extent to which this right is respected. The United Nations finds the denial of self-determination primarily in the remnants of European colonialism, and limits the concept to this application.[4] However, today the most significant limitations of national rights are not to be found in Table 2 on related territories. A broader picture of the real and putative denials of national expression existing today is offered by Table 8, *Major Peoples Without a Nation State*, and Table 9, *Major Peoples Separated from Existing Nation States*.[5] In each case, only relatively large ethnic groups (generally over one million) that have given some evidence of national consciousness are included. The tables consider only territorial peoples, and thus ignore scattered, largely urban peoples, such as Jews in the USSR or American blacks and Mexican-Americans. To be included in these tables, the ethnic group must not be the *Staatsvolk*, or dominant people in an existing state, nor can it be a truly equal party in a binational state. The first requirement excludes, for example, Serbians in Yugoslavia, Russians in the USSR, or Tagalogs in the Philippines; the latter requirement excludes the Walloons in Belgium. To reduce the tables to manageable size, in marginal cases the decision was most often to omit rather than include a people.

It is expected that many significant peoples that are not now included in the tables will develop national consciousness in the future. This is especially true in Africa, where the definitions of "a people," of ethnic-group domination, and of political consciousness are particularly difficult. The table of separated peoples assumes that a nondominant people in one state would prefer life in another state where the separated people are the dominant group or *Staatsvolk*, but such may not be the case—the Hutu of Burundi, for example, may wish to dominate their own state. Where a group would reject inclusion with its ethnic group in a neighboring state, the group has not been considered a separated people. For example, because of religious differences the Punjabi of India do not want to live in Pakistan. Some peoples could as well be included in Table 8 as Table 9: The Papuans of West Irian might wish to join the independent state of Papua New Guinea, or the Moros might rather be independent than join Malaysia.

While Tables 8 and 9 are not definitive, they suggest the size of the populations involved and the degrees of national consciousness they feel. The final column in the tables presents an evaluation of the political equality of the group in the state that incorporates it, placing this

Table 8
Major Peoples Without a Nation-State[1]

	Population (millions)	Location	National Consciousness	Political Equality/ Status of Freedom
Achehnese	2	Indonesia	high	fair/ partly free
Arabs of Chad	1.5	Chad	medium[4]	fair/ not free
Armenians	2 (plus scattered millions)	USSR	high	good/ not free
Assamese	10	India	medium	good/free
Aymara	1	Bolivia	low	fair/ partly free
Azerbaijani	4	USSR	low	fair/ not free
	5	Iran	low	fair/ partly free
Baluchis	2	Pakistan & Iran	medium[4]	poor-fair/ partly free
Bamileke	1.5	Cameroon	medium [4]	fair/ not free
Bantu of Rhodesia	6	Rhodesia	medium[4]	fair/ partly free
Bantu[2] of S. Africa	14	S. Africa	medium	poor/ partly free
Bashkir	1	USSR	low	fair/ not free
Basques	1	Spain (& France)	high[4]	good/free
Batak	2.5	Indonesia	medium	fair/ partly free
Berbers (various)	5	Algeria	low	fair/ not free
	5	Morocco	low	fair/ partly free
Bosnian Muslims	1	Yugoslavia	medium	fair/ not free
Bretons	1	France	high	fair/free
Buginese	3	Indonesia	low	fair/ partly free
Belorussians	7	USSR	low	good/ not free
Catalonians	5	Spain	high	good/free
Chuang	8	China (Mainland)	low	good/ not free
Croats	4.5	Yugoslavia	high	fair/ not free
Edo	3	Nigeria	medium	good/ partly free

Notes to the Table

1.   In several states, such as China, Indonesia and the USSR, a number of large ethnic groups have been omitted because of either their geographical dispersion or limited evidence of national consciousness. Such groups have generally not had a history of political independence beyond the local level.

2.   Many of the Bantu peoples of South Africa define themselves in tribal terms as Zulu, Xhosa, Sotho, etc. Millions who live outside of their home areas have become urban, largely de-tribalized South Africans.

3.   Although Israel itself is rated free, most Palestinian Arabs live in the occupied territories controlled by Israel or in other lands no better than partly free.

4.   Known to have had active armed movements against central government in recent years.

	Population (millions)	Location	National Consciousness	Political Equality/ Status of Freedom
Eritreans	1.5	Ethiopia	high[4]	poor/ not free
Estonians	1	USSR	high	poor/ not free
Ganda	2	Uganda	high	poor/ not free
Georgians	3	USSR	medium	fair/ not free
Gujerati	25	India	high	good/free
Hausa-Fulani	25	Nigeria	medium	good/ partly free
Hui	4	China (Mainland)	high	fair/ not free
Ibibio	3.5	Nigeria	medium	good/ partly free
Ibo	14	Nigeria	high[4]	fair/ partly free
Ilocanos	4	Philippines	low	good/ partly free
Kannada	25	India	medium	good/free
Kanuri	4	Nigeria	medium	good/ partly free
Karens	3	Burma	high[4]	poor/ not free
Kazakh	4.5	USSR	medium	poor/ not free
Kirghiz	1.5	USSR	low	poor/ not free
Kongo	2	Zaire	medium	poor-fair/ not free
	2	Angola (& Congo)	medium[4]	poor-fair/ not free
Kurds	2	Iraq	high[4]	poor/ not free
	3	Turkey	medium	poor/free
	2	Iran	high[4]	fair/ partly free
Latvians	1.5	USSR	high	poor/ not free
Lithuanians	2.5	USSR	high	poor/ not free
Luba-Kasai	1.5	Zaire	low[4]	poor/ not free
Luo	1	Kenya	medium	fair/ partly free
Makassarese	2	Indonesia	low	fair/ partly free
Malayalam	20	India	high	good/free
Marathi	45	India	high	good/free
Mayans	4	Mexico, Guatemala	very low	fair/ partly free
Mende	1	Sierra Leone	medium	fair-poor/ partly free
Miao	2.5	China (Mainland)	low	fair/ partly free
Minahassans	1	Indonesia	medium	good/ not free
Minangkabau	5	Indonesia	medium	fair/ partly free
Moluccans	1	Indonesia	high[4]	poor-fair/ partly free

Table 8—*Continued*

	Population (millions)	Location	National Consciousness	Political Equality/ Status of Freedom
Montagnards	1	Vietnam	medium[4]	poor/ not free
Nilotics of Sudan	4	Sudan	medium[4]	good/ partly free
Nkole	1	Uganda	low	poor/ not free
Nupe	1	Nigeria	medium	good/ partly free
Oriyan	20	India	medium	good/free
Oromo (Galla)	2-10	Ethiopia	medium[4]	fair/ not free
Ovimbundu	2	Angola	medium[4]	poor/ not free
Palestinians	3+	Israel, Jordan, Lebanon, Syria	high[4]	poor-fair/ partly free[3]
Pampangans	1.5	Philippines	medium[4]	fair/ partly free
Papuans	1	Indonesia	medium[4]	poor/ partly free
	1	Papua New Guinea	medium	good/free
Punjabi (India)	17	India	low	good/free
Québecois	5	Canada	high	good/free
Quechua	5	Peru, Bolivia	low	fair/ partly free
	1	Ecuador	low	poor-fair/ partly free
Scots	5	United Kingdom	high	good/free
Shan	1.5	Burma	high[4]	poor/ not free
Sidamo	2.5	Ethiopia	low[4]	poor/ not free
Sindhis	9	Pakistan	medium	fair/ partly free
Slovaks	4.5	Czecho- slovakia	high	good/ not free
Slovenes	1.5-2	Yugoslavia	high	fair/ not free
Soga	1	Uganda	low	poor/ not free
Sundanese	16	Indonesia	medium	fair/ partly free
Taiwanese	14	China (Taiwan)	low-med.	poor-fair/ partly free
Tamil	40	India	high	good/free
	2.5	Sri Lanka	high	fair/free
Tatars (various)	4	USSR	medium	poor-fair/ not free
Telegu	50	India	high	good/free
Teso	1	Uganda	low	poor/ not free
Tibetans	3	China (Mainland)	high[4]	poor/ partly free
	2	India, Pakistan, Nepal & Bhutan	medium	fair/ partly free
Tigrinya	3	Ethiopia	high[4]	poor/ not free

48

	Population (millions)	Location	National Consciousness	Political Equality/ Status of Freedom
Timorese (E)	1	Indonesia	medium[4]	poor/ partly free
Tiv	8	Nigeria	medium	good/ partly free
Turkmen	1.5	USSR (& Iran)	medium	fair/ not free
Uighur	4	China (Mainland)	medium	poor/ not free
Ukrainian	35-40	USSR	high	fair/ not free
Ulster Scots	1	United Kingdom	high	good/free
Uzbek	9	USSR	high	fair/ not free
	1	Afghanistan	medium	fair/ not free
Visayans	10	Philippines	low	good/ partly free
Welsh	2.5	United Kingdom	high	good/free
Yi (Lolo)	3	China (Mainland)	medium	fair/ not free
Yoruba	16	Nigeria	high	good/ partly free

in relation to the status of freedom of this host state as found in Table 1. These tables do not imply that the affected peoples should immediately be granted independence, or that borders should be changed. They do imply that the national rights of peoples cannot be ignored: these rights are taken into account in our evaluation of political rights. (The case for these rights is developed in *Freedom in the World 1978*, pages 180–218.) Adequate rights can be granted within the boundaries of larger states. For example, the Gujeratis of India, with internal self-government, would gain little by complete independence.

To aid in understanding the issues involved and the reasons for some of our inclusions and exclusions, Tables 8 and 9 need to be supplemented by a survey of the nature and political situation of subnational peoples by geographical region, type of polity, and country. The following treatment is necessarily brief, but it will give the reader at least an overview of the situation of those major peoples in the world today that do not have nation states.

In 1978 group rights in free states were relatively well guaranteed, although there was continued interest in expanding these rights. It is only recently that states such as France and England that proudly guaranteed individual rights removed severe limits on subnational group rights. The democracies had continued the long record of suppressing conquered cultures by dominant peoples, but where these cultures survived, there is now a revival of separatist expression. This

Table 9
Major Peoples Separated from
Existing Nation-States

	Population (millions)	Desire for Reunion or Independence	Political Equality/ Status of Freedom
Albanians of Yugoslavia	1	unknown	fair/ not free
Alsatians of France (to Germany)	1	medium	good/free
Bengalis of India (to Bangladesh)	45	low	good/free
French of Switzerland	1.5	very low	good/free
Irish of Northern Ireland	0.6	high	fair/free
Hutu of Burundi (to Rwanda)	4	high	poor/ not free
Kashmiri of India (to Pakistan)	3	med.-high	good/free
Koreans of China	1	unknown	fair/ not free
Macedonians of Yugoslavia (to Bulgaria)	1	unknown	fair/ not free
Malay of Thailand	1	unknown	fair/ partly free
Magyars of Rumania (to Hungary)	2.5	high	fair/ not free
Moldavians of USSR (to Rumania)	2.5	unknown	fair/ not free
Mongols of China	1.5	high?	fair/ not free
Moros of Philippines (to Malaysia?)	2	medium	fair-poor/ partly free
Pathans of Pakistan (to Afghanistan)	6	med.-high	fair/ partly free
Somali (of Ethiopia) (plus Kenya and Djibouti[1])	2	high	poor/ not free
Tadzhiks of USSR (to Iran)	1.5-2	low	fair/ not free
Tadzhiks of Afghanistan (to Iran)	5	low	fair-good/ not free

1. Are now the *Staatsvolk* of their own free country.

expression is meeting increasing favor; yet as late as 1960 French children were required to report to their teachers students who conversed in Breton, and in the 1970's Breton can still not be used in the regular school curricula.[6]

In recent years increasing attention has been given to the rights of the Flemish and Walloon peoples that divide the Belgian state. The British parliament accepted constitutional changes in 1978 establishing assemblies in Wales and Scotland (in early 1979 the Welsh rejected the plan by referendum and the Scots may have given it insufficient support to become law). The U.K. is still not able to resolve the conflicting claims of the Ulster Scots and Irish in Northern Ireland. In this case, to recognize the rights of one of these inter-mixed communities would be to deny the rights of the other. In France there has been more attention given to ethnic enclaves such as those of the Bretons or Alsatians as part of a general European interest in decentralization.[7] The Corsicans are pressing vigorously for increased self-determination. Violence has been suppressed, but over the last years some demands have been met. In Switzerland, the people of the Northern Jura were given a separate canton in 1978 in a national referendum climaxing a series of detailed elections. In Spain Basques, Catalans, and other peoples have recently attained a measure of self-government.

In the United States and Canada, respect for Indian and Eskimo rights has increased as pressure groups have come to represent the interests of these peoples. However, ethnicity for these native groups is broken into many small fragments; in particular, the sense of an American "Indian Nation" is largely an urban minority response. A similar progression is found in the histories of the native peoples of Australia. 1978 saw gains in all three states in the expansion of the economic and political power of native peoples in their own area. The Maori of New Zealand are perhaps the most fully and fairly incor-porated primitive group in a modern political system. The freeing of Papua New Guinea by Australia in the 1970's represented an important enhancement of self-determination. Yet it is important to note that in ethnic terms Papua New Guinea consists of a maze of small units that should in turn have their rights respected in the new state.

The problem of the self-determination of French Canada is the most outstanding issue in the developed democracies. Quebec nationalists came to provincial power in late 1976, but too much must not be inferred from this. First, their party did not stress separatism in this election to the extent it had previously, and, secondly, it did not receive a majority of the votes. Within Canada's federal system special rights have been advanced to the province of Quebec that amount to a very high degree of self-determination without independence. This includes the right to have permanent foreign missions, the growing use of French as the official language in the province, and the right to opt out of many federal social programs and replace these with provincial pro-grams.[8] The greatest denial of rights may be by the Quebec government to those favoring the English language.

The communist world has developed a unique combination of theo-retical and practical approaches to self-determination. Communist universalism has traditionally implied that there should be only one socialist system ruled by one socialist party in the world. Many communists assume that so-called ethnic conflicts are class conflicts, and represent "false consciousness."[9] From this perspective, even the East European states represent a temporary expedient—at least to the extent that their governments should be ultimately coordinated on the party level.

On another level, communist systems, especially the USSR and Yugoslavia, have emphasized the creation of ethnic administrative divisions, and to some extent the preservation of local cultures and languages. However, on the one hand these units have never been given a real chance for self-determination because of centralized party structures, while, on the other, communism has been unable to change the nationalistic tendency of the ruling people in each communist state to emphasize its own nationalism: Russians in the USSR and Han Chinese in China, as well as Serbs in Yugoslavia and Rumanians in Rumania, have come to use their power in numbers or position to deny or diminish political and even cultural self-determination to other peoples. The most frequent and devastating means has been to simply move in Russians and Chinese, respectively, until the local people no longer have a majority in their own territory. This has happened notably in Kazakhistan in the USSR, and more rapidly in Inner Mongolia and Sinkiang in the Chinese People's Republic. However, where such a policy does not succeed, the formation of subnational cultural units tends to gradually create an increasingly vital basis for unity and opposition—especially where the ruling people is not willing to give up its special privileges. In the USSR, since the non-Russian population is growing faster than the Russian, non-Soviet nationalisms may be growing more rapidly than the sense of Soviet unity. In 1978 several Republics managed to maintain the official status of their languages against a Soviet attempt at their elimination in new constitutions. Lithuanians and Ukrainians remained particularly active this year. Growing ethnic nationalism may also be observed in Yugolsavia, especially among the Croatians. In both the USSR and Yugoslavia, the central government's desire to control separatist expressions accounts for the major part of the repressive acts of the regime. An exception is Czechoslovakia, where relative harmony and a desire by Russian masters to play off Czechs and Slovaks will probably keep the interests of both groups in the state in a rough balance.[10]

Ethnic struggles in Latin America have had a muted existence. While a number of countries have large, subordinate, American Indian populations, especially Peru and Guatemala, this fact has not engendered subnational desires for self-determination.[11] Racially, Hispanic dominance is accepted—for example, by the seventy percent of Dominicans who are black and the many millions of black Brazilians or Colombians.

In most Latin American nations it appears to be passively accepted that Hispanic or Mestizo-Hispanic culture is the guiding national culture, and that mobility for the poor must involve Hispanization. It is curious that symbolic pro-Indianism—for example, in Mexico—has seldom been a movement sponsored by actual Indians. This is also true of Peru, yet here the recent glorification of the Inca past did lead to the adoption of Quechua as a second national language. More recently Bolivia has recognized both Aymara and Quechua as official languages. In Paraguay, culturally and biologically the most Indian Latin American state, Spanish and Guarani are the languages of nearly everyone, and the cultures play complementary roles in the lives of most individuals.

The main exceptions to the Hispanic-Mestizo pattern in the Americas are found in the Caribbean, where many small states are overwhelmingly black, using either French, English, or Dutch as their primary language. Where the population is not homogeneous, as in Trinidad and Tobago, Guyana, and Surinam, politics generally revolves around the ethnic clash of African and East Indian. Yet in these relatively democratic polities there is little suppression of peoples, and little separatist demand for self-determinism. A different issue, that of an island's right to self-determination, has broken up several attempts at closer unions of islands, and is even breaking up the small units that do exist (for example, St. Kitts-Nevis-Anguilla, or the Netherlands Antilles).

Small Indian tribes, particularly in the Amazon basin, continue to struggle against encroaching settlers from the dominant societies. Ruthless movement into the lands of these groups goes on today, in its most publicized form in Paraguay and Brazil, with or without government support. This is an old story of ethnic destruction along an advancing frontier that Americans should understand and oppose as we continue to try to repair the damage of the process in our own history.

In Sub-Saharan Africa, self-determination is a burning issue almost everywhere. Small elite populations rule over larger subordinated groups in Rhodesia and South Africa, five and seventeen percent of the people, respectively; in Burundi fifteen percent of the people, the Tutsi, rule over the Hutu majority. South West Africa presents a similar but more complex situation. It might also be said that Liberia is still ruled by a small elite of Americo-Liberians (three percent). Except in Burundi, a combination of external and internal pressures may soon result in turning over portions, or all, of such minority states to their majorities.

Homogeneous countries in Sub-Saharan Africa with essentially no ethnic problem include Botswana, Lesotho, Swaziland, Transkei, and

Somalia. A few African states have the developed racial or ethnic oppositions of peoples such as we are familiar with elsewhere in the world. Most notable is that in the Sudan between the Muslim, largely Arab, northern majority and the non-Muslim, largely Nilotic, south. This situation is repeated immediately to the west in Chad, although here the majority black peoples of the south are opposed by the nomadic Arab north. Continuing revolt in Chad is partially supported from Libya (which incidentally appears to have annexed a section of northern Chad without the world noticing). There is no reason, however, why Chad must be one state.[12]

In 1978 the government of the Sudan continued to show its willingness to grant a degree of autonomy to the Negro south by holding fair regional elections and by the subsequent appointment of a former rebel commander to lead the region. Although the significance was less clear, self-determination of the minority northern Arabs in neighboring Chad was recognized by the appointment of an Arab rebel leader as Prime Minister; however, by the year's end the reconciliation was falling apart.

More commonly, Sub-Saharan Africa is characterized by countries with a large number of ethnic groups. Such groups may vary widely in size and strength of group consciousness. Two types of states should be distinguished. In the first, the scattering of small groups is so extreme, and their consciousness so undeveloped, that ethnic conflict and the related question of self-determination have not been critical issues.[13] Examples are Tanzania (exclusive of Zanzibar) or the Central African Empire. Legitimate demands for self-determination may be raised later by small groups as they become more conscious, or, in the process of development, groups with related linguistic, religious, or other bonds may come to identify themselves as a people within a state.

In the second type, the scattering of peoples exists on two levels. On the first, there are some major peoples, or groups of peoples within the state, with an established subnational identity, while there are many other, generally smaller, peoples that are only rising to consciousness, or that tend to be ignored while attention is focused on the larger groups. Ghana, Uganda, and Angola belong in this type, but Nigeria is the best known example.[14] Nigeria began with a federal system based on three peoples—Yoruba, Hausa-Fulani, and Ibo. Subsequent events have caused the state to develop regionalizations that give a degree of self-determination to broader and broader ranges of peoples. In the constitutional discussion of 1978 an unsuccessful effort was made to go beyond the nineteen states this process has already produced. This process of subdivision reduces the degree of self-determination of the larger groups (and strengthens the relative power of the central government). Yet finer regionalization is fully justified by an ethnic situation in which many smaller peoples feel oppressed by their neighbors.

The Ethiopian state, emerging from the medieval age into the age of nationalism, finds itself beset internally and externally by divisive demands comparable to those plaguing the Austro-Hungarian Empire before World War I. There is no particular reason why the constituent peoples of Ethiopia, at about the state of consciousness of those in Nigeria, should find their liberty within an Ethiopian state. In both cases constituent peoples have a long history of group independence, and in some cases the experience of an independent historical state. 1978 saw the retreat of the Eritreans under the pressure of foreign arms, but the reactivation of Somali resistance. The 1978 revolt of the people of Zaire's Shaba province suggests that maintaining Zaire in its present form requires the desires for self-determination of many established and emergent peoples to be suppressed.[15] Concern for broader political issues unfortunately leads the international public to overlook the justice of their cause.

In most of the Arab Middle East and North Africa, the relation between Arabs and other peoples is similar to that of Hispanic cultures and minority peoples in Latin America. In particular, the Berbers of Morocco, Algeria, and elsewhere in North Africa have slowly lost out over the centuries to encroaching Arabs.[16] While there have been Berber revolts, the prestige of Arab culture, the carrier of Islam, is such that serious Berber nationalism seems to be absent. Much the same is the case in the northern Sudan, where a number of non-Arabic groups are gradually being Arabicized. Further east, however, we find religious ethnicity expressed in yearnings for greater self-determination among the peoples of Palestine-Israel, Lebanon, and Syria. Religion is the basis of political divisions in the former two but not officially in Syria. In Turkey, Iraq, and western Iran the primary issue is Kurdish nationalism, flaring strongly in Iraq and Iran whenever the government appears unable to suppress it. While the Kurds have a long history as an ethnic group, their first disappointment with nationalism in its modern form came at the end of World War I. Since that time, Turkey has actively tried to assimilate millions of Kurds, even by the device of relabeling them "Mountain Turks." In Iran a Kurdish Republic was suppressed at the end of World War II after brief Russian sponsorship. In the last few years, an interminable guerrilla war against Iraq was ended when Iranian support was withdrawn, but today renewed Iraqi oppression, including an attempt to scatter the Kurds, has spawned yet another resistance movement. In 1978-79 Kurdish nationalism has had a chance to grow again in Iran.

Asia is characterized by several ethnic patterns. Japan and Korea are almost entirely homogeneous. Other states with long continuity, such as China, Iran, and Thailand, have a dominant core culture and recognized boundaries, yet have had autonomist ethnic movements at the periphery. The historical states of Indochina are similarly constructed, with minorities especially important (but scattered) in Laos.[17] By the end of 1978 the Meo were reported to be largely expelled from Laos. In Burma the people of the core are continually struggling with peripheral peoples striving for their own independence. A somewhat different pattern exists in India, Pakistan, Sri Lanka, Bangladesh, and Afghanistan, where political boundaries have been superimposed arbitrarily on a geographical pattern of historical peoples that does not correspond with political boundaries. At least one-third of the population of Afghanistan is Persian speaking, while the ruling Pathans of Kabul often have their tribal homelands in Pakistan.[18] Bengalis continue to be divided between Bangladesh and India. Pakistan is now a thoroughly Muslim, pluralistic society whose dominant language and elite are from northern India. Independence movements in Pakistan have been against the centralizing state, but not clearly against a particular people, although the Punjabis are now the great majority, especially in the army. Recently the Baluchis are the most vocal in their demands. In India the adoption of Hindi alongside English as a national language goes part of the way toward developing a core culture or *Staatsvolk*.[19] Thirty to forty percent of the people speak Hindi or a closely related dialect, and both the ancient and modern Indian capitals are in the Hindi-speaking area. Indian states have been founded on regional linguistic subnationalisms; many of these, such as those based on Bengali, Tamil, and Marathi, have fully developed literatures and a corresponding subnational consciousness.

It is important to note that in both India and Pakistan the tendency of state boundaries to enhance a region's sense of identity has often led to a drive for regional self-determination at the same time as these divisions have met in large part the legitimate demands of the people concerned (especially in India). However, crosscutting allegiances of religion, caste, custom, party—and of English language among the elite—have tended to counteract the separatist tendencies of regional self-determination. It should also not be forgotten that millions of the so-called tribal peoples of India, such as the Nagas and Mizos northeast of Bangladesh, do not identify with Indian culture. India must keep these relatively small groups within its boundaries by force, much as Burma has tried less successfully with similar peoples.

Finally, in Southeast Asia there are several artificial states created by colonial masters out of previously fractured societies. Malaysia is a union of Malay states now united largely by a determined government attempt to reduce the role of the Chinese and Indians in the economy. Indonesia and the Philippines lack a dominant core culture, yet for different reason have managed to create state nationalisms for most of their peoples above the level of the particularities. The Philippines had no organized state before the Spanish conquest, but there had developed in southern Luzon a cultural core based on the Tagalog-speaking peoples. These were the people that became most fluent in Spanish and, under the Americans, in English. Although no more than twenty-one percent of Filipinos speak Tagalog, the language of the core culture, when nationalism developed a demand for a national language, the language chosen was essentially a form of Tagalog, re-christened Pilipino. By 1960 over forty percent also spoke English (compared with three percent in India). Competitive subnational groups, such as the Visayans or Ilocanos, have developed an ethnic self-consciousness, but not in a threatening manner. More important is the separatist feeling of the 3.5 million Muslims in the southern islands that are pressed hard by land-hungry Christians (especially Visayans) and supported by Muslims in the outside world. Their revolt continued to flare in 1978 in spite of the efforts of the Philippine army.

Javanese culture forms the cultural core of Indonesia, although many Indonesians have little in common with Javanese. The sense of oppression by Javanese is muted by several factors First, in most of the islands substantial ethnic identity is poorly developed, either because of socioeconomic underdevelopment (interior Sumatra or Borneo), or crosscutting allegiances. Indonesia has also been fortunate in being able to choose an old Malay *lingua franca* (converted into Bahasa Indonesia) as a national language rather than Javanese. There have been, however, movements for self-determination in outlying areas, particularly in the Moluccas, Sulawesi, and northern Sumatra.[20] These have been suppressed without significant recognition of the desires of the people. Independence movements exist in East Timor and West Irian; that in East Timor may have been largely extinguished during the year. The world's indifference to the cause of the Papuans seems particularly incongruous. They are clearly a separate people with a full right to independence; and relatively successful self-government in neighboring Papua New Guinea shows the practicality of that independence.

CONCLUSION

Although 1978 was a year of progress, there were many disappointments. Brazil, Argentina, and Pakistan did not move forward as fast as we might have hoped. Bolivia's election fizzled, and the parliamentary elections in the Philippines amounted to little. Yet there was progress, and this progress can be attributed in no small part to America's continued attention to human rights in spite of conflicting pressures, a campaign in which allies and neutrals are now also playing a part. Generally, progress is in countries only "partly free," but the campaign was not unknown even in Haiti and Uganda. It led toward the end of the year to an attempt of Kampuchea (Cambodia) to refurbish its image, an attempt that came too late.

Among those events receiving media attention, a serious failure of the human rights campaign has been the Soviet Union's seeming rejection at Belgrade of the significance of the Helsinki accords for its internal political policy. The year saw an increase in Soviet oppression of intellectual dissidents. Perhaps periods of increased repression are inevitably a part of the process of focusing more attention on basic rights. Soviet leaders obviously fear the expansion of freedoms; they fear the expansion of human rights groups; and yet they also know that repression costs them something in international regard and the good opinion of some of their own cadres. If the outside world maintains its concern for these freedoms, it will be interesting to see whether the current repressive reaction to this concern will continue to seem an attractive response to Soviet leaders. Whatever the final result for the USSR, clearly the last few years have placed human rights higher on the agenda of many governments.

As 1979 began neither Chinese leaders nor dissidents seemed fearful of a more open future. Experience suggests that for a Chinese spring to be more than another unhappy vernal interlude there will have to be continued effort on the part of the friends of freedom both within and without China. In particular, private organizations and American diplomats must strive to develop the same positive and supportive relationship to Chinese dissidents that they have to those in Eastern Europe, the USSR, or South Korea. We must know and speak up for the Chinese Solzhenitsyns and Bukovskys of the past and future. They expect it and we cannot let them down. There may be good geopolitical reasons to take seriously the desires of the rulers of the Chinese Empire; there are even better moral and long range strategic reasons for taking seriously the hopes and desires of the Chinese people or the peoples of China.

NOTES

1. For more discussion of methodology see R. D. Gastil, *Freedom in the World 1978*, especially pp. 7–30.

2. See William J. Foltz, "Political Opposition in Single-Party States of Tropical Africa" in R. A. Dahl, ed., *Regimes and Oppositions* (New Haven:

Yale, 1973); also Giovanni Sartori, *Parties and Party Systems* (Cambridge: Cambridge University Press, 1976).

3. Raymond Aron, "My Defense of Our Decadent Europe," *Encounter* (September 1977), pp. 7–50, especially p. 33.

4. See A. Rigo Sureda, *The Evolution of the Right of Self-Determination: A Study of United Nations Practice* (Leiden: Sijthoff, 1973), and Daniel Thürer, *Das Selbstbestimmungsrecht der Völker* (Bern: Stampli, 1976).

5. Those familiar with previous Surveys will note that the presentation is reversed from that in the Table of Major Subordinate Peoples in the Surveys for 1976 and 1977. Additional information and somewhat different criteria have also been used.

6. Manfred Wenner, "The Politics of Equality Among European Linguistic Minorities," in Richard P. Claude, ed., *Comparative Human Rights* (Baltimore: Johns Hopkins University Press, 1976), pp. 184–213.

7. See especially James Cornford, ed., *The Failure of the State: On the Distribution of Political and Economic Power in Europe* (London: Crown Helm, 1975), especially pp. 14–43.

8. See Richard Pious, "Canada and the Crisis of Quebec," *Journal of International Affairs*, 27, no. 1 (1973): 53–65.

9. Roman Szporluk, "Nationalities and the Russian Problem in the USSR: An Historical Outline," *Journal of International Affairs*, 27, no. 1 (1973): 22–40.

10. M. G. Zaninovich and D. A. Brown, "Political Intervention in Czechoslovakia: The Implications of the Prague Spring and Soviet Intervention," *Journal of International Affairs*, 27, no. 1 (1975): 66–79.

11. This discussion is based primarily on Crawford Young, *The Politics of Cultural Pluralism* (Madison: University of Wisconsin Press, 1976), pp. 428–59.

12. On the earlier situation see John Ballard, "Four Equatorial States," in G. M. Carter, *National Unity and Regionalism in Eight African States* (Ithaca: Cornell University Press, 1976), pp. 231–36.

13. For the factual situation see Donald G. Morrison, and others, *Black Africa: A Comparative Handbook* (New York: Free Press, 1972). The interpretation relies heavily on Young, *The Politics of Cultural Pluralism*, especially pp. 163–326.

14. This is, of course, also the situation in Chad and the Sudan, for within both sides of the basic cleavage there are subgroups that only for a time will subordinate their interests.

15. The complexities and dilemmas of the situation are well described in Young, *The Politics of Cultural Pluralism*, pp. 163–215.

16. Discussion based on Young, *The Politics of Cultural Pluralism*, pp. 373–427.

17. Frank Lebar, Gerald Hickey, and John Musgrove, *Ethnic Groups of Mainland Southeast Asia* (New Haven: Human Relations Area Files, 1961).

18. Compare Richard Newell, *The Politics of Afghanistan* (Ithaca: Cornell University Press, 1972).

19. Ainslee Embree, "Pluralism and National Integration: The Indian Experience," *Journal of International Affairs*, 27, no. 1 (1973): 41–52; also Young, *The Politics of Cultural Pluralism*, pp. 274–326, 114–21.

20. On the Moluccan movement, in addition to Young, see *Keesing's Contemporary Archives*, pp. 27537–38.

PART II
Freedom, Equality, and Culture

Freedom and Equality

Critics of the liberal concepts of political and civil freedoms frequently contrast the pursuit of these freedoms with the pursuit of equality or justice. They assert that most peoples, especially poor peoples, are primarily concerned with improving their economic and social condition, and that all peoples and individuals have a right to enjoy equal economic and social conditions, irrespective of race, religion, ethnic group, sex, or nationality. To such people, political and civil freedoms are of little importance before this equality is attained. It is often implied that in and of themselves these freedoms can make relatively little contribution to the achievement of an egalitarian society.[1]

Against this view, we urge that when seen as human rights, equality and freedom simply are different aspects of the same concept. It is particularly characteristic in the popular American tradition to assume that a "democratic attitude" is one that supports even-handedly both equality and freedom. The following discussion will show how equality and freedom support one another in this tradition, and consider the implications of their close relationship.

Freedom in the political and social realm refers to a social relationship or condition in which individuals or groups are not blocked by specific others from obtaining their separate goals.[2] On reflection it is obvious that such a *social freedom* can only be relative. Insofar as we are living in the presence of others, progress toward individual goals will frequently be blocked by others. While waiting for admission to a theatre each of us obtains the best position he can within the accepted rules of queuing. Searching for a mate every young person is blocked by the achievements of those more attractive or talented, or by the simple rejection of advances by the beloved.

The fact that we are continually blocked by others does not mean that social freedom is nonexistent, but it does mean that freedom is a condition of relative lack of interference. Freedom implies the pursuit of one's objectives within the limits set down by a society and with equal respect to the rights of other free persons within this

63

society. Thus the French Revolution's *Declaration of the Rights of Man and The Citizen* declares that "Liberty consists in the power to do whatever does not harm others." Bringing the concept up-to-date the libertarian John Hospers notes that "Every right entails a duty to refrain from violating the other person's right."[3] An unfree person must be an individual with special limits that do not apply to all, or one constrained to grant rights to others he does not enjoy himself. A free person is one who does not suffer these additional constraints. Extending freedom to all must mean that a society removes all but the most generally applied constraints from everyone. In other words, it means the achievement of equality in those rights that constitute social freedom.

In these terms let us examine what we have considered the two essential aspects of freedom: political rights and civil liberties. To have political rights means that I have a voice in selecting my leaders (or their policies) and can myself be selected as a leader. To have "full political rights" must mean that I have rights at least equal to those of others, and the extension of these rights to all is to make all equal in these rights. Civil liberties means that I have all of the liberties granted to others. It cannot mean that I am free to do anything I want, as explained above. Polities often require definite political decisions that will affect all of their members. In these cases equal political rights implies majority rule, for only in that way are the political rights of all equalized. If the majority vote for a general policy and the minority against, the way for the equality of those in the majority to be demonstrated is for the policy to be adopted. Majorities are often coalitions of minorities, yet however formed a majority must ultimately make the laws for a democratic society. Unavoidably, among these laws will be many that restrict the freedoms of all, and particularly of individuals or groups not affiliated with the majority.

Political rights would not be equal if one generation of electors could rule out the possibility of change by denying expression to present minorities that are prospective majorities. Therefore, political rights assume both equal rights to vote and equal rights to influence opinion formation. For this reason effective political rights, or political equality, must include an important arena of civil rights, or civil equality. The members of the present minority must have rights of assembly, expression, and fair trial or they cannot compete as equals against those individuals who happen at the moment to be in the majority. For if the policies of the majority constrict unequally the opinion-forming actions of the minority, then the political weight of the majority's members has been unduly expanded.

Beyond this point, the arena of civil liberties that must be guaranteed in a perfectly democratic or egalitarian society is unclear, precisely because it goes beyond the limits of guaranteeing political equality, which in turn is simply an expression of the equal respect given to the interests of all as they see them. Libertarians would have us believe that the majority has very few rights to restrict the minority. Yet that would mean in many instances that the minority would be able to establish the nature of a society's life, and thereby nullify the equality symbolized by majority rule. If forty-nine percent of the people wished to have no speed limits, to live uninhibited public sex lives, and to burn leaves in their backyards, the result would soon be a society characterized by the minority's policies. (Many in the majority would adopt the practices they disapproved, for as the "tragedy of the commons" discussion suggests, when there is no rule restricting all, it is often not in the interest of many individuals to observe rules they support on a community-wide basis.)

Although the details are far from clear, the correct basis for deciding the limits of civil liberties from the standpoint of political equality or freedom might be to guarantee to the majority control over an arena labeled "public" and to the minority control over an arena labeled "private." Civil liberties in the public arena would only be guaranteed by the demands of equality insofar as they are necessary for an adequately equal right to influence the formation of majorities. Further interference with civil liberties by the majority can be justified only to the extent that it involves the public arena of life. Defining "public" will always be a difficult and contentious legislative and judicial task, but it should not therefore be avoided.[4] The very existence of the concept establishes that there is a "private" arena of life in which the majority does not have the right of intrusion.

Ensuring a private realm can also be a mechanism for ensuring the political equality of members of the minority, a mechanism in some ways analogous to that of granting the majority control of the public arena as a means of ensuring their equality. The private arena makes it possible for those in permanent minorities to achieve within limited spheres those goals and values that are denied to them in public. The essence of a pluralistic society is that it allows subsocieties to exist in which minorities may be majorities. Those in the minority in any society (and everyone is in the minority in some respects) are always in danger of having their effective self-determination and thus freedom reduced to a level lower than the majority, unless there is a realm into which they and their fellows may retreat out of the danger of public confrontation with the society as a whole. A private arena also may make up for the fact that the limits of all communities

are more or less arbitrarily defined. Were the limits of communities
defined differently, the laws we live by would not be the same. If
the states had been nations, in 1925 Nevada would have been wet
and Utah polygamous. The existence of private realms offers partial
redress for the oppressions that result from the fortuitous nature of
arbitrary political boundaries.

The discussion must not leave in doubt the inalienability of rights
to "life and the pursuit of happiness." Surely a free person and an
equal person have these rights. These words symbolize the existence
of an essential core of humanity that no majority has a right to
take away. Civil liberties are inalienable insofar as they derive from
private rights that lie outside of the majority's arena of legitimate
control. All liberties are not inalienable in public: the policeman
may carry a gun in situations where I may not. But within a broad
realm the majority or its representatives cannot legitimately threaten
our lives or interfere with how we define and pursue our interests.

In its political dimension, then, freedom implies equality. Turning
the question around, is equality equivalent to freedom or necessary
for freedom? It would seem that a reasonable definition along the
lines of the foregoing analysis would be possible, illuminating, and
come surprisingly close to what has generally been accepted as
equality in the American tradition. Arguing that it is historical non-
sense to see equality and liberty as opposed concepts in American
history, Alexander Meiklejohn states that for the Republic's founders
they were parts of the single idea of democracy.[5] According to this
definition equality is a social relationship in which the rights of one
person to pursue his goals are not superior to those of another.

This definition of equality does not assert an equality of opportunity.
The intellectuals among the founders of the United States apparently
believed that they were establishing a system offering equality of
opportunity and that this equality would greatly reduce those inequalities of condition that characterized most societies.[6] But most
Americans have always realized that family backgrounds will make
a difference, and that chance will play an important part in the outcomes of individual lives. The favorite myth of Americans, popularized
in Horatio Alger stories, was not that virtue always triumphed but
that *given the breaks* good will and hard work would bring success.
Neither equality of condition nor equality of opportunity could really
characterize any society: the son of a president will never have the
same chances as the daughter of a miner. Up to a point Americans
want the boss to favor his son-in-law, for that is what they would
do were they in his situation.[7] But yet our tradition proclaims equality

as a goal because equality that equalizes rights rather than chances is obtainable within a free society.

The equality of opportunity that the American system provides today is meaningful but limited. Although some analysts conclude that chance is the most important determinant of economic inequalities,[8] a recent study of economic mobility points to the considerable effect of the variety of factors that make up family background, including inherited wealth. In this study twenty-five of the fifty people in the sample that came from families in the top fifth economically were themselves in the top fifth by their forties; only two of the fifty from the lower fifth had attained this level.[9] In another sample only five of fourteen from families in the lowest tenth remained there, but none had emerged from the lower half of the sample by their forties. There is upward mobility for the poor, but not surprisingly the chances of a person from a poor family for high income is not as good as the chance of a person of wealthier background.

Clearly people everywhere have wanted respect and justice. Just as clearly they have not imagined that their individual positions at either the beginning or end of life would be the same. They have not wanted this for two reasons. First, they have thought some deserved or needed more than others. This man needs more rest, that more food, this more protection, that more training. Some have wanted their income in honor, others in cattle. They have also known intuitively that unhappiness is a function of the degree to which the expectations of prior experience are disappointed. A society of truly equal opportunity would be likely to produce more unhappiness than one with more limited goals, for objective equality would become the enemy of subjective equality. Secondly, most people have realized that without incentives society would decay, and they have known that incentives must include the possibility of unequal shares of wealth, power, or prestige. Society has bargained for leadership or excellence with the coin of unequal return.

It is true that there has also been a minor populist tradition in America, the tradition of envy that insists that all should be equal in every way. This has served as necessary leaven in a world in which unjust differences in wealth and culture continue to produce widespread dissatisfaction in society. But voter preferences and popular behavior have never suggested that absolute equality is a majority desire in normal times. For example, the desire to ignore differences between bright and dull, between athletically gifted and awkward, between hard-working and lazy have been supported in the schools by liberal educationists, but opposed by the overwhelming majority of parents.[10] Taxes may be seen by some intellectuals as a way to equalize living standards; most citizens see taxes as a way to support needed government services.

The gap between the attitudes of most Americans to equality and that of the more extreme egalitarian critics of society is captured in the following quotation from a recent discussion of inequalities in education:

> ... (in a broad critique) of the American educational system Bowles and Giutis ... list four "undemocratic" elements of the capitalist system that structure work roles: (1) bureaucratic organization, (2) hierarchical lines of authority ... (3) job fragmentation, and (4) unequal reward structure. In order to maintain these elements unchanged the capitalist class controls occupational status by first requiring a pattern of noncognitive personality traits (e.g., learning to accept discipline, to be methodical, predictable, and persevering); second by discriminating in their choice of certain ascriptive characteristics of workers (race, sex, and age ...); and third by requiring certain acquired credentials such as educational degrees or seniority.[11]

The average American or European would reject these criticisms of the educational system, because they go against his training (as the quotation laments), but also, as he would say with some justification, because they defy common sense. Except for certain aspects of the discrimination specified by the critics, few American egalitarians would have ever characterized the elements of the system described above as "undemocratic." Even in theory these elements are accepted as necessary by communist states that place equality far above freedom. Experiments that have tried to organize society without most of these elements and traits are rapidly abandoned. In his later years Mao attempted to construct the society that Bowles and Giutis would approve; his attempts are now being rapidly abandoned to the cheers of the people they were meant to benefit.[12]

Equality, then, when defined as social equality, characterizes a society in which no man is by right my superior. No one blocks the attainment of my goals by virtue of superior right. I am, in other words, a free man in the sense defined above for social freedom.

In America equality and freedom can be seen as equivalent concepts, two sides of the same coin. To be equal and free does not mean that I have the highest position in the government or the most wealth in the economy, or even that no one has more money or power than I. It simply means that in my role as citizen at the ballot box, in the courts, the market place, and the home I have as many rights as anyone, and that I live in a society that guarantees this equality to me through the guarantee of political and civil freedoms.

Given this equivalence, how far must the equality of condition, the "equality of result" of recent sociology, be guaranteed in order to support effective political equality and freedom? One could make the case that only people with identical incomes and identical educations and identical prestige would have effective equivalence in political rights or freedom. I cannot, for example, support the candidate of my choice as effectively as my neighbor can if he has twice my income. From this perspective social equality as we have defined it appears to offer an insufficient basis for freedom.

The equality offered by democratic political forms when combined with the inequalities of condition must produce inequalities in political power. The claim can be substantiated that the upper class in the United States is a "governing class," at least in the sense that statistically its members control a disproportionate share of the top positions in our most important institutions.[13] This is at least as true in a socialist-seeming society such as Sweden.[14] But this fact does not necessarily conflict with democracy, as in the following definition:

> There is a democracy where rulers are politically responsible to their subjects. And there is political responsibility where two conditions hold: where citizens are free to criticize their rulers and to come together to make demands on them and to win support for the policies they favour and the beliefs they hold; and where the supreme makers of law and policy are elected to their offices at free and periodic elections.[15]

It may also be objected that political equality in the traditional democracies is essentially negated by the veto power of corporations.[16] The argument is that, essentially capitalistic, these democracies must always bend to the will of the capitalists who make possible their efficient functioning. Certainly it is true that government has less of a coercive power over economic interests in capitalistic democracy than in socialist nondemocracy. Yet the difference seems to be more in the lack of democracy in the latter than in its socialism. For whether economic activity is organized by capital or labor, by cooperative enterprise or large corporations, economic interests in any society in which they are allowed to organize and publicize will have more than an equal say in those matters that affect them directly.

The argument that corporate or business power cannot be successfully opposed in a capitalist democracy is again and again disproved by events. The political losses of business to labor reform, environmental controls, anti-discrimination statutes, and innumerable other governmental taxes and restrictions are legion. Apparently, whether one notices these recurrent defeats for business interests, large and small, depends on whether one is a businessman or not. The much touted business control over the media can also be shown to be ephemeral when one goes beyond the limits of advertising for specific products. A recent study of TV evening series suggests that they are written and directed by people overwhelmingly anti-business, and that this attitude is almost uniformly exhibited by the shows produced.[17]

But is the definition of democracy quoted above sufficient when class differences become extreme? For example, let us consider countries with majority populations of poorly paid unorganized factory workers or farm laborers living alongside extremely wealthy and influential persons. All may have an equal vote, but the frequency of voting, of political activity, or standing for office may be distinctly unequal. Rural areas with startling inequalities of income often deliver the same overwhelming majorities year after year for candidates selected by tiny elites. Clearly it would seem that social equality as we have defined it is an insufficient basis for freedom.

The reality, however, is somewhat different. The denial of political equality does not stem primarily from the sheer disparity of condition. In every instance where an elite prevents popular electoral victories, this is attained by the use of violence and coercion on a scale that is incompatible with the foregoing definition of democracy. For example, recent elections in El Salvador, Guatemala, and Nicaragua have certainly been of this kind, just as they were in the past. But when rights are not overtly denied by law or oppression the people exert their prerogatives (except perhaps a very poor minority). This fact may be demonstrated by considering those extremely poor countries where the poor play a significant role by regularly switching from supporting one group to another. India is the best example, but cases can be drawn from the recent histories of Sri Lanka, Bolivia, Costa Rica, Barbados, and Venezuela. In the American South it was not poverty that disenfranchised the blacks for generations, but specific laws and practices that denied equality and freedom to a large section of the population. With the elimination of these restraints the Southern black vote is now taken very seriously at all levels of government, even though blacks remain a minority in every state. In Northern Ireland the poorer Irish fail to achieve unification because they are a minority. In Ulster communities where they are a majority, reform of the voting system has given them local political control.[18]

It is strange how often this point is missed in discussions of equality. In his survey of the struggle for equality in the United States, J. R. Pole is quite aware of the movements, the successes and failures, that have characterized the process. Although Pole minimizes the importance of equality in civil and political freedoms, particularly in suffrage, it appears from the record he considers that essentially it was lack of equality in these rights, lack of an effective vote and of equality before the law, that has inhibited and in some areas still inhibits the fulfillment of the American dream.[19] Similarly, historians have often minimized the importance of post-reconstruction laws in the disenfranchisement of Southern blacks. The most extreme example of this tendency was Staughton Lynd's claim that without economic independence the Negroes vote in the last half of the nineteenth century could not have been meaningful. However, detailed recent study has shown that Southern blacks took the vote seriously in the 1870's and 1880's, exhibited a high level of participation, and affected policy. In most states they eventually withdrew not so much because of social pressure or violence as because the application of new laws took the right to vote away from most blacks.[20]

There remain, of course, differences in the political weight of individuals and classes, differences that democratic societies everywhere are driven to reduce by both the demands of democratic ideology and the pressure of competitive politics to expand the electorate. However, the paradox of egalitarian policy is that as soon as it gets beyond the relatively narrow arena of guaranteeing social freedom and equality, it begins to deny some freedoms while enhancing others, with the result that the advance toward the free society becomes a retreat. Ostensible advances are retreats whenever they must involve compulsion that goes beyond the provision of equal respect and freedom in law. Symbolic of such denials is the compulsory voting enacted by several democratic societies. Compulsory voting injures both those who would choose not to vote and those who would choose to vote. It harms the first by intruding on the private rights of individuals to choose how to spend their time. It also offends against the human right not to express oneself, which includes the right to expression through abstention. It offends against the rights of the voluntary voter by bringing to the polls persons who by being less interested in voting are more likely to express random preferences. Obviously this reduces the probability that the side with the majority of nonrandom preference votes will achieve an electoral majority.

Any attempt to transfer money from the better off to the less well off necessarily means that the rights of the better off must be infringed by the agents of the majority (assuming a democracy) more than those of the less well off. The obvious example is that of the progressive income tax—a point bitterly argued by its opponents when it was introduced. Less obviously, but just as surely, those benefited by such redistribution ultimately must also have their rights infringed in ways rights need not be infringed for the wealthy. Such supervision is necessary, for beyond narrow limits the majority cannot allow money to be redistributed carelessly to the poor—if it did, so many would become recipients of transfer payments that the system would collapse.[21] For this reason all truly socialist societies have stern laws against vagrancy and idleness.[22] Unemployment is banished in such societies by the simple expedient of forcing all to work—mobility and economic choice become the right of the government and not the individual. (Where this is not the case—in Yugoslavia—there is considerable unemployment and a large proportion of the workforce works outside the country.)

One-party states founded to achieve "egalitarianism" fail precisely in their inability to provide basic equality. Too often this failure is built into misunderstandings that lie at the heart of one-party systems. For example, in a recent favorable study of one-party systems in Africa arranged by the International Commission of Jurists we find three revealing statements:

> In the last resort, the extent of the freedom within a one-party state will depend upon the commitment of the party to human rights and the rule of law. If the single party and its leaders at all levels are imbued with a spirit of tolerance and concern for the protection of fundamental rights, this attitude will permeate the whole society and violations of human rights . . . will be avoided.
> A one-party state can be a truly democratic form of government where the party is freely open to all citizens who support its objectives.
> The truth is that a government will not abdicate its responsibility to formulate and implement policies it thinks best for the country. In Tanzania's commitment to social justice the stress on egalitarianism is of greater importance than public participation and fair administration, and reconciliation of them is not really possible.[23]

The first error is one any common man, anyone in politics, anyone recoiling from the transgressions of President Nixon or Mrs. Gandhi would immediately spot: *Political equality cannot rely on the good intentions of those in power.* It must be repeatedly reinforced by those who can legitimately organize the people to threaten or replace their leaders. Secondly, there is no democracy if the minorities that oppose "the party's objectives" cannot organize to form new ruling majorities in terms of alternative objectives. Finally, there is no basic egalitarianism or social justice when the government apart from "public participation and fair administration" decides what equality and justice are. It is no wonder that most African one-party systems have in fact become tools for the reachievement of economic as well as political inequality.[24]

Equality and freedom, then, can rationally be viewed as different aspects of the same dimension of civil society. Both concepts are limited and relative in their essential nature. The desire to absolutize either harms the attainment of either, while it weakens the society that alone makes either possible. So understood, the perfection of equality in freedom has been the central goal and direction of American history. It is a painful fact that a society working toward a balance in both freedom and equality may offer less economic equality and available services to the very poor and unfortunate than an enlightened despot or nondemocratic party government. Majority rule, that is, egalitarian government, implies that the interests of minorities, even poor minorities, may at times be ignored. The gain of the very poor under despotism must be at the expense of a loss of political and economic equality by the majority. But do the gains of the very poor under despotism compensate them for long for the loss of self-respect and independence that these gains entail? Evidently not, for nowhere do we know of the poor flooding across boundaries to take advantage of paternal despotisms.

NOTES

1. We addressed this criticism in *Freedom in the World 1978*, pp. 163–79. The issues raised are important enough to examine again this year.

2. Felix Oppenheim, *Dimensions of Freedom* (New York: St. Martins, 1961).

3. John Hospers, *Libertarianism: A Political Philosophy for Tomorrow* (Los Angeles: Nash, 1971), p. 58.

4. See R. D. Gastil, "The Moral Right of the Majority to Restrict Obscenity and Pornography Through Law," *Ethics* 86, no. 3 (April 1976): 231–40, and R. D. Gastil, "Societal Limits on Majority Rights," *Journal of Social Philosophy* VII, no. 1 (1976): 8–12.

5. Alexander Meiklejohn, *What Does America Mean?* (New York: W. W. Norton, 1935 [1963]), p. 117. See also Carl Becker, *Freedom and Responsibility in the American Way of Life* (New York: Knopf, 1945).

6. See Gordon Wood, *The Creation of the American Republic 1776–1787* (Chapel Hill: University of North Carolina Press, 1969), pp. 70–75.

7. See J. R. Pole, *The Pursuit of Equality in American History* (Berkeley: University of California Press, 1978).

8. Christopher Jencks, *Inequality* (New York: Basic Books, 1972).

9. John A. Brittain, *The Inheritance of Economic Status* (Washington, D.C.: Brookings Institute, 1977), especially pp. 15–23. Economic mobility may be underestimated, for the economically most mobile are often spatially mobile and so perhaps not available for a community survey of this type.

10. William Manchester, "The Law of Inversion: The Leveling of America," *New York Times,* Op Ed page, July 15, 1978. Acceptance of promotion for merit for average Americans is supported by Robert P. Quinn and Linda Shepard, "1972–73 Quality of Employment Survey," National Opinion Research Council, Ann Arbor, Michigan, 1974.

11. Paul Mantegna, *Occupations and Society* (New York: John Wiley, 1977), p. 429.

12. See *Keesing's Contemporary Archives*, 1978, pp. 29181–93.

13. See G. William Domhoff, *Who Rules America?* (Englewood Cliffs, New Jersey: Prentice-Hall, 1967).

14. Eli Ginzberg, "Sweden: Some Unanswered Questions," in D. Bell and I. Kristol, eds., *Capitalism Today* (New York: Basic Books, 1971), pp. 158–66.

15. John Plamenatz, *Democracy and Illusion* (London: Longman's Green, 1973), pp. 184–85. See Domhoff, *Who Rules America?*, page 2, for the compatibility of this definition with his governing class model of America.

16. See especially Charles Lindblom, *Politics and Markets: The World's Political-Economic Systems* (New York: Basic Books, 1977).

17. Ben Stein, *The View from Sunset Boulevard* (New York: Basic Books, 1979).

18. For example, in Londonderry (Roy Reed, "Catholics are Taking Over in Londonderry," *New York Times*, July 22, 1978).

19. Pole, *The Pursuit of Equality in American History*.

20. J. Morgan Kousser, *The Shaping of Southern Politics: Suffrage Restriction and the Establishment of the One-Party South, 1880–1910* (New Haven: Yale University Press, 1974), especially pp. 13–15.

21. The ineluctable tendency of the state to closely regulate those it aids is faced by a recent study (Willard Gaylin, *et al.*, *Doing Good: The Limits of Benevolence* [New York, Pantheon, 1978]). Representing nondependents the state cannot for long be the friend of the dependent; the more the dependent press for rights equal to those of nondependents, the greater the tendency for the state to curtail the special advantages of dependency.

22. For the Incas, see Garcilaso de la Vega, *Royal Commentaries* (London: Hakluyt Society, 1869–71). For Cuba today, see *Latin American Digest*, March 1972.

23. International Commission of Jurists, *Human Rights in a One-Party State* (London: Search Press, 1978), pp. 110, 109, and 90.

24. See, for example, "The Single-Party Syndrome," *Atlas World Press Review*, October 1978, pp. 40–41.

National Cultures
and Universal Democracy

A common criticism of the Survey and its objective of promoting civil and political freedoms in the world is the argument that the Survey arrogantly denies the right of non-Western peoples to their own definition of goals and values. Before recent events the Iranian government was particularly concerned with the development of this thesis as a counter to the attacks on its human rights record.[1] In forcing his people to accept a one-party system in 1977, President Stevens of Sierra Leone emphasized the importance of "practising the kind of parliamentary democracy that suits us best," and in "rejecting the worn-out multi-party parliamentary democracy inherited from our colonial master. . . ."[2]

The ironic twist to the self-sufficiency suggested by the latter statement is that President Stevens went on to say that "the sovereign people of Sierra Leone have today joined the ranks of the world majority of single-party states." Evidently the events of the outer world still determine internal reality, even when nations try to be most themselves. It can be no other way, for the problem of self-determination is worldwide and exists on all levels from the individual to the planetary. The growing individual strives mightily to be himself, by rejection of the opinions of his parents, but all too often falls into unquestioning acceptance of the views of his contemporaries. As Aristotle pointed out, there are only a limited number of ways to organize governments, and we can surmise that in our age regnant ideas of what is acceptable in the modern world still further limit political alternatives. These observations do not make the problem of choice easier for evolving new polities, for there is still the unrelieved need of many emerging peoples to develop their own identity so that they might avoid being swamped by indiscriminate modernization.

One way out of this dilemma is to develop a more acute consciousness of the distinction between particularist cultures and universalist civilization.[3] Civilization in this approach may be defined as the highest level of knowledge and understanding available at any one

75

time to the people of the world or a part of the world. A civilized
person is one living in terms of this level of knowledge. Civilization
in this view is always potentially universal. It is true that historians
have spoken of "Chinese Civilization" or "Indian Civilization," but
to the people of China or India, or of surrounding countries, these
were regarded as universal civilizations in terms of which all else
was to be measured. Gunpowder, printing, and porcelain moved
westward as soon as Europe could obtain them. In terms of civilization, if something was better, it was adopted. Buddhism traveled over
the Himalayas as a universal creed; eventually it became thoroughly
accepted in China as a part of Chinese civilization. There is always
borrowing among peoples. The direction of borrowing indicates where
civilization is most advanced at any one moment in history. When
Western Civilization achieved preeminence, the rest of the world soon
learned to borrow from the West, wherever it was useful.

Distinct from civilization as the totality of human creation is the
concept of "a culture," a term designating a particular way of life
of a particular group. Perhaps anthropology's greatest gift to understanding was the concept that culture (that is, history) rather than
race was the primary determinant of differences among peoples. The
distinction of civilization and culture is exemplified in the relation
of China, Korea, and Japan. Until very recently the civilization of
these countries was essentially the same (called variously Far Eastern,
East Asian, Sinic, or even "Chinese"). The religions, technologies,
scripts, and many other items of the lives of people in this region
have been very much the same for over 1,000 years. Yet the Chinese,
Koreans, and Japanese continued to be distinct peoples; each group
continued to impart to succeeding generations distinct cultural traditions. Language, literature, the ritual of daily life, ideals and goals
in Japan have persisted in spite of being embedded in Far Eastern
Civilization, and now they seem quite likely to outlive prolonged
contact with Western Civilization. It can also be suggested that
Japan's much more rapid progress after Western contact derived
from the ability of the Japanese to more clearly distinguish than
the Chinese between culture and civilization, between what was
superior in the West and what was simply different.

The relative inability of the Chinese to make this distinction was
not unusual. In the first period of any contact between peoples there
is a tendency to confuse civilization with culture, either to reject
new ways that are in fact superior or to try to imitate in all ways
the life of the people from which some useful ideas of universal value
are currently flowing. For example, in the nineteenth century enlightened individuals such as Malkom Khan in Iran or Seyyid Ahmed

Khan in India were so impressed with Western superiority that they advocated a general and even uncritical imitation of foreign ways. They were nationalists and yet they saw wholesale change as the only way to counter the overwhelming impact of the West. Later the pendulum would swing back until in India intellectuals would advocate rejecting Western technology even where it was demonstrably superior. Even today enlightened Indians may reject Western medicine in favor of Indian medicine (based in turn on Ancient Greek precepts). It is hard to find the right balance.

Human beings will eventually select what is best when best is the issue. Civilization is a selection of the best, and working out this selection must be a long and slow process, particularly for the average person. While European and American doctors may be narrow-minded and arrogant, medicine is neither Western nor Eastern, ultimately it must be as culture-free as the nuclear bomb. Marriage ceremonies, styles of clothing, and poetry, on the other hand, have many bests. There is no reason there should ever be one world culture. There are certain efficiencies in uniformity, and in some areas (for example, the language of pilots and air traffic controllers) cultural differences will be abandoned for efficiency. But for most cultural items the value of having something distinctively one's own, of one's own group, will continue to outweigh the alternative of acculturation to a universal form.

Culture, however, cannot for long conflict with the civilizational standard adopted by a people. Since civilization is progressive this means that in the process of adapting to changing civilizational levels cultures will inevitably come to abandon certain traits and beliefs that have previously characterized them. The bow and arrow will be replaced by the technically superior gun; human sacrifice will be replaced by the morally superior communion or public prayer. Most primitive peoples saw no wrong in inflicting unlimited harm on peoples outside of their own rather small moral universes; in their world genocide was common, even desirable.[4] The noble Athenians showed equal lack of compunction when they destroyed Melos. Medieval Christians and Muslims displayed similar attitudes toward destroying opponents, although their justifications indicated a significant extension of their moral universes. Modern civilization does not accept the killing or deliberate harming of human beings except as the violence is a necessary side-effect of attaining specific objectives in defensive war and police action.[5] It is only from this standpoint of modern civilization that we have hoped for universal condemnation of mass murder in Nazi Germany, Stalinist Russia, or more recently in Cambodia and Uganda. Similarly, cultures have almost universally relegated women to a secondary status, and have frequently inflicted painful or humiliating prohibitions and practices upon women. Modern civilization rejects these inequalities. Its advocates and adherents realize that all peoples will not immediately be able to accept this change; the inferiority of women is much more firmly embedded in some cultures. There is also a great deal of difference of opinion over just how far equality should be pushed beyond juridical equality and the elimination of offensive practices. But this understanding and controversy does not mean that we should renounce the universal standard of sexual equality. Slavery was accepted by most peoples in the historical past, for it did not conflict with the civilization of their time. Since the nineteenth century slavery has not been acceptable anywhere, no matter how deeply it might be embedded in a local cultural tradition.

Peter Berger has recently suggested that the discussion of universal human rights requires that we distinguish between an "exclusively Western view of the world" and a "wider consensus" derivable from an examination of the principles and values of all the world civilizations.[6] "Western Civilization" to Berger evidently means a summing or least common denominator of the cultures of Western Europe and North America. However, for many people Western Civilization is simply modern civilization, the civilization of the day to which all societies more or less must subscribe (as most of Gandhi's successors reluctantly came to see in India and as Mao's successors see in China).

In our terms Berger is advising us to search for human rights as cultural universals, or at least as universals among the most important cultures. But this is not the right way to look.

In that they speak to human desires for justice and autonomy for individuals and political subgroupings, human rights do represent at least highly generalized cultural universals. If we accept the discussion of "Freedom and Equality" above (pp. 63–74), then there is a clear basis for human rights in the historically resurgent demand of very ordinary people for equal rights. In ancient Iran leaders incited the people to rise in the name of the equality of the common man, while the Middle Ages were replete with attempts to destroy the special rights of the privileged.[7] Political democracy has ancient roots. We know of democratic institutions in ancient Greece, and are not surprised to learn this year that the king of ancient Ebla, elected for a seven-year term in 2500 B.C., ruled with a council of elders.[8] These societies did not have fully democratic institutions. Yet democratic elections and consultative processes were universal enough to give some justification to the recent claim of Senator Raul Manglapus of the Philippines that democratic rights pre-existed colonial intrusion in many parts of the world.[9]

Nevertheless, ancient cultures were not characterized by a high regard for human rights. As civilization developed these rights have gradually evolved. The universal validity in modern civilization of an infant's right to sustenance and protection by his parents is not called into question by the fact that infanticide was common in many cultures. Similarly, regardless of the depth of the history of male supremacy, in our civilization women now have the right to vote. It is simply to misread history and misunderstand what is meant by "universal" to try to derive human rights or freedom from the least common denominator of great cultures (Berger's civilizations). For in the developed form that we wish to apply them many of the rights of Modern Civilization are almost as new to the West as the East. Such rights are not, thereby, any less important or universal in their claims on our attention.

We must distinguish the universally valid political freedoms of today from those that are properly confined to particular peoples or nations. Certainly the traditions from which Western democracy sprang—Judeo-Christian on the one hand and the eighteenth-century enlightenment to name the major progenitors—were as much universalist traditions as Marxism or Buddhism. In this they can easily be distinguished from Shintoism or Zionism, doctrines expressing distinctly limited, or cultural, meanings and values. As universalist doctrines civil and political freedom are derived from the concept of the equality of all individuals. At least by the eighteenth century exploration of this natural law concept led to the conclusion that only equal access to public discussion and equal participation in a voting process could express this equality adequately in the governance of a community. Evidently this new understanding of natural law has appealed to peoples everywhere, so much so that nearly all major societies in the world today make a verbal claim that their citizens have an equal right to participate in an election process and to express their opinions on policy questions. The fact that in communist and many authoritarian countries the expression of these rights is so hedged about by restrictions as to be meaningless does not contradict the apparently universal appeal of the basic democratic rights.

To say this does not deny that much of what Americans understand as necessary to our political system is cultural rather than civilizational. In particular, our system stems from the development of common law, a law necessarily grounded in the history of a particular tradition. European polities founded on Roman law, a legislated law with a more universalist presumption, can satisfy the ultimate criteria of democracy as well. This implies that there may be other national substrata upon which democracy can build. Swiss democracy, an amalgam of peasant, almost tribal, attitudes and practices with advanced civilizational concepts including a thorough acceptance of the basic universals of democracy offers a good example for many less developed countries. South Pacific democracies such as Fiji or Western Samoa, and Botswana in Africa, or Surinam in South America provide still further examples of how the democratic universalism of respect for fundamental equality can be combined with authentic cultural traditions.

This point of view has been formalized in recent discussions of "consociational democracy" by political scientists.[10] This model of democracy, represented by the recent history of the Netherlands, Belgium, Switzerland, and Austria, is based on a grand coalition among the leaders of the major competing groups in deeply fragmented polities. The consociational solution accepts the political, regional, religious, or other divisions of societies and builds a polity on these realities. Although the full guarantees of parliamentary democracy are present in these societies, their political systems require consensus rather than simple majority rule. Minorities have, in effect, veto power over the issues that affect them most. This democratic alternative fits the traditional nonautocratic decision making mode better than simple majority decision in many underdeveloped countries. Consociational democracy avoids the cultural repressions that attempt to forcibly homogenize societies into new nations as well as the political repressions of one-party systems. A review of the record by a number of economists and political scientists suggests that authoritarian or one-party solutions have been found wanting in terms of economic growth, nation-building, or the prevention of violence.[11]

Western Civilization is often justly accused of promoting individual freedoms at the expense of traditional group rights. The contrasting concepts of rights are suggested in a recent State Department report where we find: "In Rwandan society there has always been greater emphasis on the security and harmony of one's position within family and clan structures than on individual freedom."[12] Increased mobility, impersonal legal codes, and national demands break down the authority of family, clan, village, and tribe. But where are traditional group rights most at risk? A few political systems, notably that of Western Samoa, continue to make a serious attempt to make families or clans rather than individuals the units of political action. In Africa democracies such as Botswana or Gambia recognize these social units on some political levels. They must, for leaders of democracies understand political and civil freedoms as requirements placed upon political systems to respond to the needs and desires of *all* units below the level of national government. Unlike traditional society, the modern democracy also offers the individual a chance to change group affiliations, or to emerge from the group if he desires. Denials of either individual or small group rights are most likely to occur in societies the Survey regards as "not free." For these societies regularly deny both individuals and groups the right to existence as autonomous social units with a determinative role in political life. These are the societies in which family, clan, and tribe are most rapidly weakened. Whatever continent we choose to compare democracies and nondemocracies, we will find the democracies to be the states in which autonomous group life has been preserved most effectively against the pressures of modern civilization.

Democratic political systems are more likely than alternatives to provide for the preservation and development of cultural particularism in the full range of a society's life. On the one hand, traditional authoritarian states are now rare; all are vulnerable to their lack of acceptance by a young generation anxious to participate in modern civilization. Modernist nondemocracies. on the other hand, receive their legitimacy from the claim of their ruling elites that only they can propel their nation's progress. Such elites scorn the cultural values of their masses as antiprogressive and divisive. Like Ataturk in Turkey or Reza Shah in Iran between the wars, they may see progress only through breaking the hold of religious traditions. With even more hubris they may try like Adolf Hitler to exalt artificial or defunct traditions and symbols that fit the ruler's political objectives because they lack association with groups outside the ruler's control. Democratic polities can do neither of these things. They will change, they will reject old traditions and build new ones, but only at the pace that the people approve. Only they are truly people's democracies.[13]

NOTES

1. *The Communications and Development Review* published in Teheran (1978) seems largely dedicated to this thesis. See also Jahangir Amuzegar, "Rights and Wrongs," Op Ed page, *New York Times*, January 29, 1978.

2. *Keesing's Contemporary Archives*, August 4, 1978, p. 29124.

3. See R. D. Gastil, "Culture and Civilization: In Man and Out There," *Papers of the Kroeber Anthropological Society*, 1964.

4. See Robert Redfield, *The Primitive World and Its Transformation* (Ithaca: Cornell University Press, 1953). See also the papers of N. Chagnon, F. Livingstone, and E. R. Service in M. Fried, M. Harris, and R. Murphy, eds., *War: The Anthropology of Armed Conflict and Aggression* (Garden City: Natural History Press, 1967).

5. For example, Paul Ramsey, *The Just War: Force and Political Responsibility* (New York: Scribner, 1968).

6. Peter Berger, "Are Human Rights Universal?" *Commentary*, September 1977, pp. 60–63.

7. See Edward G. Brown, *A Literary History of Persia* (Cambridge: Cambridge University Press, 1951) I:166–72, 310–13; A. Christensen, *L'Iran sous les Sassanides* (Copenhagen: Munksgaard, 1944); and Norman Cohn, *The Pursuit of the Millenium*, rev. ed. (New York: Oxford University Press, 1970).

8. *New York Times*, January 16, 1979, p. C–1.

9. Raul S. Manglapus, "Human Rights Are Not a Western Discovery," *Worldview* 21, no. 10 (October 1978): 4–6.

10. See Arend Lijphart, *Democracy in Plural Societies: A Comparative Exploration* (New Haven: Yale University Press, 1977), especially pp. 160–69, 223ff.

11. *Ibid.*, pp. 226–27.

12. United States Department of State, "Report on Human Rights Practices in Countries Receiving U. S. Aid" (Washington, D.C.: Government Printing Office, February 8, 1979), p. 142.

13. Peter Berger, *Pyramids of Sacrifice* (New York: Basic Books, 1974).

PART III

Supporting Liberalization in the Soviet Union

Introductory Note

On December 9–10, 1978, a conference was held at Freedom House on "Supporting Liberalization in the Soviet Union." Participants were: Robert J. Alexander, Bohan R. Bociurkiw, Richard W. Cottam, John B. Dunlop, Herbert J. Ellison, Lewis S. Feuer, Raymond D. Gastil, Teresa Rakowska-Harmstone, William R. Kintner, Seymour Martin Lipset, C. Grant Pendill, Jr., Leslie Rubin, Howland H. Sargeant, Leonard R. Sussman, and William C. Thoma.

The purpose of the conference and the general issues as seen by a nonspecialist were sketched in the first paper included below, "Supporting Liberalization in the Soviet Union." This is followed by the four papers delivered by specialists at the conference. Discussion follows each paper, with the bulk of the general discussion following the presentation by Professor Feuer. A summary of some of the more important results of the conference concludes this section.

Supporting Liberalization
in the Soviet Union

After the defeat of the fascist powers in World War II, the leaders of the Western democracies were soon forced to the conclusion that the primary obstacle in the way of attaining peace and freedom was the intransigence of the USSR.[1] Since 1945 the importance of this conception of international affairs has risen and fallen in response to successive waves of hope and fear. In the interim, the colonial empires of the Western powers have dissolved, the fascist states of the 1940's have become relatively stable democracies, and China has emerged as a new factor in the world. Yet thirty-four years after the end of the war, the Soviet Union remains the primary obstacle to international peace and freedom. The persistence of this "Russian problem" offers ample justification for taking another serious look at how we can remove this obstacle through both our private and public actions.

To make a start at this reexamination we need to look at alternative Soviet futures and consider why the more liberal of these should be favored by Euro-Americans. If we are to raise the probability of a desirable outcome, we need to examine what causes liberalizing change in the Soviet Union. This will lead us to identify the groups that we might wish to influence, and the tools of change that we might employ to influence these groups. Selecting an informational and ideological strategy for further emphasis, the following essay will then consider the best approaches to each of the identified groups to attain liberalization.

ALTERNATIVE SOVIET FUTURES

Before examining ways in which the directions of Soviet political development might be changed we need to consider the directions in which the Soviet polity might develop. Five alternatives cover the likely spectrum for the rest of the century. Without effective outside intervention the most likely alternative would be an *oscillating communist tyranny*, or a continuation of the Soviet Union we have seen since Stalin. In this model periods of moderate liberalization in which dissent is allowed to surface in restricted circles, and political imprisonment becomes less common are followed by periods of regression to harsher measures. Pressures to liberalize the Soviet Union derive from the desire of educated Russians over the last two centuries to live according to the standards of Europeans, from the natural desire of Russians for more freedom in thought and action (even Brezhnev is not free), and from that aspect of communist social doctrine that demands a certain humane respect for rights. Liberalization is also promoted by the fact that the liberal-leftists the Soviets hope to enlist in their support in the noncommunist world generally condemn repression (although they try to overlook leftist repression wherever possible). However, liberalization begun for these reasons is halting and eventually fails. A recurring nightmare for communist leaders is that their power rapidly erodes when liberalization is allowed to take firm root.[2] Periodically this well-founded fear causes them to reemphasize the Leninist or tyrannical side of communism. Because they can legitimize their repression only through maintaining their communist credentials their interests tie them to the ideology even if they intellectually reject it. And so the Soviet winter oscillates between periods of hard freeze and thaw.

The most probable alternative to this communist oscillation would maintain the repressive apparatus in an *authoritarian Russian Empire* purged of reliance on communism or the communist party. Many students of the Soviet Union view the USSR as more a product of the imperialist tsarist tradition than of communist ideology. If so, then a return to a precommunist tyranny, probably under military control, would be conceivable. Its intellectual basis might be a combination of Russian or Slavic nationalism with technocracy. This is most likely to occur during periods when one clique must hand the power to another and after international communism for one reason or another seems to have outlived its usefulness. Anticommunist authoritarianism might emerge from either end of the oscillation of Soviet communism—from the instabilities of liberalization or the pent-up hatreds of oppression.

These alternatives may be matched on the optimistic side by two others. First the USSR might emerge from its oscillations to create a *liberal communist union*. Recent Soviet intellectual discussion looks forward to the day when it will be possible to create a less harsh and rigid communism. Certainly the messages of the Euro-communists will continue to affect the Soviet discussion; they surely have affected the discussion in Eastern Europe.[3] In spite of ritual genuflections to communist myths, opinion leaders in the USSR must recognize the fact that the "class enemy" has long been defeated in the USSR itself, and the military strength of the Soviet Union makes the threat of imperialist aggression less plausible with each passing year. Rationally, it should be possible to liberalize the USSR without abandoning cherished communist precepts.

Most Soviet dissidents would probably prefer, however, to go much further, and create a *social democratic USSR* with the political rights and civil liberties found along the spectrum from Sweden and West Germany to Switzerland and the U.S. Many dissidents want the pluralism and full guarantees of individual rights that are found primarily in the noncommunist West.[4] These essentially noncommunist dissidents are less concerned with economics; perhaps they are not too sure how capitalism could be created or recreated in the USSR. They would probably support a gradual diffusion of power to separate economic units—the Yugoslav system as it functions in theory. In agriculture dissidents might welcome a steady expansion of private plots and the phased breakup of collectives and state farms, as and if the peasants desired this devolution.

Perhaps the knottiest problem for any liberalizing process in the Soviet future would be the conflict between Russian-Soviet nationalism and the many smaller nationalisms within the USSR. A liberalizing Soviet Union might end up a *disintegrating Soviet Union*, much as Iran has been threatened by disintegration after the Shah's removal. In theory, the dissolution of the Russian Empire could be a phased and successful process, with an emerging Russian national state preserving its great power status; in fact it might be an ugly and jerky process in which Russians would come to feel threatened on all sides.

WHY SUPPORT LIBERALIZATION?

Many may find it obvious that Euro-Americans should support the realization of the more liberal alternatives in the Soviet Union. Yet intervention in the internal affairs of other states has such a bad reputation today that the particular reasons for trying to influence events in the USSR in a liberal direction should be spelled out. In this process some readers will find that the argument for meaningful Euro-American support of enhanced freedom in the USSR is stronger than they might have thought.

My faith is that a more liberal Soviet Union would be better for the people of the Soviet Union. As I have argued exhaustively elsewhere,[5] freedom is a universal value; to the extent that people are denied social freedoms they are denied the right to live as full human beings. In no country does a "vanguard party" or elite group of sponsors have the right to inhibit the freedom of adult citizens in order to promote the ruling clique's minority and sectarian ideology. More poignantly, the machinery of repression, such as labor camps, prisons, misused psychiatric institutions, censorships, or travel restrictions, transgress the rights of individuals directly and often painfully. Any change that reduces or mitigates these conditions of oppression should be welcomed.

The present Soviet tyranny denies the group rights of many nationalities to self-determination, to pride in their own cultures and traditions. This seems particularly bitter in an age of nationalism, in which peoples outside the Soviet orbit recognize national independence as a basic right. The ascendency of the Russian language in the Soviet Empire, the domination of all sectors of its society by ethnic Russians, even in the main cities of the non-Russian republics, makes ineffective the paper self-determination of Soviet minorities. This denial of ethnic equality extends beyond the borders of the USSR to narrowly restrict the national self-determination of Czechs, Hungarians, Mongols, and others in satellite states. It is hard to imagine any liberalization that would not more fairly adjust national rights.

Although the foregoing arguments are fairly noncontroversial, to take action in support of dissidents on these bases alone would demand a great deal of Euro-American concern for the fate of others. More controversial, but less altruistically demanding, are the twin arguments that the conquest of the world by totalitarian communism is a critical danger for the next generation, and that liberalization of the Soviet Union would be one of the best ways to prevent this conquest.

There are many different approaches to assessing current trends in international force relationships. But probabilistic, that is scientific, thinking demands that we attend to the fact that *some* reasonable assessments show steady and almost irreversible communist gains in the last generation. These assessments begin by noting that more of the world is controlled today by communist states than in 1945. Eastern Europe, then China, Cuba, the states of Indochina, Angola, and Mozambique have become communist. In their train a variety of near-communist or communist-structured states have arisen and grown— Burma, South Yemen, Libya, Algeria, Tanzania, Guinea, Guinea-Bissau, to name the clearest examples. Along with these developments standards of public condemnation in the noncommunist world have shifted. Too often leftwing tyrannies are either passively accepted or applauded by the media and academia. Communist intellectuals and communist interpretations of national and international events have achieved a new legitimacy, and are widely accepted, especially among the activist young. These trends do not reflect a rapid shift in the communist favor, but their relatively halting movement, at least until recently, is not reassuring when we consider how far they have carried the world since 1945.

Militarily the United States and its allies long held significant force advantages over the Soviet Union in some areas. These advantages are lost. In the 1960's the nuclear argument was over whether or not a Western first strike made sense in defense of Europe; by the seventies the argument is whether a Soviet first strike makes sense. A strategy based on continued superiority was replaced by one assuming U.S.-Soviet equality, and then by one assuming sufficiency. The Soviet buildup that has changed the nuclear balance would not be disastrous if it were not for the fact that conventional balances have also slipped in the Soviet favor. Soviet advantage on the ground in Europe has grown with the years. Worldwide the Soviet Union in the fifties and sixties could not project its forces far afield. It had neither the air power nor naval power. Today it can. Its ability to move forces overseas is still inferior to our own, but here too the balance is shifting. There is no economic explanation for this change. The United States and its allies have increased their wealth manyfold, but American will is weak, and the will of its allies even weaker. Never have there been so many powerful states in the world quite so unwilling to make adequate defense efforts as America's allies.

For a time many analysts of worldwide force balances gained encouragement from the fact that the monolithic communist world had broken apart with the rise of Yugoslavia and China. Yet today the encouragement that can be gained from this seems slight indeed. The Soviet Union's preeminence in world power is hardly affected by the disaffection of the Chinese and other communist states. It successfully operates in Africa, Latin America, and Europe with little regard for the support or opposition of these states; even in South Asia and the Far East, the USSR remains quite successful. In addition, it is easy to overestimate the significance of communist infighting. Since all communist states accept essentially the same ideology, in most cases they will be obliged to support the same causes throughout the world. Certainly all have had to support the Vietnamese against the Americans, the Palestinians against the Israelis, and the blacks against the whites in Africa.

Finally, after the loss of nerve that accompanied defeat in Vietnam the United States has been unable to counter successive communist interventions in Africa. The successes of the Soviet Union and Cuba are likely to lead to more attempts. In spite of this no United States policy to counter the continuing communist exploitation of our weakness has emerged.

Many readers will not agree with the dismal picture of the communist threat developed above, but most will agree that the picture is too plausible to be lightly dismissed. To hedge against the possibility that such a picture will turn out to be accurate, Euro-Americans need a strategy that will improve the prospects of containing the challenge. It seems to me that since we do not have the will to raise the money or spill the blood that effective military containment will entail, this strategy must concentrate on obtaining basic change at the heart of the challenge, within the Soviet Union itself. This strategy is also recommended by the fact that the Soviet Union has been least successful internally. While dissent has not penetrated very deeply, a very large percentage of the Soviet people, and of the satellite peoples, appear apathetic and cynical communists at best.

Liberalization would reduce the military and ideological challenge posed by recent communist advances in at least three ways. First, a liberalized Soviet Union would devote a smaller share of its economic resources to the military budget. In all communist states consumer demands have remained unsatisfied. In the absence of pressing defense problems more open communist states would have to meet these needs to a greater extent. Secondly, a liberalized Soviet Union would find it harder to support ideological allies with exceptionally poor human rights records, such as Ethiopia, Cambodia, or Guinea-Bissau. Finally, in the last analysis, conquest of the world by a liberalized Soviet Union would be less of a threat to Western values than conquest by a totalitarian, Leninist state.

There are at least two other ways in which a more liberal Soviet Union would improve the world. First, a more liberal and thus less threatening Soviet Union would indirectly improve the status of freedom in the rest of the world. It would reduce the argument outside of the Soviet orbit for large military appropriations, for more oppressive intelligence services, or for sacrificing "the niceties of political freedom" in order to strengthen authoritarian regimes that can stand up to the communist challenge.

Finally, a liberalized Soviet Union would reduce the danger of both limited and all-out war. One study has pointed out the rarity of wars among democratic states.[6] Whether we trust the statistics of such studies or not, the foregoing analysis has certainly offered good reasons to believe that a liberalized Soviet Union would promote less buildup by military forces on both sides. Lower arms budgets will not prevent war, but they characterize a more peaceful environment. Since a more democratic Soviet Union also would have more in common with Euro-

America, it would tend to support more common international policies. In short, there would simply be less to fight over.

We must be careful, however, with this argument. Any change in a state may be accompanied by instabilities, especially during the transition. Violence and danger have accompanied the return of democracy to Greece, Portugal, and Spain in recent years. In the Soviet Union there may be violent resistance to the pace of significant liberalization—either by those who think it is going too fast or too slow. This is particularly true as demands for self-determination are raised, for these are apt to be more destabilizing than any others. How outsiders can assist the process of change without exacerbating internal conflict in the USSR will be the central challenge and responsibility of those who wish to be external agents of change.

WHAT CAUSES CHANGE IN THE USSR?

Those who support liberalization should have a reasonably complete theory of how and why change might occur in the USSR. The optimists of progress, the apostles of convergence, have long assumed that economic growth and the universalization of education are necessarily liberalizing. Today we have had enough experience to know that there is no automatic relationship between these factors, especially in a closed society managed from the top. Nevertheless, since the Soviet Union is not completely closed, everything else being equal the relatively high level of economic progress and education in the Soviet Union provides a basis for liberalization superior to that in many underdeveloped countries.

Communist success internally and externally helps to perpetuate its control and reinforce its dogma. It convinces both true believers and dissidents that communism as the wave of the future is essentially irreplaceable. If this is so, then lack of communist success should have the opposite effect. These are, of course, marginal effects. Unsuccessful regimes such as those of Guinea or Burma have been able to maintain themselves for years in spite of dismal performances from every point of view in a world of rising expectations. It is also possible that some types of liberalization are more probable in a successful communist state than an unsuccessful. Nevertheless, by and large effective resistance to communist external expansion would strengthen the forces for change in the USSR.

What communications are received by the many levels of Soviet society and the plausibility of these communications are a critical aspect of change. As long as the picture of the world believed by the Soviet citizenry is dependent upon what communist leaders wish them to believe, there will be no pressures for improvement in communist society. The leadership starts with an enormous advantage, for the universal Soviet education establishes in the young a favorable picture of the USSR that Soviet citizens can never completely escape, even as adults. This education offers a coherent and highly ideological, communist view of social facts and how to interpret them both within the USSR and the external world. The controlled press and radio expand and continue the development of this managed and unshaded view of reality. For most citizens the major limit on the effectiveness of such education is the disconfirmation provided by actual Soviet life. Partially to counteract the dissonance of this experience the government must make life outside of the USSR appear to be much worse. For most people this effort probably succeeds, for they have little alternative information on the outside world. Thus, cynicism about government policy internally is not likely to lead most Soviet citizens to question Soviet foreign policy or to doubt the superiority of communism. For this reason informational and educational control in the USSR may lead to widespread apathy and disaffection without producing dissidence.

Changing the information received by significant numbers of people is the way change is most likely to occur in the Soviet Union. This is why the government tries so hard to control contacts such as those occasioned by the reading of foreign publications or by foreign travel. Many liberal dissidents have had the scope of their critique greatly broadened by exposure to the reality of nationalistic or religious dissidence through personal contact in jails. Reports of demonstrations by young people who learned of the nature of the suppressions of the Czechoslovak independence in 1968 suggests what might occur with the broader dissemination of such information.

Internal dissidence comes either from natural human rebelliousness against received ideas, particularly the rebelliousness of the young, or from the gap between the idealized communist picture of the world and communist reality. But the isolated rebel will soon relapse into apathy and cynicism unless he sees some hope that opposition can produce change. This opposition will also wither unless the rebel receives the personal, emotional, and intellectual support of others with similar views. For both of these reasons the most important information for the dissident is that there are others that share his views, that he has friends inside and outside the country, and these friends are not insignificant. As a small minority party the illiberal communists can continue to rule the Soviet Union only if the majority remains fragmented into a group of still smaller, noncommunicating minorities.

Change can be promoted by external criticism. On first hearing it, this may seem either an unimportant or entirely mistaken proposition. Perhaps the argument becomes more acceptable if I turn the proposition around and consider the prospects for Soviet liberalization should everyone in the world praise current Soviet society. It is easy to see that the prospects would be dim; it would be hard for a Soviet citizen to oppose a system all the world praises. External criticism has certainly played a part in American change: no small part of the success of American liberals in removing racial barriers has been due to the difficulty Americans have felt in defending racial prejudice to liberal foreigners. Similarly, while it is true that external criticism may cause in any country a conservative reaction, a rallying-round-the-flag response, external criticism is necessary to sustain internal criticism of the status quo among at least the more educated and cosmopolitan Soviets.

Change in the USSR will proceed to the extent that the interests and information of its highly varied and crosscutting interest groups support change. First among the interest groups that should be distinguished is the ruling elite itself. Change in the interests and opinions of elites is critical in all societies and especially in one as tightly run from the top as the USSR. For our purposes two changes are of particular importance. First, change in the elites' understanding of how they should, or most safely and profitably can, rule. The liberal initiatives of Malenkov and Khrushchev are examples at the very top of this process in the Soviet Union. More dramatically, recent changes in Spain have largely been brought about by the change in attitudes of the elite majority under the symbolic leadership of the King. Equally important may be change in the ruling elite's self-confidence that they should rule. Loss of self-confidence in the ruling class is the classic precursor of revolution identified by Crane Brinton in his famous analysis of the English, American, French, and Russian revolutions.[7]

Interacting with liberalizing elements in the ruling class are members of the highly educated, primarily liberal, dissident groups. Like the rulers themselves these dissidents are far more cosmopolitan, far more exposed to the accomplishments of alternative political and economic models, than average Soviet citizens. However, since they live much more than the ruling elite in a world of ideas, they are able and willing to go considerably beyond this elite in imagining what might be.

Less cosmopolitan groups or classes of dissidents should not be forgotten. First are the members of unofficial, illegal, or disfavored fundamentalist or evangelical religious groups. Largely from working class and rural backgrounds, these people oppose the spiritually dry communist world with their very different value and belief systems. Their politics are anti-politics—freedom for them would mean being left alone to worship as they please. More passive, but latent, religious dissidence must exist among millions of Orthodox Russians who reject atheism. Nationality movements embrace people from all levels of society, although in the literature we naturally hear more from the better educated. Once in power, some nationalist dissenters might turn out to be Leninists analogous to the Rumanian communists. For the time being, however, their efforts may be enlisted on the side of liberalizing change. And if self-determination receives support from cosmopolitan dissenters and external advocates of change, the political ideas of nationalists may be kept comparatively liberal.

The military services are centers of power. In spite of vigorous and remarkably successful ideological efforts to maintain party control over the services, the interests and allegiances of Soviet officers are not the same as those of the party. Most military leaders are less exposed to foreign or conflicting ideas than top civilian leaders, but they are also less likely to be dedicated communist ideologues. Institutionally the services are strongly organized into opposing hierarchies of loyalty. From the experience of other societies we can infer that the experiences, loyalties, and views of the generals should be differentiated from those of the colonels, and those of the colonels from those of more junior officers. Just what beliefs and loyalties these different levels will demonstrate under changing circumstances is hard to predict.

Below these special interest groups we must consider the average people of the USSR. It is particularly important to note that except where they have direct experience average Soviet citizens must perforce accept the world view their leaders give them. If we divide the nonelite citizens into blue collar and white collar classes, with unskilled and semiskilled manual labor and peasants in the former, some differences can be hypothesized. Most important is the likelihood that cynicism and dissatisfaction, as well as precommunist and noncommunist traditions and beliefs, will be most common among blue collar groups. They include the people who do the work but have the least say in the Soviet system. It may be that the economic security brought by communism has benefited these groups the most. But these gains were mostly the experience of earlier generations; today Soviet workers and peasants will be most cognizant of what the Soviet system has not provided. They will be particularly aware of their lack of effective political or economic power, even in factories and collectives.

THE TOOLS OF CHANGE

The tools of change may be thought of either as the groups that may affect or effect change, or the means that these groups might use to bring their influence to bear. The first group that should be distinguished is composed of the *liberal influentials* working within the system. The group includes all leaders that will influence decisions in a somewhat more liberal direction than others. Their gradual or rapid rise to greater influence is critical in any process of change. Quite different than the liberal influentials are the *internal dissidents.* Such persons demonstrate the regime's faults and the fact that there are persons in society who oppose the system. Although a vital force, they do not have power themselves to effect change. They are supported by *external dissidents,* either voluntary or involuntary exiles that continue to try to influence events in the USSR and its satellites.

Liberalization in the Soviet Union may also be affected by *external nongovernmental organizations,* through the support of dissidents, the publications of their works, and so on. Such organizations publish studies of the Soviet Union and its policies in an attempt to bring to the attention of external and internal publics the denials of freedom that occur in the Soviet Union and the nations it supports internationally. Indirectly, the *external media* bring pressure for change by both their neutral observations of the behavior of Soviet and satellite governments and their reporting of criticisms of, or dissents from, this behavior.

The actions of *external governments* overlap with those of nongovernmental groups. External governments have much greater leverage on the Soviet government because the Soviet Union must obtain their cooperation or acquiescence to attain many of its objectives. In theory foreign governments that take human rights seriously can exchange internal improvements in the freedom of Soviet or satellite citizens for items desired by the communist government. A relation of this kind has been most explicit in the exchanges that West Germany has made of consumer items for the release of prisoners by the East German government.[8] External governments also have the power to influence change through their general military and economic policies. At the extreme we might cease trading with the Soviet Union until the conditions of the dissidents are improved in specified ways. Such embargoes on trade are standard practice by many nations in regard to no less oppressive regimes—for example, Cuba, Uruguay, or Rhodesia. Indirectly, external governments influence change by assuring the maintenance or increasing success of the alternative models of political organization by which they are governed.

The means of influencing Soviet change include both violent and nonviolent approaches. The violent may include the terrorism that was so effective against the tsarist state, or guerilla war financed from within or without the USSR. These include the broad range of CIA and paramilitary "dirty tricks." Although in recent years it is doubtful that such tricks have been tried on a large scale, they have certainly played a part in anticommunist strategy everywhere. Violence also includes forceful opposition to the Soviet Union or what we regard as its direct or indirect agents. The Korean and Vietnamese wars were attempts at such opposition. Another form of violence is the threat of violence, the deterrence policy that operates on several levels from subconventional war to nuclear holocaust.

If Soviet and communist advances through the use of violence are relatively slow or contained, and if nuclear deterrence works, further employment of violence by Euro-Americans to effect Soviet change seems unlikely. We do not have the will for large wars, and thereby fear small ones. Very low level terrorist or guerilla efforts have proven generally unsuccessful against communist regimes even when and where they could be justified on moral or political grounds.

The means to effect Soviet change that are likely to be most useful and acceptable in the next few years are informational, ideological, and organizational. I have pointed out above the many ways in which information may be used to open up Soviet society through increasing the knowledge of the Soviet people about dissidence and its repression in the USSR and about what really goes on in the freer states of the West. Ideological communication must also occur, however, if the information on alternatives is to focus and sustain dissent. Those who would change the Soviet Union must have some idea of what it might be changed to. Ideology in this sense might be as simple as the democratic amalgam of the concepts of pluralism and inalienable individual rights with the assumption that individuals and groups will pursue their own interests unless there is an opposition with contrary interests to expose their faults and counter their power. Information must also be supplemented by organizational activity that makes possible the concerting of efforts and a feeling of common purpose among all of those who would liberalize the USSR.

The objectives of information, ideology, and organization must be tailored to the interests and education of the varying interest groups in the USSR if they are to be effective. Dissidents must be provided with hope of change that will keep up their courage. They must develop convincing analyses of the viability and legitimacy of alternatives to current oppression. Most important they must be provided aid in extending their appeal, in making linkages to new groups of people, in opening more channels for information flow within and without the country. At the same time they must be enabled to develop their influence without mobilizing disabling repression. Cynically one might argue that martyrs are often the true instigators of change. However their effect can only occur if there is a sufficient knowledge within and without the society of the martyrdom, and closed societies can largely obstruct or defuse such knowledge.

For liberals and elites in the ruling classes information must provide continuing evidence that the system is not really meeting their needs, that it is not working, and that change must occur. Believing in the inevitability of change will not be sufficient to enlist their support, however, unless it can also be shown that change will not be disastrous for them. For this last and key message to be developed the dissidents must do a good deal of soul searching. They must make a convincing case that they would establish a society of national reconciliation and not revenge.

For the masses of the Soviet Union the message of the agents of change must offer a vision of a better society beyond communism. This "better" will be both materialistic, the consumer dream they have been denied so often, and idealistic. The popular idealistic component will emphasize a future society without continual government interference with private interests, starting with ethnic and religious interests.[9] The essence of the message to average Soviet citizens must be to discard the concept of the "masses." Communism has long obscured the fact that there are no masses. Nations are principally made up of highly varied groups of people, without elite tastes or national importance, that have a kaleidescope of interests, abilities, and goals. To give them a meaningful world their individuality and particularity must be recognized. Since most of these people also want to be part of the whole, to be patriots, the appeal to nonelite groups must strive to separate the concepts of patriotism and communism.

CONCLUSION

After thirty years of containment the USSR remains a critical security threat to the United States and its allies. While there has been some liberalization in the Soviet Union, the regime is repressive internally, it continues to violently compel the subservience of its communist neighbors (and does not accept the legitimacy of those who oppose it), and it continues to expand its military power to compel obedience within its realm and potentially to increase this realm. While there is no immediate threat, the West is weary, and if force balances slip much further Soviet leaders may find the temptation to assert themselves forcefully in the Western world irresistible. This may lead them to embark upon a course that neither we nor they can ultimately control. Clearly the United States and its allies want the confrontation to end, and to end without disaster, but equally clearly we do not have a theory of how present policies and trends will reach that end. In a sense the United States and its allies are mired in a worldwide Vietnam; without a theory of success against determined opponents, the continuing costs of the struggle may eventually be more than the democratic societies are willing to bear.

One solution, or hope, lies in the possibility of a liberalization of the Soviet Union. While it is recognized that as there are continuities between Tsarist and Soviet Russia so there would be between Soviet and liberalized Russia, there are several arguments that a liberalized USSR would allow the superpower confrontation to subside in a way far more meaningful than it has under the label of detente. First, ruling circles in a liberal Soviet Union would be much less likely than they have in the past to support a military suppression of nationalist tendencies in the satellites. As neighboring communist states develop their own policies, a buffering group of relatively neutral states (some no longer communist) would emerge in Eastern Europe, and the massive military threat to Europe of the Warsaw Pact would greatly diminish. Secondly, since a liberalized Soviet Union would not be able to deal summarily with independence movements of nationalities within its borders, its internal preoccupations would increase. Third, a liberalized USSR would not be able to consistently devote the quality and quantity of its economic and scientific capability to military forces that it has in the past. Fourth, there may be something in the argument that democratic states do not engage in war nearly as easily as non-democratic.

But how likely is a liberal Soviet Union? In order to examine this question we have suggested several models of the Soviet future, ranging from more of the same to a liberalizing Euro-communism or social democratic USSR. Directing Soviet change toward either of these latter models requires that we develop a theory of how liberalizing change might occur in the USSR. Clearly it will not be automatic. It will result from changes in the balance of interests and perceptions of key groups. These include the ruling elite, the military, liberal dissidents, nationalist and religious dissenters, and the general public. Those in power will support change if they feel the necessity or inevitability of liberalization, and if they believe in the possibility of their surviving it. Those out of power must feel that there is hope for change, that there are viable alternatives to socialist tsarism.

Control over information, ideology, and organization is the major way in which the present balance of interests is maintained. Change requires an information policy that promotes maximum development of the tools of change, conceived as categories of people—dissidents and disaffected among the elite and masses, liberal elements in the ruling classes themselves, external dissidents, nongovernmental organizations, and external governments—and conceived as means of influence, such as publications of dissident thought or comparisons of Soviet society with others. To supplement the highly abstract discussion presented above we will need in the future to look closely at the relative effectiveness of different programs to affect information flows, such as Voice of America, Radio Liberty, the distribution of standard publications, or the support of emigre groups. It may be, for example, that ideas reaching the Soviet Union by way of Eastern Europe are more effective than those imparted directly. Finally, it is important to consider the different informational needs of the interest groups identified in the USSR. Of particular importance is the difference between the needs of liberal dissidents and those of the noncosmopolitan majority. Organizationally and ideologically the key problem becomes the need to develop improved linkages between groups identified with each of these classes.

The foregoing is a sketch of the problem. The following papers and the discussions they engendered will take the reader a good part of the way toward understanding the directions we must go in working toward its solution.

NOTES

1. The revisionist thesis that the U.S. rather than the USSR was the obstacle is hardly convincing. But even were it true, from the West the USSR was perceived as the obstacle, and this perception is what primarily concerns us here.

2. This is, of course, what happened in Czechoslovakia. See Frank Kaplan, "Czechoslovakia's Experiment in Humanizing Socialism," *East European Quarterly* (Fall 1977).

3. For East Germany see *Der Spiegel*, January 2 and 8, 1978, for the manifesto of the "League of Democratic Communists." For the opinions of the Charter 77 group in Czechoslovakia, see *Keesing's Contemporary Archives*, 1978, pp. 28785–88.

4. What the Soviet dissidents want is of course a much disputed topic, as the discussion below indicates.

5. See R. D. Gastil, *Freedom in the World 1978* (Boston: G. K. Hall, 1978), "Freedom and Democracy: Definitions and Distinctions," pp. 111–26. See also John Rawls, *A Theory of Justice* (Cambridge, Massachusetts: Harvard University Press, 1971). See also above, pp. 63–82.

6. Compare Dean Babst, "A Force for Peace," *Industrial Research*, April 1972, pp. 55–58.

7. Crane Brinton, *The Anatomy of a Revolution* (New York: Random House, 1965).

8. *Amnesty International Briefing*, "German Democratic Republic" (October 1977), p. 7.

9. See Peter Berger, *Pyramids of Sacrifice* (New York: Basic Books, 1974).

The Struggle for National Self-Assertion and Liberalization in the Soviet Union

Teresa Rakowska-Harmstone

The Soviet Union is formally a federal state, reflecting the multi-national character of its population which is composed of more than one hundred different ethnic groups; but the national character of the Soviet state and society is distinctly Russian, because of the hegemonial role played in the country by the Great Russian ethnic group. The Russians constitute fifty-three percent of the total population (1970 Census), and their quantitatively dominant status has been reinforced by their qualitative weight—high on the relative scale of economic and social development—and the politically ruling status that has survived untouched the transition from the Russian Empire to the Soviet socialist state. The Soviet federation is in fact a unitary state, because of the monopoly of political power exercised by the unitary Communist party, the centralized character of the system reflected in the official formula describing it as "national in form and socialist in content." Moreover, the new "socialist" norms and patterns of behavior are heavily infused with Russian cultural content, a result of the Russian historical dominance.

The non-Russian national groups, twenty-one of which number more than one million people each,[1] are therefore effectively denied the exercise of their national rights, much as the people at large are denied the exercise of their civil rights because of the nature of the communist political system, despite formal guarantees embodied in the USSR Constitution. While many of the smaller and less culturally cohesive national groups appear to be assimilating into the prevalent Soviet

---

Teresa Rakowska-Harmstone is professor of political science, Carleton University; she is an authority on the Soviet Union, especially Soviet nationalities.

100

(Russian) patterns, the drive for national self-determination by the larger groups, particularly those that have Union Republic status under the Constitution, had become apparent in the nineteen fifties and has visibly accelerated in the sixties and the seventies.[2]

In the area of national relations the pressures for national rights are more broadly based and potentially much stronger than are the pressures for liberalization in the sphere of civil rights. They are spearheaded by modernized national elites most of whom participate in the party-state power structure, unlike the small and persecuted groups of dissidents who speak for human rights. The two types of pressures are closely interrelated. Both seek decentralization of political power and greater subsystem autonomy, and concessions in one sphere stimulate demands in the other. But they are not always complementary and frequently work at cross purposes. The national pressures are directed primarily at a devolution of power from Moscow to the national republics, a trend that does not necessarily imply greater recognition of civil and individual rights by the republics' national elites—examples of suppression of minority rights by militant nationalism abound worldwide. Yet the fear of a nationalist explosion is a major factor inhibiting greater liberalization. The two types of pressures tend to merge only when both the national and civil rights demands are voiced by the same groups and individuals. A partial overlap of this kind has occurred in the Ukraine and in the Baltics. Civil and national rights' demands coincide fully only in the cases of persecuted minorities that do not have formal autonomy, such as the Jews, the Germans, and the Crimean Tatars.

The denial of effective national rights to minority groups is as characteristic of the system as is the ban on political pluralism of which it is a natural concomitant. Nevertheless, the picture of ethnic relations in the Soviet Union is more complex than a general statement of this kind would indicate, because of the internationalist nature of the ruling ideology and because of the constitutionally guaranteed "national forms" for the country's ethnic groups. These are reflected in the administrative subdivisions and in the party's cultural policies. From the point of view of their ability to exercise formal national rights and to benefit from formal cultural autonomy the non-Russian ethnic groups fall into three distinct categories, a gradation that has to be understood if an effective policy designed to assist Soviet minorities in their struggle for national self-determination is to be developed.

The fourteen non-Russian Union Republic nations—which range from the forty million Ukrainians and over nine million Uzbeks and Belorussians to the one million Estonians—have formal administrative structures and territorial economic bases, as well as the use of national languages and culture forms, for the expression of ethnic interests. With their power structures penetrated by the Russians, none of the republics has any real political autonomy or any significant input into decision making at the federal level, and their cultural policies are directed from Moscow in an attempt at "internationalist" socialization. But the existence of formal autonomy has served to solidify their people's sense of separate national identity, and their national languages and cultures have increasingly become the vehicle for national self-assertion. The autonomous republic nations, most of which are smaller in size and less culturally cohesive, also have national state and culture forms, but in most cases assimilatory pressures have been stronger and trends towards gradual assimilation have set in. The third and distinct category are the national groups that are denied formal statehood and culture trappings, either because of dispersal or as a punishment. Here we have examples of classic suppression of minority rights that have become known internationally, because of the resistance of the groups affected. Although the Jews are the best known group the category includes Volga Germans, Crimean Tatars, and Meskhetian Turks.[3] The latter groups have tirelessly and repeatedly attempted to use formal legal remedies provided by the system to alleviate their national plight, but without success. They also have appealed to international public opinion.

Scholars generally agree that national elites and their perception of their group's relative status in the overall order of things play a crucial role in national self-assertion. So it is not surprising that in the Soviet Union ethnic elites are in the forefront in the articulation of national demands. Primarily, these are the political elites of the Union Republic nations. They are Soviet educated and participant in the power structure, but they face increasing frustrations because of the discrepancy between the rhetoric of "equal partnership," and their own and their group's actually inferior status vis-à-vis the ubiquitous Russians. They increasingly perceive that emphasis on ethnic identity is strategically most salient in articulating demands and in building the support of local constituencies.[4] Ethnic conflict has visibly intensified between the republics' national elites and the Russian dominated central authorities, but the pressures appear for the present to be directed at winning greater autonomy within the system, rather than at challenging the principle of the party's monopoly of political power, the touchstone of the system that precludes development of pluralism.

The struggle for greater autonomy manifests itself in the political, economic, and cultural spheres. Politically, there are growing pressures to promote ethnic elites within the power structure and to increase their participation in policy making. This is reflected in attempts to place ethnic personnel in key power positions in the republics (at the expense of Russian central cadres), and to gain greater representation at the federal level. Through the sixties and seventies republican elites made some headway in the republics and also improved their ex officio standing in Moscow. In the economic sphere, which is an exclusive federal preserve under the command planning system, there is evidence of a struggle between the republics and the central planners over resource allocation and economic policies, but so far the primacy of federal interests has consistently prevailed. On the cultural front, ethnic demands have been most pressing and most clearly articulated, centering on the greater use of national languages in education (especially in higher and technical education), and in the media, and in an effort to maximize national content in cultural offerings. Prominent here have been the demands for a more objective treatment of national historiography, especially in relation to the role of national heroes and their struggle with Russian imperialism.[5] In general, the ethnic elites are fighting to gain the "equal partnership" which they have in theory but which is absent in practice. To this end they invoke repeatedly not only the constitutional and legal provisions formally on the books, but also Lenin's myth, particularly the Leninist theory of national self-determination, and his interpretation of the rights of non-Russian nations in a socialist state.

The evidence suggests that nationalism is essentially confined within the Union Republics, although members of national elites have been able to join the federal establishment in increasing numbers, inclusive of membership or candidate membership in the Politbureau.[6] Cut off from national constituencies there, and isolated (there are no indications that members of different ethnic groups seek each other's support in federal politics), they tend to merge into the prevalent Russian coloration and pursue federal policies with the zeal equal to that of the Russians. Ethnic leaders who represent their republics ex officio speak for the republican interests, but on the whole the non-Russians' involvement in factional politics at the top reflects the primacy of personal and factional rather than nationalist considerations.

In the republics there is little doubt that the members of national political elites advocate greater recognition of their group's national rights. Their attitudes, however, are ambiguous. They represent their own people vis-à-vis the Russian "feds," but they also implement central policies at home. Those in leading positions are totally identified with the system of which they are a part. This is not to say that, if able to achieve a measure of national self-determination, they would not press for full sovereignty, or would not be receptive to liberalization. The espousal of more democratic forms, however, would be conditioned by their specific national political culture (more democratic in the Soviet West), and their exposure to examples and pressures from outside, as well as pressures from their own constituencies.

Ethnic nationalism may grow in strength as broader ethnic strata emerge in increasing numbers from the republics' mass-based educational systems. The development of cultural elites and a national professional and technical intelligentsia are particularly important. As national demands become more outspoken, there are more and more purges of national "chauvinists," some found even in the ranks of political elites. Although persecuted, "bourgeois nationalists" are no longer physically liquidated, except in extreme cases, and provide nuclei of nationalist counterelites in each republic. Young people are becoming increasingly aware of their ethnic identity as they leave schools and face competition with Russians in the market place. For some of them, particularly in the eastern republics, the growing perception of being "second best" is enhanced by inadequate facility in the Russian language. The purged "counterelite" and many of the frustrated young tend to gravitate toward civil/human rights dissident movements. Some of them cross, or are forced to cross, the border of "socialist legality."

The phenomenon of a coalition between the national and civil rights and religious dissidents has been visible in the Soviet West—in the Ukraine, Lithuania, Latvia, and Estonia, although sporadic cases have also appeared in the Caucasus—in Georgia and Armenia. So far there has been no evidence of civil rights movements in Central Asia, except for the members of the deported national groups, such as the Crimean Tatars or Volga Germans. Nevertheless, the situation may change rapidly, because of the population explosion there, a problem which is compounded by cultural alienation between the Moslem Central Asians and the Russians. Central Asians also have had a massive cultural revival based in Islam, and are increasingly coming in contact with coreligionists abroad through contacts stimulated by Soviet foreign policy. As it emerges now, the Central Asians' predominant aspiration seems to be for a type of national communism, as in Yugoslavia.

International and foreign policy considerations are an important aspect of national relations in the Soviet Union. The extension of the "socialist commonwealth" to Eastern Europe has encouraged Soviet ethnic elites to seek greater autonomy of a type closer to the East European model. The policy of support for national liberation movements in the Third World has also served to embolden domestic demands for self-determination. Both have constrained the party's hand in seeking to repress growing ethnic nationalism for fear of reverberations in Eastern Europe, among the nonruling parties, and in the Third World. Voices calling for the abolition of the Republics in the name of integration already achieved and efficiency in economic management have been muted by the adoption in 1977, finally, of a new constitution which introduced no basic changes in the federal structure. Growing nationalism in Central Asia is particularly important not only because of the population explosion among Soviet Moslems, but also because of its proximity to China (which champions the national rights of the Soviet minorities), and to Iran (with its revival of fundamentalist Islam), and in view of the Soviet Middle Eastern policy. To Moslem countries Central Asian republics are presented as models of both noncapitalist development and successful symbiosis between Islam and communism. The reverse side of the coin is the impact of relations with the Moslem world on Central Asian nationalism, and a potential influence there of militant Islam.

What can we do to support the struggle for national self-determination in the Soviet Union? Direct contact or assistance is obviously not possible but a wide range of measures is available at governmental and nongovernmental levels. These should aim primarily at letting the Soviet government and Soviet minority groups know that we recognize the problem of national oppression in the Soviet Union and that we strongly support the national self-determination of Soviet peoples. In general terms three major directions for further effort may be identified:

1. Development and expansion of research in ethnic relations in the USSR on a broad and even basis—that is, systematic collection of data on all Soviet national groups, their status and their particular grievances and demands vis-à-vis the central authorities, and analysis of the reasons for and the dimensions of the ethnic conflict, the ways that it manifests itself, and future trends. So far, research into ethnic problems in the Soviet Union has been sporadic, carried on by a few individuals, and geared, in many cases, to particular groups or stimulated by glaring cases of national oppression. The problem is universal—despite the gradation discussed above—and we need to be able to analyze the situation as it evolves across the full spectrum of Soviet nationalisms. This includes the revival of Great Russian nationalism that has accompanied the growth in national self-assertion of the non-Russians. Research of this kind requires the knowledge of other major Soviet languages as well as Russian, funding, and institutional connections.

2. Wide dissemination of the findings both at the popular and scholarly level. It is particularly important that the gap between the theory and practice in the treatment of Soviet national groups be

emphasized in order to counteract the steady propaganda barrage coming out of the Soviet Union, claiming that the national problem has been solved, and that fraternal unity characterizes the relations between equal and sovereign Soviet nations and nationalities integrated into the new "Soviet people." That is also important in order to mobilize American public opinion in support of governmental pressures to stimulate the Soviet government to live up to the letter of its own law and ideological principles, and to the letter of international instruments of which it is a signatory. Further, it is important for purposes of mobilizing international public opinion not only in the West, but in the Third World, where the USSR has been posing as a champion of national self-determination and a leading supporter of national liberation movements.

3. Development of a pattern of communication with Soviet ethnic elites and national dissidents—primarily through broadcasting but also through printed media (insofar as possible)—under the provisions of Basket III of the Helsinki agreement, to indicate that we are aware of their existence and demands. This should include not only information about outside events, but also wide coverage of information about what is happening in the Soviet Union. Political control of all media there poses a formidable barrier to internal exchange of information, and prevents coordination of efforts aiming at greater recognition of national rights. Unless we have both the capability and will to offer tangible and effective support, past experience in Eastern Europe suggests extreme caution in establishing this type of communication lest it stimulate nationalist explosions.

In specific terms various initiatives can be undertaken at governmental as well as nongovernmental levels. Governmental action, based on international agreements as well as on newly articulated Human Rights principles, would be directed at two basic aims: official recognition of the fact that the Soviet Union is not just "Russia," but a federation of several national groups in a multiethnic society; and support for the de facto implementation of the provisions on national rights and status embodied in the Soviet Constitution and in international instruments, beginning with the Charter of the United Nations. Achieving these aims would be particularly important in assisting and encouraging Soviet ethnic political elites in pressing for greater autonomy and thus political decentralization. It would also serve to extend an umbrella of international recognition and protection to dispersed national groups and national dissidents, an umbrella that would make acts of national repression increasingly inconvenient for Soviet authorities. But initiative in support of national rights should be carefully weighed in the light of current evidence (hence the importance of research), because the volatile nature of nationalism and fear of its destabilizing potential may trigger reactions by the Soviet government opposite to those intended.

Several types of *governmental* actions come to mind:

a. An invitation to the Soviet republics to utilize constitutional provisions giving them the right "to enter into relations with other states, to conclude treaties with them, to exchange consular and diplomatic representatives and to take part in the work of international organizations" (art. 80). While any such exchanges would probably include only "loyal" personnel, this type of recognition would go far in stimulating ethnic elites to press more energetically for the closing of the gap between the legal provisions and the actual practice. One could also recall the constitutional rights to secession (art. 72). While this would seem unthinkable in the U.S. diplomatic practice, one should remember Soviet exhortations in support of Puerto Rican independence. Invoking Soviet constitutional provisions in defense of minority rights would be an effective weapon for stimulating international public opinion and supporting demands for national autonomy in the Soviet Union.

b. *In private,* the U.S. government could ask for specific benefits for Soviet nationalities as a *quid pro quo* in concluding specific deals and arrangements with the Soviet Union in areas where such deals are seen as particularly advantageous by the Soviet leaders, such as specific trade items and technological transfer. Linkages of this kind can be counterproductive if publicized, however, as seen in the experience of the Jackson-Vanik amendment. For reasons of domestic and international prestige, publicity tends to foreclose options for Soviet leaders that would otherwise remain open for bargaining purposes.

c. In educational and scientific exchanges the government could press for increased ethnic balance. It might ask for the participation of specific minorities, especially those that are at the bottom of the scale of socioeconomic indicators in the Soviet Union.

d. Interested agencies could monitor violations of national rights in the Soviet Union, protesting them in the international forums with maximum publicity. Examples of this type of action have been provided by the Soviet Union in numerous cases, as in the recent campaign against Israel in international organizations.

Nongovernmental action in support of national rights in the Soviet Union would serve primarily the purpose of stimulating national and international public opinion, but would also increase awareness among Soviet national groups that their plight is known and appreciated in the West. Here again, several types of initiatives are possible.

a. Establishment of research centers as well as monitoring services with adequate publicity outlets to study, analyze, and discuss problems in Soviet national relations. Various types of nongovernmental groups, including universities, foundations, and business firms could be interested in this type of initiative.

b. Imposition of *quid pro quo* and ethnic key requirements in academic and other types of exchanges.

c. Activities on behalf of minority rights to be developed by political parties on the lines suggested by Professor Feuer (below, pp. 161–72).

d. Organized action on behalf of specific Soviet minority groups by ethnic/religious associations of the same ethnic origins. The pattern has already been established by Jewish-American groups on behalf of Soviet Jewry's rights and emigration. Ukrainian, Polish, German, and Baltic associations could develop support and publicize activities on behalf of the respective groups in the Soviet Union. Coordinated over a multiethnic spectrum this type of activity could have significant political clout in mobilizing congressional support. This activity would also facilitate communication with ethnic elites and national dissidents in the Soviet Union, as many members of ethnic associations in North America have retained individual contacts and channels of communications with relatives and friends in the Soviet Union.

Nongovernmental activities, free from constraints of official policy, could be far more wide-ranging than governmental activities, and would facilitate and pave the way for governmental action.

The potential for change in the Soviet Union inherent in the growth of ethnic nationalism is high, but it carries with it a threat to political stability. National pressures are formidable and accelerating, but so far have proceeded on a slow timetable. Concessions made to either national minorities or civil rights demands, the effects of which are inextricably interwoven, may well develop a "snowball" effect, threatening the maintenance of the system. As Yugoslavia demonstrates, a gradual decentralization of power in favor of the national republics with a parallel improvement in the sphere of civil rights is possible within the constraints of a communist system, and so far has been manageable despite destabilization potential, But conditions in the Soviet Union differ. The ethnic mix is different and, by all indications, the Russians whose nationalism has also grown in intensity, do not see the need to give up their dominant status. Soviet leaders' perception of their international role as the leader of the world communist movement also intervenes, because nationalism has proved to be the most important single obstacle on the road to the consolidation of this leadership. In the domestic context the national problem is perceived by some as being basically intractable; there is a standing temptation to resort to repression and forced assimilation rather than risk concessions and their possible outcomes at home and abroad. At the same time there are benefits to be gained by partial concessions to national political elites in exchange for their willingness to integrate into the Soviet "internationalist" model. Both points of view have appeared in the debate on the national problem that is carried on within the framework of general consensus on the paramountcy of system maintenance and stability.

The new Soviet global role as superpower has made the leadership more conscious of international public opinion. Widely publicized support for the national rights of Soviet ethnic groups coming from the West, as well as greater awareness in international forums of their violation, may stimulate some concessions within the limits set by the perceived need for control. From the point of view of overall improvement in the civil rights situation, Western support for national rights might be most effective if focused on championing the cause of persecuted minorities, included in this analysis in the third category. Broad support for the right to national self-determination of the Union Republic nations (while parallel to that extended by the Soviet Union to national liberation movements) would clearly invoke a specter of destabilization. Unless carefully synchronized with the pace of internal developments as well as with changes in the overall balance of power, such support might result in repressions both on national and civil rights fronts.

NOTES

1. The Soviet Constitution recognizes four types of autonomous units in the descending order of importance: Union Republics (SSR), Autonomous Republics (ASSR), Autonomous Regions (AO), and Autonomous Areas. In the 1970 Census the Russians numbered 129 million people and were represented in the federal structure by the core Union Republic, the Russian Soviet Federated Socialist Republic (RSFSR), which extends from the Western borders to the Pacific, and includes most of those minority groups with a national status inferior to that of a Union Republic. Characteristically, the Russians' leading position is reflected in the absence of a Russian branch party organization comparable to those of all other nationalities with Union Republic status; they are represented directly in the federal party structure of the Communist Party of the Soviet Union (CPSU). (Branch party organizations for other national groups are strictly for administrative convenience, because under the CPSU Statutes [1919 and 1961] the party is a unitary and not a federal organization. It represents the "socialist" part of the formula, "national in form and socialist in content"; the government structure represents the "national" part.)

Of the twenty-one national groups which numbered over one million people in 1970, fourteen have the status of a Union Republic; (the requirements for Union Republic status are: population above one million, an economic base, a border location and a "common psychological make-up"): the *Slavs* (other than the Russians): Ukrainians (40.7 million) and Belorussians (9.0 million); the *Central Asians*: Uzbeks (9.2 million), Kazakhs (5.2 million), Tadzhiks (2.1 million), Turkmen (1.5 million) and Kirgiz (1.4 million); the *Caucasians*:

Azeri (4.4 million), Armenians (3.5 million) and Georgians (3.2 million); the *Balts*: Lithuanians (2.6 million), Latvians (1.4 million), and Estonians (1.0 million); and the *Moldavians* (2.7 million). Four of the twenty-one are Autonomous Republics within the RSFSR: Tatars (5.9 million—the Tatar group includes the Volga Tatars in the Autonomous Republic as well as the Crimean Tatars, who lost their autonomous status during World War II and were resettled in Central Asia); Chuvashi (1.7 million), Mordvinians (1.2 million) and Bashkirs (1.2 million). Three of the twenty-one groups are geographically dispersed and do not have formal autonomous rights: the Jews (2.1 million), the Volga Germans (1.8 million) and the Poles (1.1 million). The Volga Germans had an Autonomous Republic prior to World War II, but it was abolished and its population was deported eastward for alleged collaboration with the invaders. The Germans were belatedly rehabilitated in the sixties, but their Autonomous Republic was not restored. This also happened to the Crimean Tatars and some smaller national groups. The autonomous units of some of the latter have been restored and resettlement permitted.

The major Soviet nations and nationalities are highly differentiated in terms of culture and historical traditions as well as by their level of economic and social development. The "West" is Protestant and Catholic as well as Orthodox, and stands highest on the scale of modernization; the "East" is Moslem and underdeveloped. All have retained a high degree of cultural cohesion and a high concentration of ethnic settlement in and around the original national area.

2. Considerable literature already exists in the English language on the subject of national self-assertion of the non-Russian groups in the USSR. Among the general monographs, the most comprehensive include: Erich Goldhagen, ed., *Ethnic Minorities in the Soviet Union* (New York, 1968); Edward Allworth, ed., *Soviet Nationality Problems* (New York, 1971); Zev Katz et al., eds., *Handbook of Major Soviet Nationalities* (New York, 1975); and George W. Simmonds, ed., *Nationalism in the USSR and Eastern Europe in the Era of Brezhnev and Kosygin* (Detroit, 1977). See also *Problems of Communism*, Special Issue: "Nationalism and Nationalities in the USSR," XVI, 5 (September–October 1967).

3. For recent history of the last two groups see Peter J. Potichnyi, "The Struggle of the Crimean Tatars" (pp. 302–19), and S. Enders Wimbush and Ronald Wixman, "The Meskhetian Turks: A New Voice in Soviet Central Asia" (pp. 320–39), in *Canadian Slavonic Papers*, XVII, 2 & 3 (Summer and Fall 1975).

4. Compare N. Glazer and D. F. Moynihan, *Ethnicity, Theory and Experience* (Cambridge, Mass., 1975), the Introduction.

5. See T. Rakowska-Harmstone, "The Dialectics of Nationalism in the USSR," *Problems of Communism*, XII, 3 (May–June 1974), pp. 1–22.

6. Major Republics and Republic "clusters" are represented in the Politburo according to an apparent "ethnic key." At least one or more Ukrainians and Belorussians are members. Central Asia is usually represented by a Uzbek first secretary (there is now also a Kazakh first secretary); the Caucasus, by one of the Republics' secretaries. Baltic Republics do not seem to rate a representative, nor does Moldavia. The Republics' first secretaries are always members of the CPSU Central Committee; and an ex officio membership of heads of the Republics' governmental hierarchies in the equivalent federal bodies was adopted in 1958; it is now included in the 1977 Constitution.

Comments and Discussion

Following the presentation, *Feuer* pointed out that many emigres feel a horror at the prospect of the general destabilization of the Soviet Union that would follow nationality secession. They fear rightist or populist nationalisms that might eventuate in fascism and the subsequent suppression of their own minorities. In light of this, he asked whether there was not a danger in alienating Russian intellectuals by supporting the cause of the nationalities.

Several expert participants argued strongly that these worries were not justified. They pointed out that most dissidents had come to accept the right of national self-determination as expressed in the Soviet Constitution. They saw liberalization in this sphere as intertwined with the question of liberalization in the media and arts and the general achievement of the rule of law. This was certainly the position of Sakharov and Bukovsky. *Bociurkiw* reported a survey of the nationality of those in the most restrictive labor camps for political prisoners: of 271 prisoners forty-one percent were Ukrainians, twenty-one percent Baltic, and twenty-one percent Russians. With this kind of mixture acceptance of the self-determination desires of the minority nationalities had to become a common ground for the movement. In this respect the emigre community is not necessarily representative of the dissident community.

It was also suggested that by and large the nationalities had shown little evidence of rightist, and certainly not of fascist tendencies. The right-wing elements within the emigre community should not be taken as representative of the political mixture in the USSR today. It was suggested that one of the major mistakes of Westerners at the time, and of Soviet experts even today, has been not to recognize the nature or importance of the national independence movements of 1918-1920 on the periphery of the Russian Empire. None of these were fascist, all were social democratic or social revolutionary, and all were crushed because the choice was believed to be between restoration of the Imperial monarchy or bolshevism. (This provides within Soviet society another basis for the historiographic struggle among elites referred to in the presentation).

It must be recognized that there are many variations among the nationalities in their goals and situation. The Baltic peoples are acquainted with multiparty, liberal democracy; they think in terms of reestablishing these systems, perhaps in the form of a Baltic Federation. While national feeling is very strong here, in Belorussia the people are so Russified that a potentially mobilizable popular basis for secession is questionable. The western Ukraine has experience as a part of central Europe; its people may have a potential desire for closer association of the Ukraine with the countries to the west, including Poland. Here nationalism is extremely anti-Russian and often has religious roots. In the eastern Ukraine, dissidence is more inclusive, more leftist, less intense. The strength of the nationality movement in the Caucasus is suggested by the recent public demonstrations in Georgia and Armenia in favor of restoring the favored position of their languages to the new constitutions of the Republics. The demonstrations were successful, a remarkable achievement given past experience.

The Muslim peoples in Transcaucasia and Central Asia might establish rightist regimes if they seceded. Here Islam is a common cultural determinant and hatred of Europeans goes very deep. The establishment of a conservative religious state in Iran might influence Central Asian nationalisms in an illiberal direction.

Whether nationalism and liberalism naturally go together was discussed inconclusively. Because of the secessionist hopes held out in the Soviet Constitution, most Soviet dissidents tie nationalism and liberalism together as supporting concepts. The logic of the situation suggests that Russian nationalists should feel threatened by anything that would disintegrate the Russian dominated USSR. This fear should make them turn against both liberalism and separatist nationalisms. As a result some Russian nationalists are opposed to the national self-determination of minorities, but others, such as Solzhenitsyn, support the secession of those nationalities that wish to leave. Their idealism might well decline as larger segments of the population become involved in a threatened destabilization of the Empire.

In commenting on the foregoing discussion, *Rakowska-Harmstone* remarked that there was another sense in which the situation might change. If one concentrated, as she had in her talk, on the ruling elites, one naturally saw a conservative desire to achieve communism without Russian domination. Legally these elites can push for nationalist advantage only if they espouse socialist nationalism and reject bourgeois nationalism. This situation may have led her to overstress the conservative nature of nationality movements, especially in Central Asia. If there actually were a devolution of power to the Republics, it might well bring in a new stratum of leaders, perhaps closer in thinking to that of the dissident liberals, especially in the Soviet "West." There is certainly a "dissemination of new expectations" into all areas of the USSR, and this gives a basis for hope.

Two further questions were asked of the speaker. First, since for military service the only expanding manpower pool in the USSR consists of Central Asians, will this make a problem for continued Russian control? The answer was that in 1938 nationality units were abandoned; at least since this time the army has been considered to be a major means of integration. Only Russian is spoken in the military services. For this reason and because of their generally low educational level Central Asians are mostly incorporated into infantry and auxiliary labor battalions. Control is firmly in Russian or Slav hands. In a recent survey Rakowska-Harmstone found ninety-five percent of the generals to be Slav, of which about eighty percent were Russian. Ukrainians have a chance to rise in the military, but usually become Russified.

Evidence for a Muslim cultural revival in Central Asia included the fact that Central Asians continue to follow Muslim customs in private, even the elite. Intermarriage is rare, with Muslim women almost never marrying Slavs, out of a communal sense of cultural superiority. Muslim women came out during the war, but today there is only token participation in the labor force. For example, in the Soviet Union women generally make up a major portion of the work force in textile factories, but not in Central Asia. Muslims refuse to accept urban life on Soviet terms; they continue to make pilgrimages to holy shrines; and persist in their support of itinerant mullahs and unauthorized congregations.

This was followed by a short discussion of the relative strength of the nationalities within the Soviet power structure. Rakowska-Harmstone pointed out that the key to the balance has always been that in each Republic the First Secretary of the Party is a representative of the people of the Republic and the Second Secretary is a representative of the Central Party. First Secretaries have always been on the Central Committee of the CPSU, but this is such a large body that this does not give the nationalities great weight. Their relative powerlessness nationally is suggested by the Central Committee Secretariat which is staffed almost exclusively by the Russians. There was some improvement in the ethnic balance of power in the system under Khrushchev, particularly in favor of Ukrainians, but there has been little change since then. The Ukrainian influx reflected the personal power base of Khrushchev, first, and Brezhnev later, rather than a recognition of the need to include Ukrainians *qua* nationality.

In conclusion, the feeling of most participants was that Americans should support, or at any rate not oppose, the aspirations of the Soviet nationalities within the general framework of supporting Soviet liberalization. They felt that these nationalisms would grow in strength regardless of what we did. Their growth may not necessarily lead to secession, but may also lead to a more genuine federation. In many cases nationalism would directly support the overall goal of liberalization. Within this conclusion, most participants recognized that the movement toward nationalist goals could lead, where successful, to intolerance of minorities in specific cases, or, where unsuccessful, to increased suppression of non-Russians by Russians. We must also live with the fact that liberalization that raises the specter of nationality secession in the USSR will be destabilizing within the Soviet Union and thus also unavoidably destabilizing internationally. But if we are to do anything at all to support positive change in the Soviet Union the destabilization accompanying change must be recognized and plans formulated for minimizing its negative effects.

Religious Dissent in the Soviet Union: Status, Interrelationships, and Future Potential

Bohdan R. Bociurkiw

INTRODUCTION

While *any* external manifestation of religious beliefs has been viewed by Soviet authorities as tantamount to dissent from the state doctrine of Marxism-Leninism, for the purposes of our discussion religious dissent may be defined as an overt repudiation of the existing relationship between the Soviet state and institutional religion. More specifically, religious dissent has been directed against the long standing Soviet practices of political discrimination among churches and against believers, and of subjecting religious groups to far-reaching governmental control over their internal activities, statutes, and personnel. Insofar as this policy violates both the Soviet constitutional principles and the international human rights norms providing for freedom of conscience and worship—religious dissent may well be considered as a distinct subcategory of the human rights movement in the Soviet Union.[1]

As for the Soviet regime, it has from its very beginning viewed religion as a political problem, religious doctrines as hostile ideologies, and churches and sects as competing with the Communists for influence over society and "objectively" obstructing the process of "Communist construction." On the other hand, once the governmental authorities and the policy established effective controls over the registered religious organizations and approved their statutes and leadership, religious dissent could not but be seen as a threat to Soviet control over religious

Bohdan R. Bociurkiw is professor of political science, Carleton University; he is an authority on the Soviet Union, especially Soviet religious movements.

organizations. Hence what Levitin-Krasnov has called a "monstrous paradox: a state church within a system of an atheist state"[2]—a situation that casts the Communist regime in the role of a protector of "established" faiths against their own dissenters and schismatics.

This paper will examine the genesis, scope, and social base of the principal currents of religious dissent in the USSR, analyze their objectives and strategies, and explore the interrelationships between movements of religious protest and those struggling for national and political rights. Special attention will be focused on the effect of religious dissidence on Soviet church policy and its contribution to the evolution of Soviet society towards greater tolerance of nonconformity in values and beliefs.

THE GENESIS, SCOPE, AND SOCIAL BASE OF RELIGIOUS DISSENT

Religious dissent in the contemporary USSR is represented by three generations of dissenters corresponding roughly to three distinct periods in Soviet church policy. The "oldest" category consists mainly of the remnants of those elements of the Russian Orthodox Church that refused to accept Metropolitan Sergii's 1927 compromise with the regime[3] and who have since considered the "official" Church as devoid of divine grace and dominated by the enemies of Christ. This surviving Russian Orthodox underground movement has been known as the "True Orthodox Church," and more recently, as the "True Orthodox Christians."[4] The "middle generation" of religious dissent consists of those groups which were in effect outlawed since World War II because they were considered bourgeois nationalist or anti-Soviet (for example, the Ukrainian Catholics or Uniates in the Western Ukraine[5] and the Jehovah's Witnesses), as well as several factions that split away from their respective religious groups after the latter accepted Soviet conditions of legalization, including changes in their doctrine or practices, merger with other denominations, and extensive governmental controls (for example, the Pentecostalists and Adventists-Reformers).

The "youngest generation" of dissenters which, undoubtedly, has been influenced both by the earlier dissent currents and by the general intellectual ferment in post-Stalin USSR, dates from the massive anti-religious campaign instigated by Khrushchev's regime during 1959-64. The campaign resulted in closing more than half the houses of worship and the overwhelming majority of monastic and theological institutions in the country.[6] This latest wave of dissent emerged first from the ranks of the beneficiaries of Stalin's "New Religious Policy"—the Russian Orthodox Church and the Evangelical Christians-Baptists—who have, more recently, been joined by protesters from several other religious groups, including Roman Catholics (especially in Lithuania), Georgian Orthodox, adherents of the Armenian Gregorian Church, and Jews.

There were two immediate stimuli to the rise of this last wave of religious dissent. One was the gross violations of legality perpetrated by the authorities in the course of the antireligious campaign, and especially their use in this connection of the very government agencies designed to enforce Soviet laws on religion—the Council for the Affairs of the Russian Orthodox Church and the Council for the Affairs of Religious Cults.[7] The other stimulus for Orthodox and Baptist protesters was the apparent failure of their respective ecclesiastical leaders—the Moscow Patriarchate and the All-Union Council of the Evangelical Christians-Baptists, respectively—to defend the legal rights of their churches, a failure which the dissenters interpreted either as their leaders' timidity and moral weakness, or as a sign of their collusion with the atheist authorities. For some Lithuanian and Ukrainian Catholics, an additional source of discontent became, since the early 1960's, the Vatican's "détente" with the Kremlin and the Moscow Patriarchate, which generated fears that out of ignorance, naiveté or wishful thinking about "reunion" of the East—the Holy See was making deals with the atheist authorities and abandoning its harassed flock within the USSR.[8]

Individual currents of religious dissent have been drawing on different sources of societal support. Within the Russian Orthodox Church one could discern two parallel currents. One was an intellectual current articulating believers' demands which has been represented by a group of urban clergymen (Archbishop Ermogen, priests Gleb Iakunin, Nikolai Eshliman, Sergii Zheludkov, Dimitrii Dudko, Aleksandr Men and others) and lay Orthodox intellectuals (Anatolii Levitin-Krasnov, the late Boris Talantov, Lev Regelson, Vadim Shavrov and others) closely connected with the mainstream of political dissent.[9] The other, "grassroots," current was involved in numerous confrontations with the local authorities over the believers' rights; it has been largely based on the urban workers, women, and pensioners with virtually no intelligentsia participation and perhaps even an anti-intellectual bias; among its animators there might have been some "unregistered" clergy and dispersed monastics with links to the remnants of the "True Orthodox Christians." In recent years the intellectual current has been winning numerous adherents among cultural and scientific intelligentsia, as well as among young intellectuals and students who have been gathering in private religious-philosophical study circles that emerged in several major urban centres.[10] Significantly, as Russian Orthodox dissent took on increasingly nationalist connotations, Orthodox dissidents in the

Ukraine, such as priest Vasyl Romaniuk, laymen Valentyn Moroz and Levko Lukianenko, came to identify themselves with the suppressed Ukrainian Autocephalous Orthodox Church,[11] rather than the legally existing Russian Church which failed to adapt its orientation and structure to the multinational composition of its large flock.

Even more nationalist in orientation and far more widely based among the population have been the Lithuanian and Ukrainian Catholic dissent movements. As in Poland, the close historical association of religion and nationality, as well as widespread nationalist sentiment has made Lithuanian Catholic dissent a massive movement of religious protest, a movement which brought together a majority of the legally operating Lithuanian clergy symbolically headed by the banned bishops Steponavicius and Sladkevicius, and the extralegal monastic organizations, a section of lay intelligentsia, and broad strata of working class and rural believers.[12] The Ukrainian Catholic dissent, while deprived of a legal organizational structure, has remained a powerful popular movement in Galicia and the Carpatho-Ukraine, where it has been active both within the forcibly imposed Orthodox Church as well as in the "catacomb" Greek Catholic Church. On the fringes of the "catacomb church" there emerged, since the mid-1950's a small eschatological sect of *Pokutnyky* (Penitents), a peasant-based movement, which has been preaching, along with a mixture of Mariology, mysticism and Ukrainian nationalism, a complete repudiation of the "Antichrist" regime. With the Vatican-Soviet détente, the *Pokutnyky* completely broke away from Rome and the mainstream Uniate Church in the western Ukraine.[13]

The more recent dissent movement within the Georgian Orthodox Church (Valentina Pailodze, Zviad Gamsakhurdia and others), while undoubtedly reflecting widespread concern of believers over the decimation of the Church and the far-reaching corruption among its leaders, appears to have been based on the intelligentsia.[14] This seems to be the case with the Armenian religious-nationalist dissidents.

Almost totally devoid of intelligentsia participation, dissent currents within the Evangelical sects of Western origin have been based on clusters of worker and peasant supporters. In contrast to the traditional national churches, these sects have tended to dismiss the nationality question as an obstacle to Christian unity, taking a cosmopolitan position that, in most cases has favored Russian as the sectarian lingua franca. The largest of these groups, the Council of Churches of Evangelical Christians-Baptists (which split away from the official ECB organization in 1965) has recently started publishing also in Ukrainian, presumably in response to pressures from its large Ukrainian following.[15] The most adamant stand against differentiation along nationality lines has been taken by the Adventist dissident leader V. A. Shelkov—on behalf of the clandestine "All-Union Church of True and Free Adventists of the Seventh Day"; Shelkov has quoted Scriptures to argue for a merger of nations and a common language.[16] On the other hand, the largely western Ukrainian based Jehovah's Witnesses have employed the Ukrainian language in their clandestine publications, despite their indifferent stand on the national-cultural grievances of the Ukrainians.

While intimately related to Jewish national identity, Judaism in the USSR has not apparently recovered from the dual impact of secularization and administrative antireligious measures. With a relatively small percentage of believers among the Soviet Jewry (especially in the large urban centers of Russia, the Ukraine, and Belorussia),[17] the grievances of religious Jews have largely been absorbed into a wave of Zionist revival, Hebrew study circles, and the Jewish emigration movement. At the same time, a number of Russified Jewish intellectuals embraced Christianity, most of them in the Russian Orthodox form (for example, Aleksandr Ginsburg, Lev Regelson, Fr. Aleksandr Men).

Little information is available about religious ferment among the Moslem population. It is known that Islamic religious values remain widespread, often merged with a sense of national identity (with *musulmanin* frequently denoting a "pan-Turkic nationality" as opposed to both Europeans and new national designations introduced for the Moslems under the Soviet rule). According to official Soviet sources, the great majority of Moslem religious communities operate illegally or without official registration.[18] Surprisingly, the massive Crimean Tatar movement for repatriation to Crimea and restoration of national autonomy has had, as far as can be established from the available documents, virtually no religious connotations. This is not true of the recent Bashkir-Tatar *samizdat*.[19]

THE STRATEGIES OF RELIGIOUS DISSENT

It was symptomatic of the changing mood of Soviet society during the post-Stalin era—with the general weakening of fear and of the sense of isolation and political inefficacy—that the dissenters did not resign themselves to passive opposition or retreat into the "catacombs," but rather chose to challenge openly the legality of the regime's antireligious measures through public protests and confrontations with the authorities designed to attract maximum publicity for their cause at home and abroad. At first the protest took the form of petitions to the authorities, letters to the press, and delegations dispatched by believers to plead before governmental and ecclesiastical authorities. Frustrated in their appeals to socialist legality and unable to secure any meaningful response from their own church leaders, the believers subsequently turned to more desperate measures of self-defense by physically blocking the closing of churches and monasteries, staging demonstrations and courting beatings, arrests, fines, and prison sentences through acts of civil disobedience to what they believed to be illegal orders of Soviet officials.

The early common denominator of the different religious dissent movements has been their demand for *zakonnost* (the rule of law) and *glasnost* (open or public operation by the government authorities). Baptist, Orthodox, and Catholic dissidents demanded that the authorities strictly observe their own Constitution and published legislation on "cults," however restrictive, that the state cease discriminating among religious groups and against believers, and that government agencies for religious affairs conduct their operations publicly, in conformity only with published laws and regulations on religion; and that illegally suppressed congregations, "prohibited" clergy, closed houses of worship, monastic institutions, and theological schools be restored to their respective religious groups. The "prohibited" denominations, most notably Ukrainian Catholics, Council of Churches of Evangelical Christian Baptists (CC ECB), Pentecostals, and others have been demanding legalization and equality in status with the recognized religious groups.

Progressively, as the authorities responded to these demands with administrative harassment and selective judicial and extra-judicial repressions, the range of the dissidents' aspirations widened and their methods radicalized. Following the more militant Baptist dissidents, movements of religious protest now demanded important revisions in Soviet religious legislation that would allow "religious propaganda" to be on equal terms with that of the atheists; to end the legal ban on the private religious instruction of minors; to restore to religious groups the right to undertake charitable works and to organize specialized religious circles; and for the Soviet state and school system to assume a position of neutrality vis-à-vis both believers and nonbelievers, in line with Lenin's pre-1917 pronouncements on this question.

Increasingly, dissident demands turned from appeals to Soviet legislation and authorities, to invoking international human rights declarations, covenants, and conventions that spell out the principles of the freedom of conscience, religion, and religious education. More and more protest literature that documented Soviet violations of international commitments were being addressed to international organizations, foreign churches, other governments, and world public opinion.

In the process, religious *samizdat* has emerged as an alternative, uncensored communication network linking the dissidents with their actual and potential followers within the USSR and serving as a bridge between the movements of religious protest and the world public opinion. Its voice multiplied thousandfold via Western radio broadcasts beamed at the Soviet Union (Radio Liberty, BBC, Deutsche Welle, VOA, Radio Vatican, Radio Andes, Radio Monte Carlo, etc.), religious *samizdat* provided the dissidents with a surrogate organizational structure. Largely devoid of political resources and restricted in articulating their demands directly to the Soviet policy makers, the dissidents have been relying more and more on the inputs reaching the Soviet authorities from abroad—from governments, churches, and other organizations, or opinion leaders reacting to the Soviet violations of international and their own guarantees of freedom of conscience. Apart from the mainstream human rights periodical, the *Chronicle of Current Events*, which has extended its coverage to violations of believers rights,[20] individual currents of religious dissent have launched their own periodicals, most notably the dissident Baptists (*The Fraternal Newsletter, Herald of Salvation, Bulletin of the Council of the ECB Prisoners' Relatives*) and the Lithuanian Roman Catholics (the *Chronicle of the Catholic Church in Lithuania* [1972–] and several more periodicals[21]).

Unlike the Orthodox and Roman Catholic dissidents, the other major dissident movements have either maintained their underground organizational networks since their "descent into the catacombs"—for example, the Ukrainian Catholic Church, the Adventists-Reformers, and the Jehovah's Witnesses—or have formed separate organizations after they had completely split away from their registered organizations (for example, the Council of Churches of the ECB, established in 1965). As they became the target of administrative and police reprisals, dissident Baptists proceeded to form a specialized organization (the Council of the ECB Prisoners' Relatives) to collect, document, and disseminate information about the Soviet persecution of their members. Moscow has become the focal point for the transmission to the outside world of religious *samizdat*, with the mainstream human rights movement (especially the cluster of dissident groups centered around Andrei Sakharov) becoming the chief intermediary between religious dissenters and the Soviet Union's Western journalistic and diplomatic communities. Western tourists, emigrants from the USSR, some Soviet travelers abroad, and even occasional international telephone and mail connections have also been relied upon to expose Soviet violations of religious rights to international publicity.

The Helsinki Conference and the wide publicity given by the Soviet media to its Final Act[22] opened a new stage in the evolution of the human rights movement in the USSR. After the initial pessimism about the outcome of the European summit meeting, Soviet dissidents—prodded by the "grassroots" protesters invoking the Helsinki "guarantees"—have taken advantage of the human rights pledges of the Final Act to develop a new, remarkably successful strategy aimed at internationalizing their grievances at the time when a large segment of the Western public opinion was having second thoughts about the wisdom of the Helsinki "deal." The new strategy involved the monitoring of the Soviet Union's compliance with the Final Act and bringing to the attention of all the Act's signatories Soviet violations of individual and group rights of its own citizens. According to the letter of the Act, if not in the Kremlin's official view, these violations were now a matter of international concern and subject to international review at the forthcoming Belgrade Conference.

Especially explicit language of the Final Act concerning freedom of "conscience, religion, or belief," including "the freedom of the individual to profess and practice religion," has inspired a series of the widely publicized protest letters from two leading Orthodox dissidents, Fr. Gleb Iakunin and Lev Regelson, to the World Council of Churches, Patriarchs Demetrios of Constantinople and Pimen of Moscow, and various foreign church figures. Beginning with their October 16, 1975, letter to the WCC Assembly at Nairobi (November-December 1975), Iakunin and Regelson undertook to publicize the plight of believers of different faiths *and* of human rights activists in the USSR, calling upon the WCC and individual churches to raise their voices in defense of religion and human rights in the USSR.[23] The ecumenical approach taken by the two Orthodox dissidents had been carried a step further by early 1976 in an unprecedented *joint* appeal to the Soviet Government (with a copy sent to the WCC) signed by leading figures of the Russian Orthodox, Lithuanian Catholic, Baptist, Adventist, and Pentecostal dissent movements and endorsed by a numer of lay human rights advocates.[24] The appeal catalogued the contradictions between Soviet legal norms and administrative behavior and international human rights norms formally accepted by the USSR. The document demanded that the Soviet state cease interfering in religious affairs, equalize the rights of believers and atheists to disseminate their beliefs, and place religious organizations on the same legal footing as other voluntary organizations in the USSR; in other words, the dissident spokesmen demanded the separation of the state not only from the church but also from the ruling atheist doctrine, and, implicitly, from the Communist Party as well.

INTERRELATIONSHIPS WITH MOVEMENTS FOR POLITICAL AND NATIONAL RIGHTS

The new strategy of religious dissenters called not only for the coordination of their efforts but also for a close alignment with the entire human rights movement in the USSR which, having been decimated by the post-1971 arrests, banishments, and emigration, was given a new lease on life by the Helsinki Final Act and was now attracting an unprecedented amount of attention from Western media and politicians. The rise of the Helsinki Monitoring Groups in Moscow (May 1976), the Ukraine and Lithuania (November 1977), Georgia (January 1977), and Armenia (April 1977), which brought together in a loosely coordinated network the principal currents of the human rights movement in the USSR, was accompanied, on December 27, 1976, by the formation in Moscow of a Christian Committee for the Defense of Believers' Rights. Though composed of Russian Orthodox dissidents only—Fr. Gleb Iakunin, Hierodeacon Varsonofii Khaibulin, and Viktor Kapitanchuk[25]—the Committee undertook to speak out openly on behalf of all persecuted Christians in the USSR, in close association with the Moscow Helsinki Group. Specifically, the Committee's founding "Declaration" invested it with four tasks: to study and supply information on the legal situation and actual position of religion and believers; to provide believers with legal advice whenever their rights have been violated; to raise such cases before the appropriate state institutions; and to promote the liberalization of Soviet legislation on religion.[26] Since 1976, the Committee has addressed a number of appeals and protests in defense of different religious groups and individual victims of Soviet antireligious repressions, as well as in support of the persecuted human rights advocates; the Committee has intervened on behalf of numerous local believers and compiled and transmitted abroad, by fall 1978, several volumes of documents illuminating the position of different religious communities and individual Christians and Jews in the Soviet Union.[27] During 1977 it appealed to both Soviet authorities and world churches against the antireligious implications of the new draft Constitution of the USSR which recognized Marxism-Leninism, and hence atheism, as an integral component of the Soviet state.[28] In a number of appeals and declarations the Committee was joined by the Moscow, Ukrainian, or Lithuanian Helsinki Group members, Andrei Sakharov, the Working Commission to Investigate the Abuse of Psychiatry for Political Purposes, the Committee for the Defence of Workers' Rights, as well as representatives of the dissident Adventists and Baptists.[29] On November 21, 1977, the Committee cosigned with a number of these groups a joint appeal to the Belgrade

Conference calling on the Western signatories of the Helsinki Accords to review specific areas of human rights violations in the Soviet Union, especially "violations of religious freedoms, including freedom of churches from state control and the freedom of religious education," as well as "discrimination against believers in education and employment, judicial and psychiatric repressions of believers, and the seizure of children from their religious parents."[30]

Similar defense committees have been in existence among the dissident Evangelical Christians Baptists—the much older "Council of the ECB Prisoners' Relatives" dating since the 1960's—and among the "True and Free Adventists." The latter formed in 1976 a "Group for a Legal Struggle Against the Dictatorship of State Atheism and the Investigation of the Facts of the Persecution of Believers in the USSR." On May 11, 1978, the Adventist Group announced to the public their existence, objectives, and composition (seven members headed by Rostyslav Halest'kyi [Galetskii]). In its Declaration issued on that date, the Group listed its objectives in much more radical terms than those employed by other similar bodies. It pledged to collect information and complaints from both Adventists and other believers, "persecuted for their purely religious convictions, life and activities"; to investigate facts of violence and arbitrariness of the dictatorship of state atheism; to collect documentation on the Soviet violations of human rights and Helsinki Accords for presentation to the forthcoming Madrid Review Conference; to enlighten believers about their legal rights and to uncover "secret instructions and resolutions" employed for the "suppression of the genuine religious freedom," to render every assistance to the victims of religious persecution and their families; and to combat the "illegal, criminal, and sinful" union of the "state religion of atheism-materialism-evolutionism" with the Soviet state.[31]

Among Lithuanian Catholics (and for the benefit of other Catholics as well), the functions assumed by the above mentioned bodies have been successfully performed by the *Chronicle of the Catholic Church in Lithuania* with its clandestine network of editors, informants, reproducers, and distributors. In November 1978 a separate Catholic Committee for the Defense of Believers' Rights was organized in Lithuania, and its membership and objectives were announced at a press conference in Moscow.[32] In contrast, no similar body or periodical has emerged within the large underground Ukrainian Catholic (Uniate) Church, which, after it had recovered in part from the *pogrom* of 1945–49, has deliberately followed a strategy of inconspicuous, apolitical, and strictly religious activity with a view towards securing from the state the legalization of its canonic organization, a strategy which has generated some tensions among the Uniate clergy and believers and has not so far dispelled the regime's hostility towards this "nationalist church."

Another arena for collaboration between religious dissidents and political and national rights advocates has been provided by the Helsinki Monitoring Groups. Thus Orthodox and Jews have been joined by nonbelievers in the Moscow Group; Jews have joined the Roman Catholics and the Georgian Orthodox, respectively, in the Lithuanian and Georgian Groups; with the Ukrainian Helsinki Monitoring Group are Ukrainian Orthodox, Uniates, agnostics, and a Baptist.

Besides their overall civil rights orientation, the Helsinki Groups in the non-Russian Republics have been serving as spokesmen for the national rights of their respective peoples, combining the defense of their political, cultural, and linguistic rights with that of their national religion. This has been particularly true of the Lithuanian Group working in close liaison with the Catholic opposition and its mouthpiece, the *Chronicle of the Catholic Church in Lithuania*, and several nationalist circles and periodicals. Similarly, in the Ukraine, Georgia, and Armenia, the Helsinki Groups closely combined defense of national rights with that of their national churches.

The close relationship between religious dissent and the movements for political and nationality rights in the USSR has derived from the increasing realization of the interdependence of religious and political liberalization, and the growing conviction that freedom of conscience cannot be secured without the realization of political freedoms under a rule of law. This belief is shared by all ideological shades of dissent in the USSR except for small extremist fringes on the far right[33] and the "loyalist" left.[34] At the same time, a recognition of the historical interdependence of national identity and culture with national religion has brought about an increasing overlapping of religious and national dissent. In a parallel way, a search for national roots, for an alternative belief system and an absolutist moral code has brought a growing number of seemingly "homogenized" products of Soviet socialization back to their traditional religions, a process that has taken on the dimensions of a minor religious revival among the scientific-cultural intelligentsia in Russia and other Republics of the USSR.

THE IMPACT OF RELIGIOUS DISSIDENCE ON THE STATE AND SOCIETY

The emergence of dissent in the ranks of the Russian Orthodox Church, the Evangelical Christians-Baptists, and the Catholics and the increasing ferment within several other religious groups, as well as activation of the Uniate Church and other underground groups, presented the regime with a serious challenge not only to its church policy but also to internal security, especially in view of the possible confluence of religious dissent with the civil rights and nationality rights movements.

The Soviet response to this combined challenge was to combine harsh repressions against the most active religious dissenters with concessions to "loyal" religious groups so as to intimidate the dissident rank-and-file and to make the official churches more attractive to them. Deliberate misinformation was spread by the state-controlled media about the movements of religious protest and the banned churches with a view towards generating popular hostility against dissenters. To ward off increasingly vocal criticism of Soviet violations of the believers' legal rights (the principal cause of religious dissent) and to conceal the official treatment of the dissidents, the regime has been relying on censorship and broadcast jamming devices at home, while compelling spokesmen of the "loyal" churches to endorse for the benefit of foreign critics the Kremlin's denial that religious persecution occurs in the USSR.

The toughening since mid-1965 of the regime's reaction to political dissent, could not but affect its treatment of religious dissidents. Growing manifestations of dissent, spreading to nearly all denominations in the USSR, added urgency to the problem of tightening administrative and legal controls over religious activities. In December 1965 the two governmental agencies for the Russian Orthodox Church and other denominations were merged into a single, more powerful Council for Religious Affairs under Vladimir Kuroedov.[35] In March 1966 the Republican legislation on religious cults was amended to impose more severe prison sentences and higher fines for the "violation of the laws on the separation of the Church from the State."[36] In September of the same year an amendment to Chapter Nine of the Russian Criminal Code expanded the definition of "crimes against the administrative order" to deal with all overt manifestations of dissent.[37] Under the new, toughened provisions of the Criminal Code[38] the Soviet authorities launched a campaign of administrative harassment, arrest, trial, and deportation against religious dissidents, especially the more militant Baptists *initsiativniki,* Adventists, and Pentecostalists. Between the early 1960's and spring 1977, over one thousand dissident Baptists have been imprisoned,[39] some more than once, with many more subjected to administrative fines and various forms of harassment by the police. As of December 1, 1976, sixty-nine followers of the ECB Council of Churches were held in prisons, camps, or places of exile, including the Secretary General of the Council, Georgii Vins.[40] At least twenty-six Pentecostalists were held in forced labor camps as of August 1976.[41] A similar fate was shared by a number of "True and Free Adventists," including the leader of the Church, the eighty-two-year old V. A.

Shelkov, arrested in Tashkent in March, 1978.[42] A number of clergymen and believers from the principal Christian churches have been
imprisoned in recent years, including Ukrainian Orthodox priest Vasyl
Romaniuk, Russian Orthodox layman and organizer of religious-
philosophical seminars Aleksandr Ogorodnikov, Lithuanian Catholic
activists Nijole Sadunaite and Viktoras Petkus, Ukrainian Catholic
priest Mykhailo Vynnytskyi, and Georgian Orthodox laymen Zviad
Gamsakhurdia and Merab Kostava.

Other forms of reprisals employed by the authorities against religious
dissenters have included deprivation of parental rights for a strict
religious upbringing of children;[43] confinement without trial to psychiatric prison hospitals for indefinite terms with mind destructive "treatment";[44] as well as obviously staged burglaries, arson, beatings, assaults,
suicides and even murders—none of them cleared up by the police.[45]

To confer a semblance of legality on its more restrictive religious
policy, the Government proceeded to amend its 1929 "Law on Religious Associations" by incorporating most, if not all, of its hitherto
secret (though publicized by religious dissidents) "instructions" of
1961 and 1968 into the June 23, 1975, decree of the Russian Supreme
Soviet Presidium,[46] which was closely followed by parallel enactments
in other Union Republics.

While token gestures have been made by the Soviet authorities in
response to foreign protests in the cases of individual religious dissidents or selected dissident congregations,[47] the principal beneficiaries
of religious dissent seemed to be the "established," "loyal" religious
groups: fearful of further gains by the dissidents, the regime relaxed its
pressure on the recognized churches and sects and, in a few cases,
offered some concessions to them to blunt the dissident criticism of
ecclesiastical "collaboration" with the atheist authorities. Clearly,
further losses would have been suffered by the legally operating churches
were it not for the dissidents and the instant publicity they have been
giving to Soviet violations of religious rights. In the final analysis, however, it was the long maligned and harassed rank-and-file believers who
have been benefiting most from the dissident efforts and sacrifices, not
merely in terms of the easing of Soviet antireligious pressures, but
also in a moral, psychological sense, as they are being infused by the
dissident voices and their echoes abroad with a new sense of dignity,
hope, and self-efficacy.

FUTURE POTENTIAL

The long-range effect of religious dissidence on Soviety society at large
is perhaps even more significant. More than any other current of oppo-

sition, religious dissent has been working at the grassroots level as an articulator of alternative belief and value systems, more intelligible and existentially relevant to ordinary peasants and workers than the ideologies and programs of political dissent. The progressive attrition of the official "faith" has created a growing spiritual and moral vacuum which could not be filled by larger doses of Soviet "patriotic education," nor compensated by the consumerism of developed socialism, nor by the alarmingly growing alcoholism. Religion—not of the official variety represented by the loyal ecclesiastical establishment, but that of the confessing, persecuted churches—has been making inroads in a rapidly modernizing society that, by conventional sociological wisdom, should be abandoning rather than rediscovering religious values. This process has been significantly enhanced by the incapacity of the Soviet regime, for all its physical might, to accept the challenge of religion at the level of ideas, to allow a free philosophical confrontation between religion and official Marxism-Leninism, to let the individual choose between the two; instead, the regime has been exclusively relying on "administrative methods," violence, and propaganda to silence the voices of religious dissent. Despite its formidable apparatus for political socialization and mobilization, the Party has not been able to infuse the masses with a militant antireligious fervor: on the contrary, even Soviet surveys of workers' attitudes towards religion have revealed a surprisingly high level of tolerance for religious believers ("as long as they are not doing harm to anybody, they should be left alone to practice their beliefs").[48] In other surveys, a large proportion of the population studied has identified religious rites and traditions with their national cultures.[49] Greater societal tolerance of both diverse religious beliefs and agnosticism suggests not only the far-reaching loss of credibility by the official doctrine, but also a continuing process of "secularization," differentiation in values and beliefs that could not but favor the tendencies towards a liberalization of the Soviet system.

NOTES

1. This notion of religious dissent in the USSR appears to be shared by the principal works on the subject: D. Konstantinov, *Religioznoe dvizhenie soprotivleniia v SSSR* (Religious Resistance Movement in the USSR) (London, Ont., 1967); M. Bourdeaux, *Religious Ferment in Russia: Protestant Opposition to Soviet Religious Policy* (London, 1968); and *Patriarch and Prophets: Persecution of the Russian Orthodox Church Today* (New York, 1970); W. C. Fletcher, "Religious Dissent in the USSR in the 1960s," *Slavic Review*, Vol. 30, No. 2 (June 1971), pp. 298–316, and his *The Russian Orthodox Church Underground, 1917–1970* (London, 1971). See also T. Beeson, *Discretion and Valour: Religious Conditions in Russia and Eastern Europe* (Glasgow, 1974); B. R. Bociurkiw and J. W. Strong, eds., *Religion and Atheism in the USSR and Eastern Europe* (London and Toronto, 1975); R. T. DeGeorge and J. P.

Scanlan, eds., *Marxism and Religion in Eastern Europe* (Dortrecht, Holland, 1976); M. Bourdeaux et al., eds., *Religious Liberty in the Soviet Union: WCC & USSR, A Post-Nairobi Documentation* (Keston, Kent, 1976); U.S. Congress, House, Committee on International Relations, *Religious Persecution in the Soviet Union* (Washington, D.C., 1976); U.S. Congress, Commission on Security and Cooperation in Europe, *Basket Three: Implementation of the Helsinki Accords.* Vol. II: *Religious Liberty and Minority Rights in the Soviet Union* (Washington, D.C., 1977); V. S. Vardys, *The Catholic Church, Dissent and Nationality in Soviet Lithuania* (Boulder, Colo., 1978); and *Documents of the Christian Committee for the Defense of Believers' Rights in the USSR* (5 vols.; San Francisco, 1977–78).

2. *Dialog s Tserkovnoi Rossiiei* (Dialogue with Religious Russia) (Paris, 1967), p. 109.

3. For the background and analysis of Metropolitan Sergii's loyalty declaration of 29 July 1927, see W. C. Fletcher, *A Study in Survival: The Church in Russia, 1927–1943* (London, 1965), chapters 1–2.

4. The most extensive discussion of these movements appears in Fletcher, *The Russian Orthodox Church Underground*, chapters VII and VIII.

5. On the liquidation of the Uniate (Greek Catholic) Church in the Western Ukraine, see this writer's "The Uniate Church in the Soviet Ukraine: A Case Study in Soviet Church Policy," *Canadian Slavonic Papers*, Vol. VII (1965), pp. 83–113; and "The Catacomb Church: Ukrainian Greek Catholics in the USSR," *Religion in Communist Lands*, Vol. V, No. 1 (Spring 1977), pp. 4–12.

6. See this writer's "De-Stalinization and Religion in the USSR," *International Journal*, Vol. XX, No. 3 (Summer 1965), pp. 312–30; "Religion in the USSR after Khrushchev," in J. W. Strong, ed., *The Soviet Union under Brezhnev and Kosygin: The Transition Years*, pp. 135–36; and "The Rights of Religious Groups in the Soviet Union to Organize Their Activities and to Express Their Beliefs," Statement in *Détente. Hearings before Subcommittee on Europe of the Committee on Foreign Affairs, House of Representatives, 93rd Congress, 2nd Session* (Washington, D.C., 1974), pp. 343–53. Compare D. A. Lowrie and W. C. Fletcher, "Khrushchev's Religious Policy, 1959–1964," in R. H. Marshall, Jr., ed., *Aspects of Religion in the Soviet Union 1917–1967* (Chicago, 1971), pp. 131–55. Drastically reduced totals of churches or congregations for individual religious groups are shown in *Spravochnik propagandista i agitatora* (A Reference Book of Propagandist and Agitator) (Moscow, 1966), pp. 149–50.

7. The legislation setting out the organization, powers and responsibilities of the two Councils was not published for general use; the most extensive description of the Councils' role appears in A. Kolosov, "Religiia i tserkov v SSSR" (Religion and the Church in the USSR) in *Bolshaia Sovetskaia Entsiklopediia* (Greater Soviet Encyclopaedia), Vol. 50 SSSR (Moscow, 1948), cols. 1775–90. In December 1965 the Council for the Affairs of the Russian Orthodox Church and the Council for the Affairs of Religious Cults were merged together into a Council for Religious Affairs, under Vladimir Kuroedov. The legislation setting out the organization and frame of reference of the new Council was also not made public. Extracts from the secret decrees of the Council of Ministers of the USSR dated March 17 and May 10, 1966, appear in a collection of laws, decrees, and instructions *"for internal use only,"* V. A. Kuroedov and A. S. Pankratov, eds., *Zakonodatelstvo o religioznykh kultakh* (*Sfornik materialov i dokumentov*) (Legislation on Religious Cults. Collection of Materials and Documents) (2nd ed., rev.; Moscow, 1971), pp. 78–83.

8. See, for example, *The Chronicle of the Catholic Church in Lithuania*, No. 4, 1972; No. 18 (August 1975); No. 19 (October 1975). Compare this writer's "The Catacomb Church," pp. 9–12.

9. See Bourdeaux, *Patriarch and Prophets*; this writer's statement in *Religious Persecution in the Soviet Union*, pp. 8–26; and E. A. Vagin, "Religioznoe inakomyslie v segodniashnei Rossii" (Religious Dissent in Today's Russia), *Russkoe vozrozhdenie*, No. 1 (1978), pp. 50–70. For a slanderous Soviet press attack on Russian Orthodox dissidents, see B. Roshchin, "Religious Liberty and Slanderers" in *Literaturnaia gazeta*, April 13 and 20, 1977, translated in U.S. Congress, Commission on Security and Cooperation in Europe, *Basket Three: Implementation of the Helsinki Accords* [Hearings]; Vol. II: *Religious Liberty and Minority Rights in the Soviet Union* (Washington, D.C., 1977), pp. 249–55.

10. On the Moscow and Leningrad religious-philosophical circles and seminars, see *Vestnik Russkogo Khristianskogo Dvizheniia*, No. 119 (1976), pp. 281–334; No. 121 (1977), pp. 294–300; and No. 123 (1977), pp. 169–74. Some of the materials of the Leningrad study circle has appeared in the local *samizdat* journal, "*37*," launched in January 1976.

11. On this Church, see this writer's "The Ukrainian Autocephalous Orthodox Church: A Case Study in Religious Modernization," in Dennis J. Dunn, ed., *Religious Modernization in the Soviet Union* (Boulder, Colo., 1977), pp. 310–47.

12. See this writer's "Religious Dissent in the USSR: Lithuanian Catholics," in DeGeorge and Scanlan, *Marxism and Religion in Eastern Europe*, pp. 147–75; and Vardys, *The Catholic Church, Dissent and Nationality in Soviet Lithuania*.

13. Compare this writer's "Religion and Nationalism in the Contemporary Ukraine," in G. W. Simmonds, ed., *Nationalism in the USSR and Eastern Europe in the Era of Brezhnev and Kosygin* (Detroit, 1977), pp. 81–93.

14. On Georgian Orthodox dissenters, see P. Reddaway, "The Georgian Orthodox Church: Corruption and Reversal," *Religion in Communist Lands*, Vol. 3, Nos. 1–5, 1975, pp. 14–23; as well as documents published *ibid.*, Vol. 3, No. 6, 1975, pp. 34–36; and Vol. 4, No. 4, 1976, pp. 48–51.

15. See the "Foreword" to the first Ukrainian-language book published by the clandestine "Khristianin" Publishing House, *Pisni spasennykh* (The Songs of the Saved) (1975).

16. See V. A. Shelkov, "Edinyi ideal" (The Only Ideal), *Materialy samizdata*, No. 17/76 (May 21, 1976), AS2439.

17. The number of Judaic believers in the USSR has been estimated by various Soviet sources at two to ten percent of the total Jewish population.

18. According to *Spravochnik propagandista i agitatora* (Moscow, 1966), p. 149, along with the officially recognized 400 mosques, "about 1,000 unregistered congregations worship in [private] residences."

19. See Kukshar (Ufa), "Declaration" on the oppression of Tatars-Bashkirs (linguistic, economic, and religious) of April 1977 in *Materialy samizdata*, No. 1 (January 6, 1978), AS3085.

20. Similarly, documentation on religious persecution (especially against the Ukrainian Uniates) has appeared in the now suppressed *Ukrainian Herald* (8 issues), 1970–72, 1974).

21. Including *Dievas ir Tevyne* (God and Country) and *Tiesos Kelinas* (The Road of Truth).

22. Unlike other international human rights documents, the Helsinki Final Act was published in full in the principal Soviet newspapers.

23. Published in full in *Religion in Communist Lands*, Vol. 4, No. 1 (1976), pp. 9–14.

24. Reproduced in full in "Soprotivlenie religioznym presledovaniiam" (Resistance against Religious Persecution) in *Volnoe slovo* (Frankfurt a.M.), No. 24, 1976, pp. 63–82. Conspicuously missing among the signatories of this appeal were representatives of the Ukrainian Uniates, the largest banned religious group in the USSR. The appeal also failed to mention their plight.

25. A year later, on December 29, 1977, after having been threatened with criminal proceedings by the KGB, the Committee co-opted a fourth member, Vadim Shcheglov, who was empowered in the event of arrest of the three founding members, to continue its work and to announce the names of the already approved alternative members of the Committee. *Documents of the Christian Committee for the Defense of Believers' Rights in the USSR* (Moscow, 1977; reproduced in San Francisco by the Washington Street Research Center, 1978), Vol. 1, pp. 41–42.

26. *Ibid.,* pp. vii–viii.

27. Three volumes of Russian texts with English summaries of documents, and a volume of selected documents from Vols. 1 and 2 in English translation, as well as Part I of Vol. 5, have been released by the Washington Street Research Center in San Francisco since February 1978.

28. *Ibid.,* Vol. 1, pp. 22–27, 30.

29. See, in particular, a joint 1977 declaration welcoming the formation of an international association to monitor the observance of the Helsinki Accords (HAIG) and announcing their membership in this association (*ibid.,* Vol. 1, pp. 28–29).

30. Reproduced in full in U.S. Congress, Commission on Security and Co-operation in Europe, *The Right to Know, The Right to Act: Documents of Helsinki Dissent from the Soviet Union and Eastern Europe* (Washington, D.C., May, 1978), pp. 74–85.

31. See *Gruppa ot Vsesoiuznoi Tserkvi Vernykh i Svobodnykh Adventistov Sedmogo Dnia po pravovoi borbe i rassledovaniiu faktov presledovaniia veruiushchikh v SSSR,* Document No. 31 (May 11, 1978): *Soobshchenie* (Announcement) and *Deklaratsiia deiatelnosti* (Declaration of Activities), 2 pp. Note the elimination of the phrase "against the Dictatorship of State Atheism" from the "Group's" name once it surfaced into the open.

32. The Committee includes five priests—Svarinskas, Tamkevicius, Zdebskis, Velavicius, and Kauneckas. See *Radio Liberty Research,* RL 265/1978 (November 22, 1978), 3 pp. Significantly, on November 25, 1978, members of the "Movement for the Defence of the Rights of Man and Citizen" in Poland issued a Declaration pledging its "full solidarity [with] and fervent regards" for the Catholic Committee, invoking the "centuries-long Lithuanian-Polish friendship" and calling for "joint efforts" to make the Church in both countries a "Church of a vocal and living confession of faith."

33. Compare an unpublished paper by John B. Dunlop, "Contemporary Russian Orthodox Dissent," presented at the Kennan Institute in June 1978. For two widely contrasting views of the Russian right, see Alexander Yanov, *The Russian New Right: Right-Wing Ideologies in the Contemporary USSR* (Berkeley, Calif., 1978), and D. Pospielovsky, "Russkii natsionalism v segodniashnei istoricheskoi obstanovke" (Russian Nationalism in the Contemporary Historical Circumstances), *Posev,* Vol. 34, No. 12 (December 1978), pp. 10–15, 41–43.

34. Represented by Roy Medvedev and the contributors to his *samizdat* publication *Dvadtsatyi vek* (The Twentieth Century). In recent years, some liberal and nationalist dissidents have accused Medvedev of wittingly or unwittingly aiding the regime in undermining the human rights movement in the USSR.

35. In this connection, Kuroedov announced that the new Council was given "a much greater role to play and greater responsibility in controlling observance of the laws on [religious] cults" (*Izvestiia*, August 30, 1966).

36. *Vedomosti Verkhovnogo Soveta RSFSR*, No. 12 (March 24, 1966), p. 220. Aiming at religious dissidents, the decree extended the *corpus delicti* to include "the preparation for purposes of mass dissemination of handbills, letters, leaflets, and other documents making appeals for the nonobservance of the legislation on religious cults."

37. *Ibid.*, No. 38 (September 22, 1966), p. 819.

38. In particular, Articles 142, 190–1, 190–3, and, especially Article 227 ("Infringement of person or rights of citizens under appearance of performing religious ceremonies") providing for a maximum sentence of five years imprisonment or exile.

39. As estimated by Peter Reddaway in his testimony before the U.S. Congress Commission on Security and Cooperation in Europe, on April 27, 1977, in *Basket Three: Implementation of the Helsinki Accords*, Vol. II, p. 5.

40. *Biuleten Soveta rodstvennikov uznikov Evangelskikh Khristian-Baptistov v SSSR* (Moscow), No. 39, 1977, pp. 37–45.

41. Testimony of Evgenii Bresenden, a representative of Soviet Pentecostalists, who emigrated from the USSR in September 1975 (*ibid.*, p. 30).

42. See Documents Nos. 27 (April 20, 1978) and 28 (April 27, 1978) on searches and arrests, issued by the Adventist's "Group . . . for the Legal Struggle and Investigation of the Facts of the Persecution of Believers in the USSR" as well as *Documents of the Christian Committee*, Vol. 2 (1978), pp. 235–73.

43. See testimonies and documents in *Basket Three: Implementation of the Helsinki Accords*, Vol. II, pp. 19–35, 232–35, 244–48, 262–72.

44. See *ibid.*, p. 23.

45. See *Documents of the Christian Committee*, especially Vol. I, pp. 111–47, and Vol. II, pp. 246–73.

46. *Vedomosti Verkhovnogo Soveta RSFSR*, No. 27 (June 3, 1975), pp. 487–91. The amended law has been translated by John B. Dunlop and published in U.S. Congress, House, *Religious Persecution in the Soviet Union* (Washington, D.C., 1976), pp. 69–75.

47. For example, individual dissident Baptist and Pentecostal congregations were registered by the authorities *independently* of the official All-Union Council of the Evangelical Christians-Baptists. For recent developments in this respect, see *Keston News Service*, 1978 *passim*.

48. See *Voprosy formirovaniia nauchno-ateisticheskikh vzgliadov* (Problems of the Formation of Scientific-Atheist Views) (Moscow, 1964), p. 43; *Nauka i religiia*, No 2, 1966, pp. 2, 7; P. I. Kosukha, "Pro kharakter i prychyny proiaviv relihiinosty sered molodi" (On the Character and Causes of Religious Manifestations among the Youth), *Pytannia ateizmu* (Questions of Atheism), Vol. 4 (Kiev, 1969), pp. 111–21; and E. Protasov and D. Ugrinovich, "Issledovanie religioznosti naseleniia i ateisticheskoe vosspitanie" (The Study of the Religiosity of the Population and Atheistic Upbringing), *Politicheckoe samoobrazovanie* (Political Self-Education), No. 11, 1975, pp. 109–16.

49. See Christel Lane, *Christian Religion in the Soviet Union: A Sociological Study* (London, 1978), pp. 192–217.

Comments and Discussion

Professor *Bociurkiw* added to his paper comments on the character of external support for religious movements in the Soviet Union and some support strategies he thought that outsiders might usefully follow. As to the first, he thought that the record was not a good one. He praised the work of Keston College outside of London and of the *Glauben in der Zweiten Welt* organization in Zurich, but these were unfortunately very small and underfinanced groups. The record of the major established churches was lamentable. Not till the Nairobi Assembly did the World Council of Churches speak out. The record of the Vatican has been equally poor; the Lithuanian and particularly Uniate Catholics have often felt abandoned. Vatican secret diplomacy may help at times, but it is not enough. The World Baptist Alliance has similar problems. Like the Russian Orthodox Church within the World Council of Churches, the official leaders of the Russian Baptist Church plead that they can participate in the World Baptist Association only if there is no criticism of the USSR. The exploitation of religion by Soviet propaganda is very well supported. It is estimated that a major part of the donations to Soviet churches is diverted to the Soviet Peace Fund. This is used in turn to lavishly support the world travels and gifts to foreign friends of Soviet church leaders. Thus, by granting limited freedom and privileges to a few religious leaders the Soviets are able to cut off significant criticism by the major churches and their international connections.

Professor Bociurkiw identified four approaches for external supporters of religious liberty in the USSR. First, Western governments, human rights organizations, and churches should bring steady pressure on Soviet officials, emphasizing the fact that the Soviets have acceded to international agreements guaranteeing religious liberty. The Soviets are more likely to respond positively to such pressure than they would be to pressure in the area of individual political rights. A new generation is progressively taking over the reins of the USSR, a generation that is less ideologically oriented, and less devoted to atheism. Restrictions on religion are also much less oppressive in such other Soviet orbit countries as East Germany or Poland. The second approach

133

should be to take to task the official church organizations for not standing up for elemental religious rights. The third approach should be to give added support to the prohibited churches. They need more attention in the media and public opinion. Westerners going to the Soviet Union should bring along Bibles and prayer books for these churches, and should make a point of attending services in the unofficial churches. Finally, a greater effort should be made to promote the study of the religious situation in the Soviet Union and of church-state relations. Most study centers have to live from hand to mouth.

After reiterating the difficulty of such estimates, particularly in a society in which religious belief can lead to loss of position and block future success, Bociurkiw estimated that there were thirty to sixty million Orthodox believers. After World War II there were about 17,500 Orthodox churches. This was down to 7,500 by the 1960's, with, at the most, 6,500 now operating, and 5,900 priests. True Orthodox Christians should be estimated in the tens of thousands; Jehovah's Witnesses perhaps in the thousands, mostly concentrated in the western Ukraine. Though their own estimates are much higher, Pentecostals and Adventists may together number one hundred thousand. There are probably at least 500,000 "official" Evangelical Christians-Baptists (not including the dissident Baptists). The Ukrainian Uniate (Greek Catholic) Church had a membership of three and one-half to four million before they were banned in the late 1940's. Founded at the end of the sixteenth century, the Uniate Church was banned because of its close ties with the Ukrainian national movement; it may preserve a large part of its membership for the same reason.

Asked to specify more exactly the present status of religion and the extent of its persecution, Professor Bociurkiw pointed out that the recent growth of sectarianism may be explained by the vacuum left behind by Khrushchev's antireligious campaign, particularly in urban centers and industrial areas. At the same time, the attrition of the official ideology has contributed to a growing interest in religion, especially among young intellectuals. The revival of the nationalities had also sparked religious interest. For example, a secularized Jew may become a Zionist, learn Hebrew, and end up a believer. In the face of this growth in religious interest the regime has eased somewhat its antireligious pressure on the officially recognized denominations in terms of the administrative closing of churches—except for the "unregistered" Western sects. At the same time for selected cases, chiefly those that seem to threaten the regime's control, there have been severe reprisals. Roughly, one thousand persons have been imprisoned for religious activities since 1960, mostly people from the most rapidly growing and militant sectarian groups.

Bociurkiw added that in some fields such as science or art, one could function as a believer. But a writer cannot if he wants to be published; a teacher found to be a believer is immediately fired. It is very difficult for a known believer to enter a university, partly because such a person will be expelled from the Komsomol, and a negative Komsomol recommendation would adversely affect one's chances for acceptance at a university.

Dunlop observed that the antireligious campaign of 1959–1964 had tended to galvanize Russian nationalism in reaction. For example, a direct result of this campaign was the All-Russian Society for the Protection of Historical and Cultural Monuments with twelve and one-half million members. He also wanted to emphasize the importance of the fact that the Christian Committee for the Defense of Believers' Rights, although founded in 1976 in association with the Helsinki monitoring groups, had not had any of its members arrested. He believed this might be because too many believing Russians would be offended by such arrests. He also pointed out that several churches have been opened recently in the vicinity of the Chinese border, perhaps for the use of the Soviet troops stationed there. This could stem from the World War II attitude toward the Russian church as a pillar of patriotism.

The discussion briefly returned to consider the unusual strength of the Lithuanian Church and its less intense persecution. It was suggested that this relative freedom might be credited to the policies of the First Secretary of the Lithuanian Communist Party, Snieckus, who remained in office from 1940 to 1974. He has been credited with being able to protect Lithuanian national interests while maintaining the confidence of Moscow, and it is quite possible he has also protected the Church.

Cottam related the results of an interviewing effort in Afghanistan two years ago. One finding of the study was that it was widely believed that the Muslim Brotherhood (Ikhwānī) were very strong and were a rightist CIA organization. He was also told that Ikhwānī were numerous in Central Asia. He later found that the Ihkwānī were in fact strong at the University of Kabul, but that they were leftist if anything. He also learned from the students about the strength and intentions of the religious dissident movement in Iran. This information turned out to be remarkably accurate. Cottam wondered if we should take seriously the suggestion of Ikhwānī strength in Central Asia, and asked if the Soviets see the Ikhwānī as CIA and right wing. *Bociurkiw* answered that the Ikhwānī were described in Soviet sources as very reactionary, although he had not seen a mention of a CIA connection. More generally, the Soviets tend to lump religion, right-wing views, American support, and Zionism together; and of course they often tie dissidents to the CIA. He suggested that Soviet spokesmen making these connections generally believe them.

Reform and Repression in the USSR: The Western Influence

Herbert J. Ellison

> Pour un mauvais gouvernement le moment le plus dangéreux
> est celui où il commence a se transformer.   Montesquieu

It is probably wise to begin with a dictionary definition of the word reform: "The amendment of some faulty state of things, especially of a corrupt or oppressive political institution or practice; the removal of some abuse or wrong."[1] In this broad sense of the word there has certainly been a great deal of reform in the Soviet Union over the past quarter century. But reform means change, and change from existing political institutions and practices is always unsettling, particularly for a poor government, as Montesquieu's dictum suggests. The appetite for reform, particularly in a society where it has been suppressed, can grow with explosive force when the suppression is reduced or ended. Moreover, what the intending reformer sees as "a corrupt or oppressive political institution or practice," fit only for abolition, a defender of the established order might see, indeed rightly see, as an essential pillar of that order. Hence on the Soviet scene, as elsewhere in political affairs, a reform initiative frequently begets its opposite—an effort at repression, for repression is usually an effort to halt a process of change which is unacceptable to the governing power. And where a powerful censorship of the Soviet type prevails, not only action but the written and spoken word as well are repressed in order that even ideas of change can be controlled.

In writing about reform and repression in the Soviet Union we shall be concerned not only with the attitudes toward reform of the

---

Herbert J. Ellison is professor of history, University of Washington; he is an authority on modern Russia and the Soviet Union.

governing elite, but also with those of the regime's internal critics. For one of the major developments of the post-Stalin Soviet Union was the revival of the public conversation about reform and reform needs.[2] In addition to the increasing outspokenness of the various technical specialists, who posed reform ideas on educational, economic, legal, and other questions from their official positions and in officially sanctioned publications, there appeared as well an extensive literature of unofficial social and cultural criticism and related reform ideas.[3] Most of this literature appeared in underground or *samizdat* publications, a revival of the critical traditions and perspectives of the prerevolutionary intelligentsia. Both groups of reform spokesmen, official and unofficial, contributed in their own ways to a considerable broadening of the reform discussion.

Another part of the task is to inquire about the impact of the West upon the process of Soviet reform. One of the distinctive features of the Stalin era had been the effort to seal off the Soviet Union from external cultural and intellectual influences. The gradual and partial reopening to news and ideas from the West, in publications, broadcasting, travel, and other forms, revived an influence which, like the tradition of intelligentsia criticism, had lain dormant for many years.

In the general features which our opening definition of reform implies there is little in the post-Stalin Soviet Union to distinguish it from the dynamic process of reform and repression in other societies. But the Soviet reform process has been profoundly influenced by three unique factors: the scope of revolutionary change and the severity of oppression in the Stalin era; the pervasiveness of the political power and the close link between that power and the abuses toward which the reformers' energy is directed; and the fact that the governing elite see themselves, and act, as the leaders of a continuing revolution, domestic and international. The impact of these special factors upon the Soviet reform process needs closer examination.

The scope and pace of the revolutionary change in Soviet society during the Stalin era is probably without equal in the history of any society. The change included the total socialization of the economy, the most disruptive feature of which was the forcible collectivization of over twenty million peasant farms. It included an equally forceful mobilization of urban labor with drastic reductions of living standards for the entire population as the government channeled the maximum investment into industrial expansion through the mechanism of a highly centralized, planned "command economy." Abandoning the critical caution of the 1920's, Stalin forced Soviet reality into conformity with party theory, and not only in economic policy and institutions. The command economy was matched by a command culture with the literary, artistic, and scientific intelligentsia compelled to mold their work to a forcefully enunciated and brutally enforced "party line" as their political leaders instructed them in the construction of a literature, art, and science appropriate to "the era of construction of socialism." No less formidable pressure was applied to the national minorities. Their political and cultural leadership was purged and their cultural and educational institutions remolded to conform to the policy of building Soviet nationhood. Even religious believers experienced an unprecedented intensity of persecution, as the government undertook massive closures of churches, synagogues, and mosques, seminaries and religious schools, and harassed both religious leaders and followers.

So sweeping a social and cultural change was bound, of itself, to require an unprecedented scale and severity of coercion. But the coercion went far beyond the requirements of even the revolutionary objectives. The hallmark of the Stalin era was an enormously expanded and pervasive police force and purges on a fantastic scale which literally gutted the ranks of party, military, and economic leadership, and extended to the mass of the population as well.

The Stalin legacy has been, beyond any doubt, one of the most unmanageable ingredients in the Soviet reform process. In his famous secret speech to the party leadership at the XX Party Congress in 1956 Khrushchev attempted simultaneously to endorse the main institutional changes of the Stalin years and to repudiate the leadership cult ("personality cult"), the excesses of police power, the personal dictatorship, and the impact of both upon the purges, the conduct of World War II, the treatment of certain of the small nationalities, and the Soviet-Yugoslav conflict. The speech was clearly an attempt to reaffirm the main institutional changes since 1928, to rekindle dedication to the communist goals within the party, and to attribute all of the major leadership failures and abuses of the preceding generation to Stalin's paranoid and despotic personality.

Initially, the most explosive impact of the speech was not in Russia, but in Eastern Europe and China. But only five years later (1961), and for reasons that remain uncertain, Khrushchev went much further with his denunciation of Stalin, offering appalling details of his personal role in the 1930's purges and his other abuses of power, and seeking to efface all possible evidence of his legacy from the surface of Soviet life. By early 1963, however, faced with a flood of literature critical of abuses of the Stalin years, he felt compelled to hold the line, reaffirming at the XXII Party Congress "Stalin's contributions to the Party and to the Communist movement."[4] The post-Stalin era has witnessed a slow but definite process of rehabilitation of Stalin, as evident in official references to his rule, and especially in a gradual removal from the successive editions of the official party history of virtually all negative allusions to his policies during those years.[5]

The central point is that de-Stalinization raised a host of questions and problems for which the defects of Stalin's character were simply not a sufficient explanation. It raised questions about Stalin's fellow leaders (Khrushchev sought to tar his own former colleague with this brush in 1961), questions about the enormous human cost of the Stalin era, and very specific questions about the cost of policy errors in two particular periods—the First Five-Year Plan (especially the collectivization of agriculture) and the Second World War. The growing scholarly inquiry into both these periods during the 1960's was cut off abruptly, as was the belletristic literature with its uncomfortable candor about the Stalin years.[6] In effect, the leaders acknowledged simultaneously the danger of close examination of the realities of the Stalin years and the need to rehabilitate the reputation of the man whose policies were fundamental to the system within which they governed. This recognition inevitably set tight limits to subsequent reform efforts.

A second special feature of the Soviet reform context is that the pursuit of perceived abuses in policies or institutions comes very easily into conflict with some extension of a pervasive political power. For example, the religious believer who seeks a literal application of the constitutional guarantee of separation of church and state quickly learns, if he needed to do so, that the Party is determined to sustain, indeed extend, the structure of administrative controls that it uses to regulate the leadership, administration, and facilities of religious organizations, for that structure is a crucial instrument in the continuing effort to contain, and eventually to eliminate, the influence of religion in Soviet life.[7] Or the intending reformer of the law soon discovers that the prefatory qualifications upon general rights in the constitution and the vague categories of crime in the criminal code are sternly defended by the political power, for broadly stated qualifications upon constitutional civil rights and vaguely defined political crimes sustain a broad and flexible administrative capability to deal with political opposition.[8] Analogous experiences result from efforts to reform the apparently irrational centralism of economic administration or the seemingly pedantic regulation of scholarly research and writing—such is the pervasiveness of the political power in communist societies generally, and in Soviet society particularly. What the intending reformer sees as the removal of a specific and separable abuse, the power controllers often see as an attempt to weaken a system of power.

Thirdly, there is the fact that the governing elite of Soviet society see themselves not as the beleaguered and privileged defenders of a static power structure, but as the leaders and organizers of a continuing communist revolution, domestic and inernational. One can illustrate the consequences of this outlook with the example of policy regarding agriculture. Reform-minded intellectual critics outside the leadership are denied the opportunity to write, or to publish, scholarly history or fiction dealing with the foundations of Soviet agricultural institutions in the era of collectivization, and thus open for question underlying premises of that policy.[9] But meanwhile the leadership continues to implement the main institutional remodeling of agriculture—the transformation of the kolkhozes after the pattern of the sovkhozes through consolidation into larger units, and the conversion of *kolkhozniki* from cooperators to paid agricultural laborers with fixed wages, pensions, and so forth. With free discussion of both past and current conditions in Soviet agriculture one might well expect the raising of serious doubts about the fundamental effectiveness and economic viability of existing agricultural institutions; with a party monopoly of power and communication the issue does not even surface in public discussion and the old policy continues into the new, whatever its actual shortcomings. In this way the Party monopolizes the process of institutional change.

Similar observations can be made about Party policy in other key areas. For example, the structure of policies devised to implement Soviet nationalities policy—the language and educational policies, the regulation of literature and history, religious policies, and so forth— have changed but little in the post-Stalin years, in spite of a considerable onslaught by nationalist intellectuals using both legal and *samizdat* publishing opportunities.[10] The latter effort achieved impressive successes, as the decision to publish an official rebuttal to Ivan Dzyuba's underground book on Soviet nationalities policy provocatively titled *Internationalism or Russification?* clearly demonstrated.[11] But, meanwhile the thrust of Stalin era policy continues, maintaining Russian as the language of higher education throughout the country, encouraging education of non-Russian children in Russian-language schools by means direct and indirect, pressing forward with centralization of educational and economic administration, and concentrating critical fire in cultural and other publications upon the evils of "local nationalism" while the abuses of central power are ignored and the glories of Soviet nationality are extolled.[12]

The foreign observer often fails to appreciate the comprehensive and long-range policy of the Soviet leadership, a policy which could properly be described as a long revolution. In this perspective collectivization only began the movement toward a fully socialist agriculture and a fully proletarianized peasant, and the efforts to that end still continue. Similarly, the integration of many nationalities into a new Soviet nationhood, the gradual triumph of "scientific" atheism, and the final elimination of "alien" currents from cultural and intellectual life are all aspects of building communism and creating the new Soviet Union. The main point is that the harsh treatment of opposition is not solely, or even basically, a policy of reaction, of using censorship and other means of repression to exclude negative criticism of established policies or circulation of alternative policy concepts, essential though that effort is. It is a dynamic policy of institutional change pursuing essentially the same social vision as that which motivated Soviet society in the Stalin years.

In effect, then, the Soviet Communist Party claims a monopoly of reform initiative. It defines reform as a continuation of the revolutionary process, the remolding of culture and institutions to conform to the Party's ideological vision of the good society. Conversely, any reform notion challenging the official concept of reform is by definition counter-reform or reaction. But the retention of the monopoly of reform is crucially dependent upon retaining another monopoly, that of communications and information. In many ways the most momentous development in Soviet life in recent years was the challenge to the Party's monopoly of information and ideas, and the means of their communication. Without serious inroads into that monopoly it was impossible to expand the definition of reform beyond the restrictive limits of the official usage. But such inroads did come, both through the relaxation of controls over official publications and, vastly more significantly, through the widespread appearance of unofficial publications, or *samizdat*. These innovations led to the gradual articulation of ideas and proposals for reform that in many areas of national life constituted a fundamental challenge to the official policies. The scope and seriousness of that challenge can best be appreciated against the background of official reform measures and reform notions.

The achievements of official reform policy in the post-Stalin Soviet Union are in many ways very impressive. The vast structure of Stalin labor camps has been disbanded, and with it most of the structure of arbitrary justice (most notably the MVD Special Boards). The enormous empire of the MVD was reduced to the more limited secret police responsibility of the KGB, an organization which was, at least until 1969, deprived of its predecessor's power of ideological surveillance. Most of the coercive labor legislation of the Stalin years has been abolished, and free mobility of industrial labor substantially restored.

The long-neglected and exploited peasant has attained a very large increase of income and has been granted (1975) internal passports with full rights of mobility. Extremely narrow applications of the doctrine of "socialist realism" have given way to a much broader concept of the aesthetic forms and intellectual substance of literature and the arts. Some of the more arbitrary and destructive forms of party ideological intervention in the sciences, particularly in biology, agronomy, and physics, have been rectified, and much has been done to restore domestic scholarship and international scholarly ties in such fields as economics and sociology. A simultaneous expansion of the school system has done much to extend and improve school opportunities, especially in rural areas. These reform initiatives were combined with a huge expansion and technical modernization of the national economy, a steady and sizable rise in living standards, and a significant shift in investment priorities that brought a great improvement in desperately bad housing conditions. Such are the broad outlines of a considerable reform achievement.

But the unofficial reform discussion in the *samizdat* literature went much further than the official, and its contents reveal a dissatisfaction with fundamental elements of established institutions and policies. This literature challenged not just the application but the rationale of official censorship, the validity of the doctrine of socialist realism in literature and the arts, and of political partisanship (*partiinost'*) in intellectual life generally.[13] Scientists proclaimed the internationalism of science, its independence of class and national boundaries and ideological limitations.[14] Nationalists repudiated the Soviet nationalities policy and its guiding concept of internationalism. Religious believers challenged the structure of official religious policy as incompatible with separation of church and state. Critics of the economy called for at least a partial desocialization and a radical decentralization. Political critics proposed extensive constitutional reform, with restatement and effective protection of civil and political rights, and reduction of the monopoly role of the Communist Party of the Soviet Union, and the removal of the system whereby the Party has absorbed the role of the Soviets.

By the mid-1960's the Soviet leadership faced not only a challenge to its monopoly of communication and information, but explicit challenges to the basic policies and institutions inherited from the Stalin era. In substantial part the main developments were the consequence of the government's own reform efforts. There had been relaxation of the ideological control structure and a simultaneous expansion of the information about both the Soviet Union and the world outside, past and present. The opportunity to undertake broader exploration of the history and literature of the Russians, and of other peoples of the USSR, and the chance to explore more openly and critically the conditions and problems of the Soviet economy, polity, and society were essential preparation for asking questions about the main elements of government policy and for critical examination of its key elements—the Party dictatorship, the command economy and centralized socialism, the structures of ideological direction of cultural and intellectual life, the policy of socialist internationalism as it affected the nationalities, official atheism, and the world role of Soviet power. That very important exploration, and the reform notions which it generated, was what the Party leadership set out to control or suppress from the mid-1960's onward.

The latest phase in the reimposition of controls has been marked by virtually complete destruction of the leadership and press of the dissent movement (from 1972 onward), and a massive campaign of intimidation, vilification, imprisonment, and exile of participants. An immensely significant aspect of the process is its accompaniment by a forceful reaffirmation of Soviet control over the states of Eastern Europe—Czechoslovakia serving in 1968 as the practical example of the Brezhnev Doctrine—and by the very rapid emergence, over the past decade, of the Soviet Union as a full-fledged superpower with parity or superiority over its American rival in nuclear weaponry, conventional land forces, and naval power. As so often in earlier periods of Soviet history, a period of counterreform and repression is also a period of dynamic and aggressive foreign policy. Another important parallel with earlier times is the fact that dissident intellectuals pressing the cause of internal reform were also sharp critics of the most offensive and dangerous elements of Soviet foreign policy—including the anti-Israeli policy, the invasion of Czechoslovakia, the armaments policy, and much else. The information monopoly and the single official line on key foreign policy questions were challenged just as were key aspects of domestic policy.

To repeat, then, what the Soviet leadership faced, from the middle 1960's, was an aggressive challenge to its monopoly of communication, ideas, and information, and explicit challenges to the basic institutions and policies inherited from the Stalin era. That leadership obviously felt it imperative to take decisive action to meet the challenge and to silence or control the mounting chorus of intellectual dissent. The task was now vastly more complex than in the Stalin era: society was more urbanized and educated, technical means of internal and external communication were greatly improved, and instruments of coercion available to the leadership were more limited. But beginning with the Daniel-Sinyavsky trial in 1966, these means have been ever more aggressively mobilized, and have included a wide range of administrative measures against dissenters (loss of housing, employment, educational opportunities, and so forth), as well as imprisonment in psychiatric hospitals and conventional prisons, and forced emigration. Even the police power was again expanded for the task with the reinstitution of KGB powers of ideological control in 1969.

The central task was to rebuild and reconsolidate the crumbling official control of communications and information, and to isolate or expel, discredit and silence those who had dared offer reform ideas which challenged the basic elements of the system. The new control system had to be imposed with a maximum of subtlety, since much of the outside world was now watching with interest to see how the Soviet leaders would behave, and even sympathetic observers, such as the heads of foreign communist parties, would be sharp critics of too obvious repression. Every effort was made internally to vilify dissenters, portraying them as traitors to their own people and lackeys of foreign intelligence agencies.[15]

Reading only the Soviet press in recent years one could conclude that the post-Stalin reform process might easily have been kept within "sensible" and manageable limits had it not been for the superbly clever and persistent efforts of disruptive "bourgeois ideologues" and of Western intelligence agencies and their sponsoring governments. There has undoubtedly been a Western impact upon the reform process, and upon the process of counterreform or repression, to which we must now turn attention. But precisely because Soviet official attacks upon internal critics seek to discredit and dismiss them as agents of hostile foreign powers, it is vital to stress that the roots of the reform process were internal.

The abuses against which reform-minded intellectuals directed their criticism were both internal and quite real. The break between the Party and the intellectuals came typically at the point where the Party sought both to limit and control the discussion of abuses and recommendations for reform. Even at the early stage of the process there was, of course, a Western impact, if only in the passive form of representing an alternative—a free society. The Western impact was vastly increased, over the course of the late 1950's and 1960's, as the exchange of people and information was expanded and Soviet intellectuals gained a broader sense of conditions in the West and of the contrast with their own problems and development. But otherwise the Western impact was largely indirect and facilitative, especially the publication of works by Soviet intellectual dissidents denied internal publication, and the broadcasting of general international news and news of internal dissent within the Soviet Union. In effect, the main Western impact was to make it either more difficult, or impossible, for the Soviet government to set limits upon the internal reform debate and upon the information available to the participants.

One of the most important roles of the West in facilitating the internal debate was the provision of information which helped Soviet intellectuals to regain contact with elements of their own cultural and political history. Publication and distribution of important works in philosophy, economics, and history, long banned in the USSR, was an important effort. But even without foreign assistance the effort went forward internally. For many Russian intellectuals the landmark philosophical and cultural debates among the intelligentsia of the late nineteenth and early twentieth century were a vital starting point for a fundamental critique of official communist ideology.[16] And the rediscovery of Dostoevsky, in the aftermath of the Stalin era, would provide a powerful impetus to religious renewal and reform. The West might provide models of new technology, or economic organization, of scientific scholarship, or of legal and constitutional notions. But for many Soviet intellectuals the task of reform must begin with national moral renovation, and in this sphere there was an ample store of native religious and secular thought to provide guidance.

In those spheres for which the Western models have had wide appeal to Soviet reformers—technology, economic organization, scientific scholarship, and law and constitutionalism—it is significant that the impact has been extremely limited where there is any conflict with established ideological or organizational dogmas. The economic reform schemes of the sixties are a dim memory: the centralist command economy of the Stalin years maintained its dominance. In scientific scholarship the impact has been greater, facilitating the freeing of biology and agronomy from the clutches of ideology.[17] But the concept of empirical research in social and political questions, divorced from ideology and arriving at generalizations by a process of inductive reasoning from research data, has been severely trounced in politics and sociology.[18] The fate of the democratic movement in general, and of the human rights movement in particular, and the failure of the efforts at constitutional reform, as well as the character of the new Soviet constitution, give eloquent testimony to the difficulty of transplanting alien structures and concepts to the Soviet system.

One is faced, then, with the essential "contradiction." The appeal of the Western cultural and political model to reform-minded Soviet intellectuals is enormous, and yet that model conflicts with the established system at virtually every key point. One reads the reform program offered by Andrei Sakharov in a recent work with a sense of the impassable gulf between the aspirations it expresses and the possibility of their realization within the present Soviet society.[19]

In one way it is comforting to recall the speed with which reform ideas and the reform initiative developed among the Soviet intelligentsia in the aftermath of the Stalin era. But one must also remember that the peak of this process came with a combination of loosening up of the official thought control structures, encouragement from above (as in the two Khrushchev de-Stalinizations), and a relaxation of police surveillance upon illegal activities such as the *samizdat*. The control structures have been rebuilt and repression is today in full swing. In such a context, what does past experience suggest would be the best policies in the West, public and private, to encourage the revival and continuation of the reform initiative?

My suggestion would be quite simple: first, to make every effort to continue the work of repressed underground journalism, most importantly the *Chronicle of Contemporary Events*, to spread word of the continuing process of repression, the fate of its victims, and the violation of civil and political rights that accompany that repression; and secondly, to work for the maximum circulation of the ideas and views of leading figures in the dissent movement of the past fifteen to twenty years, as well as the continuing commentary upon Soviet and foreign events and conditions by members of that movement now in exile. I would repeat my earlier comment that the prerequisite to control of the reform movement by the Soviet government is a monopoly of information. At the moment, only the democratic governments have the capacity to deny that monopoly of the printed and broadcast word to the Soviet government.

In his important study, *Detente and the Democratic Movement in the USSR*, Frederick Barghoorn makes a significant concluding statement:

> Both the security of the United States and its allies and the continued vitality of the civil political culture that we cherish require conditions, such as freedom of information and political competition, which the Soviet elite regards as incompatible with its political purposes.[20]

There is surely little chance of introduction of political competition: though in an important sense the formulation of policy alternatives by intellectuals in the 1960's was an incipient form of political competition, it has been almost completely stopped at present. The internal limits upon information are much greater than only a few years ago, and seem to be increasing. Here the opportunities for Western influence continue to be greatest. It is significant that Andrei Sakharov, in

My Country and the World, also gives the highest priority to efforts to broaden communication. He writes:

> A concern for the greater openness of the socialist countries—for the freedom to exchange people and information—must be one of the central tasks of the coordinated policy of the Western countries.

> It is precisely the openness of the socialist countries, plus a balanced disarmament, that can guarantee the security of Europe and the whole world.[21]

In this context Sakharov laments the inattention of the outside world to the important matter of free communications and the means of expanding it:

> ...at present I fear they (the Western countries) are not putting enough pressure on the socialist countries....

> It is essential to revoke the UN General Assembly's shameful banning of free television from satellites. (Hundreds of millions of people watch television, and they have the right to see what they want to.) It is also essential that foreign radio broadcasting to the USSR be expanded and improved....[22]

These are unsettling words from two very thoughtful and well-informed observers of the socialist countries and of the East-West relationship. The one asserts that the survival of free societies is vitally linked to freedom of information and this is amply confirmed by his Soviet counterpart. Yet Sakharov laments the lack of a consistent and coordinated policy and notes regretfully the banning of free television communication. Both men deplore the failure to make adequate use of resources of communication freely available, and Barghoorn stresses the urgent need to bargain vigorously with the Soviets when they are in pursuit of the knowledge and resources of the West:

> We can be sure that if the West allows Moscow to get what it needs ... easily—by, for example, making available advanced computer and energy technology on easy credit terms, without demanding in return concessions in respect to Western interests—Moscow will exploit such opportunities ruthlessly.[23]

But is is not necessary to gain Soviet approval for use of the most important asset—information, ideas and the means for their communication—that Western societies possess. The foregoing comments have repeatedly stressed the importance of the Soviet government's monopoly of communication of information and ideas for its control of the reform initiative. It is undoubtedly correct to emphasize the importance of objective, factual reporting as the necessary main content of broadcasting to the USSR. I would suggest, however, that more specific clues as to what is needed and desirable can be obtained from the main themes, and the main concerns, of the writings produced by the intellectual dissent during recent years. *Samizdat* provided wide opportunity for acquiring hitherto unavailable information, but also for development of systematic criticism of established policies and institutions and for the formulation of alternative ideas of both. The *samizdat* writers' main concerns have been not just the legal system and civil rights that have received much Western attention recently, but major issues such as the position of the various nationalities, the historical origins of problems of key sectors of the socialist economy, the problems and aspirations of religious believers, the structures of intellectual and cultural control, and the main elements of Soviet foreign policy and relations with foreign communist parties.

To contribute to continued communication on these issues is the best possible service that free countries can do for the future of the cause of reform in Soviet society. We must sustain and broaden acquaintance with the reform ideas articulated in recent years; we must encourage continuation of fertile and creative discussion among both Soviets resident in the USSR and those intellectual emigres that the Soviet leadership has released or expelled in hope that their intellectual resistance would be neutralized by emigration.

NOTES

1. *Shorter Oxford English Dictionary.*

2. An interesting study of the interaction between the political leadership and leaders of important groups in Soviet society is provided in Joel J. Schwartz and William R. Keech, "Group Influences and the Policy Process in the Soviet Union," *The American Political Science Review*, 62, No. 3 (September 1968), pp. 840–51.

3. This assertion is based on reading of Soviet publications in a variety of fields. When Soviet intellectuals encountered the still quite restrictive official censorship, they often turned to the underground (*samizdat*) press. The latter is the subject of an extensive literature. Among the more useful works are: Peter Reddaway, *Uncensored Russia* (American Heritage Press, 1972); and Rudolf L. Tökes, *Dissent in the USSR: Politics, Ideology and People* (Baltimore and London, 1975).

4. Roy A. Medvedev and Zhores A. Medvedev, *Khrushchev: The Years in Power* (New York: W. W. Norton, 1978), p. 148.

5. Sidney I. Ploss, "Soviet Party History: The Stalinist Legacy," *Problems of Communism* (July-August 1972), p. 32.

6. Critical discussion of collectivization was quite extensive in scholarly journals in the early 1960's, but had been replaced by supportive commentary

by the mid-60's, such as F. Vaganov, "Preobrazovanie sel'skogo khoziaistva," *Kommunist*, No. 3, 1966, p. 95. In literature the terrible consequences of forced collectivization continued to appear somewhat longer, as in V. Tendriakov's *Death, Moskva*, No. 3, 1968, p. 37. The brilliant scholarly critique of Stalin's conduct of Soviet military preparation for World War II, published by Alexander Nekrich in 1965, became the object of bitter denunciation by the journal *Istoriia KPSS* in 1966. See Alexander Nekritch, *L'armee rouge assassinee* (Paris, 1968), p. 22.

7. This question is presented with a number of examples in Peter Reddaway, "Freedom of Worship and the Law," *Problems of Communism* (July-August 1978), pp. 21ff.

8. Even Khrushchev ran headlong into entrenched power interests in his 1959 effort at constitutional reform. See Jerome M. Gilison, "Khrushchev, Brezhnev and Constitutional Reform," *Problems of Communism* (September-October 1972), p. 69, which opens with the statement that "The story of constitutional reform in the Soviet Union is essentially the story of a reform that failed."

9. The 60's and early 70's brought considerable attention in literature to the painful costs of collectivization, but writers were sternly cautioned by a critic in *Literaturnaia Gazeta* in 1974 to remember that "in taking up major social and political questions in an artistic work, *questions that our party has resolved once and for all* (italics mine), a writer must without fail adhere to the standpoint of a Marxist historian. . . ."

10. A brief summary of the reform and counterreform currents in Soviet nationalities policy is contained in Teresa Rakowska-Harmstone, "The Dialectics of Nationalism in the USSR," *Problems of Communism* (May-June 1974), pp. 17–19.

11. See Ivan Dzyuba, *Internationalism or Russification?* (New York, 1974), p. xix.

12. Evidence of continuity of pre- and post-Stalin policies in language and education is provided in Yaroslav Bilinsky, "Education of the Non-Russian Peoples in the USSR, 1917–67: An Essay," *Slavic Review*, xxvii, No. 3 (September 1968), p. 411.

13. The most powerful challenge to socialist realism was Andrei Sinyavsky's (Abram Tertz, pseud.) *On Socialist Realism* (New York, 1965).

14. Zhores Medvedev wrote of the Stalin era's "erroneous tendency to classify sciences as bourgeois on the one hand, and proletarian or socialist on the other." *The Rise and Fall of T. D. Lysenko* (New York, 1971), p. 248.

15. A writer in *Molodoy Kommunist* (No. 1, 1969, p. 59) asserted that "*Samizdat* comes into being at the direct instigation of Western intelligence and is actively supported by it."

16. See, for example, Peter B. Reddaway, "The Search for New Ideals in the USSR: Some First-Hand Impressions," in William O. Fletcher and Anthony J. Strover, *Religion and the Search for New Ideals in the USSR* (New York, 1967), pp. 83–90.

17. Loren R. Graham, *Science and Philosophy in the Soviet Union* (New York, 1974), pp. 252–56.

18. See Rolf W. Theen, "Political Science in the USSR," *Problems of Communism* (May-June 1972), pp. 64ff.

19. I refer here to Sakharov's *My Country and the World* (New York, 1975) in which he concludes with a reform program that includes such reforms as the right to strike, an end of censorship, the right of secession of Soviet republics, a multiparty system, and so forth (pp. 101–102).

20. Frederick Barghoorn, *Detente and the Democratic Movement in the USSR* (New York, 1977), p. 173.

21. Sakharov, *My Country and the World*, pp. 106–107.

22. *Ibid.*

23. Barghoorn, *Detente and the Democratic Movement in the USSR*, p. 173.

Comments and Discussion

The discussion following Professor Ellison's presentation focused on varying interpretations of the strength of the ideological commitment of Soviet leaders both internally and externally, and prospects for change in the Soviet Union in the near future.

Bociurkiw proposed that the post-Khrushchev period represented a non-utopian, conservative, less ideological period. The entrenchment of the formula of a "developed socialist society" in the new Soviet Constitution is symbolic of this new conservatism. He identified four aspects in the post-Stalin reforms. First was the establishment of the party hegemonies over the bureaucracies, especially over the secret police. Next was the establishment of bureaucratic pluralism in which the principal functional elites have a fairly stable input up to the level of the Central Committee. Central Committee membership and position increasingly goes with function, so that the leadership choices of those at the top become very limited. In the last few years there have been very few changes in the distribution of seats among major functional groups. Third, a limited degree of socialist legality has been established. There are now fewer arrests than under Stalin. Finally, since Khrushchev consumer aspirations have been more fully taken into account by increasing the availability of goods.

These changes led Bociurkiw to disagree with Ellison's characterization of the Brezhnev period as one of continuing revolution. He saw it rather as a transitional regime, in which there was still talk of revolution but movement was actually in the direction of a conventional superpower. Internationally, the USSR now seemed more interested in developing client states than communist states. Discussions with middle level Soviet bureaucrats today can go on for days without hearing mention of ideology. Ideology is gauche. More important is the pervading sense of being a big power, of running the world as equals to the Americans. This suggests that in the coming generation the elite is likely to be more nationalistic, technocratic, and pragmatic. Such an elite can be expected to make concessions in religious questions, perhaps even on the question of the nationalities, but not on individual political rights.

Although he agreed with much in this position, *Ellison* reminded us that the latest phase of Soviet politics was always called a conservative phase. What Bociurkiw was saying about the Brezhnev years was reminiscent of what Isaac Deutscher and others were saying about the Khrushchev years, or the opinions of contemporaries in the late 1930's on the characteristics of Stalinism. Of course, there has always been a mixture of Russian nationalism with Marxism in the development of the Soviet Union. Rosa Luxemburg saw this right from the beginning. Such a mixture does not imply a postideological period.

The official ideology was still dynamic; Soviet leaders were willing to incur the costs of adhering to its limits. Wage policy in recent years was not just practical politics, but stemmed from a commitment to egalitarianism. Khrushchev's antireligious policy had not been pragmatic politics. Therefore, Ellison sees Bociurkiw's evidence as indicating little disposition to downplay ideology. Evidently Khrushchev thought the system could get along without Stalinist controls, but party leaders soon found they simply could not. In the 1960's intellectual dissenters challenged every aspect of the ideology: its messianic foreign policy, its proletarian internationalism, nationalistic policy, conception of party supremacy, even socialism. But in no case did the party leadership respond by abandoning its ideological position.

Several participants doubted the role of ideology in Soviet foreign policy. Most saw Soviet foreign policy as expansionist or at least threatening, but some thought this was merely Russian imperialism in Marxist-Leninist garb. Going much further *Cottam* doubted whether messianic or expansionist goals were expressed in Soviet foreign policy. For example, he thought their Middle Eastern and arms policies, or their intervention in Czechoslovakia could be interpreted as the actions of a status quo state. In developing strategy and tactics for Soviet liberalization Cottam emphasized how important it was to get this issue straight.

Ellison found Cottam's status quo, nonideological interpretation of Soviet foreign policy reminiscent of earlier phases in the interpretation of Soviet intentions and motivations. In the 1920's many observers were convinced that communism had lost its international dynamic. In World War II many became convinced that the Soviets were essentially status quo nationalists. This conviction was shattered by events after the war, but was again revived with the Soviet policy of peaceful coexistence. Ellison was puzzled when this position was again advanced today. A regular reading of the Soviet press provides a very different picture. Soviet journalists consistently express support for communist revolutions abroad. They take a long view. They seek (as *Kintner* adds) a "fundamental restructuring of the international system." From this perspective Soviet papers see progressive changes in the "correlation of forces" as developing a new basis for this restructuring. They applaud the erosion of NATO and view positively the development of the strength of communist parties in Western Europe—parties which continue to receive generous support from the Soviet Union. Of course, in Soviet policy the interpenetration of ideology, nationalism, and cynical opportunism is always evident. Wittfogel said of Leninism that it had "erected opportunism into an ideological principle."

Rakowska-Harmstone also rejected the status quo interpretation of Soviet policy. Soviet books and other publications present a very aggressive stance. Recently the Soviets have tried to place many states in a dependent relationship—Angola and Mozambique have recently become members of Comecon. The Soviet military buildup has been remarkable; the USSR has developed a global outreach. In the last few years their navy has developed an ability to deny the shipping lanes and to intervene anywhere in the world, for example in Angola. The Soviets have built their Warsaw Pact forces far beyond the requirements of the situation in Europe today. The military problem of Soviet aggressiveness is also a matter of changing attitudes. John Erickson who has many contacts with the Soviet military thinks that they are now "feeling their oats." This is especially true of the younger generation, well trained and without the trauma of World War II. They are increasingly impatient with the pussy-footing policies of their elders.

The dynamic of the current Soviet situation raises on the domestic front the probability of heightened aggression in the 1980's. The USSR faces a declining rate of growth which they cannot make up with human or technological productivity. By the mid-eighties the Soviets will not be able to meet the demand of consumers, economic growth, and military growth. If for these reasons in the 1980's Soviet military leaders feel their relative military power has peaked, they may decide it is time to press for military victory. Soviet leaders are also under pressure on civil rights, particularly by workers and intellectuals in Eastern Europe. But they try to offset these problems by expansion, by maintaining their momentum elsewhere.

Lipset also questioned the assumption that ideology was dead in either Soviet foreign or internal policy. Ideologies are necessary to great states and have a remarkable lasting power. Ideology might have been thought dead in the Roman Empire a hundred years after it was Christianized, or in the Middle East a hundred years after it had been Islamized. It is a mistake to think ideology is dead in America now even two hundred years after the Declaration of Independence. In the nineteenth century we opposed monarchy everywhere. We are the only country in the world dominated by the antistate, Protestant sects. Our long nonrecognition of the Soviet Union and Communist China derives from this Protestant moralism, as did both the support for and opposition to the Vietnam War. Of course, the moralism and democratic fervor of our ideology determines only a small part of American policy. But it is a significant part. Knowing this of ourselves, Lipset believes ideology should be expected to play a major role in Soviet thinking. Both Americans and Soviets want to moralize the world in terms of their own ideologies.

Feuer suggested that one reason ideology seemed less important today in the Soviet Union was its very success. Many of its basic assumptions had become thoroughly internalized. In his own study of four hundred recent Soviet Jewish emigres in Toronto he had found a striking contrast between this generation and the older immigrant generations. Jews in the past had arrived as potential entrepreneurs, and they quickly established private businesses of their own. The new immigrants came expecting to be absorbed in large bureaucracies. Not one had established a business at the time of the study (one did shortly afterwards). Similarly, students in Soviet schools may hear a variety of views at home, but they soon learn that only certain views will be accepted by their teachers and fellow pupils. Feuer thought we should note the implication of the guiding belief (mentioned above) of many apparently nonideological bureaucrats that the Soviet Union is going to become the greatest nation in the world, for this assumption hides within it a deep faith that in critical ways the Soviet social system will ultimately prove itself superior to all others. The bureaucrats may not talk much of Marx, but the ideology seems to still be there.

Bociurkiw pointed out that it was in any event a mistake to think of Marxism-Leninism as a package. It consisted of the superimposition of many pre- and post-revolutionary types of belief. Clearly communist belief systems can change: they changed after the break with China, and after the rise of Eurocommunism. Today there is a new mix that makes reversion to Stalinism unlikely.

Another reason there will not be a reversion to Stalinism is the revolution in communications technology in the last generation. Transistor radios have been available for twenty years. (*Sargeant* added that under Stalin only three percent of households had radios that could receive foreign broadcasts, while today fifty percent were estimated to have such radios.) The new media have truly revolutionary potential, for they allow ordinary people to make a daily contrast of the *is* and the *can be*. There are areas of dissatisfaction in Soviet life that have barely been touched on by broadcasts up to now. Labor dissatisfaction and peasant dissatisfaction on the collectives and state farms are only now reaching *samizdat*. There was nothing comparable to this ability to spread information in the nineteenth or early twentieth century. Jamming, even when it occurs, is largely restricted to the cities. This potential should lead us to pay more attention to studying the great silent majority and their inevitably rising and quite differentiated dissatisfactions.

Gastil suggested that in this regard the Iranian revolution of 1978 should have some lessons for us. In the past it has been hard for revolutions to not be essentially elite affairs, for it was hard for large numbers of people to become directly involved in their early stages. But today there are cassette players, radios, television sets, and widely available, inexpensive, and instantaneous means of duplicating written materials or pictures. Perhaps for this reason the Iranian revolution from below has been so effective that middle class Iranian intellectuals are beginning to talk like conservative Muslims just to be part of the action. From the evidence of this conference it appears as though the impetus for change might also shift to the lower classes in a process of rapid change in the Soviet Union. This suggests the value of encouraging intellectual dissidents to relate their interests to the interests of broader groups as Bociurkiw suggests.

In discussing what hope there was for change in the USSR, *Cottam* pointed to an apparent contradiction in Ellison's paper. On the one hand, the Khrushchev years were years of uncertainty, of testing, years that Ellison said would not be repeated. Ellison described the dissidents as only a small group of intellectuals and found no trend we could contribute to. The only conclusion seemed to be to "forget it." On the other hand, the paper wished to revitalize the uncertainty of the Khrushchev years. Ellison saw the primary problem of the party to be its loss of the monopoly over information it had previously enjoyed, and pointed out how foreign broadcasts might further erode this monopoly.

In response, *Ellison* admitted that he was pessimistic about the possibility of rapid political change in the USSR. The process of reform in the nineteenth century had inevitably been a very slow process. The monopoly power structure of that day could not be brought down overnight, and the tsar's power structure was amateurish compared to that of the contemporary Soviet system. Therefore, unless a revolution occurs, he was pessimistic about rapid change. But with all this the challenge of the intellectuals should be kept alive. They are a force for long-run change, and future opportunities may arise to which they can make a decisive contribution.

Rakowska-Harmstone suggested that the reforms of the Khrushchev era were moderated or reversed because of systemic constraints. After the initial reforms further change was blocked by the party's monopoly of power. Ideology played a decisive part because through legitimizing the party's monopoly of power it stymied pluralism, making it impossible for the reformers to break either economic or political monopolies. Soviet society had become what Chalmers Johnson describes as a "transfer-goal culture," that is a culture in which the system sets out to achieve certain goals and in the end the system becomes the goal. The same systemic restraints led to an effort at a reassertion of the party monopoly after 1971 in Yugoslavia. In Czechoslovakia many leaders had become disillusioned with the "Prague Spring" even before the Soviet intervention, because it too threatened the breakdown of party monopoly. Chinese liberalization faces the same systemic problem today.

Thus, in spite of widespread recognition of need for reforms, especially in economics, change is blocked by fear of political pluralism. (One way reformers try to get around this is to try to substitute the computer for the market.) Although the dynamics of reform continually press Soviet leaders toward further change, the leaders simply will not cut their own throats. Several anecdotes were added by the group to reinforce this point. Bociurkiw, in particular, quoted a communist functionary as describing Leninism as "an organizational science for winning, organizing, and maintaining power." Leninism for this purpose was unlikely to be abandoned.

Alexander thought it might be useful to view the Stalin period from the cost-benefit perspective of an economist. In the Stalin era many people, including the elite, had incurred heavy costs from the terrorism and unpredictability of the system. Initial de-Stalinization benefited almost everyone and the costs were low. However, once the terror was gone the benefits for the power holders of further change were not great. Efficiency might be enhanced but they have been doing quite well without this added efficiency. The conclusion is that there will be no fundamental change unless a leading group sees the costs of change likely to be less than the benefits. How they will come to this conclusion is unclear, unless the impetus comes from Eastern Europe.

Dunlop suggested that Soviet leaders have handled the post-Khrushchev period quite brilliantly from their own perspective. There has been a "freezing up" of dissent. Dissenters have been exiled to the West, or sent to mental hospitals and labor camps. The mental hospital alternative is fully in accord with ideology. In Marxist theory about the only way to classify people who oppose the system at this late date is as insane. It also provides a strong deterrent that can be presented in the guise of humanitarianism, of caring behavior. At the same time commitment avoids a trial and allows for indefinite confinement.

Several other participants felt that the post-Khrushchev leadership has done very well internationally, and can show a continuing expansion of influence and power. Another discussant viewed incarceration in mental hospitals as an only partially effective replacement for Stalinist terrorism. He thought the group underestimated the problems that ending terrorism had created for the system. This led to the optimistic conclusion that the general decline in terror could not help but change the system. The generation now ruling inaugurated de-Stalinization to escape terror, yet they cannot entirely forget the terror. This may help to explain their extraordinary conservatism. More than anything they want stability. But what will happen now when a new generation arises that lives without the memory of terror?

The discussion turned briefly to this new generation. *Feuer* felt they were conformist, still living in fear of today's controls, or at any rate ideologically neutralized. As they grew older they became careerists. *Ellison* referred to the Yevtushenko line, "He knew the earth turned on its axis/but he had a family." The passivity of careerism might, however, only be temporary. In the United States the generations of the fifties, sixties, and seventies were very different from one another. Change could be rapid. Perhaps a basis for a new generation had been laid in the information and education explosion coupled with the less fearful contemporary society.

Several questions of tactics were also addressed to the speaker. *Rubin* outlined two approaches that Americans might take. One was a naive but direct challenge: the United States has had a successful society for two hundred years; this society is the model for much of the world; the Soviets should adopt this model in restructuring the USSR. Alternatively, Americans could be more sophisticated and careful, making tactical suggestions for change here and there. Americans should bring ideological pressure only when there is a clear likelihood of success. Both approaches were useful, but Rubin felt Americans were generally overly tentative and humble in discussing political alternatives.

Ellison agreed that we should always be very clear about what we stand for. President Carter's policy on human rights is such a direct affirmation; the administration's actions have not been as consistent as they might have been, but the general statements are very good. However, although U.S. political models are important, as he had pointed out in his paper the Soviet intellectuals had themselves developed an ample political literature. It was on this literature that we should concentrate our ideological attention. For example,

Andrei Sinyavsky has produced a remarkable work on the political control of intellectual life. We should see to it that his viewpoint is known and discussed in the USSR. We could facilitate this by means such as broadcasts. In addition to disseminating the work of the best minds among the dissidents we should use the radio to provide commentary on the best of Western literature and social science.

In addressing the fear that pressing for liberalization might raise the danger of war, Ellison agreed that it would be foolish for the United States to take a belligerent or hostile stance, or to foment revolt and revolution at every opportunity. He also thought it would be most useful and least threatening if in our communications with the elite we start from where they are. We should stress, as Rakowska-Harmstone suggests in her paper, examples such as Yugoslavia that are closer to their own experience and assumptions.

A question of the possibility that Soviet generals might at a future date replace party leaders drew a general response of disbelief. *Dunlop* thought it was a possibility. He felt that a nationalist junta might be less expansionist internationally, for example in Africa.

A question on the importance of the dissident labor organizations, an area often ignored, drew the response that there was only the barest beginning of independent labor organization. The Week's article (*Freedom at Issue*, September/October, 1978) gave a good summary. *Dunlop* added that a leading Soviet dissident, now in the West, told him that with the arrest of the labor leader Klebanov the movement may have been dealt a death blow. *Ellison* added that he did not feel that the intellectuals had ignored the labor question. Sakharov, for example, emphasized the need for a free labor movement as a check on the state employer.

Gastil suggested that the ruling elite appeared to have lost confidence in their right to defend the system as vigorously as they had in the past. He gave the example of a Lithuanian Catholic cross that had been erected against the party's wishes. In response the party sent out a group at night to remove the cross. When questioned why at night, the answer was that of course the people taking the cross down lived in the community and they did not want to be seen taking it down. More generally recent Soviet repression of dissidence has been halting and incomplete. If the government had quickly jailed each dissident as he arose, the outside world would be much less aware of dissidence in the USSR today. But it did not. Is not this characteristic of recent Soviet repression a sign of the hesitancy and lack of confidence at the top that has been described by Brinton and others as characteristic of a prerevolutionary situation?

Ellison felt that lack of confidence at the top was not the explanation. Khrushchev's memoirs suggest that he really did not like terror. Rejecting terror as stupid and out of control, he wanted to govern by more organized means. The government now brought opponents to trial. The Soviet government now has to deal with a different population than Stalin faced, and they have to act in the light of world attention. The fact that they are now more careful and controlled does not imply that Soviet leaders lack confidence in their basic rectitude.

For the group as a whole this range of problems remained unresolved. The workers and peasants represent an enormous, evolving, increasingly sophisticated and perhaps dissatisfied enigma, an enigma complicated by the fact these are highly differentiated groups when examined carefully. Students, teachers, and other intellectuals are today largely quiescent and conformist in the face of carefully managed but not draconian controls. The power elite, imbued with ideology and dependent upon it for power, are increasingly modern* or liberalized* in their attitudes. Yet they cannot go beyond glacial change without seriously threatening their legitimacy. Whether they can maintain adequate control of a society faced with this skein of contradictions remains unclear.

---

* The participants would have said "pragmatic." Yet Stalin's terror was also pragmatic, as was his about-face on religion. "Modernist" or "liberalized" seems to better capture the change in attitude suggested in Ellison's reference to Khrushchev's memoirs.

American Activists and Soviet Power: Supporting Liberalization in the Soviet Union

Lewis S. Feuer

W e may take it as axiomatic that a genuine peace with the Soviet Union will not be secured until a liberal democratic government finally prevails in its borders. For so long as the Soviet Communist Party exercises its dictatorship, the strategy of secret attack that only a totalitarian regime can effectively pursue still remains an ever-present alternative. There is no parliamentary or administrative opposition in the Soviet Union to sound warnings against the rulers, no critical press to report on governmental and military plans. Under such circumstances, whatever agreements are signed, they remain feeble instruments toward peace until a liberal government alters the spirit of political power in the Soviet Union. It is in America's own highest interest therefore to enquire: What can American scholars and scientists, sportsmen and sight-seers do to advance the situation of liberals in the Soviet Union, to enhance their feeling of self-confidence, to remind them that though their numbers are small, their echo from the United States is large?

The present weakness of the dissident, or democratic, human rights movement in the Soviet Union is clear enough. Compare, for instance, the handful of persons that gathered in the courtyard in Moscow to protest the trial of the dissident Anatoly Shcharansky with the numerous protest meetings that took place throughout Czarist Russia during the trial in 1913 of Mendel Beiliss. For Beiliss lawyers, doctors, students, workers, and peasants held meetings and demonstrations; the streetcar workers in Kiev collected money for the Beiliss family.

Lewis S. Feuer is professor of sociology, University of Virginia; a social critic of East and West, he is an authority on Soviet intellectual dissent.

The Assembly of the St. Petersburg Bar sent a telegram to the defense counsel at Kiev. By contrast, the band of Moscow Human Rights dissidents seem pitifully isolated from the general Soviet population, which thus far has stood detached from the Human Rights movement.

The essential difficulty that confronts a Soviet liberal movement is that among the people there is no sense of a social alternative, no sense of the direction that social reform might take. The suggestion of a multiparty system does not evoke enthusiasm. When I met in Moscow in 1963 with a group of about twelve university students in an underground circle, they said they wanted more freedom to read what they liked and that they wished to see the Party run by educated men; but they expressed no wish for a pluralistic party system. And the dissident literature, the *samizdat*, indicates that this is still the prevalent view among the Soviet dissidents. One evening I met with two unusual persons, American women who had come to Russia in the 1930's as adolescents; they had lived through the horror of the purges, seen their husbands and fathers vanish in labor camps, and after the war, had themselves spent years as prisoners. Yet they were terrified by the notion of multiple parties: "It's bad enough already with one party," they said. Somehow they feared the total collapse of the entire system if there was not a single party to drive people on; they seemed afraid that all sorts of horrors might break out from the otherwise ungovernable Russian masses if their instabilities were ignited by party conflicts. To many Soviet intellectuals a Pugachev uprising seems potential in every Russian crowd.

This suggests it is wisest not to hold up American society to the Soviet people as a practical model. America's achievements and freedoms seem so great to them as to belong to another realm, and to fill them with a hopelessness. In recent years a new generation of Soviet emigrants have become the writers for the station Radio Liberty in Munich. Sharp and militant, they emphasize the contrasts between American free society and Soviet dictated existence. But the listeners' reports come back: "Don't tell us how bad things are. We know for ourselves how bad they are. Please just give us information. We want to know what's going on in the world."

We might formulate what could be called a "principle of proximate criticism," that in depicting the shortcomings of Soviet society, we do so in terms of a model which is in the sphere of what Soviets conceive as politically possible. Radio Liberty might advantageously stage debates in which workers' self-management in Yugoslavia would be contrasted with planned controls in the USSR; or the relatively free emigration of Yugoslav workers with the ban on Soviet emigration; or the relatively free circulation of Western literature in Yugoslavia with the Soviet avenues closed to "ideological coexistence." Soviet liberalism will grow more naturally if its advocates speak within the framework of the socialist tradition rather than in the context of a confrontation between liberal capitalism and totalitarian socialism. The "truth of the defeated" needs a re-awakening for Soviet liberals. For instance, the character and politics of the tragic figure of Nikolai Bukharin, the kindly "favorite of the party," might well be redrawn for its significance to the Soviet people; it was Bukharin who made the last futile efforts, under Stalin's dictatorship, to preserve the life and liberty of such as the poet Osip Mandelsstam. Gradually the Soviet personality, so much modelled on Lenin's character, must be disenthralled, "de-Leninated," as Soviets come to learn of the realistic appraisals of Lenin's methods and character by thinkers who knew him personally, such as Rosa Luxemburg and Bertrand Russell. Since the education of the Soviet character proceeds largely through imitation of Lenin and Marx, we must bear in mind that a drastic critique risks the disorienting of moral goals. Therefore we must look to the socialist pantheon itself to provide substitutes that are more liberal, tolerant, and universally human. Edward Bernstein and Jean Jaurès are routine symbols in Soviet education as "revisionist heretics." The Soviet youth might be encouraged to learn that they were men of moral stature who felt that even a socialist society would degenerate if it practices the amorality that the end justifies any means. They might learn that "revisionism" is the ever self-correcting spirit of science.

Curiously, the Soviet people must still be acculturated to the notion of debate. Nothing is so rare in the Soviet Union as a genuine debate, since every discussion they broadcast moves to a preordained common conclusion. Plato could never have written a dialogue in the Soviet Union because no political, philosophical, or artistic question can be left unanswered or unanswerable.

Weak though the Soviet dissident movement may be, Soviet leaders are probably more sensitive than ever before in their history to Western criticism. For the likelihood of a future Soviet-Chinese conflict remains undiminished, and the fears the Russians express of a developing Chinese imperialism mirror their anxiety that their own imperialism will clash with the Chinese. Uneasy with an unstable eastern border, Soviet leaders are prepared to tolerate Western Eurocommunism, despite all its divagations, provided that its parties and possible governments continue to endorse the basic propositions of Soviet foreign policy. The main objective of Soviet foreign policy has always been to avoid concurrent enemies, and to make use of temporary coalitions to isolate the primary enemy. The Soviet leaders are keenly aware that the various Soviet classes have become restive as information has spread concerning American achievements in space, on the moon, and in economic prosperity. The Soviet leaders consequently aspire toward the "crypto-legitimacy" that an American association can bring them. No Soviet regime can point to a legitimacy grounded in a democratic election, for all Soviet citizens know there has not been a free election since that for the Constituent Assembly which the Soviet regime suppressed in 1918; the rhetoric that Soviet democracy is a superior form has acquired the meaninglessness of monotony. Therefore the Soviet leaders seek an external legitimation: if they cannot provide a free democracy themselves, they can point to their treaties with freely elected democratic governments, and take pride that their foreign minister is the most often received visitor at the White House. Soviet rulers are also troubled that they are confined to a plateau of technological achievement. The Soviet social structure has after sixty years not liberated itself from the fetters of its mode of production, nor developed a technology superior to that of Western capitalism. Soviet rulers undoubtedly regret that they initiated and propagandized a space race, which they then lost, thereby underscoring their technological inferiority. Once again, cooperation with Western technologists is desired by the Soviet Union as it was in 1928 when the First Five Year Plan was made possible by Western technological aid.

Thus, the present period is one where a Western contribution to the strengthening of an embryonic Soviet liberalism is truly possible. And for the first time Western individuals and institutions are in a position to act independently to help the otherwise isolated Soviet liberals.

The Olympic games, for instance, are to open in Moscow on July 19, 1980. More than 300,000 foreign tourists are expected to attend, of whom the largest contingent, perhaps 20,000, will be American. The Soviet authorities are, of course, planning to isolate the Americans as much as they can by housing them in new apartment buildings that are being constructed from the outskirts of Moscow to fifteen or twenty miles away. The Executive Council of the American Federation of Labor proposed, last August, that the U.S. Olympic Committee "take the lead among nations in moving the 1980 Moscow Games to a country which respects human rights and the true Olympic spirit." But clearly American public opinion would like to give the Russians a chance, hoping that "they'll get good" under the games' beneficent influence. But since Americans will be journeying to Moscow, let them journey as free Americans and not renounce their freedoms while on Soviet terrain. Every American could take with him to the Soviet Union a copy of a book by one leading Soviet dissident—Solzhenitsyn, Zhores Medvedev, Nadezhda Mandelsstam, or many others—to present as a gift to a Soviet friend. If planefuls of tourists were to do this (and it is perfectly legal in principle) Soviet authorities would think twice before they decide to provoke an American tourists' demonstration at their Sheremetyevo Airport (newly reconstructed by German companies). Would American lovers of sport, with their dedication to the ideal of a fair chance in competition for everybody, have the courage necessary for such simple actions that can crack an iron curtain grown rusty?

At the overseas airports in the United States, on the critical days, volunteer distributors, perhaps assisted by agencies such as Freedom House and (if political miracles still occur) the American Civil Liberties Union, would be at hand to distribute such books. Every traveler might also be provided with a booklet setting forth his rights under the Soviet Constitution and some sample questions they might raise with Soviet sports fans. These might form the basis for exchanges like the following:

Question: Why doesn't your government allow you to listen to Radio Liberty? No Western country jams your broadcasts.
Answer: We must protect our people from lies and filth.

Question: Why don't you trust your citizens to listen to all sides of questions? Didn't denial of freedom of speech make Stalin's crimes possible?
Answer: The Party will not allow a cult of personality again.

Question: Why have you never tried the thousands of KGB men and officials who took part in the frame-ups of the Stalin Era?

Question: Why don't you allow relatives, friends, and correspondents into the trials of dissidents?

Question: Why has an Uzbek never been elected a full member of the Politburo? Why isn't there a woman in the Politburo?

Question: Why don't you allow an American lending library and reference room to be opened in Moscow? We allow your Soviet Bookshop to sell your books, even anti-American propaganda, on Fifth Avenue. Shouldn't there be equal rules in competition?

A few hundred American tourists demanding the elementary liberties afforded in any Western civilized country would do more to advance the practice of liberties in the Soviet Union than any resolution enacted from the sanctuary of the United States Congress.

Or let us consider the contribution that our universities might make. It is customary for universities to pay the fare and expenses of professors who present papers at scholarly and scientific conferences, including those in the Soviet Union. Would the universities and their faculties announce that they will not finance scientists to attend congresses that invite delegations from countries that exclude dissidents, even those of the highest scientific qualifications, from participating? Would the faculty of the University of Virginia resolve that it will not finance the journey of any professor to attend a scientific meeting in the Soviet Union so long as the meetings were closed to papers presented by qualified scientists who are Soviet dissidents? Certainly universities would not allow their athletes to participate in athletic contests from which a participating country denied athletes the right to compete because of race.

At international congresses Soviet and Communist delegations are now more vulnerable to the pressure for liberalization than ever before. Communist countries send delegations of scholars and scientists that are carefully chosen and organized, each with its political head (and committee) to decide on policy and make decisions. For instance, at the Washington Congress in 1962, the Soviet head of delegation decided to identify Daniel Bell as the chief ideological enemy of Soviet sociology; whereupon, speaker after speaker then intoned his name with a veneer of hatred. At the Toronto Congress in 1974 the Soviet delegation rounded up votes with Bolshevik discipline to elect the English leftist, T. R. Bottomore, to the presidency of the International Sociological Association. Defining their objectives in political terms, upon returning to their countries members of communist delegations publish articles and write reports announcing: "We utterly routed the bourgeois sociologists, and proved the supremacy of our socialist system," or "We utterly defeated the bourgeois linguists, and proved the superiority of our Soviet society and its linguistic science."

A new situation, however, has arisen at the international congresses. On Soviet soil the Soviet authorities can suppress people like Solzhenitsyn, or Pavel Litvinov, or Valery Chalidze, or Medvedev. But what are they to do if Solzhenitsyn, Litvinov, and Chalidze appear at a political science congress to present papers on human rights in the Soviet Union? Or if Solzhenitsyn appears at a literary congress to discuss the problems of the writer working under the controls of the Soviet bureaucracy and censorship? For the first time in modern history, meeting places exist where Soviet spokesmen may be obliged to face the Soviet dissidents, and engage them in argument without the advantage of a police threat. International science congresses can become international parliaments of the world's intellectual class.

Perhaps Soviet delegates would boycott sessions where Soviet dissident emigrants are the scheduled speakers, but how will they handle the contradictions and corrections that the emigrants might raise from the floor to challenge Soviet speakers? Are they to make themselves look silly by denouncing such questions as "provocations," that favorite Soviet word of last resort, always used when Soviet speakers cannot respond with facts because the facts are so incriminating?

And then there are the book displays that now haunt the Soviet delegates with the prospect of counter-exhibits. When the International Sociological Association convened in 1974 at Toronto, several of the Soviet emigrant community displayed their emigrant literature on a table adjoining that of the Soviets. Soviet delegation leaders were aghast. Every once in a while a Soviet delegate maneuvering toward the emigrant display, and making sure that nobody was watching, would pocket some pamphlet, book, or leaflet, all of which had been arranged to facilitate such expropriation. When the Soviet chiefs complained to their Canadian colleagues, they pusillanimously had the Soviet dissidents transferred to the dining hall lobby. Nevertheless, the Toronto Ukrainian and Jewish student groups continued to hand out their leaflets on Soviet repression right on the floor of the big meetings, and neither Canadian nor Western fellow travelers felt it expedient to try to do anything about it.

A document smuggled out of Czechoslovakia reveals how worried Soviet and satellite Communists are by possible confrontations at international congresses with Western liberals and emigrant dissidents. When the Czech sociologists returned home, they submitted a report to the Central Committee of the Czechoslovak Communist Party, a copy of which found its way into the pages of the journal *Listy*, the organ of the Czechoslovak Socialist Opposition published in Rome. According to the Czech report, "in most parts of the Congress . . . the ideological supremacy of sociologists from the socialist countries was achieved," although the report acknowledged, some sections were neglected "in order to avoid a split of their forces." Also, it notes "the representatives of bourgeois ideology proved unable to present a united front. Instead, they frequently became engaged in arguments among themselves" (for example, D. Bell and A. Touraine). Interestingly, the report complains that one segment of the Polish delegation rebelled, "refused to comply with instructions issued by the official leader of the delegation, Prof. V. Markiewicz." Evidently, in this heady, infectious atmosphere of Western freedom, "part of the vice-presidency" was thus lost in the voting for officers, provoking "indignation from the delegations of the other socialist countries." But what troubled the Communist report most was, in their words, the direct confrontation by critics:

> Open attacks on the socialist countries came . . . mainly from organized Zionist and reactionary Ukrainian groups who have settled in Toronto. . . . Anticommunist elements made attempts to arrange a sale of anti-Soviet literature (Solzhenitsyn, Dzyuba, and others) near the Soviet exhibition. When after a protest from the Soviet delegation, the Canadians banned their activities from the grounds of the Congress, the provocateurs moved into the building of the University of Toronto occupied by the Secretariat of the Congress. Here they organized various petitions and campaigns against the so-called imprisonment of intellectuals in the USSR.

My own efforts to raise the problem of the repression of liberties in the Soviet Union before the Congress were cited by the Czech Communists. I had published an Open Letter to the Soviet Sociologists in the *Toronto Star* when the Congress began, welcoming them to a free city in which they could even distribute questionnaires if they wanted (without being arrested as Professor Frederick Barghoorn of Yale was in the USSR). My letter reminded several of the Soviet "sociologists" of things they had said in public discussion in Moscow— how Konstantinov had denied that anyone wanted to leave the Soviet Union, or that there was any anti-Semitism there; that Osipov, defending the fact that the works of Sartre or Freud could not be secured by students, had refused to believe that Soviet Communist books could be bought in North American bookshops; that Momjian had insisted there was no freedom in the Western countries. The Czech Communist report wrote of the effect of my "open letter":

> Just before the opening of the Congress, a professor of Sociology at the University of Toronto, L. S. Feuer, who maintains contact with the Zionist groups, attempted to foment anti-Soviet propaganda in an "open letter" to Academician F. V. Konstantinov. In the text, he rekindled a "protest" against the persecution of individuals in the USSR. The wide publication of the letter in the local press surpassed that of all other reports from the Congress.

The Czech Communist report was grateful and thankful to Western fellow travelers who had helped prevent leading emigrés from presenting papers at the Congress. As the report put it: "Some of them were perhaps barred from attending by Western sociologists in an attempt to avert an open political confrontation which would have an adverse outcome." It praised the "French sociologist Chombart de Lauwe" for having "prevented the emigré Stomiska from attending, even though his name was on the prepared list of speakers." The Czech Communists also noted that though a Hungarian revisionist's name had appeared on the program, he had not arrived at the meeting, a fact which Hungarian emigrés had protested. The Communist delegation was relieved, in its words, that "the emigrés present at the Congress were of lesser reputation," and that they mostly discussed "nonpolitical themes," and that they made no attempt to speak as Czechoslovaks, but as Americans, for instance, or Canadians. To meet the threat latent in the emigré presence, the report continues: "The Czechoslovak delegation met every evening in order to assign duties for the next day; our comrades, usually two or three, were sent to all sections where possible attacks could be expected and should be effectively confronted."

Toward the end of the meeting, when a leaflet was distributed protesting the arrests of Soviet and Czechoslovak intellectuals, the Czech and Soviet delegates were aroused because its signature included the name of Thomas B. Bottomore, the English leftist, whom they had just helped to elect as president of the International Sociological Association. Whereupon there ensued a high-level international political-academic-ideological intrigue. As the Czech Communists described it:

> After a meeting with the Soviet comrades, we prepared an answer. ... According to the wish of our Soviet comrades, R. Richta and T. Vasko paid a visit to T. B. Bottomore, and explained to him the provocative intent of such campaigns. T. B. Bottomore received them very warmly, attentively listened to their explanation and categorically denied signing the above mentioned leaflet. He then promised to inform us about any such future campaigns, to seek information from us and to refrain from involvement in any actions directed against us. He expressed great interest in maintaining close and sincere cooperation with us. He gave the Soviet delegation a similar confirmation about not signing the leaflet. This scandal was not followed by any other provocation.

Thus the Soviet ideological chieftains regard every international scientific congress as an ideological battlefield in which liberal scholars and ideas are to be fought tactically, organizationally, even with deceit and the corruption of the society's officers. Yet for precisely these reasons, every scientific and scholarly conference is an opportunity for liberal scholars to make them a forum for free and unfettered scientific thought, and a meeting place in which those scholars denied a voice in the Soviet Union because of their dissidence can present their evidence and views before the objective judgment of the world's scientific community. To insist on the free character of international scientific congresses will assist greatly the beleaguered enclaves of free-minded scientists and scholars in the Soviet Union. Merely making use of slogan-words such as "freedom" will not however mean much at scientific congresses in Moscow. When the International Historical Congress convened in Moscow in 1970, a Yale professor defended his participation by saying that he would dare use the word "freedom" in his paper. Many a professor today probably intends to utter some such word in a lecture hall of Moscow State University. Unfortunately such linguistic missiles are very quickly defused by the Soviet ideological carapace. "Freedom" is translated into the Leninist language: "proletarian freedom" will be endorsed, "bourgeois freedom" will be repudiated; the professor may even find himself enthusiastically applauded as he defends, for example, the "freedom" of Thomas More, seen in the USSR as the representative of the embryonic progressive bourgeoisie of the sixteenth century. But the "freedom" of dissidents in the Soviet Union will be dismissed as the last stand of anarchistic, decadent bourgeois. A paper considering contemporary problems of freedom, including those in the Soviet Union, could conceivably upset Soviet smugness, though in that case a boycott of Soviet listeners would probably be promulgated by its congress chief.

The American social science community continues to follow a curious double standard of morality with regard to Soviet infractions of freedom. Take, for instance, the recent decision of the American Political Science Association to participate in the World Congress of the International Political Science Association in Moscow in the Summer of 1979. The American political scientists had two momentous issues to resolve at their convention in New York in September 1978. First, they voted not to hold their next convention in Chicago because the state of Illinois had not as yet ratified the proposed Equal Rights Amendment for women. Then, they had to decide on whether to have the American Political Science Association withdraw from participation in the Moscow World Congress: "The international academic community," the motion explained, "has become increasingly concerned about the violations of human rights and academic freedom in the Soviet Union, particularly as they have affected the rights to emigrate, freely travel abroad for scholarly purposes, scholarly access to foreign materials, as well as the restrictions placed on the freedom to do research of Soviet scholars who have voiced disagreements with these policies." But the American political scientists voted down the anti-Moscow Congress resolution. The familiar array of arguments was adduced, to wit, that the resolution smacked of "cold war," that the Congress was an opportunity to influence Soviet political scientists through informal discussion and interchange, that one should not shut off intellectual contacts. Why this reasoning did not apply even more to a political scientists' boycott of the state of Illinois was never clearly explained. After all, since American political scientists can speak English, they presumably can be more persuasive in Chicago than they can be in Moscow where almost none of them will be able to speak Russian, and they will be about as effective as a spiked fieldpiece aiming at a concrete wall. The "leftist latitudinarian" attitude still prevails among some well-known American political scientists, whose "fellow travelerism" evolves into "fellow tourism." On the other hand, the Council of the American Political Science Association did leave open a possible change of site from Moscow "in case of the denial of visas to bona fide political scientists." Practically speaking, however, this was an unenforceable proviso. The customary practice of the Soviet authorities is not to issue visas until almost the eve of departure; hence, an authentication of a denial of visa would (at the earliest) reach the political scientists when the meetings in Moscow would almost be over, and change of location out of the question.

The American Political Science Association abounds in large numbers of "activists," young academics who pride themselves on their past participation in "sit-ins," seizures, and occupations of campus buildings in the late sixties and early seventies. Advocates of direct action to dramatize and theatricalize issues, their targets have thus far been confined to university buildings, though their actions were once presumably directed against a system. In New York, at their September meetings, they attended sessions to listen again to such spokesmen as Daniel Ellsberg, and they helped enact a resolution on behalf of a Marxist professor allegedly denied an appointment at Maryland because of "improper political pressures."

Certainly the congress in Moscow of the International Political Science Association offers to the "generation of activists" a test of their character and the authenticity of their principles. Planefuls of quondam "activists" will be arriving at the Moscow Airport. Will they then be prepared to bring in their suitcases the books of Marxist dissidents, such as Zhores and Roy Medvedev, such books as the *Rise and Fall of T. D. Lysenko* and *Let History Judge*? Would they be prepared if their "free speech" were constrained to stage the first "sit-in" in Soviet history? Or were such actions designed only to "confront" such foes as deans, librarians, and professors, and never to be entertained in the face of the genuine no tomfoolery power of the Soviet dictatorship? Are Western political activists "active" only when they feel secure against the background of the liberties of Western political societies? Is political "activism" the luxury of children of liberal society, to be shelved in the Soviet arena in favor of discreet silence? Thus the question of contributing to the liberalization of the Soviet Union should be on the agenda of many an "activist" alumnus.

Lastly, what further measures can the United States government and American political parties take to strengthen the American stand on human rights?

The present policy of the United States government toward the advance of human rights in the Soviet Union and elsewhere is best described as fitful. When a situation in some given country deteriorates badly, or some outstanding case receives the attention of foreign correspondents, or a distinguished emigrant reaches our shores and is received by the president or vice president, there is considerable discussion. But such a policy, since it is not part of an ongoing, institutionalized effort, is bound finally to be neglected, either in the press of other business or because of no evident fruitfulness. And after a while, since almost the entire dissident elite of the Soviet Union will have been expatriated, cases involving outstanding writers may become rare. The persecuted humble teacher, musician, motion picture actor, worker, or farmer goes undocumented.

Then too the National Committees of the Democratic and Republican Parties might well consider the formation of International Affairs Offices similar to the one which for many years has been maintained by the American Federation of Labor-Congress of Industrial Organizations, and has made a remarkable contribution toward defending the liberties of workers throughout the world. The Soviet regime, making use of the fiction that it is legally not responsible for propaganda published by its Communist Party, subsidizes a huge outpouring of anti-American and antiliberal propaganda. The United States government, by contrast, has on the whole avoided such direct ideological and systemic debate. The American political parties, as nongovernmental organizations, are the natural vehicles for such debate with the Soviet Communist Party. Indeed, since it is the pluralistic party structure that the one-party, Soviet Communist Party proposes in due course to annihilate, the task of reply belongs to our political parties. What puzzles many Soviet liberals and dissidents is the question: Why are the Americans so weak in defending their own society? Why do they ignore the Soviet charges and allegations that conjure up in their children's minds the picture of a depressed, exploited, utterly depraved society?

Comments and Discussion: Strategy and Tactics for Liberalizing the USSR

Since Professor Feuer's paper dealt primarily with questions of strategy and tactics for supporting liberalization in the Soviet Union, discussion of his paper flowed naturally into the tactical discussion.

In commenting on Feuer's presentation *Rakowska-Harmstone* thought that the dissident effort should be viewed more optimistically. The population where *samizdat* was circulating was not large, but it was important. Beyond this narrow group there was bound to be increasing questioning of the regime. The Soviet people are more educated today. They read, and to do technical jobs they have to think. This means there is a mass audience that knows the system is not working as well as it should. The rate of economic growth is falling. Of course, there are ways to improve the system's performance without basic alteration. But every change will imply another. The process will be a slow one, a kind of ripple effect. It will increase in power as the people learn more of the very different, more open atmosphere in Hungary, of the Czech experiments, of the evolution in Poland. The sheer circulation of information about this outside world is very important.

Rakowska-Harmstone agreed with Feuer's "principle of proximate criticism." Our world is a moonscape for people on the other side; we must accept their frame of reference, ride the wave of their dissatisfactions, emphasize the greater liberalism of Yugoslavia or Eurocommunism. On nationalities one can find many passages in Lenin that support arguments for increased democratization, equality, and self-determination among nationalities. Ivan Dzyuba's* *International-*

---

* Ukrainian journalist and party member who prepared a manuscript, originally for internal party circulation, condemning strongly the suppression of national autonomy of the non-Russian groups and contrasting it with Lenin's views on national self-determination. It was later published in the West. Dzyuba was arrested and eventually recanted.

173

ism or Russification is a good example of using Lenin to support self-determination.

Rakowska-Harmstone felt that Feuer overemphasized the difference between the strength of recent dissidence and that of prerevolutionary times. The populists of the nineteenth century also failed to get through to the peasants. Demonstrations are smaller today simply because the present system is much more effective in its repression. The penalties for dissent are simply too harsh for broad participation.

Sargeant added to the discussion remarks on many years of experience with Radio Liberty which went on the air just two days before Stalin's death. He emphasized the fact that the Voice of America (and other official radios) look at the world through American eyes; their mission is to project the values of American society. An institution such as Radio Liberty, on the other hand, is most effective when the broadcaster is looking at the world through the eyes of a former Soviet citizen, or a Soviet citizen out of the country interacting with people from Western democracies.

Since 1956 many studies have been made of the effectiveness of Radio Liberty and of change in the attitudes of people in a closed society. The latest study gathered data from 1974 through 1977. Performed by several European social science research organizations, it was a study serving all the Western radios. It consisted of the analysis of conversations held with 4,000 travelers from the Soviet Union. None were emigres; all were planning to return. The sample is skewed in that it is relatively urban and highly educated, and has a high proportion of communist party members (twenty-three percent). By using computer techniques the sample can, however, be made fairly representative of the country as a whole. Although the majority came from the large cities of western USSR, respondents represent most parts of the country.

The results provide the best available indicator of the awareness of *samizdat*. They show that nearly half of the adult population of the Soviet Union are aware of *samizdat*. Surprisingly a high percentage of those in the Caucasus and Central Asia know of *samizdat*, although Sargeant had seen very little material from these areas. Most who had heard of *samizdat* had not actually seen an example; only five hundred respondents referred to a specific example or said they had seen an example and very few of these were from the Transcaucasus or Soviet Central Asia.

The results suggest that over twenty million Soviet adults have heard Western broadcasts describing *samizdat*; still, most respondents had only heard of *samizdat* from official Soviet information sources. Although most respondents were opposed to *samizdat*, over six million of the estimated twenty million that had heard of it over the radio were estimated to be strongly in favor. The hostile comments of the majority were very strong; they saw the writers of *samizdat* as betrayers of the homeland or instruments of Western imperialism. But still a remarkably large group think *samizdat* is a good thing.

It is very difficult to show the effectiveness of communication like that of Radio Liberty except by hindsight. A story illustrates this point. In the 1840's and 1850's there was published in New England *Elizabeth Peabody's Aesthetic Papers*, a journal of its time. In a rather complicated sequence of events a peripatetic Englishman, probably a remainder man of his day, who had lived in the Orient, in Canada, and the United States, found himself living in South Africa. Becoming short of money he left behind for his lodging bill a trunk. In that same lodging house was a young Indian lawyer, who acquired the collection of manuscripts, magazines, and books from this trunk including *Mrs. Peabody's Aesthetic Papers* containing an essay on "Civil Disobedience" by Henry Thoreau. Around 1915, this young lawyer, who had been very active in working for the rights of indigent miners in South Africa, returned to India. The civil disobedience that Gandhi organized may have had some connection with the happenstance of *Elizabeth Peabody's Aesthetic Papers* and Mr. Thoreau's essay; the linkage cannot be proven. Similarly, we have no way of knowing that broadcasting *samizdat* leads to active reform or positive evolution, whether liberal or illiberal. Still, in all of the papers that have been presented here, there are two clear themes: we cannot afford to discontinue our efforts to communicate; we must find more ingenious and imaginative ways to do it.

Sargeant's experience pointed to a need to subdivide the audience and subdivide again. There is no hope for a service like Radio Liberty if it simply deals with a mass audience. It must attempt to find elites; it must even attempt to find military audiences. Radio Liberty found that it could reach military officers who were on occupation duty in Poland and Hungary, often in the context of their curiosity or lack of it about the society and culture in which they were temporarily living. It was even found that when there were tank maneuvers, Soviet soldiers would listen to Radio Liberty broadcasts with earphones in the tanks. Sargeant did not know what effect you can have on military officers, but felt that to neglect them as a special audience was a losing proposition. We have to try in very specific ways that will interest them. As military doctrine becomes more technical, it is necessary to find people who can talk in technical terms of developments in which technicians will be interested. The fundamental tactic is the recognition of who it is we want to communicate with, and then to find the very special content that will interest them.

Lipset supported Feuer's emphasis on international academic conferences. The Soviets do treat these conferences as though they were ideological Olympics: they delegate people to attend certain sessions because there are "trouble spots"; they consider the election of convention officers as a major ideological battleground. He had doubts, however, that they accomplished much by all this. Sometimes they provide a negative education for naive American academics who have no idea what a totalitarian society is like.

Lipset also commented on the study just described by Sargeant. He felt its reliability was suggested by the fact that if one broke down the answers into attitudes toward different issues in Soviet society by the social characteristics of respondents, the same divisions show up as are found in comparable studies of the West. If we remember there is a strong degree of political reliability among the respondents or they would not be allowed to leave the Soviet Union on trips, it is remarkable that a large proportion were very critical of aspects of Soviet society. A breakdown of the results shows that the small group of Jews in this sample, presumably the most politically reliable Jews, were almost totally hostile. Communist party members were naturally the most pro. Classified by academic specialties, the social scientists were the most hostile, the engineers were pro. The same pattern, the same kind of people who are conservatives in American society were most likely to favor the regime in the Soviet society. Workers and peasants, a small group in the sample, were very pro. This pattern clearly reflects real divisions within the society.

Lipset had never been to the Soviet Union, but from his experience he offered several examples reenforcing the Survey's impressions. For example, the Soviet head of a section of the Institute for the Study of the USA spoke to Lipset's class recently. In answer to a question on Soviet dissidents he pointed out that, "American communists don't reach anybody, dissidents reach everybody." "What do you mean they reach everybody?" He said they all listen to foreign radio and talk about it, and *samizdat* articles are constantly discussed.

Another indication of intellectual attitudes is suggested by Lipset's discussion a few years back with the deputy head of the Law Institute in Moscow, a Lithuanian. He got into a ridiculous discussion of how many Jews there were in the Soviet Union. Lipset said two or three million, and he said, "No, ten or fifteen million." They went back and forth. Finally the Soviet official said, "Look, I have lived in Moscow for twenty years. I don't care about the statistics. The majority of Moscow is Jewish. I've been to parties." It finally turned out that what he meant was that many people who are half Jewish or one-quarter Jewish, say they are Jewish. He claimed that people will mention some Jewish ancestry, or report themselves as Jews, as a way of disassociating themselves from the system. Of course, to some extent they simply want to get out.

Lipset also reported the result of a meeting at Stanford of academics who had been in the Soviet Union recently, especially scientists. Complaining of inefficiency, one Soviet host reportedly asked for suggestions on improving the Soviet system. An American's response was to suggest that a free market system should be introduced. The Soviet said, "Everybody knows that; I was looking for something original." Similarly, Soviet academics apparently avoid fellow-traveling American academics who visit Moscow. They object to their naiveté as to the real nature of the Soviet system, much preferring Americans who offer realistic critiques of the system. A major complaint of young economists was the inadequacy of their training; they did not get access to American materials until the end of the study program.

No social scientists have shown up as dissidents.* Apparently if they opposed the ideology in any way their careers would be over; for natural scientists opinions on social questions can often be overlooked by their superiors. The social scientists, however, conduct mobility and social stratification research, ostensibly to document Soviet equality. This research often presents quotes from Lipset along with obligatory refutations. But in the process the Soviet writers present long quotations from Lipset's work, and their results often support Lipset's conclusions. It is hard to believe these writers do not know what they are doing.

Soviet social scientists write about the problem of getting young people to improve their attitude to work. College students feel they should never be expected to do menial work. The social scientists point out that in American colleges students work their way through college, and that this might indeed improve attitudes to work. It also appears that attitudes toward freedom among social scientists are not too different from what we find in the West. Even Soviet propagandists see the need for free speech and criticism to counteract the inefficiencies of bureaucratization.

These people do not actively oppose the system. In general, there are few actual dissidents, but the society as a whole feels very brittle. Remember that Milosz in the *Captive Mind* thought almost everyone in Eastern Europe believed in the system, but subsequent events showed this to be false.

---

* But compare their dissidence as poll respondents, above, page 176.

Lipset suggested that the type of interviews carried out in the past by the Harvard Russian Research Center with Soviet emigres might be useful today. The Center's studies used Soviet emigres of the late 1940's as informants, not as representative samples. They tried to get the emigres to describe what went on at their level of association in the system. He believed comparable research ought to be done today with Soviet emigres. The fact that they are heavily Jewish gives some bias, but all are not Jews, and most Soviet Jews, secularized and assimilated, are in contact with the general Soviet population. By again asking people what goes on at their level of society, Lipset thought better informed images of Soviet society could be obtained. As far as he knew it is not being done. (It was pointed out, however, that Israeli authorities object to having people come to interview emigres, because of the danger of jeopardizing the exodus.)

In response *Feuer* mentioned that a Detroit interview sample of emigres was very closely studied by Gittelman and published, and that the Toronto Jewish community has had a running study of its people. These tended to confirm Sargeant's evidence that there was widespread acquaintance with Radio Liberty. Solzhenitsyn and even Sakharov said that this was their principal means of knowing what was going on in the world of thought. Radio Liberty has a program in which they read *samizdat* very slowly so that people in the Soviet Union can type down this material and give it to friends. This is a major means of diffusing *samizdat* literature.

Feuer was still not convinced of the political significance of *samizdat*. What does it mean when half of the Soviet population knows or has heard of *samizdat* or come in contact with it? Any poem not in an official journal that is handed around among little circles of friends is *samizdat*. There is a good deal of this. We have a lot of this kind of "samizdat" in the United States. Because it is officially suspect in the USSR, it has the mystery surrounding a forbidden world of ideas— poems, philosophic essays, and metaphysical essays. There is a lot of trash that simply appalls the editors of *samizdat* collections. It is poor writing that nobody would want to publish.

There are small friendship circles throughout the Soviet Union, face-to-face associations where people trust each other to handle *samizdat* documents. Their efforts can be heroic: they will hand out portions of a book that they want reproduced which they may have gotten from some Westerner, and each one goes home and types up a chapter during the night, and then they put them together to form a book. But if one asks the realistic political question, what has been the significance of this activity in political terms, or where does it stand in comparison to similar stages in past Russian political movements, the conclusion has to be negative. Is there anything comparable to Herzen's paper circulating as an official organ of the opposition? People knew what it stood for. It had a program. Do they have anything corresponding to *Iskra,* a group of emigres really pushing a program and getting their illegal papers circulated inside the country? Feuer again pointed out the lack of significant numbers at demonstrations, even compared to the 1880's or 1890's in Russia. He again pointed to the intellectuals' distrust of the masses.

Feuer shares the enthusiasm for Radio Liberty. Its impact is suggested by the fact that a chief objective of Soviet foreign policy is to get Radio Liberty off the air. It bothers them and they do not know what to do about it. They want a closed society, and here is an agency which keeps pumping in information. Yet after all these years of transmitting there is no single action in the Soviet Union that one can directly connect to an informational stimulus. Radio Liberty has saved the morale of Soviet intellectuals, giving them a sense that they are a part of the Western world community, that people outside are interested in what they are doing, but there are no signs of a political effect.

Feuer believes that Soviet intellectuals know what they are doing in presenting long quotations in critical reviews. A magazine called *Foreign Literature,* consisting of hostile reviews of Western books, has been prized by Soviet scholars, especially for those reviews that include the longest quotations from the author before reaching the obligatory refutation. The reviews were the closest the readers could get to reading the books. We admire the ingenuity it takes to do this sort of thing. Leo Strauss once wrote an essay on persecution and the tricks of writing under the eyes of the Inquisition. Such heroism is wonderful, but it did not knock out the Inquisition. It is a technique of maintaining one's human dignity under oppressive circumstances, but sadly it has little political meaning.

True, many people now say they are Jews. Actually Tania Litvinov had already done that when she told the Writers Union that she wanted to inscribe herself as Jewish. This meant what? She was on her way out of the Soviet Union. And what has been happening to the authors of *samizdat*? And to the dissident group? The greatest of the dissidents are out of the country. The Soviet Union is pleased that they call themselves Jews because they can now tell people like Sinyavsky that you have to call yourself a Jew and then you can get out of the country. The emigration has weakened the dissident movement. There was a great quarrel between Sakharov and Chalidze, who had decided to leave the Soviet Union. Solzhenitsyn, who was still in the Soviet

Union at the time, berated Chalidze for his leaving the country. But the decision being made more and more by the intellectuals is to get out. What does it mean to leave the USSR? One does not get out of a country if he thinks social change is in the making and he will be able to take part in a great reconstruction of the society. If the dissidents felt that, they would stay. Their exodus is a sign that they have given up on any real hope for change. Of course, we can hope some Soviet Gandhi is going to read the right book and all this will change. But essentially the problem is not lack of books. American books get around: there are tourists who leave books, the American embassy is always facilitating the circulation of books. The problem is that Gandhi was dealing with the British Christian empire. Here you are dealing with the Soviets who, if it really comes to a crunch, are not going to hesitate to use repressive measures. Marxian ideology legitimates extreme measures. This is a difference we have to recognize.

Lipset agreed with Feuer's description of the situation, but there remained the question of what is under the iceberg. In World War II the actions of the people in the Ukraine were remarkable. There is no other case in history where as large a number of people joined the army of the enemy because of their attitude toward the system. Read the German reports of the way they were welcomed, even by the Jews, before they started their repressive measures. The Jews simply did not believe the Russian press. It had lied so much on other matters that they would not believe what it said about a cultured people like the Germans. When the Germans came into Jewish towns and villages, the Jews were out there cheering.

Feuer felt that the lesson of the events in the Ukraine was that people will seriously defect only when the Soviet Union is defeated militarily or goes through a terrible diplomatic defeat. Khrushchev fell mainly because of the Cuban defeat he sustained in 1962. His prestige was so weakened that he could be toppled. If something of this sort takes place, then opposition to the regime can crystallize. But at the moment the tide is going the other way.

Relative to the probability of significant change occurring within the Soviet intelligentsia and our possible contributions to it, *Ellison* recalled his academic year in Leningrad in the early 1960's. He observed the enthusiasm of many students, a feeling of an opening up, of a second de-Stalinization period. His contacts were primarily with students who were either especially interested in Russian history or actually working in Russian history. They seemed remarkably eager to break out of the confines of the official intellectual controls in their field of study. They were taking their clues from what was already available to them, but they needed to go beyond that. They felt that anything described negatively but on which they were given little information must somehow be interesting. They were very interested in the presentation by official histories of the negative view of the neo-Kantian movement in the 1890's and the early years of the twentieth century, the movement out of which the philosopher Berdyaev came eventually. Not surprisingly within a few years the works of Berdyaev were worth a king's ransom on the black market. People were interested in rediscovering the Russian cultural past, especially through figures of this kind. Another work that was just beginning to be discussed (as it was mentioned negatively in the official histories) was Viekhi's *The Signposts*. Published in the aftermath of the 1905 revolution, it was a crucial turning point in the history of Russian intelligentsia. Later this work, or *samizdat* copies of chapters from it, became one of the hottest items. While interest in these works did not have any immediate political relevance, the later interest that developed in Bukharin's *Notes of an Economist* did. Many people became interested in where the collectivization system came from, why it had been opposed, what was wrong with it, and what alternatives communists had proposed.

Ellison suggested that the approach of proximate criticism should include increasing the possibility of reading, and hearing comment upon, major episodes in the historical sequence of events that led to Soviet communism or the development of Soviet communism. In reading some of the literature on national dissent, Ellison noted that the writers were really interested in what Lenin had to say about the national question. They were interested in those who had disagreed with the nationality policies that were adopted. If more Soviets can be given access to this literature, and many have gained access, it will positively affect cultural attitudes.

Ellison agreed with Lipset that many Soviet academics are disappointed with their poor intellectual training in the social sciences. For example, an Africanist had complained to Ellison that instead of doing fieldwork in Africa, he had to do it in Siberia. Later Ellison had the experience of having a Soviet Africanist present a paper to a group of university Africanists in the U.S. The presentation suggested that instead of doing fieldwork Soviet Africanists were scavenging what they could from Western literature, and were using even this badly. Ellison thought that there was a clue here. Perhaps a radio commentary that talked about Soviet scholarship in such areas, and of Western perceptions on its quality would be useful. Such programs would speak directly to a limited but very important academic audience in the Soviet Union that is aware that objective scholarship is still very tenuous in the Soviet Union, especially in the social sciences, and is eager to know more about Western perceptions of what they are doing. Soviet scholarship has made tremendous strides in the post-Stalin years. The weakening of *samizdat* and the emigration of a number of dissidents does not destroy this gain. The base still remains, inquiring attitudes remain, whatever the reimposition of control structures. Perhaps we could serve the further evolution of this scholarly community.

Bociurkiw wished to confirm Sargeant's observation that one needed to treat Soviet society as highly heterogeneous and complex. It has distinct political subcultures. As mentioned before, in the western fringe of the Soviet Union that has been annexed since 1939-40, the multiparty system makes sense; in fact, *samizdat* from the Baltic states argues for this system. In certain areas of the older USSR, for example, Armenia and Georgia, the level of civic culture is much more supportive of multiparty institutions than neighboring Azerbaijan or Central Asia. Soviet society is also very heterogeneous in terms of the social make-up of the society. For example, even if there is not necessarily sympathy in all groups of intelligentsia for a multiparty system, at least they have exposure either through *samizdat* or travel to the operation of the system, whereas other less mobilized strata would hardly know what a multiparty system means. But these strata may want other institutional changes that would eventuate in multiparty rule.

An institution such as a multiparty system is an end product or a consequence of a great many other things. And if one were to try to influence Soviet society, one has to start with the pieces, with the attitudes or value orientations of Soviet citizens. Eventually the other things will come.

Among the concerns of ordinary people that should be emphasized privacy is highly valued, especially by those who have insufficient housing, who live on collective farms or in workers' quarters, or are in the lower ranks of the intelligentsia. Dignity, individual dignity, is *very* highly valued. Equality and legality should be emphasized. The Soviet system exhibits conspicuous class inequality, and there is a deep desire for more equality in treatment. Few Soviets actually desire illegality, except perhaps some members of the police and party. Among political prisoners there is concern for legality. The value of tolerance should be stressed, both in relation to religion and, by extension, to dissident views and other social values. Many people, such as workers, students, believers, or even disabled veterans would like to form voluntary associations without interference from the government. We should also speak to the developing socioeconomic aspirations of the Soviet citizenry, an area largely ignored. The only recent case in the Soviet Union in which there were large-scale disorders requiring significant use of troops and subsequent massive reprisals was at

Novocherkask in 1962 when meat and butter prices were raised by Khrushchev. Unfortunately this is an area that is poorly reported in *samizdat*.

In terms of social alternatives, the slogan of Kronstadt, of "soviets without the commissars," of the separation of the party from the state, or of a state truly governed by soviets of peoples deputies seems widely appreciated, especially among the lower strata of the population. Many want socialist democracy without the party, not a multiparty system, but a nonparty system. Whoever said that one party is bad enough, but two parties or three parties are even worse, would probably hold this view. These are the present values and wants on which eventually a civic culture can be built that would evolve into a multiparty system. Such systems cannot be built directly on the shambles of civic culture that the Soviet system has produced.

Bociurkiw agreed with Feuer's conclusion that there is a widespread sense of political inefficacy among the dissidents, a widespread doubt has overtaken some of the best minds in the dissident movement among the prisoners. A study of Ukrainian political prisoners now in the camps suggests that the majority of the intellectual vanguard of prisoners has renounced Soviet citizenship and decided that they want to leave. They argue that "there is no hope in the system. We are finished. If we survive the camps, they will find other ways to repress us. We cannot live under this regime any more in the Soviet Union." It is a very sad, tragic phenomenon; it will weaken and it does weaken the movement of the dissidents. On the other hand, General Grigorenko claims that there are other people coming up, younger people with even less fear of authority than those now in the camps. These tend not to be intellectuals.

Samizdat is a many-splendored thing. It tends now to be predominantly copies of written materials documenting persecution. Literary activity has become less important, perhaps because of the emigration of so many writers. Bociurkiw emphasized the need to study *samizdat* seriously.

Bociurkiw said that although the Radio Liberty collection of *samizdat* in Munich was the best, they did not have adequate resources to analyze it properly or even prepare a subject index. He has developed a small project on the Ukrainian materials, but an attempt to establish a larger center for *samizdat* research has just fallen through for lack of funds. *Sussman* briefly discussed the center being developed at Freedom House for the collection, translation, and dissemination of *samizdat* literature. Much of the material would be coming from Radio Liberty.

Since so much emphasis had been placed by the conference on

the role of Radio Liberty, *Sussman* thought it well to warn the group
of the danger posed to Radio Liberty and Radio Free Europe by the
World Administrative Radio Conference (WARC) of the International
Telecommunications Union to be held in 1979. The conference will
reassess the domestic and international radio spectrum, and include
regulations for satellite communications. Resulting assignments and
regulations will apply for the next twenty years. The Soviet Union has
continued to try to block out our transmissions to communist states.
In a small WARC last year they obtained the agreement of most
countries that the principle of "prior consent" should apply to all
transmissions that cross national borders. We have not yet signed
this agreement.

At the 1979 WARC the complete group of issues will be raised. For
the first time the Third World countries have formed a unified front to
gain more of the transmission spectrum. Since the United States and
the USSR together control a major share of the spectrum, we will have
some common interests with the Soviets on this issue. However, American spokesmen must defend a wide variety of both governmental and
commercial interests. Since we lack a large domestic constituency for
Radio Liberty and Radio Free Europe, all of us should try to raise
our voices to meet this challenge.

Relating his broad experiences in academic, intelligence, and national
security planning to the issues before the conference, *Kintner* thought
it useful to remember the long history of attempts such as we were
undertaking. In particular, the National Security Council's memo-
randum Number 68 published in 1950 emphasized essentially three
themes: containment of the Soviet Union along the lines proposed by
Kennan; the enhancement of our military position; and the necessity to
liberalize the Soviet Union if we were to build a peaceful world, a
position similar to that taken by the Gastil paper. Because of the
Korean War, the United States was able to build up its military potential. Perhaps in the 1950's we were relatively stronger than we have
been since. Kintner felt that by now we should see that containment
had not worked well; it had broken down on several fronts. He did
not think our efforts to liberalize the Soviet Union had been very
successful.

A major reason for our inability to effect the liberalization of the
USSR has been our unwillingness to aggressively engage in ideological
conflict. From the very beginning of the Cold War American decision-
makers, including many in the State Department, were inclined to deemphasize ideology because they simply believed we had no ideology.
Ideological offensives were regularly blocked. The proposal in the
early 1950's that we distribute worldwide a realistic biography of

Stalin was vetoed because it would be thought offensive. A detailed program to exploit cleavages in Soviet society after the death of Stalin was developed. But when Stalin died, the program was ignored. When the Soviets lost control of East Germany for two days in June 1953 the United States did nothing to exploit the situation. The open skies proposal was more successful. While the proposal was partly for intelligence, it was also meant as a way of more generally opening up the closed society.

The cultural exchange program was developed but little exploited. What Kintner and others had desired was a massive program. For example, twenty thousand young Americans would go to the USSR and twenty thousand Soviet youth come here. The Soviets could not police such a program effectively. But the State Department opposed the proposal on their standard ground that they did not want to propose anything unless they believed in advance that the Soviets would accept it. The result is that the Soviets have largely dictated the nature of the programs. The typical person they send is middle-aged, with a wife and children in Moscow. The likelihood of defection or other trouble is further reduced by the selection of fully committed supporters with a relatively powerful position and comfortable way of life back home.

Now we find ourselves in a slipping military relationship in which the Soviets are becoming increasingly arrogant. The Gastil paper pointed out that if we can't improve the military situation perhaps we can exploit the societal vulnerabilities of the USSR. This is true, but the chances of doing it are minimal unless changes in U.S. government policy are made. Private organizations can do a great deal, but without government backing using the psychological element of our relationship to the USSR to strengthen our security relationship has little chance.

Cottam's discussion of the tactical and strategic issues involved in trying to liberalize the Soviet Union drew heavily on his work on international bargaining relationships and on analogies between attempts to liberalize the Soviet Union and the problems of liberalizing Iran. His point of departure for this analysis differed from that of most participants in that Cottam does not regard the present Soviet system as a threat to world peace or American values. He believes, however, that continued repression in the USSR is a sufficient reason for Americans to be interested in Soviet liberalization.

Cottam advanced the view that making human rights a *central concern* in American foreign policy pronouncements has been a mistake. It is a mistake, first, because most of those who make decisions in large bureaucracies are going to have little sense of history. Therefore, when they promote a policy such as human rights they have little sense of what will follow. For example, in Iran and many other countries human rights pronouncements predictably had a revolutionary impact. Yet this surprised and dismayed many American advocates of human rights.

Secondly, an attempt to make human rights a central aspect of foreign policy is inescapably open to the charge of hypocrisy. Foreign policy will always represent a variety of internal pressures. This makes it impossible to have a sophisticated, single purpose strategy. Policy will always be a compound of compromises. In general, since the public pressure in support of human rights in any particular country is weak, other pressures will determine policy toward that country. Therefore, making human rights a central concern of declaratory policy unavoidably leads to policy profiles such as we see today where there is great concern for human rights in the Soviet Union, but never a mention of the problem in China. So it was not surprising to Cottam that on a recent visit to Poland academics had seemed to regard Carter's human rights initiatives as a cold war throwback to Dulles, engineered by the evil spirit of Brzezinski.

Finally, of all of the instruments of interference in other polities that we have the human rights instrument is the bluntest and least controllable. For example, once the policy started a process of change in Iran a momentum developed that was uncontrollable. The administration found the result dangerous to its other concerns, but it could do little except simply stop talking about human rights.

A human rights policy that our government follows in response to internal pressures is quite a different matter. For example, if a significant part of the Senate should oppose sending arms to a particular country until the human rights situation improves, then the country buying the arms will understand the need of the U.S. administration to be provided evidence of improvement in human rights conditions. This puts the administration in an excellent bargaining position. Such popular or congressional pressure also greatly enhances the bargaining leverage within the U.S. administration of those giving priority to human rights.

The group had convinced Cottam of the prospects for destabilization in the USSR. Referring to the Iranian analogy again, Cottam pointed out that the Shah had used two means for maintaining his stability: coercion and the satisfaction of material wants. What the Shah lacked was legitimacy. To Cottam a government has legitimacy when in a crisis it is able to manipulate symbols in such a way that it can gain popular support. Most governments need this control device. Usually it is based on an ability to manipulate national and religious symbols effectively. In Iran the Shah lacked an ability to appeal to national symbols because politically conscious Iranians saw the present Shah coming to power as a result of American support, just as Reza Shah had established the regime in the previous generation on the basis of British support. The Shah had, in addition, needlessly thrown away his ability to manipulate Islamic symbols.

Similarly, the hollow ring of communist ideology among educated Soviets today implies that if liberalization occurs in the USSR, that is, if the government reduces its reliance on coercive control, then the Soviets must rely primarily on material rewards to maintain support. Obviously such reliance makes a society vulnerable to material crises. For example, the Shah was undermined in Iran by inflation that damaged the standard of living of many people. A similar material setback in the USSR could be very destabilizing.

Given this analysis, a crisis in the Soviet Union, however it occurs, is likely to force a return to emphasis on the Russian Orthodox Church and Russian nationalism, as it did in World War II. The foreign policy implications of such a change are probably negative. Therefore, in strategic terms we should be humble about what we are doing to international stability by underwriting destabilization in the USSR.

Assuming that there are relatively liberal or at least moderate elements in the Soviet elite and that external and internal events affect their bargaining power within the system, Cottam would make a guiding principle of a liberalization policy the strengthening of the position of these elements. In deciding on how to strengthen the position of liberal elements the foreign policy analysis that one adopts is critical. Cottam contrasted the policies one would adopt if he assumed the Soviet Union followed an aggressive policy with those one would adopt if he assumed, as Cottam did, that the Soviet Union was a status quo power that appears aggressive when it is in fact only fearful. Taking the example of "playing the China card" (which the administration played shortly after the conference), if the former analysis is correct, playing the card will weaken belligerent forces in the USSR. It will show that the U.S. has the will to stand up to them, to counter their every move. If belligerence is not paying off, the Soviet elite will select leaders favoring alternative policies. If on the other hand, the Soviet Union today is a fearful status quo power, playing the China card will weaken Soviet liberals, for it will reinforce the argument that the United States is a fundamentally hostile power bent on the destruction of the Soviet system. Since the official American response to the USSR is by all odds the most important in producing liberalization, a nonromantic analysis of Soviet foreign policy is critical.

Our central purpose must be to change perceptions in the USSR, to confirm those of people moving the way we desire and to disconfirm the perceptions of others. In this Radio Liberty is important but government is more important.

Private organizations should think in terms of making it profitable for the Soviet Union to liberalize and unprofitable for them not to. Cottam advocated tying further development of trade to evidence of liberalization, the policy that has been advocated, for example, by Senator Jackson. This policy must be built up from below, by developing public and congressional pressure. Coming directly from the administration the bargaining potential of tying human rights to trade would be low; it would appear more as a plot.

Under questioning, Cottam agreed that in the short run such a policy might increase pressure on the dissidents. They would appear as the cause of the trade problem and be increasingly repressed. Such a U.S. policy would, after all, directly threaten those in power. However, in the longer term, such a policy should lead to a replacement of those in power by liberal elements anxious both for trade and a more liberal polity. There will undoubtedly be people hurt by the initiation of a policy as strong as that of linking trade with human rights. As Kintner has said (above) consciousness of these risks has led to a very hesitant policy in the past. But with hesitant policies we will accomplish little.

Cottam reaffirmed the importance of a supportive outside milieu for human rights. When Soviets visit the U.S. they should hear what we think of their system, and not hear only polite remarks. As and if we develop increasingly friendly contacts with the USSR the problem of Americans ignoring the human rights situation in the USSR will be exacerbated. For example, as soon as American businessmen see trade possibilities expanding they will become the champions of a more positive view of Soviet society. Much the same will be true of academics. Cottam reminded the academics in the room that they had had the good fortune of studying the society of a repressive enemy. From his own experience it was much harder to study a repressive ally. When an allied regime denies access to its American critics, these critics find few friends at home. Indeed, most of the critic's fellow scholars in the U.S. will for various reasons be strong in their praise of the repressive regime. Human rights organizations should recognize and try to deal with this problem worldwide.

The work of private organizations in the U.S. in defense of human rights will not be effective if they appear self-serving, as they often do. A human rights group that allows itself to be identified with either the right or left is dysfunctional. The concern of Jewish groups for Jews in the Soviet Union is clearly self-serving, as is true of the human rights activities of many other nationality and emigre groups.*

Finally, a private human rights strategy should emphasize institutional development. The idea of international political party involvement is a good one. For example, there is a good deal of interest in the Middle East in the treatment of Muslims in the USSR. In Europe there are other constituencies, for example, Eurocommunists that want to bring pressure on particular issues. If different peoples could place pressures on their governments on those issues that have internal constituency support, then the cumulative effect on the USSR would be significant. It would in turn improve the bargaining position of those Soviet leaders who want to liberalize the USSR.

In response to Cottam *Alexander* agreed on the danger of over-emphasizing human rights in American foreign policy, but he felt human rights should be an important element of policy. Except under Kennedy and Carter, in Latin America U.S. foreign policy has suffered from a lack of interest in human rights. Without human rights America seemed at times to have no policy, to simply respond to whatever special interest (such as business, labor, or military) was dominant in a particular situation. The result created many resentments. Now if someone wants to support a particular project, party, or investment in Latin America he often has to prove his case in the face of human rights considerations, and this is not always possible. Since Carter, violations of the human rights of many people have been curtailed. Pinochet in Chile has freed almost all his political prisoners; Stroessner's Paraguay has freed most of its political prisoners; rights have improved in Brazil. In Nicaragua if we do not do more explicitly in human rights terms we may have an international war on our hands, and then we will really have lost out. Our best friends in Latin America are those who want democracy; they are our true ideological allies; we must at least give them moral support.

Ellison supported Alexander's reply to Cottam. In particular, he doubted if consideration of a variety of other values in policy meant that it was necessarily hypocritical to emphasize human rights. It

---

*However, it may be that such self-serving groups are the only way to enlist major popular support for human rights causes. Cottam himself suggests in the next paragraph employing the Middle Eastern interest in the oppression of Muslims in the USSR in a general campaign of human rights pressure on the Soviet regime. See also Rakowska-Harmstone's discussion (above) of the importance of getting American ethnic communities of Soviet background to attempt to influence public and Congressional opinion.

was true human rights was not very controllable—advocating freedom had the same problem—but within a context of rational policies we needed to have principles and hold to them.

In response to Alexander *Cottam* suggested that human rights policy succeeds in Latin America because it is not an important region of confrontation. When it is applied rhetorically to an area of confrontation the question of hypocrisy becomes very important. It cheapens human rights and destroys its vitality everywhere.

Bociurkiw added that his conclusion as to America's human rights policy was that it was better to have an imperfectly applied universalistic formula than to be denuded of legitimizing formulas in foreign policy. In the Soviet bloc the Carter policy has had a tremendous impact, an impact increased by a seeming American willingness to admit making mistakes. The announcement of the Carter policy came at a very critical time for the dissidents; it served to draw them together without antagonizing any of them.

The human rights policy has served as a kind of moral rearmament for American policy. Of course, any policy includes a good deal of cynicism. Cynicism and self-interest may in fact be the only intellectually honest positions. But a nation does not win supporters by appealing only to its own national self-interest. In Iran today Bociurkiw judged that America was reaping a harvest of technological, value-free, political thinking.

Bociurkiw did not see liberals in the Soviet government. He thought rather that talk of liberals was a game Soviet leaders played with us. He felt that although elites should be targeted the liberalization effort must be directed to the whole society, for the significant changes must come from within that society. The liberalization effort must place potential brakes on the ability of the Soviets to divert major resources to armaments or to become increasingly aggressive. This requires a certain delegitimization of Soviet authoritarianism. To promote this we need to assist the development of several trends. First is the trend toward supporting the values and concerns of the ordinary people, as Bociurkiw had mentioned previously. Of course, this also requires support for civil rights, national aspirations, and religious rights. The second direction of change that we should assist is the development of autonomous groups, or intermediate structures. These cannot help but restrict the arbitrary actions of government, and, as they develop, to lay the basis for the future evolution of an alternative kind of system. Third, we should try to make an impact on the elites of the Republics—the only link between the ruling elites and the masses is in national aspirations.

Dzyuba and others in the national dissent movement have stressed the inferior, second-class nation status imposed on Ukrainians, Belorussians, Baltic peoples, and others. Bociurkiw suggested that this kind of criticism hurt the Ukrainian party elite, and suspected this was true in many Republics. *Samizdat* documents from the Ukraine ask, for example, why the Rumanians who fought against the USSR should have separate statehood and the Ukrainians should not. Members of the Soviet nationalities also notice the many small countries in the U.N. and ask why they cannot be equally independent. They may not be interested in dissolving the USSR but in transforming it into a confederation or loose federation promised by the Soviet Constitution. The United States might aid this evolution by pointing out that the only affected U.N. members that did not take part in Helsinki and similar conferences are the Ukraine and Belorussia. Perhaps the United States could even urge their invitation to future conferences, including the 1980 Madrid Conference of the Helsinki signatories.

Experience gained from the observation of Soviet-American exchanges led another participant to the conclusion that our goal in influencing the USSR must be liberalization rather than revolution. Liberalization means supporting the kind of program that has occurred in Poland since 1957 rather than events in Hungary in 1956 or Czechoslovakia in 1968.* To achieve our goals we need to have ideals such as pluralism or majority rule, but we cannot directly pursue these goals. We must develop indirect means to achieve them. The source of change must be found in internal forces. As Kintner pointed out, we tried to use external means, but these were simply not supported.

The focus of the liberalization campaign should be on the elites, the new elites, the national elites, and the religious elites. The masses are heavily controlled, and there is little we can do to affect them. Most important are the current party elites or "liberal influentials." We must concentrate on trying to strengthen the bargaining position of the liberals within the elite. The dissidents are important, perhaps even growing in importance, but should not be our main focus.

The elites or potential elites can be split into three generations. The older generation is now in power or retired. World War II and Stalinism are the great experiences of their lives; still fearful, their highest value is stability. The younger generation, in their twenties

---

* Unrest and riots have, however, played an important role in sustaining or instigating liberalizing change in Poland; the Hungarian Revolution of 1956 may be one reason for subsequent liberalization there. (Rakowska-Harmstone)

and thirties, know little of the war or Stalinism. They are often materialistic, cynical, without ideals, interested in clothes and cars. In between, the generation now in its forties is pessimistic and technocratic, they want a more rational, enlightened society, yet they also worry about the lack of control and the nihilistic values of the young. Thus, this generation suffers acutely from a general schizophrenia, exhibited, for example, in a tendency of Soviets in conversation one day to docilely repeat what they are supposed to say, and the next day to suddenly begin to ridicule the system.

Since this middle generation will be the next elite, we must know how to deal with them. Threatening their position is dangerous. Psychologists tell us schizophrenics react to threats belligerently. It is true that revolution often occurs when a leadership group loses confidence. But gradual change such as we are talking about can perhaps occur only when leaders feel some self-confidence, at least enough to make them willing to experiment.

Tactically, a liberalization program should first provide hope to dissidents. It would include giving increased access to information to a variety of people with a variety of needs. Soviet Africanists, for example, might be given access to increased educational opportunities.

In our interactions with Soviets, Americans should strive more to be themselves, do what they want, be innovative, tell what they think. This does not necessarily mean being dogmatic or assertive. Accustomed to a highly pluralistic society it goes against the grain of many Americans to say, "This is what we feel." We feel that people have different points of view, that is what we really feel. This looks weak, but the message gets through. Soviets come to understand that Americans can respect different points of view and still hold together. Homogeneity is not necessary for strength.

In foreign policy Americans should make their positions clear, be consistent, and firmly hold the line. Only holding the line will allow the internal ferment to do its work. We might make a practice of answering more directly the continual ideological attacks that Soviet leaders make upon us. We might revitalize Lodge's "twenty-four hour rule" of the 1950's: no verbal attack from the Soviets should remain unanswered for twenty-four hours. This might deter Soviet leaders from casually launching their persistent verbal attacks.

We should also emphasize conference tactics. For example, the Soviets often do something that Americans intending to attend a conference do not like. The Americans can choose one of five responses: stay home and keep quiet; stay home but publicize the reason; attend and stay quiet; attend and discuss their concerns; attend and aggressively develop their position (distribute books, engage in sit-ins, etc.). The best choice is for Americans to attend the conference but make clear their objections. The Soviets need information and contact. Many Soviets suspect a deep gap between ideology and reality, and they crave more information to fill in what they do not know.

Summary and Conclusions

Conferences of this kind are as valuable as the information and analysis that they produce. Consensus is a valuable but by no means necessary result. In this conference there were several areas in which significant disagreement was apparent. Those interested in supporting Soviet liberalization will find some of the most useful suggestions for further action emerge from this disagreement.

Most of the group believed that the Soviet Union was carefully but persistently pursuing the ideological goal of bringing the world under both Soviet and communist domination. Fear that an illiberal Soviet Union will continue toward this goal was one of the main reasons that Freedom House sponsored the conference. However, some participants doubted that communist ideology was more than a convenient smokescreen for the pursuit of Russian national interest. One member felt that Soviet foreign policy was status quo oriented. If he is correct then the American policy most conducive to liberalization in the Soviet Union will not be the relatively strong, confrontational policy most participants favored.

An analogous cleavage developed between those who viewed the Soviet Union today as largely denuded of ideological conviction and those who viewed the Communist Party of the Soviet Union as still in active pursuit of the revolutionary and utopian goals mapped out years ago in Marxist-Leninist terms. Those who believed the Soviet Union was becoming a conventional authoritarian state with a communist glaze were more likely to see the current governing elite reaching accommodations internally with religious and nationalist dissidents. Such compromise would appear more difficult to those who believed ideology was still an active component of Soviet official life, and who saw reform coming only out of an extended struggle of ideas.

Several participants believed that America's public and private actions should be directed toward supporting the position of relatively liberal, less aggressive, elements within the governing Soviet elite. The evolution of their position would be sustained by increasing the availability of information from the outside world as well as by

194

adopting U.S. foreign policy strategies that strengthen the credibility of liberal Soviet interpretations of the world. However, several expert participants doubted the reality of this distinction, believing that a markedly liberal governing Soviet elite does not exist.

This difference of opinion was closely related to two others. First, some felt that the efforts of outsiders must be directed primarily at changing the information, attitudes, and relative strength of a variety of elites, including the intellectual elites, dissident and passive. They felt that average people in the Soviet Union were highly controlled and essentially conservative. Others felt that much more attention should be directed toward nonelite groups. They pointed out that average Soviet citizens have a wide variety of increasingly strong interests in privacy, dignity, political equality, national identity, religious freedom, and organizational independence. Secondly, most participants felt that outsiders should direct major attention to support of the national ambitions of the peoples of the Soviet Republics. National feelings in the Soviet Union have large constituencies, reaching even into the ruling elites of the Republics. It was conceivable that the next generation would see a general loosening up of the Soviet Union in which the Republics attained a status similar to that of the satellites. This group saw increased respect for the nationalities as being inseparable from the general goal of liberalizing Soviet society. However, a minority of the participants believed that national aspirations, both Russian and, reciprocally, those of other nationalities, were more than likely to lead to a repressive and illiberal Soviet Union.

Many felt that the dissident movement was a very important force in Soviet history, and that its preservation and strengthening could lead to the progressive liberalization of the USSR. By continually questioning the legitimacy of the regime the dissidents focus the innumerable discontents of the population as a whole, eventually forcing governing elites to develop new bases of legitimacy more in accord with the democratic standards acceptable in the modern world. Some participants, however, preferred to emphasize the fact that the dissident effort remained remarkably weak and fragmented, especially when compared with that in prerevolutionary times. To them the Soviet population seemed conservative and passive. From this perspective the purpose of supporting dissidents became not so much to suport tendencies toward liberalization coming from many sources in Soviet society as it was to keep alive a critical minority that might help to prevent the ever-present danger that the Soviet Union would slide back into Stalinism.

There were, of course, many tactical differences. Some proposed relatively aggressive tactics, such as American activists distributing

dissident literature or staging sit-ins in Moscow. Other strong approaches included an American foreign policy that tied trade or
technology transfer to human rights improvements, or that encouraged
repeated reference to the constitutional rights to secession of the
Republics, or attempted to develop direct relations with them. Many
participants would emphasize that such tactics should be used with
great care, if at all. The probability of negative Soviet reactions, at
least in the short run, loomed larger to them. They believed there
were other approaches that had as good a chance of achieving liberalizing objectives, such as emphasis on improving communication,
increasing information available to the Soviets, marshalling world
opinion against human rights violations, and remaining steadfast in
the external confrontation.

There was general consensus on several important questions. All
participants believed in continued support for the dissidents and the
dissemination of *samizdat* literature. All believed that opening up
the Soviet Union to more information about the world, to more
contact with outsiders, was desirable. The role of communications
media such as Radio Liberty was viewed as particularly important.
These means should be strengthened if possible, and upcoming
threats to their continued operation through international agreement
resolutely opposed. The idea was generally accepted that there should
be more research on the nature, extent, and varieties of dissent in
the USSR.

Most participants accepted, with varying degrees of enthusiasm,
the "principle of proximate criticism," the idea that the liberalizing
ideas most likely to be accepted by any Soviet audience were those
not too far from the assumptions of the socialist world. Thus, it is
more useful to disseminate the writings and concepts of the liberal
early Marxists such as Bukharin, of the Eurocommunists today, of
the Czechs of 1968, or of the Yugoslavs, than it is to try to convince
most Soviets of the value of a multiparty state or a free market.
On the other hand, it was obvious to all that there were significant
variations among both the geographical areas and social strata of
Soviet society as to their receptivity to ideological alternatives. The
people of the Baltic states, for example, would be immediately interested in multiparty, Western democracy.

All participants believed that support of religious dissidents was
desirable and productive. Relatively numerous and from many classes,
they form a means of contact between the very small group of
intellectual dissidents, who have Western contacts, and the general
population of the Soviet Union. Religion was also an area in which
the Soviet government appeared particularly vulnerable both externally

and internally. Moreover, emphasis on religious oppression was an avenue by which relatively large numbers of Americans, Europeans, Middle Easterners, and others could become more than intellectually concerned with Soviet oppression.

Most participants accepted President Carter's placing of human rights among the major concerns of American foreign policy. Even those who disagreed with this emphasis, in general terms, did not deny that the administration's human rights policy had had a positive effect on dissidence in the Soviet Union and Eastern Europe. Carter's policy helped to reinforce the legalistic case of many dissidents that depend on reference to the Helsinki accords and the Universal Declaration of Human Rights for their legitimization.

There was a consensus that our goal could not be more than the gradual liberalization of the Soviet Union. At the same time there was a consensus that change often came in response to crisis situations, brought about by the failure of either the external or internal policies of rulers, or simply by problems of transition from one set of rulers to another. A strategy for liberalizing the Soviet Union must strive both to develop the internal forces within the USSR that can take positive advantage of such critical periods and to develop new concepts of the role that the United States and its allies might most usefully play in such periods.

All agreed that private individuals and organizations could make a contribution to Soviet liberalization. But most thought that their contribution would be relatively ineffective without the active support of the American government and the American public. The development of the international activities of Western political parties may become a useful alternative means to influence the process. In any event, the task of a private organization is as much that of developing public support for liberalization and devising publicly acceptable strategies that the government could adopt in support of liberalization, as it is directly promoting liberalization through the use of its own limited resources.

PART IV

Country Summaries

Introduction

The following country descriptions summarize the evidence that lies behind our ratings for each country. They first bring together for each country most of the tabular material of Part I. Then, political rights are considered in terms of the extent to which a country is ruled by a government elected by the majority at the national level, the division of power among levels of government, and the possible denial of self-determination to major subnationalities, if any. While decentralization and the denial of group rights are deemphasized in our rating system, these questions should not be ignored. The summaries also contain consideration of civil liberties, especially as these include freedom of the media and other forms of political expression, freedom from political imprisonment, torture, and other forms of government reprisal, and freedom from interference in nonpublic group or personal life. Equality of access to politically relevant expression is also considered. In some cases the summaries will touch on the relative degree of freedom from oppression outside of the government arena, for example, through slavery, labor bosses, capitalist exploitation, or private terrorism; this area of analysis is little developed at present.

At the beginning of each summary statement the country is characterized by the forms of its economy and polity. The meanings of the terms used in this classification may be found in Part I, "The Relation of Political-Economic Systems to Freedom," and its accompanying Table 7. The classification is highly simplified, but it serves our concern with the developmental forms and biases that affect political controls. The terms employed in Part I and Table 7 differ from those used in the following summaries only in that the capitalist-socialist term in the former discussion is divided into two classes in the summaries. *Mixed capitalist* systems, such as those in Israel, the Netherlands, or Sweden, provide social services on a large scale through governmental or other nonprofit institutions with the result that private control over property is sacrificed to egalitarian purposes. These nations still see capitalism as legitimate, but its legitimacy is accepted grudgingly by many in government. *Mixed socialist* states such as Iraq or Poland proclaim themselves to be socialist but in fact allow rather large

201

portions of the economy to remain in the private domain. As in Table 7 the terms *inclusive* and *noninclusive* are used to distinguish between societies in which the economic activities of most people are organized in accordance with the dominant system and those dual societies in which they remain largely outside. The system should be assumed to be inclusive unless otherwise indicated.

Each state is categorized according to the political positions of the national or ethnic groups it contains. Since the modern political form is the "nation-state," it is not surprising that many states have a *relatively homogeneous population*. The overwhelming majority in these states belong to roughly the same ethnic group; people from this group naturally form the dominant group in the state. In relatively homogeneous states there is no large subnationality (that is, with more than one million people or twenty percent of the population) residing in a defined territory within the country: Austria, Costa Rica, Somalia, and West Germany are good examples. States in this category may be ethnically diverse (for example, Cuba or Colombia), but there are no sharp ethnic lines between major groups. These states should be distinguished from *ethnically complex states*, such as Guyana or Singapore, that have several ethnic groups, but no major group that has its historic homeland in a particular part of the country. Complex states may have large minorities that have suffered social, political, or economic discrimination in the recent past, but today governments in such states treat all peoples as equals as a matter of policy. In this regard complex states are distinguishable from *ethnic states with major nonterritorial subnationalities,* for the governments of such states have a deliberate policy of giving preference to the dominant ethnic group at the expense of other major groups. Examples are Burundi or China (Taiwan).

Another large category of states is labeled *ethnic states with (a) major territorial subnationalities(y)*. As in the homogeneous states there is a definite ruling people (or *Staatsvolk*) residing on its historic national territory within the state. But the state also incorporates other territories with other historic peoples that are now either without a state, or the state dominated by their people lies beyond the new border. As explained in *Freedom in the World 1978* (pp. 180–218), to be considered a subnationality a territorial minority must have enough cohesion and publicity that their right to nationhood is acknowledged in some quarters. Events have forged a quasi unity among groups only recently quite distinct—as among rebels in the Southern Sudan. Typical countries in this category are Burma and the USSR; more marginally states such as Peru or Laos are also included. *Ethnic states with major potential territorial subnationalities* fall into a closely related category. In such states—for example, Morocco or Bolivia—many individuals in the ethnic group have merged, with little overt hostility, with the dominant ethnic strain. The assimilation process has gone on for centuries. Yet in these countries the new consciousness that accompanies the diffusion of nationalistic ideas through education may reverse the process of assimilation in the future, especially where the potential subnationality has preserved a more or less definable territorial base.

There are a few truly *multinational states* in which ethnic groups with territorial bases coexist in one state without a clearly definable ruling people or *Staatsvolk*. In such states the several "nations" each have autonomous political rights, although these do not in law generally include the right to secession. India and Nigeria are examples. One *trinational* and a few *binational* states complete the categories of those states in which several nations coexist.

The distinction between truly multinational states and ethnic states with territorial subnationalities may be made by comparing two major states that lie close to the margin between the categories—the ethnic Russian USSR and multinational India. In the USSR, Russian is in every way the dominant language. By contrast, in India Hindi speakers have not achieved dominance. English remains a unifying lingua franca, the languages of the several states have not been forced to change their script to accord with Hindi forms, and Hindi itself is not the distinctive language of a "ruling people"—it is a nationalized version of the popular language of a portion of the population of northern India. (The pre-British ruling class used a closely related language with Arabic, Persian, and Turkish infusions; it was generally written in Persian-Arabic script.) Unlike Russians in the non-Russian Soviet Republics, Hindi speakers from northern India do not have a special standing in their own eyes or those of other Indians. Calcutta, Bombay, and Madras are non-Hindi speaking cities, and their pride in their identities and culture is an important aspect of Indian culture. By contrast, many Soviet Republics are dominated by Russian speakers, a situation developing even in Kiev, the largest non-Russian city.

Finally, *transethnic heterogeneous states*, primarily in Africa, are those in which independence found a large number of ethnically distinct peoples grouped more or less artificially within one political framework. The usual solution was for those taking over the reins of government to adopt the colonial approach of formally treating all local peoples as equal, but with the new objective of integrating all equally into a new national framework (and new national identity) as and when this would be possible. Rulers of states such as Senegal or Zaire often come from relatively small tribes, and it is in their interest to deemphasize tribalism. In some cases the tribes are so scattered and localistic that there is no short-term likelihood of secession resulting from tribalism. However, in other cases portions of the country have histories of separate nationhood making the transethnic solution hard to implement. In a few countries recent events have placed certain ethnic groups in opposition to one another or to ruling circles in such a way that the transethnic state remains only the *formal* principle of rule, replaced in practice by an ethnic hierarchy, as in Uganda or perhaps Sierra Leone.

The descriptive paragraphs for political and civil rights are largely self-explanatory. Subnationalities are generally discussed under a subheading for political rights, although the subject has obvious civil liberties aspects. Discussion of the existence or nonexistence of political parties may be arbitrarily placed in one or the other section. These paragraphs only touch on a few relevant issues, especially in the civil liberties discussion. An issue may be omitted for lack of information, because it does not seem important for the country addressed, or because a particular condition can be inferred from the general statement of a pattern. It should be noted that we have tried to incorporate the distinction between a broad definition of political prisoners (including those detained for violent political crimes) and a narrow definition that includes those arrested only for nonviolent actions—often labeled "prisoners of conscience." At the end of each country summary we have included an overall comparative statement that places the country's ratings in relation to those of others. Countries chosen for comparison are often neighboring or similar ones, but juxtaposing very different countries is also necessary for tying together the system.

The following summaries take little account of the oppressions that occur within the social units of a society, such as family and religious groups, or that reflect variations in the nonpolitical aspects of culture. In particular, the reader will note few references in the following summaries to the relative freedom of women. This may be a serious gap in the Survey, but with limited resources we felt that it was better to omit this range of issues than to only tangentially include it. We suspect that including the freedom of women would not affect the ratings a great deal. Democracies today have almost universally opened political and civic participation to women on at least a formal basis of equality, while most nondemocratic societies that deny these equal rights to women also deny effective participation to most men. In such societies granting equal rights may have limited meaning. It is little gain for political and most civil rights when women are granted equal participation in a totalitarian society.

AFGHANISTAN

Economy: noninclusive socialist   **Political Rights:** 7
Polity: socialist one-party   **Civil Liberties:** 7
Population: 18,000,000*   **Status of Freedom:** not free

An ethnic state with major territorial subnationalities

Political Rights: Afghanistan is now ruled by a single party proclaiming communist goals. The government's control in rural areas is contested; revolts in some provinces were reported late in the year. Soviet officials have a great deal of influence on the government and Soviet officers may command military units.

Subnationalities. The largest minority is the Tadzhik (thirty percent), the dominant people of the cities and the western part of the country. Essentially lowland Persians, their language remains the lingua franca of the country, although it has been government policy to require equal use of the language of the Pathan majority, especially in the bureaucracy. About ten percent of the population belong to Uzbek and other Turkish groups in the north.

Civil Liberties. The press is government owned and under rigid censorship. Antigovernment organization or expression is forbidden. Conversation is guarded and travel is restricted. The continuing strength of Islam in law and society mitigates the absolutism of the central government. There are perhaps thousands of political prisoners; there have been political executions. The objectives of the state appear totalitarian, but the degree of their achievement, especially outside of the cities, is unclear.

Comparatively: Afghanistan is as free as Vietnam, less free than Iran.

ALBANIA

Economy: socialist   **Political Rights:** 7
Polity: communist one-party   **Civil Liberties:** 7
Population: 2,600,000   **Status of Freedom:** not free

A relatively homogeneous population

Political Rights. Albania has been a communist dictatorship under essentially one-man rule since 1944. While there are a number of elected bodies, including an assembly, the parallel government of the communist party (three percent of the people) is decisive at all levels; elections offer only one list of candidates. Candidates are officially

---

* Population estimates for all countries are generally derived from the 1978 World Population Data Sheet of the Population Reference Bureau, Washington, D.C.

designated by the Democratic Front, to which all Albanians are supposed to belong. In the 1970's several extensive purges within the party have apparently been designed to maintain the power of the top leaders.

Civil Liberties. Press, radio, and television are completely under government or party control, and communication with the outside world is minimal. Media are characterized by incessant propaganda, and open expression of opinion in private conversation is rare. Political imprisonment is common; torture is frequently reported. All religious institutions were abolished in 1967; religion is outlawed; priests are regularly imprisoned. Apparently there are no private organizations independent of government or party. Economic disparities are comparatively small: all people must work one month of each year in factories or on farms, and there are no private cars. Private economic choice is minimal.

Comparatively: Albania is as free as Kampuchea, less free than Yugoslavia.

ALGERIA

Economy: socialist
Polity: socialist one-party
Population: 18,400,000

Political Rights: 6
Civil Liberties: 6
Status of Freedom: not free

An ethnic state with a potential subnationality

Political Rights. Algeria has combined military dictatorship with one-party socialist rule. Elections at both local and national levels are managed by the party; they allow no real opposition to the system, although individual representatives and specific policies may be criticized. Recent elections resulted in highly questionable percentages (over ninety-nine percent). (In some areas these results appear to have been simply fabricated.) However, the pragmatic, puritanical, military rulers are probably supported by a fairly broad consensus. *Subnationalities*: About twenty percent of the people are Berbers: revolt in their areas in the Kabylia (1963–64) suggests continuing desire to run their own affairs.

Civil Liberties. All media are government controlled; no opposition voice is allowed. Private conversation appears relatively open. Although not independent, the regular judiciary is unlikely to be capricious. There are political prisoners, and no appeal from the decisions of the special Revolutionary Courts for crimes against the state; there are reports of torture. Land reform has transformed former French plantations into collectives. Although government goals are clearly socialist, many small farms and businesses remain. Eighty percent of the people are illiterate; many are still very poor, but extremes of wealth have been reduced. Islam's continued strength provides a counterweight to governmental absolutism; there is little religious freedom beyond Islam.

Comparatively: Algeria is as free as Mauritania, freer than Iraq, less free than Morocco.

ANGOLA

Economy: noninclusive socialist	**Political Rights:** 7
Polity: socialist one-party	**Civil Liberties:** 7
Population: 6,400,000	**Status of Freedom:** not free

A transethnic heterogeneous state with major subnationalities

Political Rights. Angola is ruled by a communist-style socialist party in which military commanders may wield considerable power. The ruling party has relied heavily on Soviet equipment and Cuban troops to win the recent civil war and to stay in power. In 1977 a serious revolt within the top level of the ruling party decimated its leadership. *Subnationalities*: The party is not tribalist, but is opposed by groups relying on particular tribes or regions—especially in Cabinda, the northeast, and the south central areas. The UNITA movement among the Ovimbundu people actively controls much of the south and east of the country.

Civil Liberties. There is no constitution; the nation remains in a state of war, with power arbitrarily exercised, particularly in the countryside. The media in controlled areas are government owned and do not deviate from its line. Political imprisonment and repression of religious activity are reported. Private medical care has been abolished, as has much private property—especially in the modern sectors. Agricultural production is held down by peasant opposition to socialization.

Comparatively: Angola is as free as Vietnam, less free than Zambia.

ARGENTINA

Economy: capitalist-statist	**Political Rights:** 6
Polity: military nonparty	**Civil Liberties:** 5
Population: 26,400,000	**Status of Freedom:** not free

A relatively homogeneous population

Political Rights. Ruled today by a military junta, Argentina oscillates between democracy and authoritarianism. The military's last intervention probably had initial popular support because of the high level of both right- and left-wing terrorism, and the corrupt and ineffective regime it replaced. But the continued use of violence by the regime and its supporters to silence opposition has eroded this support. The regions are now under direct junta control. The government has only limited control over its security forces.

Civil Liberties. Private newspapers and private broadcasting stations operate; they report unfavorable events and criticize the government. Yet both self-censorship and newspaper closings are common. Censorship of media and private expression also occurs informally through the threat of terrorist attacks from radical leftist or rightist groups (with the latter apparently supported by, or associated with, elements of the military and police). The universities are closely controlled. While courts retain some independence, arbitrary arrest, torture, and execution occur. The church and trade unions continue to play a strong opposition role, although there is frequent pressure on the unions. For non-Catholics religious freedom is curtailed.

Comparatively: Argentina is as free as Chile, freer than Uruguay, less free than Brazil.

AUSTRALIA

Economy: capitalist   **Political Rights:** 1
Polity: decentralized multiparty   **Civil Liberties:** 1
Population: 14,300,000   **Status of Freedom:** free

A relatively homogeneous population with small aboriginal groups

Political Rights. Australia is a federal parliamentary democracy with strong powers retained by its component states. With equal representation from each state, the Senate provides a counterbalance to the nationally representative House of Representatives. There have been recent changes in government, with the Labour Party gaining control in 1972 only to lose it again in 1975. As shown by recent events, the British appointed Governor General retains some power in constitutional deadlocks. Trade unions (separately and through the Labour Party) and foreign investors have great economic weight. The states have separate parliaments and premiers, but appointed governors. The relative power of rural peoples and aborigines has recently been strengthened, particularly through the establishment of the new Northern Territory.

Civil Liberties. All the newspapers and most radio and television stations are privately owned. The Australian Broadcasting Commission operates government radio and television stations on a basis similar to BBC. Although Australia lacks many formal guarantees of civil liberties, the degree of protection of these liberties in the common law is similar to that in Britain and Canada. Freedom of choice in education, travel, occupation, property, and private association are perhaps as complete as anywhere in the world. Relatively low taxes enhance this freedom.

Comparatively: Australia is as free as the United Kingdom, freer than Italy.

A U S T R I A

Economy: mixed capitalist   **Political Rights:** 1
Polity: (centralized) multiparty   **Civil Liberties:** 1
Population: 7,500,000   **Status of Freedom:** free

A relatively homogeneous population

Political Rights. Austria's parliamentary system has a directly elected lower house and an upper (and less powerful) house elected by the provincial assemblies. The president is directly elected, but the chancellor (representing the majority party in parliament) is the center of political power. The two major parties have alternated control since the 1950's but the government often seeks broad consensus. The referendum is used. Provincial legislatures and governors are elective. *Subnationalities*: Fifty thousand Slovenes in the southern part of the country have been granted rights to their own schools at Yugoslav insistence.

Civil Liberties. The press in Austria is free and varied, while radio and television are under a state-owned corporation that by law is supposed to be free of political control. Its geographical position and neutral status by treaty places its media and government in a position analogous to Finland, but the Soviets have put less pressure on Austria to conform to Soviet wishes than on Finland. The rule of law is secure, and there are no political prisoners. Banks and heavy industry are largely nationalized.

Comparatively: Austria is as free as Belgium, freer than Greece.

B A H A M A S

Economy: capitalist   **Political Rights:** 1
Polity: centralized multiparty   **Civil Liberties:** 2
Population: 225,000   **Status of Freedom:** free

A relatively homogeneous population

Political Rights. The Bahamas have a parliamentary system with a largely ceremonial British Governor General. The ruling party has a large majority, but there is an opposition in parliament (receiving about forty-five percent of the vote). Most islands are administered by centrally appointed commissioners. There is a strong independence movement in Abaco Island, one of the more important islands in the group.

Civil Liberties. There are independent newspapers, but through restricting income and preventing hiring or keeping desired employees, the government has exerted pressure on the opposition press. Radio is government owned and is not completely free of government control. In other respects Bahamas' freedoms seem reasonably secure.

Comparatively: Bahamas is as free as Venezuela, freer than Grenada, less free than Barbados.

BAHRAIN

Economy: mixed capitalist-statist
Polity: traditional nonparty
Population: 280,000

Political Rights: 6
Civil Liberties: 4
Status of Freedom: partly free

The citizenry is relatively homogeneous

Political Rights. Bahrain is a traditional shaikhdom with a modernized administration. At present the legislature is dissolved, but powerful merchant and religious families place a check on royal power. There are local councils. *Subnationalities:* The primary ethnic problem has been the struggle between the Iranians who once ruled and the Arabs who rule now. This resolved, the opposition of the ruling Sunni and majority Shi'ite Muslim sects remains.

Civil Liberties. The weak press is both government and private. Radio and television are government owned. In general freedom of expression and assembly are cautiously expressed. A climate of fear does not exist. The legal and educational systems are a mixture of traditional Islamic and British. Short-term arrest is used to discourage dissent, but there are a few long-term political prisoners. In security cases involving violence fair and quick trials are delayed and torture occurs. Rights to travel, property, and religious choice are secured. There is a long record of disturbances by workers groups, although union organization is restricted. Many free social services are provided. Citizenship is very hard to obtain and there is antipathy to foreign workers (but unlike neighboring shaikhdoms most people in the country are citizens).

Comparatively: Bahrain is as free as Kuwait, freer than Saudi Arabia, less free than Turkey.

BANGLADESH

Economy: noninclusive capitalist-
    statist
Polity: centralized multiparty
Population: 85,000,000

Political Rights: 4
Civil Liberties: 4
Status of Freedom: partly free

A relatively homogeneous population with Hindu and Bihari minorities

Political Rights. Bangladesh returned to elective government in 1978. At the head of a broad coalition the incumbent military ruler received 75 percent of the vote for president against an organized opposition. Previous experience suggests some validity to opposition criticism of the process. There is presently no parliament but there are elective local positions. (Subsequent parliamentary elections in 1979 appear to raise the rating of Bangladesh.) *Subnationalities*: Fighting with minor tribal groups along the border continues; the Bihari minority suffers discrimination.

Civil Liberties. The press is private, government, and party. Official censorship was removed by the end of the year, although self-censorship remained. Radio and television are government controlled. The existence of a broad spectrum of political parties allows for the organization of dissent. There have been numerous arrests and executions following coup attempts during recent years, and torture is reported. It appeared that by the end of 1978 there were few prisoners of conscience. Evidence suggests the courts decide against the government in many cases. In spite of considerable communal antipathy, religious freedom exists. Travel is generally unrestricted; labor unions are active but do not have the right to strike.

Comparatively: Bangladesh is as free as Brazil, freer than Burma, less free than India.

BARBADOS

Economy: capitalist
Polity: centralized multiparty
Population: 250,000

Political Rights: 1
Civil Liberties: 1
Status of Freedom: free

A relatively homogeneous population

Political Rights. Barbados is governed by a parliamentary system, with a ceremonial British Governor General. Power alternates between the two major parties. Local governments are also elected.

Civil Liberties. Newspapers are private and free of government control. There are both private and government radio stations, but the government-controlled radio station also controls the only television station. There is an independent judiciary, and general freedom from arbitrary government action. In spite of both major parties relying on the support of labor, private property is fully accepted.

Comparatively: Barbados is as free as the United Kingdom, freer than Jamaica.

BELGIUM

Economy: capitalist
Polity: decentralized multiparty
Population: 9,900,000

Political Rights: 1
Civil Liberties: 1
Status of Freedom: free

A binational state

Political Rights. Belgium is a constitutional monarchy with a bi-cameral parliament. Elections lead to coalition governments, generally of the center. Linguistic divisions have produced considerable instability. *Subnationalities*: The rise of nationalism among the two major peoples—Flemish and Walloon—has led to increasing transfer of control over cultural affairs to the communal groups. However, provincial governors are appointed by the national government.

Civil Liberties. Newspapers are free and uncensored. Radio and television are government owned, but the director of each station is solely responsible for programming. The full spectrum of private rights is respected.

Comparatively: Belgium is as free as Switzerland, freer than France.

BENIN

Economy: noninclusive socialist
Polity: socialist one-party
Population: 3,400,000

Political Rights: 7
Civil Liberties: 7
Status of Freedom: not free

A transethnic heterogeneous state

Political Rights. Benin is a military dictatorship. Although theoretically a one-party socialist state, it is doubtful that party organization is very substantial. Regional and tribal loyalties may be stronger than national. Elections and parliament do not exist nationally. There are controlled local assemblies.

Civil Liberties. All media are rigidly censored; most are owned by the government. Opposition is not tolerated; criticism of the government often leads to a few days of reeducation in military camps. The rule of law is very weak. Private schools have been closed, Jehovah's Witnesses are banned, independent labor unions forbidden. Potential dissidents are not allowed to leave the country. Economically, the government's interventions have been in cash crops and internal trade, and industries have been nationalized; control over the largely subsistence and small entrepreneur economy remains incomplete.

Comparatively: Benin is as free as Congo, less free than Nigeria.

B H U T A N

Economy: preindustrial
Polity: traditional nonparty
Population: 1,300,000

Political Rights: 5
Civil Liberties: 5
Status of Freedom: partly free

An ethnic state with a significant subnationality

Political Rights. Bhutan is a hereditary monarchy in which the king rules with the aid of a council and the indirectly elected National Assembly. There are no legal political parties and the Assembly does little more than approve government actions. Villages are traditionally ruled by their own headmen, but districts are directly ruled from the center. The Buddhist hierarchy is still very important in the affairs of the country. In foreign policy and defense Bhutan is largely dependent upon India. *Subnationalities*: The main political party operates outside the country, agitating in favor of the Nepalese minority (about 250,000) and a more open system.

Civil Liberties: The primary newspaper is government owned and radio broadcasting is hardly developed. The legal structure exhibits a mixture of traditional and British forms. Traditional agriculture, crafts, and trade dominate the economy.

Comparatively: Bhutan is as free as Maldives, freer than Burma, less free than India.

B O L I V I A

Economy: noninclusive mixed
    capitalist
Polity: military nonparty
Population: 5,000,000

Political Rights: 5
Civil Liberties: 3
Status of Freedom: partly free

An ethnic state with major potential subnationalities

Political Rights. Bolivia is ruled as a military dictatorship with some party support. In 1978 a disputed presidential election was followed by two military coups. The resulting government appears more responsive to popular protest and political parties; an election is planned in 1979. Provincial and local government is controlled from the center, but there are strong labor, peasant, and religious organizations in many areas that exert quasi-governmental power. *Subnationalities*: Over sixty percent of the people are Indians speaking Aymara or Quechua; these languages have recently been given official status alongside Spanish. These peoples remain, however, more potential than active nationalities.

Civil Liberties. The press and most radio and television stations are private. Although the government sometimes interferes, and self-censorship is practiced, there is general freedom of the press. An organized private group fights human rights violations. Freedom is also restricted by the climate of violence, both governmental and non-governmental. Normal legal protections have often been denied during frequent states of siege, but it is possible to win against the government in the courts. By mid-1978 there were no known prisoners of conscience. There are now no travel restrictions. Peasant and union organizations are powerful. The people are overwhelmingly post-land-reform, subsistence agriculturists. The major mines are nationalized; the workers have a generous social welfare program, given the country's poverty.

Comparatively: Bolivia is as free as Nigeria, freer than Paraguay, less free than Colombia.

BOTSWANA

Economy: noninclusive capitalist
Polity: decentralized multiparty
Population, 750,000

Political Rights: 2
Civil Liberties: 3
Status of Freedom: free

A relatively homogeneous population

Political Rights. The republican system of Botswana combines traditional and modern principles. The assembly is elected for a fixed term and appoints the president who rules. There is also an advisory House of Chiefs. There are nine districts, led either by chiefs or elected leaders, with independent power of taxation, as well as traditional power over land and agriculture. Elections continue to be won overwhelmingly by the ruling party as they were even before independence, yet there are opposition members in parliament, and electoral processes appear reasonably fair. There is economic and political pressure from both black African and white neighbors. *Subnationalities*: The country is divided among several major tribes belonging to the Batswana people, as well as minor or refuge peoples on the margins. The latter include a few hundred comparatively wealthy white farmers.

Civil Liberties. The radio and most newspapers are government owned; however, there is no censorship, and South African media present an available alternative. Rights of assembly and expression are respected. Judicially, civil liberties appear to be guaranteed, although on the local scale the individual tribesman may have considerably less freedom.

Comparatively: Botswana is as free as Colombia, freer than Zambia, less free than Fiji.

BRAZIL

Economy: capitalist-statist   **Political Rights:** 4
Polity: decentralized multiparty   **Civil Liberties:** 4
   (military dominated)   **Status of Freedom:** partly free
Population: 115,000,000

A complex but relatively homogeneous population with many small territorial subnationalities

Political Rights. Brazil has been governed by a president, essentially elected by the military, and a popularly elected but weak assembly. Legislative elections in 1978 gave a majority to the opposition, although the opposition did not gain legislative majorities. Party organization is controlled, but the opposition party is authentic; serious opposition also exists within the ruling party itself. There are independently organized elected governments at both state and local levels, though the army has interfered a good deal at these levels in recent years. *Subnationalities*: The many small Indian groups of the interior are under both private and public pressure. Some still fight back in the face of loss of land, lives, and culture.

Civil Liberties. The media are private, except for a few broadcasting stations. The powerful press is now largely free of censorship. Leading newspapers have won censorship cases in the courts. Although political imprisonment and torture occurred in 1978, the atmosphere of terror had largely dissipated. At the end of the year the special powers of repression of the central government were officially abrogated. Private violence against criminals and suspected communists may continue outside the law. Opposition voices are regularly heard— including parliamentarians, journalists, and officials of the church. Strikes occur. There is considerable large-scale government industry, but rights to own property, to religious freedom, to travel, and education of one's choice are generally respected.

Comparatively: Brazil is as free as Mexico, freer than Uruguay, less free than Jamaica.

BULGARIA

Economy: socialist
Polity: communist one-party
Population: 8,820,000

Political Rights: 7
Civil Liberties: 7
Status of Freedom: not free

A relatively homogeneous population

Political Rights. Bulgaria is governed by its communist party, although the facade of a parallel government and independent candidates is maintained. The same man has essentially ruled over the system since 1954; elections at both national and local levels have little meaning. Both economically and politically the country is subservient to the Soviet Union. *Subnationalities*: The Muslim Turkish minority of about one million is persecuted in several ways.

Civil Liberties. All media are controlled by the government or its party branches. Citizens have few if any rights against the state. There are thousands of prisoners of conscience, many living under severe conditions. The detained may also be banished to villages, denied their occupations, or confined in psychiatric hospitals. The most common political crimes are illegally trying to leave the country, criticism of the government, and illegal contacts with foreigners.

Comparatively: Bulgaria is as free as Mongolia, less free than Hungary.

BURMA

Economy: noninclusive mixed
    socialist
Polity: socialist one-party
Population: 32,200,000

Political Rights: 7
Civil Liberties: 6
Status of Freedom: not free

An ethnic state with major territorial subnationalities

Political Rights. Burma is a one-party socialist, military dictatorship. The government's dependence on the army makes its strengths and weaknesses more those of a military dictatorship than those of a communist regime. Elections are held at both national and local levels; the only candidates likely to win are those nominated by the single party. *Subnationalities*: The government represents essentially the Burmese people that live in the heartland of the country. The Burmese are surrounded by millions of non-Burmese living in continuing disaffection or active revolt. Among the minorities in the periphery are the Karens, Shan, Kachins, Mon, and Chin.

Civil Liberties. All media are government owned, with alternative opinions expressed obliquely if at all; both domestic and foreign publications are censored. Organized dissent is forbidden; in part, this policy is explained by the almost continuous warfare the government has had to wage since independence against both rebellious subnationalities and two separate communist armies. This state of war has been augmented since the 1960's by the attempts of civilian politicians to regain power by armed force or antigovernment demonstration, as well as recent plots within the army itself. There are probably thousands of political prisoners. The regular court structure has been replaced by "people's courts." Religion is free; union activity is not; emigration is difficult. Although the eventual goal of the government is complete socialization and there are to be steady moves toward agricultural collectivization, an official announcement in 1977 temporarily reserved significant portions of the economy for private enterprise.

Comparatively: Burma is as free as Iraq, freer than Kampuchea, less free than Thailand.

B U R U N D I

Economy: noninclusive mixed
Polity: socialist one-party
      (military dominated)
Population: 4,000,000

Political Rights: 7
Civil Liberties: 7
Status of Freedom: not free

An ethnic state with a majority, nonterritorial subnationality

Political Rights. Burundi is ruled by a Supreme Revolutionary Coun- cil led by a military officer, with the assistance of the single party. There is now no elected assembly. *Subnationalities*: The rulers continue to be all from the Tutsi ethnic group (fifteen percent) that has tradi- tionally ruled; their dominance was reinforced by a massacre of Hutus (eighty-five percent) after an attempted revolt in the early 1970's.

Civil Liberties. There are both government and church newspapers, and radio is government controlled. Lack of freedom of political speech or assembly is accompanied by political imprisonment and reports of brutality. Under current conditions there is little guarantee of indi- vidual rights, particularly for the Hutu majority. In recent years Hutu have been excluded from the army, secondary schools, and the civil service. There are no independent unions. Traditional group and individual rights no doubt persist on the village level: Burundi is not a highly structured modern society. Travel is relatively unrestricted. Religion is free, education controlled. Although officially socialist, private or traditional economic forms predominate.

Comparatively: Burundi is as free as Somalia, less free than Kenya.

CAMBODIA

(See Kampuchea)

CAMEROON

Economy: noninclusive capitalist   Political Rights: 6
Polity: nationalist one-party   Civil Liberties: 6
Population: 8,000,000   Status of Freedom: not free

A transethnic heterogeneous state with a major subnationality

Political Rights. Cameroon is a one-party state ruled by the same person since independence in 1960. The government has steadily centralized power. Referendums and other elections have little meaning; voters are given no alternatives and provide ninety-nine percent majorities. Provincial governors are appointed by the central government. An attempt has been made to incorporate all elements in a government of broad consensus. *Subnationalities*: The most significant opposition has come from those opposing centralization, particularly movements supported by the country's largest ethnic group, the Bamileke (twenty-six percent). Other ethnic groups are quite small.

Civil Liberties. The media are government controlled. Although newspapers are occasionally outspoken, they must run the hurdles of a double censorship. Freedom of speech, assembly, and union organization are limited, while freedom of occupation, education, and property are respected. There are many prisoners of conscience, often ill-treated and detained without trial. Allegations have been made of torture. Internal travel and religious choice are relatively free; foreign travel may be difficult. The government has supported land reform; although still relatively short on capital, private enterprise is encouraged wherever possible.

Comparatively: Cameroon is as free as Gabon, freer than Niger, less free than Nigeria.

CANADA

Economy: capitalist   Political Rights: 1
Polity: decentralized multiparty   Civil Liberties: 1
Population: 23,600,000   Status of Freedom: free

A binational state

Political Rights. Canada is a parliamentary democracy with alternation of rule between leading parties. The provinces have their own democratic institutions with a higher degree of autonomy than the

American states. *Subnationalities*: In an attempt to prevent the breakup of Canada, the government has moved toward granting French linguistic equality; French has become the official language in Quebec. In addition, Quebec has been allowed to opt out of some national programs and maintains its own representatives abroad.

Civil Liberties. The media are free, although there is a government-related radio and television network. The full range of civil liberties is generally respected. In Quebec rights to choose education and language for many purposes have been infringed. There has been evidence of the invasion of privacy by Canadian security forces in recent years, much as in the United States. Many judicial and legal structures have been borrowed from the United Kingdom or the United States, with consequent advantages and disadvantages.

Comparatively: Canada is as free as the United States of America, freer than Italy.

CAPE VERDE ISLANDS

Economy: noninclusive socialist
Polity: socialist one-party
Population: 330,000

Political Rights: 6
Civil Liberties: 6
Status of Freedom: not free

A relatively homogeneous state

Political Rights. The party ruling the Cape Verde Islands also rules Guinea-Bissau. Established and originally led by Cape Verdeans, the party achieved its major preindependence success on the mainland. Its secretary-general is president of the Cape Verde Islands, and a key political issue is how soon the two states will merge. Only this party has taken part in recent elections; other parties are banned.

Civil Liberties. Neither private nor government media may criticize the government. Prisoners of conscience are frequently detained, often without trial; rights to organized opposition, assembly, or political expression are not respected. For its region Cape Verde's seventy-five percent literacy is very high. The Islands' plantation agriculture has been largely nationalized, but endemic unemployment continues to lead to emigration. Religion is relatively free, although under political pressure; labor unions are government controlled.

Comparatively: Cape Verde Islands is as free as Tanzania, freer than Ethiopia, less free than Seychelles.

CENTRAL AFRICAN EMPIRE

Economy: noninclusive capitalist   **Political Rights:** 7
Polity: nationalist one-party   **Civil Liberties:** 7
Population: 1,900,000   **Status of Freedom:** not free

A transethnic heterogeneous state

Political Rights. The Central African Empire is ruled as a military dictatorship, although it has incorporated the single party of the previous regime in its political structure. There are at present no representative institutions. Prefects are appointed by the central government in the French style. The country is heavily dependent on French economic and military aid.

Civil Liberties. All media are government or party controlled; there is no legal opposition voice. Freedom of political expression is denied even for the use of the mails. Brutal treatment of prisoners and arbitrary arrest have been common features of the administration. Political trial procedures offer the defendant no protection. Independent unions are not allowed. Since there is no state ideology religious freedom is generally respected, as are other personal and economic freedoms.

Comparatively: Central African Empire is as free as Congo, less free than Cameroon.

CHAD

Economy: noninclusive capitalist   **Political Rights:** 6
Polity: military nonparty   **Civil Liberties:** 6
Population: 4,300,000   **Status of Freedom:** not free

An ethnic state with a major territorial subnationality

Political Rights. Chad is a military dictatorship. Provincial governors are centrally appointed. *Subnationalities*: Ethnic struggle pits the ruling southern Negroes (principally the Christian and animist Sara tribe) against a variety of northern Muslim groups (principally nomadic Arabs). As a gesture of conciliation in 1978 a former Muslim rebel was appointed premier. (In early 1979 Muslims appeared to further increase their power in government.) The government of Chad has remained in power with French military help, while the rebels have received Libyan support.

Civil Liberties. The media are controlled by the government. Anyone writing an article thought to damage Chad's relations with its neighbors may be imprisoned. There are many political prisoners; most have been directly involved in the civil war. Religious freedom is respected. Not an ideological state, traditional law is still influential.

Comparatively: Chad is as free as Saudi Arabia, freer than Central African Empire, less free than Sudan.

CHILE

Economy: capitalist
Polity: military nonparty
Population: 11,000,000

Political Rights: 6
Civil Liberties: 5
Status of Freedom: not free

A relatively homogeneous population

Political Rights. Chile is a military dictatorship. However, a plebiscite confirming government policy held at the beginning of the year allowed an opposition vote of twenty percent. All power is concentrated at the center, and there are no elective positions. An appointive Council of State is supposed to represent most sectors of society.

Civil Liberties. All media have both public and private outlets; newspapers are primarily private. The media, although censored and often threatened with closure, express a considerable range of opinion, occasionally including direct criticism of government policy. While one can win against the government in the courts, there have in the last few years been hundreds of political executions and "disappearances." Many persons have been imprisoned, and torture has been commonly employed. Recently there has been less arbitrary arrest and ill-treatment. Rights to private property have been greatly strengthened both in the country and city, with government control of the economy now being limited to copper and petroleum.

Comparatively: Chile is as free as Yugoslavia, freer than Czechoslovakia, less free than Bolivia.

CHINA (Mainland)

Economy: socialist
Polity: communist one-party
Population: 930,000,000

Political Rights: 6
Civil Liberties: 6
Status of Freedom: not free

An ethnic state with peripheral subnationalities

Political Rights. China is ruled as a one-party communist state. At the top is the collective leadership of the Politburo. A National Peoples Congress is indirectly elected within party guidelines. At its nine-day meeting in 1978 it approved a ten-year plan, adopted a new constitution, and appointed a new State Council. Actual power is diffused among several factions in both the party and the army. *Subnationalities*: The several subnationalities on the periphery, such as the Tibetans, Uighurs, or Mongols, are allowed some separate cultural life. Amounting to not more than five percent of the population, non-Chinese ethnic groups have tended to be diluted and obscured by Chinese settlement or Sinification.

Civil Liberties. The media have been rigidly controlled. Still, a limited underground literature has developed. The new constitution defines civil liberties more clearly, placing an emphasis on legal procedures that has been lacking until recently. This seems to herald a movement toward socialist legality on the Soviet model. Nevertheless, all court cases are explicitly decided in political terms. There remain hundreds of thousands or millions of political prisoners or "exiles," including those in labor-reform camps. Although the numbers may have been reduced, political executions were still reported in 1978. Thirty million Chinese may have been systematically discriminated against because of "bad class background"; in 1978 these disabilities started to be dismantled. Poster campaigns, demonstrations, and evidence of private conversation show that pervasive factionalism has allowed elements of freedom and consensus into the system, especially at the lowest levels. Economic, educational, and cultural freedoms have recently become significant.

Comparatively: China (Mainland) is as free as Tanzania, freer than Mongolia, less free than Korea (South).

C H I N A   (Taiwan)

Economy: capitalist-statist	**Political Rights:** 5
Polity: centralized dominant-party	**Civil Liberties:** 5
	Status of Freedom: partly free
Population: 16,900,000	

A quasi-ethnic state with a majority nonterritorial subnationality

Political Rights. Taiwan is ruled by a single party organized according to a communist model (although anticommunist ideologically). There is a parliament to which representatives from Taiwan are elected in fairly free elections; a few members oppose the regime but no real opposition party is tolerated. However, most parliamentarians continue to be persons elected in 1947 as representatives of districts in China where elections could not be held subsequently. The indirect presidential election is *pro forma*, but the election of a Taiwanese as vice president in 1978 was significant. Promised elections scheduled for December were cancelled and accompanying liberalizations were reversed after U.S. recognition of Peking. Important local and regional positions are elective, including those in the provincial assembly which are held by Taiwanese. *Subnationalities*: The people are eighty-six percent native Taiwanese (speaking two Chinese dialects), and an opposition movement to transfer control from the mainland immigrants to the Taiwanese has been repressed. Since nearly all Taiwanese are also Chinese, it is difficult to know the extent to which non-Taiwanese oppression is felt.

Civil Liberties. The media include government or party organs, but are mostly in private hands. Newspapers and magazines are subject to occasional censorship or suspension, and practice self-censorship. A major opposition paper was forced to sell out to a government supporter in 1978. The year saw a number of new publications and new suppressions; in late 1978 major papers began to regularly and fairly present opposition views; after U.S. recognition of the People's Republic, stricter controls on domestic and foreign publications were imposed. Television remained one-sided. Rights to assembly are limited. There are several hundred political prisoners, but there has been only one recent political execution and reports of torture are now rare. Union activity is restricted; strikes are forbidden. Private rights to property, education, and religion are generally respected; there is no right to travel to the mainland.

Comparatively: China (Taiwan) is as free as Singapore, freer than China (Mainland), less free than Malaysia.

COLOMBIA

Economy: capitalist
Polity: centralized multiparty
Population: 25,800,000

Political Rights: 2
Civil Liberties: 3
Status of Freedom: free

A relatively homogeneous population with scattered minorities

Political Rights. Colombia is a constitutional democracy. The president is directly elected, as are both houses of the legislature. Although campaigns are accompanied by both violence and apathy, there is little reason to believe they are fraudulent. Members of the two principal parties are included in the government and the list of departmental governors. Both of the leading parties have well defined factions. There is one major third party; among the minor parties several are involved in revolutionary activity. The provinces are directly administered by the national government.

Civil Liberties. The press is private, with some papers under party control, and quite free. Radio and television include both government and private stations. Personal rights are generally respected; courts are relatively strong and independent. Riots and guerrilla activity have led to periodic states of siege in which these rights are limited. Assemblies are often banned from fear of riots. In these conditions the security forces have violently infringed personal rights, especially those of peasants or Amerindians in rural areas. Although many persons are rounded up in antiguerrilla or antiterrorist campaigns, people are not imprisoned simply for their nonviolent expression of political opinion. Torture occurs. The government encourages private enterprise where possible.

Comparatively: Colombia is as free as Turkey, freer than Ecuador, less free than Venezuela.

COMORO ISLANDS

Economy: noninclusive capitalist   **Political Rights:** 5
Polity: decentralized nonparty   **Civil Liberties:** 4
Population: 300,000   **Status of Freedom:** partly free

A relatively homogeneous population

Political Rights. The Comoran government came to power by armed attack in 1978. Subsequently, the voters approved a new constitution and president. The majority probably support the new system—the previous ruler had become very oppressive and the new president was prime minister in the recent past. However, the ninety-nine plus percentages in both elections make them unacceptable tests of informed popular choice. (Late 1978 contested parliamentary elections will raise the Survey rating.) The new constitution grants each island an elected governor and council. (The island of Mayotte is formally a part of the Comoros, but it has chosen to be a French dependency.)

Civil Liberties. Radio is government owned; there is no press. Discussion appears to be free. There are political prisoners resulting from the recent coup. Religious freedom has been restored along with most private civil liberties. The poor population depends almost entirely on subsistence agriculture and emigration.

Comparatively: Comoro Islands appears to be as free as Kenya, freer than Seychelles, less free than Mauritius.

CONGO

Economy: noninclusive mixed   **Political Rights:** 7
Polity: socialist one-party   **Civil Liberties:** 7
     (military dominated)   **Status of Freedom:** not free
Population: 1,500,000

A formally transethnic heterogeneous state

Political Rights. Congo is ruled as a one-party military dictatorship. After the assassination of the president a ruling military committee suppressed the previous constitution, including the assembly and regional government. *Subnationalities*: Historically the country was established out of a maze of ethnic groups, without the domination of some by others. However, the army that now rules is said to come from tribes with not more than fifteen percent of the population.

Civil Liberties. The news media are heavily censored. Executions and imprisonment of political opponents are common; trials exhibit little interest in justice. Only one union is allowed; it is not allowed to strike. Religious groups are limited. At the local and small entrepreneur level private property is generally respected; many larger industries have been nationalized.

Comparatively: Congo is as free as Benin, less free than Cameroon.

COSTA RICA

Economy: capitalist
Polity: centralized multiparty
Population: 2,100,000

Political Rights: 1
Civil Liberties: 1
Status of Freedom: free

A relatively homogeneous population

Political Rights. A parliamentary democracy, Costa Rica has a directly elected president and several important parties. This structure is supplemented by an independent tribunal for the overseeing of elections. Elections are fair; in 1978 they brought the opposition to power. Provinces are under the direction of the central government.

Civil Liberties. The media are notably free, private, and varied; they serve a society ninety percent literate. The courts are fair, and private rights, such as those to movement, occupation, education, religion, and union organization are respected.

Comparatively: Costa Rica is as free as Ireland, freer than Colombia.

CUBA

Economy: socialist
Polity: communist one-party
Population: 9,700,000

Political Rights: 6
Civil Liberties: 6
Status of Freedom: not free

A complex but relatively homogeneous population

Political Rights. Cuba is a one-party communist state on the Soviet model. Real power lies, however, more in the person of Fidel Castro and in the Russian leaders upon whom he depends than is the case in other noncontiguous states adopting this model. Popular election at the municipal level has recently been introduced. Provincial and national assemblies are elected by municipalities but can be recalled by popular vote. The whole system is, however, largely a show: Political opponents are excluded from nomination by law, many others are simply disqualified by party fiat; no debate is allowed on issues; and once elected there is no evidence the assemblies oppose party decisions.

Civil Liberties. The media are state controlled and publish only as the state directs. In 1978 the government began to release its thousands of political prisoners, but mostly into exile. Torture has been reported only in the past, and hundreds who have refused to recant are held in difficult conditions. There are hundreds of thousands of others who are formally discriminated against as opponents of the system. There appears to be some freedom to criticize informally. Freedom to choose work, education, or residence is greatly restricted; the practice of religion is discouraged by the government.

Comparatively: Cuba is as free as Tanzania, freer than Czechoslovakia, less free than Mexico.

CYPRUS

Economy: capitalist
Polity: decentralized multiparty
Population: 650,000

Political Rights: 3
Civil Liberties: 4
Status of Freedom: partly free

A binational state (no central government)

Political Rights. At present Cyprus is one state only in theory. Both the Greek and the Turkish sectors are parliamentary democracies, although the Turkish sector is in effect a protectorate of Turkey. Elections have seemed reasonably fair in both sectors, but in the violent atmosphere pressure has been applied to all nonconforming groups or individuals. *Nationalities*: Greeks and Turks now live almost exclusively in their own sectors. Eighty percent of the population is Greek, sixty percent of the land is in the Greek sector.

Civil Liberties. The newspapers are free and varied in both sectors, with the constraints mentioned above. Radio and television are under the respective governments or semigovernmental bodies. The usual rights of free peoples are respected in each sector, including occupation, labor organization, and religion. Because of communal strife and invasion, property has often been taken from members of one group by force (or abandoned from fear of force) and given to the other. Under these conditions rights to choose one's sector of residence or to travel between sectors are denied.

Comparatively: Cyprus is as free as Malaysia, freer than Syria, less free than Turkey.

CZECHOSLOVAKIA

Economy: socialist
Polity: communist one-party
Population: 15,200,000

Political Rights: 7
Civil Liberties: 6
Status of Freedom: not free

A binational state

Political Rights. Czechoslovakia is a Soviet-style one-party communist state, reinforced by the presence of Soviet troops. Elections are noncompetitive and there is essentially no legislative debate. *Subnationalities*: The division of the state into separate Czech and Slovak socialist republics has only slight meaning since the Czechoslovak Communist Party continues to run the country (under the guidance of the Soviet Communist Party). Although less numerous and poorer than the Czech people, the Slovaks are probably granted their rightful share of power within this framework.

Civil Liberties. Media are government or party owned and rigidly censored. However, some private and literary expression occurs that is relatively free. Rights to travel, occupation, and private property are restricted. Heavy pressures are placed on religious activities, especially through holding ministerial incomes at a very low level and the curtailing of religious education. There are a number of political prisoners; exclusion of individuals from their chosen occupation is a more common sanction. The beating of political suspects is common. Those accused of political crimes are invariably convicted.

Comparatively: Czechoslovakia is as free as Rumania, freer than Bulgaria, less free than Poland.

DENMARK

Economy: mixed capitalist
Polity: centralized multiparty
Population: 5,100,000

Political Rights: 1
Civil Liberties: 1
Status of Freedom: free

A relatively homogeneous population

Political Rights. Denmark is a constitutional monarchy with a unicameral parliament. Elections are fair. Since a wide variety of parties achieve success, resulting governments are based on coalitions. Districts have governors appointed from the center and elected councils; local officials are under local control.

Civil Liberties. The press is free (and more conservative politically than the electorate). Radio and television are government owned but relatively free. All other rights are guaranteed, although the very high tax level constitutes more than usual constraint on private property in a capitalist state. Religion is free but state supported.

Comparatively: Denmark is as free as Norway, freer than Finland.

DJIBOUTI

Economy: noninclusive capitalist	**Political Rights:** 3
Polity: centralized multiparty	**Civil Liberties:** 4
Population: 115,000	**Status of Freedom:** free

Independence led initially to a Somali majority ruling over a territorial Afar minority

Political Rights. Djibouti is a parliamentary democracy under French protection. In the elections of 1977, only one list of parliamentary candidates was presented, a list dominated by the majority Somali people. The opposition (Afar) party encouraged the casting of blank ballots. Resulting governments have included representatives of all political parties and ethnic groups and appear to be broadly representative.

Civil Liberties. Law is based on French codes and modified overseas French practice. The media are mostly government owned and apparently apolitical. There is no censorship. Continuing violence between Somali and Afar has led to many arrests, accusations of police brutality, and the banning of a radical Afar party. Not all of those arrested have been violent.

Comparatively: Djibouti is as free as Guatemala, freer than Somalia, less free than Israel.

DOMINICA

Economy: capitalist	**Political Rights:** 2
Polity: centralized multiparty	**Civil Liberties:** 3
Population: 75,000	**Status of Freedom:** free

A relatively homogeneous population with a minority enclave

Political Rights. Dominica is a parliamentary democracy with competing political parties. The ruling party has, however, been in for several years and questions have been raised over electoral and campaign fairness. The rights of the native Caribs are said not to be fully respected.

Civil Liberties. Press is private and the radio public. Pressures against the press are said to exist although it is generally free and critical. Law and order legislation and practice has been strict in the past, but there is a rule of law and no cases of simple political imprisonment.

Comparatively: Dominica is as free as Colombia, freer than Guyana, less free than Barbados.

DOMINICAN REPUBLIC

Economy: capitalist
Polity: centralized multiparty
Population: 5,100,000

Political Rights: 2
Civil Liberties: 2
Status of Freedom: free

A complex but relatively homogeneous population

Political Rights. The Dominican Republic is a presidential democracy on the American model. Fairly contested elections in 1978 were won by the opposition. The ensuing regime has greatly reduced military influence. Provinces are under national control, municipalities under local.

Civil Liberties. The media are privately owned and free. Public expression is generally free; the spokesmen of a wide range of parties openly express their opinions. The communist party was recently legalized, but in some rural areas opposition meetings have been harassed. In the recent past guerrilla activity has led to government violence in which rights have not been respected. Torture and beatings in the prison system and semigovernmental death squads have been reported. However, such events have not happened recently. There are few, if any, prisoners of conscience. Labor unions operate under constraint.

Comparatively: Dominican Republic is as free as Italy, freer than Guatemala, less free than Barbados.

ECUADOR

Economy: noninclusive capitalist
Polity: military nonparty
Population: 7,800,000

Political Rights: 5
Civil Liberties: 4
Status of Freedom: partly free

An ethnic state with a potential subnationality

Political Rights. Ecuador is governed by a military junta temporarily accepted by a number of the political parties. The legislature has been dissolved for many years, and the provinces are under military governors. Multiparty elections in 1978 produced no clear victor;

a run-off will be held in 1979. There were limited restraints on candidacy. *Subnationalities*: Perhaps forty percent of the population is Indian and many of these speak Quechua. However, this population does not at present form a conscious subnationality in a distinctive homeland.

Civil Liberties. Newspapers are under private or party control and quite outspoken, although there is some self-censorship. Radio and television are mostly under private control. Although often repressed, unions remain powerful and independent. Leaders of a broad range of parties continue their publications and indoor meetings; they hold outdoor rallies, though not in the streets. Such freedoms are best guaranteed in the cities and may at times be inconsistently denied. There are few if any prisoners of conscience. The court system is not strongly independent, and imprisonment for belief can be expected to recur. Accusations of torture have been made in the past. Although there are state firms, particularly in major industries, Ecuador is essentially a capitalist and traditionalist state.

Comparatively: Ecuador is as free as Peru, freer than Argentina, less free than Mexico.

E G Y P T

Economy: mixed socialist
Polity: centralized dominant-
          party
Population: 39,600,000

Political Rights: 5
Civil Liberties: 5
Status of Freedom: partly free

A relatively homogeneous population with a communal religious minority

Political Rights. Egypt is a controlled democracy. Within limits political parties may organize: communist and religious extremist parties are forbidden, and pressure forced the dissolution of an important moderate party that emerged during the year. The recent presidential election was an uncontested referendum, but parliamentary elections were contested by competing lists. In 1977 parliament expelled a member for criticizing the president, with the vote 281 to 28; again a level of contest unknown in one-party states. Yet a 1978 referendum to allow greater suppression of critics received an unlikely ninety-eight percent majority. *Subnationalities*: Perhaps two million Coptic Christians live a distinct communal life.

Civil Liberties. The Egyptian press is mostly government owned. After a short period of relative freedom, 1978 saw the suppression of a major opposition paper and increasing pressure on all papers. Radio and television are under government control. A fairly broad range of literary publications has recently developed. There is limited freedom of assembly. Severe riot laws have led to large-scale imprisonment, but the independence of the courts has been strengthened recently. Many prisoners of conscience have been arrested in the last few years; few were still in detention at the end of 1978. In both agriculture and industry considerable diversity and choice exists, although within a loose socialist framework. Unions have developed some independence of the government. Travel and other private rights are generally free.

Comparatively: Egypt is as free as Panama, freer than Saudi Arabia, less free than Cyprus.

EL SALVADOR

Economy: capitalist
Polity: centralized multiparty
    (military dominated)
Population: 4,400,000

Political Rights: 5
Civil Liberties: 5
Status of Freedom: partly free

A relatively homogeneous population

Political Rights. Formally, El Salvador is a constitutional democracy on the American model, with a directly elected president. Although there are several parties, in the 1970's the government has blatantly interfered in elections; the boycott by the major opposition party of the 1978 elections seemed justified. As a result there is now no effective parliamentary opposition. In rural areas a bloody struggle has developed between pro- and anti-government peasant organizations.

Civil Liberties. Newspapers and radio are largely in private hands. Except during a state of siege, the media have been free of formal censorship, but under strong pressures. There are major opposition papers. The rule of law weakens with distance from the capital; government detention and probable murder of opponents has affected all groups. Political imprisonment and torture occur. Violence accompanying election disturbances and rural guerrilla war reduces the security of law. Right-wing terror against peasants, priests, and labor leaders reduces effective civil liberties. Although still a heavily agricultural country, rural people are to a large extent involved in the wage and market economy.

Comparatively: El Salvador is as free as Maldives, freer than Haiti, less free than Guatemala.

EQUATORIAL GUINEA

Economy: noninclusive capitalist-   Political Rights: 7
statist   Civil Liberties: 7
Polity: socialist one-party   Status of Freedom: not free
Population: 300,000

An ethnic state with a territorial minority

Political Rights. Equatorial Guinea is a dictatorship with control organized along one-party lines. By the end of 1977 this ostensibly Marxist regime was backed by Cuban, Russian, and Chinese advisors. Before his usurpation of power the dictator was elected president in the late 1960's. *Subnationalities*: Regional autonomy has been abolished, further reducing the self-determination of the island Bubi people vis-à-vis the ruling Fang.

Civil Liberties. The media are very weak and largely government owned. There is no freedom of speech or press; judges serve at the whim of the president. Executions, massacres, imprisonment, torture, and forced labor are common, leading perhaps one-third of the population to flee the country. The main established religion, Catholicism, has been prohibited. The country is to a considerable extent dependent on plantation agriculture.

Comparatively: Equatorial Guinea is as free as Uganda, less free than Gabon.

ETHIOPIA

Economy: noninclusive mixed   Political Rights: 7
Polity: military nonparty   Civil Liberties: 7
Population: 30,000,000   Status of Freedom: not free

An ethnic state with major territorial subnationalities

Political Rights. Ethiopia is ruled by a military committee (the Dergue) that has successively slaughtered the leaders of the *ancien régime*, and then many of its own leaders. Several "parties" have been formed, but they are more accurately described as revolutionary factions with rapidly shifting, leftist ideologies. Popular control in the villages may be significant. By the end of 1978 the government had succeeded with the aid of Cuban and other communist forces in bringing most of the country under control of the central government.

Subnationalities: The heartland of Ethiopia is occupied by the traditionally dominant Amhara and acculturated portions of the diffuse Galla people. In the late nineteenth century Ethiopian rulers united what had been warring fragments of a former empire in the heartland, and proceeded to incorporate some entirely new areas. At this time the Somali of the south came under Ethiopian rule; Eritrea was incorporated as the result of a UN decision in 1952. Today Ethiopia is crosscut by linguistic and religious divisions: most important is separatism due to historic allegiances to ancient provinces (especially Tigre), to different experiences (Eritrea), and to the population of a foreign nation (Somalia).

Civil Liberties. Personal rights as we know them are unprotected under conditions of despotism and anarchy. Political imprisonment, forced confession, execution, and torture are common—by the government, its supporters, and, no doubt, some of its opponents. Many thousands have been killed aside from those dying in civil war. What independence there was under the Ethiopian monarchy (of churches, the media, and unions) has been largely lost, but lack of centralized control has led to some pluralistic freedom in expression and to increased local control, benefits supported in some degree by the land reform that the revolution has accomplished. The words and actions of the regime indicate little if any respect for private rights in property.

Comparatively: Ethiopia is as free as Kampuchea, less free than Sudan.

F I J I

Economy: noninclusive capitalist
Polity: centralized multiparty
Population: 600,000

Political Rights: 2
Civil Liberties: 2
Status of Freedom: free

A binational state

Political Rights. Fiji has a complex political structure designed to protect the interests of both the original Fiji people and the Indian people, who now form a slight majority. The Lower House is directly elected on the basis of both communal and national rolls. The Upper House is indirectly elected by a variety of electors (including the council of chiefs, the prime minister, and the opposition leader). Local government is organized both by the central government and by a Fijian administration headed by the council of chiefs. In 1977 the opposition won its first election, but was unable to hold together a majority that could rule. This inability led to its decisive defeat in a subsequent election later in the year.

Civil Liberties. The press is free and private, but radio is under government control. The full protection of the rule of law is supplemented by an ombudsman to investigate complaints against the government. Right to property is limited by special rights of inalienability that are granted to the Fijians and cover most of the country. The nation may be about evenly divided between a subsistence economy based on agriculture and fishing and a modern market economy.

Comparatively: Fiji is as free as Gambia, freer than Tonga, less free than New Zealand.

FINLAND

Economy: mixed capitalist
Polity: centralized multiparty
Population: 4,800,000

Political Rights: 2
Civil Liberties: 2
Status of Freedom: free

An ethnic state with a small territorial subnationality

Political Rights. Finland has a parliamentary system with a strong, directly elected president. Since there are a large number of relatively strong parties, government is almost always by coalition. Elections have resulted in shifts in coalition membership. Soviet pressure has influenced the maintenance of the current president in office for over twenty years; by treaty foreign policy cannot be anti-Soviet. The provinces have centrally appointed governors. *Subnationalities*: The rural Swedish minority (seven percent) has its own political party and strong cultural ties to Sweden. The Swedish-speaking Åland Islands have local autonomy and other special rights.

Civil Liberties. The press is private. Most of the radio service is government controlled, but there is an important commercial television station. Discussion in the media is controlled by a political consensus that criticisms of the Soviet Union should be highly circumspect. Those who cross the line are often admonished by the government to practice self-censorship. There is a complete rule of law.

Comparatively: Finland is as free as Greece, freer than Turkey, less free than Sweden.

FRANCE

Economy: capitalist
Polity: centralized multiparty
Population: 53,400,000

Political Rights: 1
Civil Liberties: 2
Status of Freedom: free

An ethnic state with major territorial subnationalities

Political Rights. France is a parliamentary democracy. However, the directly elected president is more powerful than the premier and assembly. There is also a constitutional council that oversees elections and passes on the constitutionality of assembly or executive actions on the model of the United States Supreme Court. The multiparty system ensures that governments are generally coalitions. *Subnationalities*: Territorial subnationalities continue to have few rights as ethnic units and have little power under a rigidly centralized provincial administration. However, the recent election of a Paris mayor for the first time in a century and hesitant steps toward regionalization has slightly improved the situation. At present the Alsatian minority seems well satisfied, but there is a demand for greater autonomy among many Bretons, Corsicans, and Basques.

Civil Liberties. The French press is free, although often party-related. The news agency is private; radio and television are divided among a variety of theoretically independent companies under indirect government control. In spite of recent changes there is still an authoritarian attitude in government-citizen relations, publications may be banned at the behest of foreign governments, and arrest without explanation still occurs, particularly of members of subnationalities. Among other nationalistic restrictions is that forbidding Bretons the use of the Breton language in family or given names. France is, of course, under the rule of law, and rights to occupation, residence, religion, and property are secured. Nevertheless, both through extensive social programs and the creation of state enterprises France is quite far from a pure capitalist form.

Comparatively: France is as free as Germany (West), freer than Spain, less free than the United Kingdom.

G A B O N

Economy: noninclusive capitalist
Polity: nationalist one-party
Population: 535,000

Political Rights: 6
Civil Liberties: 6
Status of Freedom: not free

A transethnic heterogeneous state

Political Rights. Gabon is a moderate dictatorship operating in the guise of a one-party state, with noncompetitive elections characteristic of this form. Candidates must be party approved. Major cities have elected local governments; provinces are administered from the center.

Civil Liberties. All media are government controlled, and no legitimate opposition voices are raised. There is no right of political assembly, and political opponents may be imprisoned. Only one labor union is sanctioned. The authoritarian government generally does not care to interfere in private lives, and respects religious freedom and private property.

Comparatively: Gabon is as free as Jordan, freer than Angola, less free than Ghana.

GAMBIA

Economy: noninclusive capitalist
Polity: centralized multiparty
Population: 600,000

Political Rights: 2
Civil Liberties: 2
Status of Freedom: free

A transethnic heterogeneous state

Political Rights. There appears to be a fully functioning parliamentary democracy, although the same party and leader have been in power since independence in 1965. In the last election (1977) the ruling party won twenty-five seats and the opposition parties seven, an increasing but still very small share. Yet there is no evidence of serious irregularities. There is local, mostly traditional, autonomy, but not regional self-rule. (The maintenance of the system may be partly explained by the small size of the government and the lack of an army.)

Civil Liberties. The private and public newspapers and radio stations provide generally free media. An independent judiciary maintains the rule of law. Labor unions are strong and independent. The agricultural economy is largely dependent on peanuts, but remains traditionally organized. The illiteracy rate is very high.

Comparatively: Gambia is as free as Papua New Guinea, freer than Senegal, less free than Barbados.

GERMANY, EAST

Economy: socialist
Polity: communist one-party
Population: 16,700,000

Political Rights: 7
Civil Liberties: 6
Status of Freedom: not free

A relatively homogeneous population

Political Rights. East Germany is a one-party communist dictatorship. Elections allow slight choice; no competition is allowed that involves policy questions. In addition, the presence of Soviet troops and direction from the Communist Party of the Soviet Union significantly reduces the sovereignty (or group freedom) of the East Germans.

Civil Liberties. Media are government owned and controlled. Dissidents are repressed by imprisonment and exclusion; the publication of opposing views is forbidden. Among the thousands of political prisoners, the most common offense is trying to leave the country illegally (or in some cases even seeking permission to leave), or propaganda against the state. Political reeducation may be a condition of release. The average person is not allowed freedom of occupation or residence. Once defined as an enemy of the state, a person may be barred from his occupation and his children denied higher education. Particularly revealing has been the use of the "buying out scheme" by which West Germany has been able to obtain the release of prisoners in the East through cash payments and delivering goods such as bananas and coffee. There is considerable religious freedom, with the Catholic and Protestant hierarchies possessing some independence. Freedom also exists within the family.

Comparatively: Germany (East) is as free as Rumania, less free than Poland.

GERMANY, WEST

Economy: capitalist
Polity: decentralized multiparty
Population: 61,300,000

Political Rights: 1
Civil Liberties: 2
Status of Freedom: free

A relatively homogeneous population

Political Rights. West Germany is a parliamentary democracy with an indirectly elected and largely ceremonial president. Both major parties have ruled since the war. The weak Senate is elected by the assemblies of the constituent states and loyally defends states' rights. Successive national governments have been based on changing party balances in the powerful lower house. The states have their own elected assemblies; they control education, internal security, and culture.

Civil Liberties. The papers are independent and free, with little governmental interference by European standards. Radio and television are organized in public corporations under direction of the state governments. Generally the rule of law has been carefully observed, and the full spectrum of private freedoms is available. Recently jobs have been denied to many with radical leftist connections; terrorist activities have led to tighter security regulations, invasions of privacy, and less acceptance of nonconformity. Arrests have been made for handling or producing inflammatory literature, or for calling in question the fairness of the courts. Government participation in the economy is largely regulatory; in addition, complex social programs and worker participation in management have limited certain private freedoms while possibly expanding others.

Comparatively: Germany (West) is as free as France, freer than Italy, less free than the United States of America.

GHANA

Economy: capitalist-statist   **Political Rights:** 5
Polity: military nonparty   **Civil Liberties:**   4
Population: 10,900,000   **Status of Freedom**: partly free

A transethnic heterogeneous state with subnationalities

Political Rights. While Ghana is currently ruled by a moderate military junta, return to civilian democracy is planned for 1979. A considerable degree of consensus appears to underlie political actions; when this broke down in mid-1978, the leader of the junta was replaced. On the local level traditional sources of power are still significant. The first district council elections in twenty-six years were held in 1978.

Subnationalities: The country is composed of a variety of peoples, with those in the south most self-conscious. The latter are the descendants of a number of traditional kingdoms, of which the Ashanti was the most important. A north-south, Muslim-Christian opposition exists but is weakly developed, because of the economic and numerical weakness and the incomplete hold of Islam in the north. In the south and center of the country a sense of Akan identity is developing among the Ashanti, Fanti, and others; since they include forty-five percent of the people, this amounts to strengthening the ethnic core of the nation. The leaders of the one million Ewe in the southeast (a people divided between Ghana and Togo) have on occasion asked for separation or enhanced self-determination.

Civil Liberties. The critical press is both government and private; there is a degree of autonomy to the government-owned radio and television systems. Journalists have continually struggled against censorship or closures; in late 1978 they were winning. Private opinion is freely expressed on most matters, and freedom of assembly has been honored in the latter part of the year. In 1978 most if not all prisoners of conscience were released and exiles asked to return. Private businesses and independent organizations such as churches and labor unions thrive. There has been a great deal of government control in some areas—especially in cocoa production, on which the economy depends, and in modern capital-intensive industry. Like Senegal, Ghana has a relatively highly developed industry and its agriculture is dependent on world markets.

Comparatively: Ghana is as free as Peru, freer than Togo, less free than Gambia.

GREECE

Economy: capitalist
Polity: centralized multiparty
Population: 9,300,000

Political Rights: 2
Civil Liberties: 2
Status of Freedom: free

A relatively homogeneous state

Political Rights. Greece is a parliamentary democracy with a theoretically strong, but indirectly elected, president The stabilization of free institutions is proceeding rapidly: recent elections have been competitive and open to a wide spectrum of parties. Provincial administration is centrally controlled; there is local self-government.

Civil Liberties. Newspapers are private and the judiciary is independent. Because of the recent revolutionary situation all views are not freely expressed (a situation similar to that in post-fascist Portugal). One can be imprisoned for insulting the authorities. Private rights are respected.

Comparatively: Greece is as free as India, freer than Turkey, less free than France.

GRENADA

Economy: capitalist
Polity: centralized multiparty
Population: 100,000

Political Rights: 2
Civil Liberties: 3
Status of Freedom: free

A relatively homogeneous population

Political Rights. Grenada is ruled as a parliamentary democracy within the British Commonwealth. In recent elections the opposition significantly increased its power; the electoral process seemed to function acceptably. (In early 1979 the opposition came to power through a coup.)

Civil Liberties. Newspapers are largely private, but radio is government controlled. In the recent past, pressures have been brought against the press, magistrates have been dismissed for opposing the government, and a progovernment "goon squad" has been allowed to beat up and otherwise terrorize the opposition. Today the judiciary seems relatively independent; the use of violence against opponents continues sporadically.

Comparatively: Grenada is as free as Turkey, freer than Guyana, less free than Bahamas.

GUATEMALA

Economy: noninclusive capitalist   **Political Rights:** 3
Polity: centralized multiparty   **Civil Liberties:** 4
Population: 6,600,000   **Status of Freedom:** partly free

An ethnic state with a major potential territorial subnationality

Political Rights. Guatemala is a constitutional democracy on the American model. In recent elections not all parties were allowed to participate nationally, and there was significant organized abstention. The 1974 presidential election results were apparently altered in favor of the ruling coalition's candidate; in 1978 counting irregularities and resulting challenges were resolved in favor of a candidate less clearly identified with the government. Congressional seats went to a variety of parties. The provinces are centrally administered. *Subnationalities*: Various groups of Mayan and other Indians make up half the population; they do not yet have a subnationalist sense of unity.

Civil Liberties. The press and a large portion of radio and television are privately controlled. The press is generally free, although rural journalists have been harassed by the police. In the cities, at least, opposition political acitivity is open. However, the continuing operation of death squads on both the right and left inhibits discussion and expression. The struggle against rural guerrillas has led to frequent denial of rights in rural areas by security forces. The judiciary is not entirely free of governmental pressures in political or subversive cases, but some members of rightist death squads have been tried. Official political imprisonment and torture occur, but the main problem is that illegal armed groups, often associated with the government, are responsible for thousands of deaths. Unions are often intimidated, but other private rights seem fairly well respected by the government. Largely an agricultural country, fifty percent of those in agriculture own their own farms.

Comparatively: Guatemala is as free as Malaysia, freer than Nicaragua, less free than Jamaica.

GUINEA

Economy: preindustrial socialist   **Political Rights:** 7
Polity: socialist one-party   **Civil Liberties:** 7
Population: 4,800,000   **Status of Freedom:** not free

A transethnic heterogeneous state

Political Rights. Guinea is a one-party socialist dictatorship. Elections for president and parliament are uncontested. Provincial and local governments are highly centralized.

Civil Liberties. All media are government or party owned and censorship is rigid. Ideological purity is demanded in all areas except religion. There are 1,000–4,000 prisoners of conscience; torture has been common and execution frequent. Everyone must participate in guided political activity. There are few recognized private rights, such as those to organize unions, develop property, or choose one's education. Private lawyers are not permitted. Movement within the country or over the border has been restricted. In 1977 in an attempt to encourage the more capable among the million people who have fled the country since independence to return, the government granted them special tax exemptions, and reintroduced capitalism in small industries, agriculture, and many services. This policy is very much in flux, and fundamental change is unlikely.

Comparatively: Guinea is as free as Ethiopia, less free than Liberia.

GUINEA-BISSAU

Economy: noninclusive capitalist
Polity: socialist one-party
Population: 600,000

Political Rights: 6
Civil Liberties: 6
Status of Freedom: not free

A transethnic heterogeneous state

Political Rights. Guinea-Bissau is administered by one party; all other parties are illegal. Constitutionally the secretariat of the party is the highest organ of the state; the party is recognized as the expression of the "sovereign will" of the people. There is apparently limited local freedom to reject candidates; the national assembly is indirectly elected. Local economic control under party guidance is emphasized.

Civil Liberties. The media are government controlled, and criticism of the system is forbidden. There are prisoners of conscience. Union activity is government directed. All land has been nationalized; rights of private property are minimal. As the system develops, many other personal rights are likely to be sacrificed, but whether an attempt will be made to adhere strictly to a communist model is unclear.

Comparatively: Guinea-Bissau is as free as Tanzania, freer than Guinea, less free than Senegal.

GUYANA

Economy: mixed socialist
Polity: centralized multiparty
Population: 820,000

Political Rights: 4
Civil Liberties: 4
Status of Freedom: partly free

An ethnically complex state

Political Rights. Guyana is a parliamentary democracy. However, in the last three elections the government has been responsibly charged with irregularities that resulted in its victory. The 1978 referendum was criticized for the way it was presented, for campaign restriction, and for the inflation of participation figures. The ruling party has been co-opting the position of the opposition communist party and may be headed toward a one-party state as it moves to the left. Administration is generally centralized but there are some elected local officials.

Civil Liberties. The media are both public and private (including party). Several opposition newspapers have been nationalized; the ability of the remainder to publish is restricted. There is a right of assembly, but harassment occurs. All private schools have recently been nationalized, and the government has interfered with university appointments. It is possible to win against the government in court; there are no prisoners of conscience. Art and music are under considerable government control. Unions retain independent power. Private property (as distinct from personal property) is no longer considered legitimate.

Comparatively: Guyana is as free as Mexico, freer than Panama, less free than Surinam.

HAITI

Economy: noninclusive capitalist   Political Rights: 7
Polity: nationalist one-party   Civil Liberties: 6
Population: 5,000,000   Status of Freedom: not free

A relatively homogeneous population

Political Rights. Haiti is a dictatorship with an ephemeral ruling party. Elections allow no opposition; the assembly has been merely for show. (Early 1979 assembly elections indicated improvement.)

Civil Liberties. The media are both private and public. During 1978 a critical press and radio emerged for several months due to outside pressure, but was subsequently silenced. Political gatherings are not permitted. A government sponsored militia has suppressed opposition; political murders, imprisonment without trial, exile, and torture have characterized the system, but were much less common in 1978. An acceptable rule of law has been in abeyance during a prolonged "state of siege." Many people attempt to flee the country illegally every year. Union activity is restricted.

Comparatively: Haiti is as free as Togo, freer than Benin, less free than Panama.

HONDURAS

Economy: noninclusive capitalist   **Political Rights:** 6
Polity: military nonparty   **Civil Liberties:**   3
Population: 3,000,000   **Status of Freedom:** partly free

A relatively homogeneous population

Political Rights. Although the government is a military dictatorship, there is continued political party activity, and halting progress toward an election in 1980. Advisory councils involving several political parties and pressure groups assist the government. Provincial government is centrally administered.

Civil Liberties. The media are largely private and free of prior censorship. Journalists have been imprisoned. Militant peasant organizations and political parties continue to function outside government control. Partisan political demonstrations are not allowed, but other forms of party activity are. The previous government imprisoned some of the peasants' most violent oppressors. Most private rights are respected—insofar as government power reaches. Labor unions are relatively strong, especially in plantation areas. There is freedom of religion and movement.

Comparatively: Honduras is as free as Peru, freer than Cuba, less free than Mexico.

HUNGARY

Economy: socialist   **Political Rights:** 6
Polity: communist one-party   **Civil Liberties:**   5
Population: 10,700,000   **Status of Freedom:** not free

A relatively homogeneous population

Political Rights. Hungary is ruled as a one-party communist dictatorship. Although there is an elective national assembly as well as local assemblies, all candidates must be approved by the party, and the decisions of the politburo are decisive. Within this framework recent elections have allowed at least a restricted choice among candidates. The group rights of the Hungarian people are diminished by the government's official acceptance of the right of the Soviet government to interfere in the domestic affairs of Hungary by force.

Civil Liberties. Media are under government or party control. Some scope for criticism is allowed, especially through papers, plays, books, and the importation of foreign productions. Prisoners of conscience continue to be detained. Control over religious affairs is more relaxed than in most communist states. Although private rights are not guaranteed, in practice there is considerable private property, and permission to travel into and out of the country is easier to obtain than in most of Eastern Europe. (In January 1979 the border with Austria became essentially open.)

Comparatively: Hungary is as free as Yugoslavia, freer than Czechoslovakia, less free than Egypt.

I C E L A N D

Economy: capitalist   Political Rights: 1
Polity: centralized multiparty   Civil Liberties: 1
Population: 223,000   Status of Freedom: free

A relatively homogeneous population

Political Rights. Iceland is governed by a parliamentary democracy. Recent years have seen important shifts in voter sentiment, resulting successively in right- and left-wing coalitions. Although a small country Iceland has pursued a highly independent foreign policy. Provinces are ruled by central government appointees.

Civil Liberties. The press is private or party and free of censorship. There are no political prisoners and the judiciary is independent. Private rights are respected; few are poor or illiterate.

Comparatively: Iceland is as free as Norway, freer than Portugal.

I N D I A

Economy: noninclusive capitalist-   Political Rights: 2
         statist   Civil Liberties: 2
Polity: decentralized multiparty   Status of Freedom: free
Population: 635,000,000

A multinational and complex state

Political Rights. India is a parliamentary democracy. The strong powers retained by its component states have been compromised in recent years by the central government's frequent imposition of direct rule. After several years of decline Indian democracy was reinstitutionalized both at the regional and federal level by the 1977 success of the Janata party in winning the first opposition victory since independence. The depth of mass interest in democracy was established by the victory, although the doubtful legality of calling immediate elections in the states where the Janata party appeared assured of victory, and an understandable mood of reprisal against those who misused power in the previous administration may have set dangerous precedents. In

1978 there was continued political instability and a recovery of opposition prospects through success in by-elections.

Subnationalities: India contains a diverse collection of mostly territorially distinct peoples united by historical experience and the predominance of Hinduism. India's dominant peoples are those of the north central area who speak as a first language either the official language, Hindi (Hindustani), or a very closely related dialect of Sanskrit origin. The other major subnational peoples of India may be divided into several groups: (1) peoples with separate states that are linguistically and historically only marginally distinct from the dominant Hindi speakers (for example, the Marathi, Gujerati, or Oriya); (2) peoples with separate states that are of Sanskrit background linguistically, but have a relatively strong sense of separate identity (for example, Bengalis or Kashmiris); (3) peoples with separate states that are linguistically and to some extent racially quite distinct (for example, Telegu or Malayalam); and (4) peoples that do not have states of their own and are often survivors of India's pre-Aryan peoples (for example, Santali, Bhuti-Lapcha, or Mizo). With the exception of the last group, the Indian federal system accords a fair amount of democratic rights to all peoples. Several peoples from groups (2), (3), and (4) have shown through legal (especially votes) and illegal means a strong desire by a significant part of the population for independence or greater autonomy (notably Kashmiris, Nagas, and Mizos). This accounting leaves out many *nonterritorial* religious and caste minorities, although, here again, the system has granted relatively broad rights to such groups to reasonable self-determination.

Civil Liberties. Recent events have shown the surprising strength of Indian attachment to civil liberties. The Indian press is strong and independent. The fact that radio and television are not independent in this largely illiterate country is disquieting. Although there have been illegal arrests and reports of torture in the recent past, in general the police and judiciary are now thought to be responsive, fair, and independent. There are few, if any, prisoners of conscience, but there are hundreds imprisoned for political violence, and demonstrations may lead to large-scale jailings. Due to the decentralized political structure there is a great deal of regional variation in the operation of security laws. Kashmir has especially repressive security policies in relation to the press and political detention; Sikkim is treated as an Indian colony, and the same might be said for other border areas. Indians enjoy freedom to travel, to worship as they please, and to organize for mutual benefit, especially in unions. Lack of education, extreme poverty, and surviving traditional controls certainly reduce the meaning of such liberties for large numbers of Indians.

Comparatively: India is as free as Portugal, freer than Malaysia, less free than Japan.

INDONESIA

Economy: noninclusive capitalist-statist

Political Rights: 5

Civil Liberties: 5

Polity: centralized dominant-party

Status of Freedom: partly free

Population: 140,000,000

A transethnic heterogeneous state with active and potential sub-nationalities

Political Rights. Indonesia is a controlled parliamentary democracy under military direction. Recent parliamentary elections showed the ability of the rather tame opposition parties to gain ground at the expense of the governing party, but the government's majority is still overwhelming. The number and character of opposition parties is carefully controlled, parties must refrain from criticizing one another, candidates of both government and opposition require government approval, and opposition activities in rural areas are restricted. In any event parliament does not have a great deal of power. Provincial governors are indirectly elected from centrally approved lists. Local assemblies are elected.

Subnationalities: Indonesia includes a variety of ethnic groups and is divided by crosscutting island identities. Although the island of Java is numerically dominant, the national language is not Javanese, and most groups or islands do not appear to have strong subnational identifications. Both civilian and military elites generally attempt to maintain religious, ethnic, and regional balance. Groups demanding independence exist in Sulawesi, the Moluccas, Timor, West Irian, and northern Sumatra, and continue to mount revolts against the government.

Civil Liberties: Most newspapers are private. All are subject to fairly close government supervision; criticism of the system is muted by periodic suppressions. Radio and television are government controlled. Freedom of assembly is restricted, but citizens are not compelled to attend meetings. There are over ten thousand political prisoners in Indonesia. Although there have been many releases of long-term prisoners lately, new imprisonments occurred in 1977 and 1978. In this area the army rather than the civilian judiciary is dominant. Torture appears to be infrequent recently, but the army has been responsible for many thousands of unnecessary deaths in its recent suppression of revolt in East Timor. Union activity is closely regulated; movement, especially to the cities, is restricted; other private rights are generally respected. The Indonesian bureaucracy has an unenviable reputation for arbitrariness and corruption, practices that must reduce the effective expression of human rights.

Comparatively: Indonesia is as free as Nicaragua, freer than Burma, less free than Bangladesh.

I R A N

Economy: noninclusive capitalist-statist
Polity: transitional nonparty
Population: 35,500,000

Political Rights: 5
Civil Liberties: 5
Status of Freedom: partly free

An ethnic state with major territorial subnationalities

Political Rights. The year saw the erosion of Iran's monarchical one-party system. Many parties reemerged, but by the end of the year the monarchy remained, sharing power only with the military and a populist religious movement that fought for the control of the streets. The political and economic life of the country was at a standstill. (Subsequently, a revolutionary regime was established amidst turmoil; it was unclear whether Iran would end 1979 with an authentic democracy.) *Subnationalities:* Among the most important non-Persian peoples are the Kurds, the Azerbaijani Turks, the Baluch, and a variety of other (primarily Turkish) tribes. Many of these have striven for independence in the recent past when the opportunity arose.

Civil Liberties. Newspapers are private. Their freedoms expanded during the year until an attempted imposition of renewed censorship under martial law led their staffs to suspend publication (resumed without official censorship in January, 1979). Other media are largely government owned but became relatively free by the end of the year. The right of assembly was largely reclaimed, although not when there was a real threat of violence. Many prisoners were released, but other political prisoners taken. Anarchy led to vigilante groups competing with the official security system.

Comparatively: Iran was as free as Poland, freer than Iraq, less free than Bangladesh.

I R A Q

Economy: noninclusive socialist
Polity: socialist one-party
Population: 12,200,000

Political Rights: 7
Civil Liberties: 6
Status of Freedom: not free

An ethnic state with a major territorial subnationality

Political Rights. Iraq is governed by the ruling party and its military leaders. The communist party is officially recognized as a part of the ruling front, but because of the present lack of elective and legislative mechanisms it appears to operate more as a faction than a political party. Several communists were executed in 1978 for overstepping these limits. Provinces are governed from the center. *Subnationalities*: The Kurds have been repeatedly denied self-determination, most recently through reoccupation of their lands and some attempt to disperse them about the country.

Civil Liberties. Newspapers are largely public or party and are closely controlled by the government. However, publication of a variety of socialist and religious points of view is allowed. Radio and television are government monopolies. Political imprisonment, execution, and torture are common, particularly for the Kurdish minority. The families of suspects are often imprisoned. Rights are largely de facto or those deriving from traditional religious law. Iraq has a dual economy, with a large preindustrial sector. The government has taken over much of the modern petroleum-based economy and, through land reform leading to collectives and state farms, has increasingly limited private economic choice.

Comparatively: Iraq is as free as Mali, freer than Mozambique, less free than Syria.

IRELAND

Economy: capitalist
Polity: centralized multiparty
Population: 3,200,000

Political Rights: 1
Civil Liberties: 1
Status of Freedom: free

A relatively homogeneous population

Political Rights. Ireland is a parliamentary democracy which successfully shifts national power among parties. The bicameral legislature has an appointive upper house with powers only of delay. Local government is not powerful, but is elective rather than appointive.

Civil Liberties. The press is free and private, and radio and television are under an autonomous corporation. Strong censorship has always been exercised over both publishers and the press, but since this is of social rather than political content, it lies within that sphere of control permitted a majority in a free democracy.* The rule of law is firmly established and private rights are guaranteed, although in

---

* For further discussion of this distinction see *Freedom in the World 1978*, pp. 111–26, and the references cited.

connection with a recent antiterrorism campaign suspects have been roughly handled and their rights curtailed.

Comparatively: Ireland is as free as Canada, freer than France.

ISRAEL

Economy: mixed capitalist
Polity: centralized multiparty
Population: 3,700,000

Political Rights: 2
Civil Liberties: 2
Status of Freedom: free

An ethnic state with microterritorial subnationalities

Political Rights. Israel is governed under a parliamentary system. Recent elections have resulted in major shifts of power among the many political parties. Provinces are ruled from the center, although there are important local elective offices in the cities. *Subnationalities*: National elections do not involve the Arabs in the occupied territories; Arabs in Israel proper participate in Israeli elections as a minority. Arabs both in Israel and the occupied territories must live in their homeland under the cultural and political domination of twentieth-century immigrants.

Civil Liberties. Newspapers are private or party, and free of censorship except for restrictions relating to the always precarious national security. Radio and television are government owned. In general the rule of law is observed, although Arabs in Israel are not accorded the full rights of citizens, and the Orthodox Jewish faith holds a special position in the country's religious, customary, and legal life. Because of the war, the socialist-cooperative ideology of its founders, and dependence on outside support, the role of private enterprise in the economy has been less than in most of Euro-America. Arabs are not allowed to buy land from Jews, and Arab land has been expropriated for Jewish settlement. Freedom House's rating of Israel is based on its judgment of the situation in Israel proper and not that in the occupied territories.

Comparatively: Israel is as free as Portugal, freer than Egypt, less free than France.

ITALY

Economy: capitalist
Polity: centralized multiparty
Population: 56,700,000

Political Rights: 2
Civil Liberties: 2
Status of Freedom: free

A relatively homogeneous population with small territorial subnationalities

Political Rights. Italy is a bicameral parliamentary democracy. Elections are generally free, but the political process is not free of corruption on both right and left. Since the 1940's governments have been dominated by the Christian Democrats, with coalitions shifting between dependence on minor parties of the left or right. The fascist party is banned. Referendums are used to supplement parliamentary rule. Opposition parties gain local political power, but regional and local power are generally quite limited.

Civil Liberties. Italian newspapers are free and cover a broad spectrum. Radio and television are both public and private and provide unusually diverse programming. Freedom of speech is inhibited in some areas and for many individuals by the violence of both right- and left-wing extremist groups. Since the bureaucracy does not promptly respond to citizen desires, it represents, as in many countries, an additional impediment to the full expression of the rule of law. Detention may last for years without trial. Since major industries are managed by the government, and the government has undertaken major reallocations of land, Italy is only marginally a capitalist state.

Comparatively: Italy is as free as Greece, freer than Morocco, less free than France.

IVORY COAST

Economy: noninclusive capitalist
Polity: nationalist one-party
Population: 7,200,000

Political Rights: 6
Civil Liberties: 5
Status of Freedom: partly free

A transethnic heterogeneous state

Political Rights. Ivory Coast is ruled by a one-party, capitalist, dictatorship. Under these constraints presidential and assembly elections have little meaning; in the most recent election there was no choice and the president received ninety-nine percent of the vote. Organized in the 1940's, the ruling party incorporates a variety of interests and forces, and there may be democratic elements at the local level in the selection of assembly candidates. Provinces are ruled directly from the center. Contested mayoralty elections have occurred recently.

Civil Liberties. Although the press is mostly party or government controlled, it presents at least a limited spectrum of opinion. Foreign publications are widely available. While opposition is discouraged, there is no ideological conformity. Radio and television are government controlled. There has been evidence of political imprisonment and police brutality in the recent past; today there may be no prisoners of conscience. Unions are controlled by the party. Travel and religion are generally free. There is a limited right to strike and organize unions. Economically the country depends on small private farms; in the modern sector private enterprise is encouraged.

Comparatively: Ivory Coast is as free as Poland, freer than Niger, less free than Kenya.

J A M A I C A

Economy: mixed capitalist   **Political Rights:** 2
Polity: centralized multiparty   **Civil Liberties:** 3
Population: 2,100,000   **Status of Freedom:** free

A relatively homogeneous population

Political Rights. Jamaica is a parliamentary democracy in which power changes from one party to another. However, political life has become increasingly violent: the last election was accompanied by murders, a state of siege, bans on political rallies, and government supervision of publicity. Regardless of who is to blame, and both sides may be, this degrades the meaning of political rights. The opposition refused to participate in by-elections in 1978 because of violence and poor electoral procedures. Regional and local administrations do not have independent power.

Civil Liberties. The free press is endangered by nationalization, government attacks, and court actions. The government has recently eliminated private ownership from radio and television in an ominous move apparently meant to counter the influence of an antisocialist newspaper. Freedom of assembly has been curtailed. The rule of law and respect for rights remain, yet in many districts a climate of fear inhibits their expression. The military intelligence unit has also been used to hinder the opposition. Aside from the media, nationalization of the economy has emphasized so far the takeover of foreign companies.

Comparatively: Jamaica is as free as Colombia, freer than Panama, less free than Surinam.

J A P A N

Economy: capitalist   **Political Rights:** 2
Polity: centralized multiparty   **Civil Liberties:** 1
Population: 114,400,000   **Status of Freedom:** free

A relatively homogeneous population

Political Rights. Japan is a bicameral, constitutional monarchy with a relatively weak upper house. The conservative-to-centrist Liberal

Democratic Party ruled with solid majorities from independence in the early 1950's until the mid-1970's. Although the Liberal Democrats have lost considerable support in recent elections, through coalitions with independents they have maintained control at the national level, and have recently showed increased strength at the local level. Concentrated business interests have played a strong role in maintaining Liberal party hegemony through the use of their money, influence, and prestige. In addition, a heavy weighting of representation in favor of rural areas tends to maintain the Liberal Party position. Opposition parties are fragmented. They have local control in some areas, but the power of local and regional assemblies and officials is limited. Since electoral and parliamentary procedures are democratic, we assume that Japan's system would freely allow a transfer of national power to an opposition group should the majority desire it, but as in Italy this is not yet proven by events. Democracy within the liberal party is increasing.

Civil Liberties. News media are generally private and free, although many radio and television stations are served by a public broadcasting corporation. Television is excellent and quite free. Courts of law are not as important in Japanese society as in Europe and America; both the courts and police appear to be relatively fair. Travel and change of residence are unrestricted. The public expressions and actions of many people are more restricted than in most modern democracies by traditional controls and Japanese style collectivism that leads to strong social pressures, especially psychological pressures, in many spheres (unions, corporations, or religious-political groups, such as Soka Gakkai).

Comparatively: Japan is as free as West Germany, freer than Italy, less free than the United Kingdom.

JORDAN

Economy: noninclusive capitalist   **Political Rights:** 6
Polity: traditional nonparty   **Civil Liberties:** 6
Population: 2,900,000   **Status of Freedom:** not free

A relatively homogeneous population

Political Rights. Jordan is an absolute monarchy in the guise of a constitutional monarchy. There are no parties; parliament provides no check on the king's broad powers, since it has not met since 1967. In 1978 an appointive National Consultative Council was established. Provinces are ruled from the center and local governments have very limited autonomy. The king is regularly petitioned by his subjects.

Civil Liberties. Papers are private but self-censored and occasionally suspended. Television and radio are government controlled. Under continuing emergency laws normal legal guarantees for political suspects are suspended, and organized opposition is not permitted. There have been long-term political prisoners and instances of torture. Private rights such as those to property, travel, or religion appear to be respected.

Comparatively: Jordan is as free as Saudi Arabia, freer than South Yemen, less free than Syria.

K A M P U C H E A (Cambodia)

Economy: socialist	Political Rights: 7
Polity: communist one-party	Civil Liberties: 7
Population: 8,000,000	Status of Freedom: not free

A relatively homogeneous population

Political Rights. Kampuchea was a one-party communist dictatorship in 1978. (Kampuchea was conquered early in 1979 by Vietnamese forces; these forces, and their Kampuchean client government, continued to struggle against the forces of the former regime when this went to press.) All power was in the hands of the party leaders. The tightly knit nature of the small communist elite was suggested by the fact that wives of top leaders also served as government ministers.

Civil Liberties. The media were completely controlled by the government. Revolutionary law offered little security to life or property; party objectives determined private residence or occupation more than private desire. Political executions were a common function of government. Since 1974 hundreds of thousands or even millions were killed as the result of brutal government policy, especially in relocation. The extreme application of ideology led to communal kitchens in villages, work teams that divided population by sex and age, and the abolition of wages. In 1978 Kampuchea was perhaps the world's most complete tyranny.

Comparatively: Kampuchea was as free as Ethiopia, less free than Thailand.

K E N Y A

Economy: noninclusive capitalist	Political Rights: 5
Polity: nationalist one-party	Civil Liberties: 4
Population: 14,800,000	Status of Freedom: partly free

A formally transethnic heterogeneous state with active and potential subnationalities

Political Rights. Kenya is a one-party capitalist state. Although the party is dominated by the Kikuyu tribe, it contains an amalgam of different tribal groups. Only the ruling party competes in elections. A few individuals are elected within this format that are publicly critical of the government. Selection of top party and national leaders is by consensus or acclamation. The administration is generally centralized, but elements of tribal and communal government continue at the periphery. *Subnationalities*: Comprising twenty percent of the population, the Kikuyu are the largest tribal group. In a very heterogeneous society, the Luo are the second most important subnationality.

Civil Liberties. The press is private. It is not censored but under government pressure to avoid criticism. Radio and television are under government control. Rights of assembly are limited. In spite of these limitations the government's critics and opponents speak out. The courts have considerable independence. All prisoners of conscience were released in late 1978. Unions are active, and private rights are generally respected. Land is gradually coming under private rather than tribal control.

Comparatively: Kenya is as free as Ghana, freer than Tanzania, less free than Mauritius.

K O R E A ,   N O R T H

Economy: socialist	**Political Rights:** 7
Polity: communist one-party	**Civil Liberties:** 7
Population: 17,100,000	**Status of Freedom:** not free

A relatively homogeneous state

Political Rights. North Korea is a hard-line communist dictatorship in which the organs and assemblies of government are merely a facade for party rule. National elections allow no choice. The politburo is under one-man rule; the dictator's son was his expected successor until recently. Military officers are very strong in top positions.

Civil Liberties. The media are all government controlled, with glorification of the leader a major responsibility. No private or public rights appear to be inviolable. There are political prisoners, and torture may be assumed to be common. However, the severity of its controls offers a considerable propaganda advantage. How little unauthorized news finds its way out of the country may be indicated by quoting in full Amnesty International's 1977 report:

> Amnesty International has carefully monitored all available information from North Korea and can only report that it contains no detailed evidence whatsoever regarding arrests, trials and imprisonment in that

country. Furthermore, there appears to be a complete censorship of news relating to human rights violations. Despite its efforts Amnesty International has not been able to trace any information, even positive, on the subject of such rights in North Korea.*

Comparatively: North Korea is as free as Albania, less free than South Korea.

KOREA, SOUTH

Economy: capitalist
Polity: centralized multiparty
Population: 37,100,000

Political Rights: 4
Civil Liberties: 5
Status of Freedom: partly free

A relatively homogeneous state

Political Rights. South Korea has a strong presidential system. The president is indirectly elected by a special elective body, and he appoints one-third of the assembly. 1978 assembly elections gave a plurality to the opposition party; however appointive members and the large number of independents prevented its gaining control. Provinces are headed by national governmental appointees.

Civil Liberties. Most newspapers are private, as are many radio stations and one television station. Because of government pressure, self-censorship is the rule. Special laws against criticizing the constitution, the government, or its policies have resulted in many prisoners of conscience; torture is used. The resulting climate of fear in activist circles is sharpened by extralegal harassment of those who are not imprisoned, and the inability of the courts to effectively protect the rights of political suspects or prisoners. Yet demonstrations and expressions of open dissent continue. Several important dissident prisoners were released at the end of 1978; they immediately resumed their attack on the government. Outside this arena private rights are generally respected. Unions are free to organize, but not to strike. Religious freedom and freedom of movement within the country are respected. Rapid, capitalistic economic growth has been combined with a relatively egalitarian income distribution.

Comparatively: South Korea is as free as Ecuador, freer than China (Mainland), less free than Bangladesh.

* *Amnesty International Report: 1977* (London: Amnesty International Publications, 1977), p. 192. *Amnesty International Report: 1978*, p. 170, has an equivalent statement.

K U W A I T

Economy: mixed capitalist-
    statist
Polity: traditional nonparty
Population: 1,100,000

Political Rights: 6
Civil Liberties: 4
Status of Freedom: partly free

The citizenry is relatively homogeneous

Political Rights. Kuwait is a traditional monarchy in retreat from an experiment in constitutional monarchy. The recent monarchical succession was uneventful. More than half the population are immigrants; their political, economic, and social rights are much inferior to those of natives.

Civil Liberties. The press is private. Self-censorship is enforced by periodic suspensions. Radio and television are government controlled. Freedom of assembly is curtailed. However, private discussion is open and few, if any, political prisoners are held. Private freedoms are respected, although foreign travel may be restricted. There is a wide variety of enabling government activity in fields such as education, housing, and medicine that is not based on reducing choice through taxation.

Comparatively: Kuwait is as free as Bahrain, freer than Saudi Arabia, less free than Lebanon.

L A O S

Economy: noninclusive socialist
Polity: communist one-party
Population: 3,600,000

Political Rights: 7
Civil Liberties: 7
Status of Freedom: not free

An ethnic state with active or potential subnationalities

Political Rights. Laos has established a traditional communist party dictatorship in which the party is superior to the external government at all levels. There is continuing subservience to the desires of the North Vietnamese party and army, upon which the present leaders must depend. There is continued resistance in rural areas. *Subnationalities:* Pressure on the Meo hill people has caused the majority of them to flee the country.

Civil Liberties. The media are all government controlled. There are many political prisoners; large numbers have been subjected to re-education camps of varying severity and length. There are few accepted private rights. It is probable that the precommunist way of life is preserved in some parts of the country.

Comparatively: Laos is as free as Vietnam, less free than China (Mainland).

LEBANON

Economy: capitalist
Polity: decentralized multiparty
Population: 2,800,000

Political Rights: 4
Civil Liberties: 4
Status of Freedom: partly free

A complex, multinational, microterritorial state

Political Rights. In theory Lebanon is a parliamentary democracy with a strong but indirectly elected president. In spite of the calamities of the last few years the constitutional system still functions to a degree under the protection of the Syrian army. Parliament meets sporadically. *Subnationalities*: Leading administrative and parliamentary officials are allocated among the several religious or communal groups by complicated formulas. These groups have for years pursued semiautonomous lives within the state, although their territories are often intermixed.

Civil Liberties. The private and party press was formerly renowned for its independence. Some papers were suspended under Syrian control, but censorship is now confined to relatively few subjects. Radio is government owned; television has been in private hands. Widespread killing in recent years has inhibited the nationwide expression of most freedoms and tightened communal controls on individuals. Few if any prisoners of conscience are detained by the Lebanese government.

Comparatively: Lebanon is as free as Mexico, freer than Syria, less free than Turkey.

LESOTHO

Economy: noninclusive capitalist
Polity: partially centralized multiparty
Population: 1,300,000

Political Rights: 5
Civil Liberties: 5
Status of Freedom: partly free

A relatively homogeneous population

Political Rights. Lesotho is a constitutional monarchy essentially under the one-man rule of the leader of the ruling political party who suspended the constitution to avoid being defeated in 1970. Opposition parties as well as the king have been repressed, yet major elements of the traditional system (chiefs) remain, and members of other parties have been introduced into the government. Although there are frequent expressions of national independence, Lesotho remains under considerable South African economic and political pressure. Lesotho is populated almost exclusively by Basotho people, and the land has never been alienated. However, a large percentage of the male citizenry works in South Africa.

Civil Liberties. Radio is government and church controlled, as are most papers. There are, however, opposition publications and South African media offer a readily available alternative. Freedom of assembly is restricted. The judiciary seems to preserve considerable independence vis-à-vis the government. There were nine prisoners of conscience in 1978. Limited union activity is permitted. Internal travel is unrestricted, as are most private rights.

Comparatively: Lesotho is as free as Indonesia, freer than South Africa, less free than Botswana.

LIBERIA

Economy: noninclusive capitalist
Polity: nationalist one-party
Population: 1,780,000

Political Rights: 6
Civil Liberties: 5
Status of Freedom: partly free

A formally transethnic heterogeneous state

Political Rights. Liberian government is formally modeled on that of the United States. However, there is no independent provincial power and there is only one significant party. Elections are characterized by lack of opposition and the easy election of the party's candidates. Although attempts are made to increase the participation of the native population, the country is still ruled by the very small Americo-Liberian community.

Civil Liberties. The press is private but consists primarily of the organs of the ruling party. Radio and television are partially government controlled. Pressure is brought against those who become too critical either through the media or other channels. The government generally acts under special "emergency powers" suspending many constitutional guarantees, yet there are few, if any, political prisoners. Travel and other private rights are generally respected. Only blacks can become citizens. Union organization is partly free.

Comparatively: Liberia is as free as Ivory Coast, freer than Gabon, less free than Senegal.

LIBYA

Economy: capitalist-statist
Polity: socialist one-party
(military dominated)
Population: 2,800,000

Political Rights: 6
Civil Liberties: 6
Status of Freedom: not free

A relatively homogeneous state

Political Rights. Libya is a military and party dictatorship apparently effectively under the control of one person. The place of a legislature is taken by the direct democracy of large congresses. Whatever the form, no opposition is allowed on the larger questions of society. Institutional self-management has been widely introduced in schools, hospitals, and factories. Sometimes the system works well enough to provide a meaningful degree of decentralized self-determination.

Civil Liberties. The media are government controlled. There are many political prisoners; the use of military and people's courts for political cases suggest little respect for the rule of law. Torture and mistreatment are alleged. Oil and oil-related industry is the major government enterprise. Although ideologically socialist, even some of the press remains in private hands. However, the year ended with a threat to eliminate the merchant class as exploitative. Respect for Islam provides a check on arbitrary government.

Comparatively: Libya is as free as China (Mainland), freer than Iraq, less free than Egypt.

LUXEMBOURG

Economy: capitalist
Polity: centralized multiparty
Population: 350,000

Political Rights: 1
Civil Liberties: 1
Status of Freedom: free

A relatively homogeneous state

Political Rights. Luxembourg is a constitutional monarchy on the Belgian model, in which the monarchy is somewhat more powerful than in the United Kingdom or Scandinavia. The legislature is bicameral with the appointive upper house having only a delaying function. Recent votes have resulted in important shifts in the nature of the dominant coalition.

Civil Liberties. The media are private and free. The rule of law is thoroughly accepted in both public and private realms.

Comparatively: Luxembourg is as free as Iceland, freer than France.

MADAGASCAR

Economy: noninclusive mixed
    socialist
Polity: nationalist one-party
    (military dominated)
Population: 8,000,000

Political Rights: 6
Civil Liberties: 6
Status of Freedom: not free

A transethnic heterogeneous state

Political Rights. Madagascar is a military dictatorship with a very weak legislature. In 1977 the parliamentary election was restricted to candidates selected by parties grouped in a "national front," a government sponsored coalition. However formed, the parliament appeared to play very little role in government in 1978. Anarchical conditions also called into question the extent to which the people are willing to grant the regime legitimacy. Emphasis has been put on developing the autonomy of local Malagasy governmental institutions, but the restriction of local elections to approved front candidates belies this emphasis.

Civil Liberties. There is a private press, but papers are carefully censored and may be suspended. Broadcasting is government controlled. Movie theatres have been nationalized. The government replaced the national news agency with one which will "disregard information likely to be harmful to the government's socialist development policies." There is no right of assembly; one must be careful of public speech. There are few political prisoners but short-term political detentions are common. Labor unions and the judiciary are not strong, but religion is free and most private rights respected. Public security is very weak. Overseas travel is restricted. While still encouraging private investment, most businesses and large farms are nationalized.

Comparatively: Madagascar is as free as Tanzania, freer than Mozambique, less free than Egypt.

MALAWI

Economy: noninclusive capitalist
Polity: nationalist one-party
Population: 5,400,000

Political Rights: 6
Civil Liberties: 7
Status of Freedom: not free

A transethnic heterogeneous state

Political Rights. Malawi is a one-man dictatorship with party and parliamentary forms. A 1978 election allowed some choice among individuals for the first time. Administration is centralized, although the paramount chiefs retain power locally through control over land.

Civil Liberties. The press is private or religious but under strict government control. The semicommercial radio service is also not free. Private criticism of the administration remains dangerous. Foreign publications are carefully screened. The country has been notable for the persecution of Jehovah's Witnesses (including a demand they join the ruling party), treason trials, expulsion of Asian groups, the detention of journalists, torture and brutality, and even an open invitation to the people to kill anyone who opposes the government. Fortunately in 1977 most political prisoners were released and pressures were relaxed on Jehovah's Witnesses. Traditional courts offer some protection against arbitrary rule, as do the comparatively limited interests of the government. Foreign travel and union activity are closely controlled.

Comparatively: Malawi is as free as South Yemen, freer than Uganda, less free than Zambia.

MALAYSIA

Economy: capitalist   **Political Rights:** 3
Polity: decentralized multiparty   **Civil Liberties:** 4
Population: 13,000,000   **Status of Freedom:** partly free

An ethnic state with major nonterritorial subnationalities

Political Rights. Malaysia is a parliamentary democracy with a weak, indirectly elected and appointed senate and a powerful lower house. The relatively powerless head of state is an elective monarch, rotating among the traditional monarchs of the constituent states. A multinational front has dominated electoral and parliamentary politics. By such devices as imprisonment or the banning of demonstrations the opposition is not given an equal opportunity to compete in elections. The states of Malaysia have their own rulers, parliaments, and institutions, but it is doubtful if any of them any longer have the power to leave the federation. *Subnationalities*: Political, economic, linguistic, and educational policies have favored the Malays (forty-four percent) over the Chinese (thirty-six percent), Indians (ten percent), and others. Traditionally the Chinese had been the wealthier and better educated people. Although there are Chinese in the ruling front, they are not allowed to question the policy of communal preference.

Civil Liberties. The press is private and highly varied. However, nothing that might influence communal relations can be printed, and editors are constrained by the need to renew their publishing licenses annually. Foreign journalists are closely controlled. Radio is mostly government owned, television entirely so. Universities have been put under government pressure and foreign professors encouraged to leave. There have been several reports of the development of an atmosphere of fear in both academic and opposition political circles, as well as widespread discrimination against non-Malays. In 1978 an attempt to establish a private university for Chinese language students was blocked. 1,500–3,000 political suspects are detained indefinitely, generally on suspicion of communist activity. Nevertheless, significant criticism appears in the media, and in parliament campaigns are mounted against government decisions. Unions are partly free and have the right to strike. Economic activity is free, except for government favoritism to the Malays.

Comparatively: Malaysia is as free as Morocco, freer than Indonesia, less free than Sri Lanka.

MALDIVES

Economy: noninclusive capitalist
Polity: traditional nonparty
Population: 140,000

Political Rights: 5
Civil Liberties: 5
Status of Freedom: partly free

A relatively homogeneous population

Political Rights. The Maldives have a parliamentary government in which a president (elected by parliament and confirmed by the people) is the real ruler. Regional leaders are presidentially appointed. Both economic and political power are concentrated in the hands of a very small, wealthy elite. Islam places a check on absolutism.

Civil Liberties. An apolitical daily newspaper is published intermittently; the radio station is owned by the government. Foreign publications are received; political discussion is limited. "Imprisonment" of political prisoners often involves internal exile; all political prisoners were released in 1978. Law is traditional Islamic law; most of the people rely on a traditional subsistence economy; the small elite has developed commercial fishing and tourism.

Comparatively: Maldives is as free as Qatar, freer than Seychelles, less free than Mauritius.

MALI

Economy: noninclusive mixed
    socialist
Polity: nationalist one-party
    (military dominated)
Population: 6,300,000

Political Rights: 7
Civil Liberties: 6
Status of Freedom: not free

A transethnic heterogeneous state

Political Rights. Mali is a military dictatorship with a recently constructed political party to lend support. The regime appears to function without broad popular consensus. *Subnationalities*: Although the government is ostensibly above ethnic rivalries, severe repression of the northern peoples has been reported.

Civil Liberties. The media are all government controlled. Antigovernment demonstrations are forbidden. Private conversation is relatively free. Political imprisonment occurred in 1978, although many prisoners from previous years were released. Religion is free. Unions are controlled; travelers must submit to frequent police checks. Private economic rights in the modern sector are minimal, but collectivization has recently been deemphasized for subsistence agriculturists, the majority of the people.

Comparatively: Mali is as free as Togo, freer than Somalia, less free than Liberia.

MALTA

Economy: mixed capitalist-statist   Political Rights: 2
Polity: centralized multiparty   Civil Liberties: 2
Population: 322,000   Status of Freedom: free

A relatively homogeneous population

Political Rights. Malta is a parliamentary democracy in which power has shifted between the major parties. The most recent election, maintaining the governing party in its position, was marked by violence. The government also altered the composition of a constitutional court in the middle of a case concerning alleged coercion of voters in a particular district.

Civil Liberties. The press is free. Broadcasting is under a licensed body; Italian media are also available. The government has concentrated a great deal of the economy in its hands, and social equalization programs have been emphasized.

Comparatively: Malta is as free as Italy, freer than Turkey, less free than the United Kingdom.

MAURITANIA

Economy: noninclusive mixed   Political Rights: 6
        capitalist   Civil Liberties: 6
Polity: military nonparty   Status of Freedom: not free
Population: 1,500,000

An ethnic state with minor territorial subnationalities

Political Rights. Mauritania is ruled by a military committee pledged to the restoration of democracy. Subnationalities: There are important subnational movements in the portion of the Western Sahara that has been recently incorporated and in the non-Arab, southern part of the country.

Civil Liberties. The media are government owned, but foreign publications and broadcasts are freely available. Members of the previous government remain in jail. Conversation is free and no ideology is imposed. Travel is generally unrestricted. Union activity is government controlled. There is religious freedom. The government controls much of industry and mining, as well as wholesale trade, but the new regime has moved to reduce government involvement.

Comparatively: Mauritania is as free as Tanzania, freer than Iraq, less free than Morocco.

MAURITIUS

Economy: noninclusive capitalist   **Political Rights:** 2
Polity: centralized multiparty   **Civil Liberties:** 4
Population: 900,000   **Status of Freedom:** partly free

An ethnically complex state

Political Rights. Mauritius is a parliamentary democracy. The last election showed an important gain for the opposition, but the government managed to retain power through coalition (and amidst controversy). A variety of different racial and religious communities are active in politics, although they are not territorially based. There are a number of semi-autonomous local governing bodies.

Civil Liberties. The press is private or party and without censorship. Broadcasting is under a single corporation, presumably private in form. Freedom of assembly is restricted: most opposition members of parliament were imprisoned briefly for illegal demonstration in 1978. The labor union movement is quite strong, as are a variety of communal organizations. There is religious and economic freedom; taxes can be quite high.

Comparatively: Mauritius is as free as Western Samoa, freer than the Comoro Islands, less free than Barbados.

MEXICO

Economy: capitalist-statist   **Political Rights:** 4
Polity: decentralized dominant-   **Civil Liberties:** 4
    party   **Status of Freedom:** partly free
Population: 66,900,000

An ethnic state with potential subnationalities

Political Rights. Mexico is ruled by a governmental system formally modeled on that of the United States; in practice the president is much stronger and the legislative and judicial branches much weaker. The states have independent governors and legislatures. The ruling party has had a near monopoly of power on all levels since the 1920's.

In the last election the president received over ninety-four percent of the vote, and the ruling party won all but one seat in the Congress. Political competition is largely confined to factional struggles within the ruling party—these are not struggles that the general public can use its vote to resolve. New laws may foster greater political competition in the future by increasing the share of representation for parties. Voting and campaign irregularities are common, particularly on the local level. *Subnationalities*: There is a large Mayan area in Yucatan that has formerly been restive; there are also other smaller Indian areas.

Civil Liberties. The media are mostly private. Although they have operated under a variety of direct and indirect government controls (including take-overs), newspapers are generally free of censorship. Literature and the arts are free. The judicial system is not strong. However, decisions can go against the government; it is possible to win a judicial decision that a law is unconstitutional in a particular application. The clergy are prohibited from political activity, but religion is free. Widespread bribery and lack of control over the behavior of security forces greatly limits operative freedom. Disappearances occur, detention is prolonged, torture and brutality have been common. Private economic rights are respected; government ownership predominates in major industries.

Comparatively: Mexico is as free as Bangladesh, freer than Nicaragua, less free than Colombia.

MONGOLIA

Economy: socialist
Polity: communist one-party
Population: 1,600,000

Political Rights: 7
Civil Liberties: 7
Status of Freedom: not free

A relatively homogeneous population

Political Rights. A one-party communist dictatorship, for many years Mongolia has been firmly under the control of one man. Power is organized at all levels through the party apparatus. Those who oppose the government cannot run for office. In the 1977 parliamentary elections, 99.9 percent of eligible voters participated; only two persons failed to properly vote for the single list of candidates. Mongolia has a subordinate relation to the Soviet Union, which it depends on for defense against Chinese claims. It must use the USSR as an outlet for nearly all of its trade, and its finances are under close Soviet supervision.

Civil Liberties. All media are government controlled, and apparently quite effectively. Religion is greatly restricted, Lamaism having been nearly wiped out. Freedom of travel, residence, and other civil liberties are denied.

Comparatively: Mongolia is as free as Bulgaria, less free than the USSR.

MOROCCO

Economy: noninclusive capitalist
Polity: centralized multiparty
Population: 18,900,000

Political Rights: 3
Civil Liberties: 4
Status of Freedom: partly free

An ethnic state with a potential Berber subnationality

Political Rights. Morocco is a constitutional monarchy in which the king has retained major executive powers. Recent elections at both local and national levels were fair and well contested in most localities. Most parties participated (including the communist); independents (largely supporters of the king) were the major winners. Opposition leaders were included in the subsequent government. The autonomy of local and regional elected governments is limited. *Subnationalities*: Although people in the newly acquired land of the Western Sahara participate in the electoral process, it has an important resistance movement. In the rest of the country the large Berber minority is a potential subnationality.

Civil Liberties. Newspapers are private or party, and quite vigorous. Recently there has been no formal censorship, although there are other pressures, including the confiscation of particular issues. Both public and private broadcasting stations are under government control. Political arrests have often followed violent attempts to overthrow the government; many of those arrested may not have been personally involved in violence. The use of torture has been quite common and probably continues; the rule of law has been weakened by the frequent use of prolonged detention without trial. There were few political arrests in 1978. There are strong labor unions; religious and other private rights are respected.

Comparatively: Morocco is as free as Malaysia, freer than Algeria, less free than Spain.

MOZAMBIQUE

Economy: noninclusive socialist
Polity: socialist one-party
Population: 9,900,000

Political Rights: 7
Civil Liberties: 7
Status of Freedom: not free

A transethnic heterogeneous state

Political Rights. Mozambique is a one-party communist dictatorship in which all power resides in the party leadership. (The Liberation Front has now officially been converted into a "vanguard party.") A series of elections from village to national assembly levels were held in 1977: all candidates were selected by the ruling party at all levels. Regional administration is controlled from the center.

Civil Liberties. The press may not yet all be government owned, but broadcasting is; all media are rigidly controlled. No public criticism is allowed. There are no private lawyers. Secret police are powerful; up to 100,000 people are in reeducation camps. Police brutality is common. Independent unions are being replaced. Heavy pressure has been put on all religions and especially Jehovah's Witnesses. Villagers are being forced into communes, leading to revolts in some areas. The emigration of citizens is restricted.

Comparatively: Mozambique is as free as Angola, less free than Tanzania.

NAURU

Economy: capitalist-statist

Polity: traditional nonparty

Population: 8,500

Political Rights: 2

Civil Liberties: 2

Status of Freedom: free

An ethnically complex state

Political Rights. Nauru is a parliamentary democracy with a recent change of government by elective and parliamentary means. Realignments have led to considerable political instability. The country is under Australian influence.

Civil Liberties. The media are free of censorship but little developed. The island's major industry is controlled by the government, but otherwise private economic rights are respected.

Comparatively: Nauru is as free as Fiji, freer than the Maldives, less free than New Zealand.

NEPAL

Economy: noninclusive capitalist

Polity: traditional nonparty

Population: 13,400,000

Political Rights: 6

Civil Liberties: 5

Status of Freedom: partly free

An ethnic state with active and potential subnationalities

Political Rights. Nepal is a constitutional monarchy in which the king is dominant. The national parliament is elected indirectly through a series of tiers of government in which the lower levels are directly elected. Elected representatives do not have a great deal of power except possibly at the village and town levels. The government's movement generally selects those elected; no political parties are allowed, but some members of the opposition have joined the government. *Subnationalities*: There are a variety of different peoples, with only fifty percent of the people speaking Nepali as a first language. Hinduism is a unifying force for the vast majority. The historically powerful ruling castes continue to dominate.

Civil Liberties. Newspapers are public and private; muted criticism is allowed of the government but not the king. Foreign publications are often banned; Indian papers remain the main source of news about the opposition. Radio is government owned. Private contacts are relatively open. Political arrests, banishment from the capital, and exile occur. The judiciary is not independent. Religious proselytizing and conversion is prohibited, and the emigration of those with valuable skills or education is restricted. The population is nearly all engaged in traditional occupations; illiteracy levels are very high.

Comparatively: Nepal is as free as South Africa, freer than Burma, less free than Malaysia.

NETHERLANDS

Economy: mixed capitalist
Polity: centralized multiparty
Population: 13,900,000

Political Rights: 1
Civil Liberties: 1
Status of Freedom: free

A relatively homogeneous population

Political Rights. Netherlands is a constitutional monarchy in which nearly all the power is vested in a directly elected legislature. The results of elections have periodically transferred power to coalitions of the left and right. There is some diffusion of political power below this level, but not a great deal. The monarch retains more power than in the United Kingdom both through the activity of appointing government in frequently stalemated situations, and through the advisory Council of State.

Civil Liberties. The media are free and private, with broadcasting more directly supervised by the government. The courts are independent, and the full spectrum of private rights guaranteed. The burden of exceptionally heavy taxes limits economic choice.

Comparatively: The Netherlands is as free as Belgium, freer than Portugal.

NEW ZEALAND

Economy: capitalist
Polity: centralized multiparty
Population: 3,200,000

Political Rights: 1
Civil Liberties: 1
Status of Freedom: free

A relatively homogeneous state with a native subnationality

Political Rights. New Zealand is a parliamentary democracy in which power alternates between the two major parties. There is elected local government, but it is not independently powerful. *Subnationalities*: About eight percent of the population are Maori, the original inhabitants.

Civil Liberties. The press is private and free. Television and most radio stations are owned by the government. The rule of law and private rights are thoroughly respected. Since taxes (a direct restriction on choice) are not exceptionally high, and industry is not government owned, we label New Zealand capitalist. Others, emphasizing the government's highly developed social programs and penchant for controlling prices, wages, and credit might place New Zealand further toward the socialist end of the economic spectrum.

Comparatively: New Zealand is as free as the United States, freer than Japan.

NICARAGUA

Economy: noninclusive capitalist
Polity: centralized dominant-party
        (military dominated)
Population: 2,400,000

Political Rights: 5
Civil Liberties: 5
Status of Freedom: partly free

A relatively homogeneous population

Political Rights. Since 1928 Nicaragua has been ruled directly or indirectly by the Somoza family. The current President Somoza was returned to power in 1974 after the constitution had been adapted to make that possible. Elections are manipulated in accordance with the government's wishes. For example, the latest legislative election produced an agreed upon 3/2 formula for representation between Somoza's ruling Liberal Party and the Conservative Party. Other parties exist but they are not recognized. Somoza's election in 1974 was certainly facilitated by the disqualification or withdrawal of the opposition candidates. Somoza control is based on economic power and control over the National Guard.

Civil Liberties. The media are private and often highly critical. Recognized and unrecognized opposition groups have the right of assembly. Censorship and violence against the media have been applied intermittently during the recent disturbances and civil wars. In the last few years large numbers have been detained for political opposition; torture, widespread killing, and brutality have occurred, especially in rural areas. The civil war in 1978 cost thousands of lives, many killed needlessly by government troops. In common with several Central American countries, the independence of the judiciary is not well developed, but the government does not always win in the courts. Union activity is relatively free and varied. The combination of economic and governmental power in the hands of one family reduces economic freedoms in a society without as much of the cushion of preindustrial forms as its comparative poverty and agricultural base might indicate.

Comparatively: Nicaragua is as free as the Philippines, freer than Cuba, less free than Guatemala.

N I G E R

Economy: noninclusive capitalist
Polity: military nonparty
Population: 5,000,000

Political Rights: 7
Civil Liberties: 6
Status of Freedom: not free

A transethnic heterogeneous state

Political Rights. Niger is a military dictatorship with no elected assembly or legal parties. All districts are administered from the center.

Civil Liberties. Niger's very limited media are government owned and operated. Dissent is seldom tolerated, although ideological conformity is not demanded. A military court has taken the place of a suspended Supreme Court, and political prisoners are held. Labor unions are closely controlled. Foreign travel is relatively open; outside of politics the government does not regulate individual behavior.

Comparatively: Niger is as free as Togo, freer than Benin, less free than Liberia.

N I G E R I A

Economy: noninclusive
        capitalist-statist
Polity: military nonparty
Population: 85,000,000*

Political Rights: 5
Civil Liberties: 3
Status of Freedom: partly free

A multinational state

---

* Population may be 68,000,000–100,000,000.

Political Rights. Government in Nigeria remains under military control. However, the tradition of decentralized power remains. The Constituent Assembly elected in 1977 produced a constitution in 1978 in accord with democratic practices. Party activity then resumed in preparation for 1979 elections. However, only those five major parties that could show national constituencies have been authorized—these included all the major civilian leaders. There are elected local governments.

Subnationalities: Nigeria is made up of a number of powerful subnational groupings. Speaking mainly Hausa, the people of the north are Muslim. The highly urbanized southwest is dominated by the Yoruba; and the east by the Ibo. Within each of these areas and along their borders there are other peoples, some of which are conscious of their identity and number more than one million persons. Strong loyalties to traditional political units—lineages or kingdoms—throughout the country further complicate the regional picture. With the new constitution proposing nineteen (or more) states, and independent institutions below this level, the present rulers seem dedicated to taking into account the demands of this complexity in a new federal structure.

Civil Liberties. Traditionally, Nigeria's media have been some of the freest in Africa. Television and radio are now wholly federal or state owned, as are all but two of the major papers, in part as the result of a Nigerianization program. However, in spite of occasional suppressions, the media continue to preserve considerable editorial independence. Political organization, assembly, and publication are now freely permitted. The universities, secondary schools, and the trade unions have been brought under close government control or reorganization in the last few years. Apparently the judiciary remains strong and independent, including, in Muslim areas, sharia courts. No prisoners of conscience are held; citizens can win in court against the government. There is freedom of religion and travel. The country is in the process of moving from a subsistence to industrial economy— largely on the basis of government-controlled oil and oil-related industry. Government intervention elsewhere in agriculture (cooperatives and plantations) and industry has been considerable. Since private business and industry are also encouraged, this is still far from a program of massive redistribution. General corruption in political and economic life has frequently diminished the rule of law. Freedom is respected in most other areas of life.

Comparatively: Nigeria is as free as Bolivia, freer than Ghana, less free than Morocco.

NORWAY

Economy: mixed capitalist　　　　**Political Rights:** 1
Polity: centralized multiparty　　**Civil Liberties:** 1
Population: 4,100,000　　　　　　**Status of Freedom:** free

A relatively homogeneous population with a small Lapp minority

Political Rights. Norway is a centralized, constitutional monarchy. Labor remains the strongest party, but other parties have formed several governments since the mid-1960's. There is relatively little separation of powers. Regional governments have appointed governors; cities and towns their own elected officials.

Civil Liberties. Newspapers are privately or party owned; radio and television are state monopolies. This is a pluralistic state with independent power in the churches and labor unions. Relatively strong family structures have also been preserved. Norway is capitalistic, yet the extremely high tax burden, perhaps the highest in the noncommunist world, the government's control over the new oil resource, and general reliance on centralized planning reduce the freedom of economic activity.

Comparatively: Norway is as free as the United Kingdom, freer than West Germany.

OMAN

Economy: noninclusive capitalist-　**Political Rights:** 6
　　　　　　statist　　　　　　　　**Civil Liberties:** 6
Polity: centralized nonparty　　　**Status of Freedom:** not free
Population: 500,000

An ethnic state with a territorial subnationality

Political Rights. Oman is an absolute monarchy with no political parties or elected assemblies. Regional rule is by centrally appointed governors, but the remaining tribal structure at the local and regional level gives a measure of local autonomy. The government is under British influence because of their long record of aid and advice. *Subnationalities*: Quite different from other Omani, the people of Dhofar constitute a small subnationality in periodic revolt.

Civil Liberties. Newspapers are public and private, broadcasting is government controlled. Except in private, criticism is not generally allowed. Although the preservation of traditional institutions provides a check on arbitrary action, the right to a fair trial is not guaranteed. Freedom of assembly and freedom of public religious expression are curtailed. There is freedom of travel; private property is respected.

Comparatively: Oman is as free as Saudi Arabia, freer than South Yemen, less free than the United Arab Emirates.

PAKISTAN

Economy: noninclusive capitalist-statist
Polity: military nonparty
Population: 76,800,000

Political Rights: 6
Civil Liberties: 5
Status of Freedom: partly free

A multinational state

Political Rights. At present Pakistan is under centralized military rule. The political parties, religious leaders, provincial leaders, and judiciary (and bar association) continue to be factors in a situation with many elements of consensus. Some party leaders have been brought into the government. (The early spring 1979 execution of the ousted prime minister for murder, whether or not justified, could tear the country apart.) Ostensibly, the present government sees itself as presiding over an interregnum before the reestablishment of an elected federal regime. *Subnationalities*: Millions of Pathans, Baluchis, and Sindhis have been represented since the origin of Pakistan as desiring greater regional autonomy or independence. Provincial organization has sporadically offered a measure of self-determination.

Civil Liberties. Newspapers are private and independent; the occasional detention of journalists and the closing of papers lead to self-censorship. Radio and television are public and have recently been granted more freedom—yet their rights can as easily be withdrawn. Thousands of members of the opposition have been imprisoned or flogged in the violent political climate. Yet there is a high level of political activity, and 1978 saw the first legal communist party of this generation. Rights of assembly are limited, as are those of travel for some political persons. Courts preserve considerable independence. Unions organize freely and have the right to strike. A renewed emphasis on Islamic conservatism curtails private rights, especially freedom of religion. Private property is respected, although many basic industries have been nationalized.

Comparatively: Pakistan is as free as Tunisia, freer than Afghanistan, less free than Bangladesh.

PANAMA

Economy: capitalist-statist   **Political Rights:** 5
Polity: military nonparty   **Civil Liberties:** 5
Population: 1,800,000   **Status of Freedom:** partly free

A relatively homogeneous population

Political Rights. Officially Panama is governed by a president elected for a six-year term by the assembly. Assembly members are elected from very unequal districts and assembly powers are very limited. Although elections are nonparty, organized opposition functions at least in major cities and for referendums. The National Guard retains major political power. The provinces are administered by presidential appointees.

Civil Liberties. Newspapers are directly or indirectly under government control. Censorship and self-censorship still exist in practice but have become less common in all media since 1977. Political parties maintain their opposition role. The judiciary is not independent; the rule of law is very weak in both political and nonpolitical areas. Although common in the past, political arrest or torture was uncommon or absent in 1978. The government owns major concerns; private property is generally respected; labor unions are under some restrictions. There is general freedom of religion, although foreign priests are not allowed. Travel is generally free.

Comparatively: Panama is as free as the Philippines, freer than Haiti, less free than Guatemala.

PAPUA NEW GUINEA

Economy: noninclusive capitalist   **Political Rights:** 2
Polity: centralized multiparty   **Civil Liberties:** 2
Population: 3,000,000   **Status of Freedom:** free

A transethnic heterogeneous state with subnationalities

Political Rights. Papua New Guinea is an independent parliamentary democracy, although it remains partially dependent on Australia economically, technically, and militarily. Elections appear fair and seats are divided among two major and several minor parties—party allegiances are still fluid. Because of its dispersed and tribal nature, local government is in some ways quite decentralized. Elected provincial governments with extensive powers have been establishd. *Subnationalities*: Development of provincial government is meant to contain strong secessionist movements in the Solomon Islands, Papua, and elsewhere.

Civil Liberties. The press is not highly developed but apparently free. Radio and television are government controlled; Australian stations are also received. The legal system adapted from Australia is operational, but a large proportion of the population lives in a preindustrial world with traditional controls, including violence, that limit freedom of speech, travel, occupation, and other private rights.

Comparatively: Papua New Guinea is as free as Portugal, freer than Malaysia, less free than Australia.

PARAGUAY

Economy: noninclusive capitalist-statist
Polity: centralized dominant-party (military dominated)
Population: 2,900,000

Political Rights: 5
Civil Liberties: 5
Status of Freedom: partly free

A relatively homogeneous state with small Indian groups

Political Rights. Paraguay has been ruled as a modified dictatorship since 1954. In addition to an elected president there is a parliament that includes members of opposition parties. Elections are regularly held, but they have limited meaning: the ruling party receives eighty to ninety percent of the vote, a result guaranteed by direct and indirect pressures on the media, massive government pressure on voters, especially in the countryside, and interference with opposition party organization. The most important regional and local officials are appointed by the president. Subnationalities: The population represents a mixture of Indian (Guarani) and Spanish peoples; ninety percent continue to speak Guarani as well as Spanish. Several small tribes of primitive forest peoples are under heavy pressure from both the government and the public.

Civil Liberties. There is a private press, and a combination of private, government, and church radio and television. In spite of censorship and periodic suppression of publications, dissenting opinion is expressed, especially by the church hierarchy and opposition newspapers. Opposition political organization continues, as do human rights organizations. Torture, imprisonment, and execution of political opponents have been an important part of a sociopolitical situation that includes general corruption and anarchy. But reports of these actions were uncommon in 1978 and nearly all prisoners of conscience were released. Union organization is restricted. The government's brutal suppression of the Aché (Guayaki) people has received widespread publicity; in 1978 this led to improvement in their position. Recognition of Jehovah's Witnesses was withdrawn in 1978. Beyond the subsistence sector, private economic rights are restricted by government intervention and control. Perhaps a majority of peasants now own land, partly as a result of government policy.

Comparatively: Paraguay is as free as Nicaragua, freer than Cuba, less free than Brazil.

P E R U

Economy: noninclusive mixed
        capitalist
Polity: military nonparty
Population: 17,100,000

Political Rights: 5
Civil Liberties: 4
Status of Freedom: partly free

An ethnic state with a major territorial subnationality.

Political Rights. Peru is ruled by a military junta of varying composition. The government responds to the pressure of a variety of organized groups, such as unions, peasant organizations, and political parties. In 1978 a constituent assembly with broad party representation was fairly elected. (Illiterates, perhaps twenty percent of the voting age population, could not vote.) At least informally its powers went beyond those of writing a constitution. Parliamentary elections are to be held in 1979. Provincial administration is not independent. *Subnationalities*: Several million people speak Quechua in the highlands, and it has recently become an official language. There are other important Indian groups.

Civil Liberties. The media are largely under government control, but journals are free and highly critical. The existence of a variety of political parties allows diverse positions to be expressed; the parties have limited access to the broadcasting services and have a limited right of assembly. Political prisoners are taken and union leaders are frequently detained, in some cases justifiably because of violence or threats of violence. Some opposition leaders were briefly exiled during the last year, but most returned; by the end of the year all prisoners of conscience appeared to be freed. Reports of torture and death during interrogation have been publicized in the recent past, and in the political arena states of emergencies have frequently weakened the rule of law. Rights to religion, travel, and occupation are generally respected. Land reform, nationalization, and experiments in compulsory worker control of factories or institutions have characterized recent years, but private property has regained governmental acceptance.

Comparatively: Peru is as free as Kenya, freer than Paraguay, less free than Guyana.

PHILIPPINES

Economy: noninclusive capitalist   **Political Rights:** 5
Polity: civilian nonparty   **Civil Liberties:** 5
Population: 46,300,000   **Status of Freedom:** partly free

A transethnic heterogeneous state with active and potential subnationalities

Political Rights. The Philippines is ruled as a plebiscitory family dictatorship with the aid of a docile assembly. The present ruler was elected in a fair election, but more recent referendums affirming his rule, his constitutional changes, and martial law have not been conducted with open competition, free discussion, or acceptable voting procedures. Previously legitimate political parties exist, but they have no part to play in current political life. Assembly elections in 1978 were held with severely restricted opposition activity and were boycotted by the major parties. The results were subject to questionable tabulations. There is some decentralization of power to local assemblies, but provincial and local officials are centrally appointed. *Subnationalities*: The Philippines includes a variety of different peoples of which the Tagalog speaking are the most important (although a minority). A portion of the Muslim (Moro) subnationality is in active revolt along the front of Christian-Muslim opposition. There are several major potential subnationalities that may request autonomy in the near future on the basis of both territorial and linguistic identity.

Civil Liberties. Newspapers and broadcasting are largely private but under indirect government control. No opposition papers or stations are allowed; diverse foreign publications are widely available. Freedom of assembly for the opposition is restricted. The courts have retained some independence although it has been much reduced. Prisoners of conscience are held; torture is used but is sporadically condemned by the top levels of government—torturers have been brought before the courts. Unions have only limited independence, but strikes are permitted. The Church still maintains its independence; private rights including that to religious choice are generally respected. The economy is marginally capitalist, but there has been rapid growth in government intervention, favoritism, and direct ownership of industries.

Comparatively: The Philippines is as free as Singapore, freer than Vietnam, less free than Malaysia.

POLAND

Economy: mixed socialist
Polity: communist one-party
Population: 35,000,000

Political Rights: 6
Civil Liberties: 5
Status of Freedom: partly free

A relatively homogeneous population

Political Rights. Poland is a one-party communist dictatorship, with noncompetitive, one-list elections. However, a few nonparty persons are in the assembly and recent sessions have evidenced more than pro forma debate. There are elected councils at provincial levels. The party apparatus operating from the top down is in any event the locus of power. The Catholic Church, academics, peasants, and workers have countervailing power. The Soviet Union's right of interference and continual pressure diminishes Poland's independence.

Civil Liberties. The Polish newspapers are both private and government, and broadcasting is government owned. The independent press occasionally differs cautiously with the government. Censorship is pervasive; yet there are legal anti-Marxist publications with limited circulations. There are prisoners of conscience, no right of assembly, nor concept of an independent judiciary. Short imprisonment, beating, and harassment are now the most common means of restricting opposition. Illegal attempts to leave Poland frequently lead to arrest, but travel is now permitted for most citizens. Strikes and demonstrations occur, and nongovernmental organizations develop; the Church is an especially important alternative institution. Most agriculture and considerable commerce remain in private hands.

Comparatively: Poland is as free as Tunisia, freer than Yugoslavia, less free than Egypt.

PORTUGAL

Economy: mixed capitalist
Polity: centralized multiparty
Population: 9,700,000

Political Rights: 2
Civil Liberties: 2
Status of Freedom: free

A relatively homogeneous population

Political Rights. At present Portugal is a parliamentary democracy with the military command playing a relatively strong role through the presidency and the Council of the Revolution. There is vigorous party competition over most of the spectrum (except the far right), and fair elections. Provincial government is centrally directed.

Civil Liberties. The most important papers and journals are private or party owned, and are now quite free. Radio and television are government owned except for one Catholic station. The government has restored the rule of law. There are probably few prisoners of conscience, yet one can be imprisoned for insult to the government or military. Long periods of detention without trial occur. Imprisonment for "fascist" organization or discussion was promulgated in 1978. The Catholic Church, unions, peasant organizations, and military services remain alternative institutions of power. The economy has a large nationalized sector, but movement is toward capitalism.

Comparatively: Portugal is as free as Greece, freer than Turkey, less free than France.

Q A T A R

Economy: capitalist-statist
Polity: traditional nonparty
Population: 250,000

Political Rights: 5
Civil Liberties: 5
Status of Freedom: partly free

A relatively homogeneous citizenry

Political Rights. Qatar is a traditional monarchy. The majority of the residents are recently arrived foreigners; of the native population perhaps one-fourth are members of the ruling family. The role of consensus is suggested by the fact that extravagance and lack of attention to affairs of state recently led the ruling family to replace the monarch.

Civil Liberties. The weak press is public and private; broadcasting is government owned. Self-censorship is practiced, but discussion is fairly open and foreign publications are available. This is a traditional state still responsive to Islamic and tribal laws that moderate the absolutism of government. The family government controls the nation's wealth through control over oil, but there are also independently powerful merchant and religious classes. Union activity is negligible.

Comparatively: Qatar is as free as the United Arab Emirates, freer than Saudi Arabia, less free than Lebanon.

R H O D E S I A

Economy: noninclusive capitalist-statist
Polity: centralized multiparty
Population: 7,000,000

Political Rights: 5
Civil Liberties: 5
Status of Freedom: partly free

An ethnic state with a majority nonterritorial subnationality

Political Rights. Rhodesia is a parliamentary democracy in which the overwhelming power has been in the hands of the white minority (four percent). Some black representatives have opposed the whites in parliament. In 1978 executive power was partially transferred to the leaders of the main black parties within the country and their followers. They have three of four positions on an Executive Council and are represented in each ministry. This transitional regime has drawn up a constitution and planned elections for 1979.

Civil Liberties. The press is private. It is under pressure to conform, but still offers a spectrum of opinion within the white community. A major black publication appeared but was later banned in 1978. Broadcasting is government controlled. For whites there is a generally fair application of the rule of law, freedom of residence and occupation (except for conscription). Black parties have general freedom of speech, assembly, and organization, as long as they do not support the guerrilla movements based outside the country. Laws allowing for racial discrimination were greatly modified during the year, especially in residence, occupation, and conscription. Much of the country is under martial law. The forced movement of large numbers of blacks into fortified villages because of the security situation has been resented by many. The war and security situation has led to political imprisonments. Both agricultural and nonagricultural economic development has moved Rhodesia most of the way toward a capitalist society, while government restrictions on movement and work of black citizens in the recent past have created a form of corporate state economy.

Comparatively: Rhodesia is as free as the Sudan, freer than Mozambique, less free than Kenya.

RUMANIA

Economy: socialist
Polity: communist one-party
Population: 21,900,000

Political Rights: 7
Civil Liberties: 6
Status of Freedom: not free

An ethnic state with territorial subnationalities

Political Rights. Rumania is a now-traditional communist state. Assemblies at national and regional levels are subservient to the party hierarchy. Elections involve only candidates chosen by the party; for some assembly positions the party may propose several candidates. Soviet influence is relatively slight. *Subnationalities*: The Magyar and German minorities are territorially based. If offered self-determination one Magyar area would surely opt for rejoining neighboring Hungary; many of the Germans evidently wish to migrate to Germany, and this movement has been developing. In Rumania the cultural rights of both groups are narrowly limited.

Civil Liberties. The media include only government or party organs for which self-censorship committees recently replaced centralized censorship. Dissenters are frequently imprisoned or placed in psychiatric institutions. Treatment may be brutal. Many arrests have been made for attempting to leave the country or importing foreign literature (especially Bibles and material in minority languages). Religious and other personal freedoms are quite restricted. Private museums have recently been closed. Independent labor and management rights are essentially nonexistent.

Comparatively: Rumania is as free as East Germany, freer than Bulgaria, less free than Hungary.

R W A N D A

Economy: noninclusive mixed
Polity: nationalist one-party
(military dominated)
Population: 4,500,000

Political Rights: 6
Civil Liberties: 6
Status of Freedom: not free

An ethnic state with a minority nonterritorial subnationality

Political Rights. Rwanda is a military dictatorship with an auxiliary party organization. A constitutional referendum and plebiscite were held in 1978, but not under conditions of freedom. Similar conditions are expected for elections to establish an assembly in 1979. There is no legislature and districts are administered by the central government. There are elected local councils. *Subnationalities*: The former ruling people, the Tutsi, have been persecuted and heavily discriminatd against, but the situation has improved.

Civil Liberties. The weak press is private or governmental; radio is government owned. Public criticism is very constrained. Political prisoners are held, and beating of prisoners and suspects may be common. Considerable religious freedom exists. Travel is restricted both within the country and across its borders. Independent labor unions were authorized in 1978. There are no great extremes of wealth. The government is socialist in intent, but missionary cooperatives dominate trade, and private business is active in the small nonsubsistence sector. Traditional ways of life rather than government orders regulate the lives of most.

Comparatively: Rwanda is as free as Gabon, freer than Burundi, less free than Zambia.

SAO TOME AND PRINCIPE

Economy: inclusive socialist
Polity: socialist one-party
Population: 85,000

Political Rights: 6
Civil Liberties: 6
Status of Freedom: not free

A relatively homogeneous population

Political Rights. Sao Tome and Principe are governed under strong-man leadership by the revolutionary party that recently led the country to independence. The degree of implementation of the post-independence constitutional system remains unclear.

Civil Liberties. The media are government controlled; opposition voices are not heard; there is no effective right of political assembly. The largely plantation agriculture has been socialized, as has most of the economy. Labor unions are not independent. On the other hand, there is an operating legal system, freedom of religion, and little evidence of brutality, torture, or political imprisonment.

Comparatively: Sao Tome and Principe appears to be as free as Guinea-Bissau, freer than Guinea, less free than Senegal.

SAUDI ARABIA

Economy: capitalist-statist
Polity: traditional nonparty
Population: 7,800,000

Political Rights: 6
Civil Liberties: 6
Status of Freedom: not free

A relatively homogeneous population

Political Rights. Saudi Arabia is a traditional family monarchy ruling without assemblies. Political parties are prohibited. The right of petition is guaranteed. Regional government is by appointive officers; there are some local elective assemblies.

Civil Liberties. The press is both private and governmental; strict self-censorship is expected. Radio and television are mostly government owned, although ARAMCO also has stations. Private conversation is relatively free; there is no right of political assembly. Islamic law limits arbitrary government, but the rule of law is not fully institutionalized. Political prisoners and torture have been reported; there appear to be few if any prisoners of conscience. Citizens have no freedom of religion—all must be Muslims. Unions are forbidden. Private rights in areas such as occupation or residence are generally respected, but marriage to a non-Muslim or non-Saudi is closely controlled. Women may not marry non-Muslims, and suffer other special disabilities, particularly in the right to travel. The economy is overwhelmingly dominated by petroleum or petroleum-related industry that is directly or indirectly under government control.

Comparatively: Saudi Arabia is as free as Algeria, freer than Iraq, less free than Syria.

SENEGAL

Economy: mixed capitalist
Polity: centralized dominant-party
Population: 5,400,000

Political Rights: 4
Civil Liberties: 3
Status of Freedom: partly free

A transethnic heterogeneous state

Political Rights. After several years under a relatively benevolent one-party system, multiparty activities begun in 1977 were expanded in 1978. In parliamentary elections during the year eighteen of one hundred seats were obtained by an opposition party. Subsequently, another important party was recognized. Decentralization is restricted to the local level.

Subnationalities: Ethnically eighty percent are Muslims; the Wolof people represent thirty-six percent of the population, including most of the elite, the urban population, and the more prosperous farmers. However, regional loyalties, both within and outside of this linguistic grouping, seem to be at least as important as communal groupings in defining potential subnationalities. In addition, rapid assimilation of rural migrants in the cities to Wolof culture has reduced the tendency toward ethnic cleavage. The fact that the ruler since independence is a member of the second largest ethnic group (Serer) and minority religion (Catholic) also retards the development of competing subnationalisms.

Civil Liberties. The press is independent, but censorship and arrests for illegal publications have occurred. Major opposition papers and journals now appear. Belonging to illegal associations is still punished. Unions have gained increasing independence. Religion, travel, occupation, and other private rights are respected. Although much of the land remains tribally owned, government-organized cooperatives and dependence on external markets have transformed the preindustrial society.

Comparatively: Senegal is as free as Morocco, freer than Ghana, less free than Gambia.

SEYCHELLES

Economy: mixed capitalist
Polity: nationalist one-party
Population: 65,000

Political Rights: 6
Civil Liberties: 5
Status of Freedom: partly free

A relatively homogeneous population

Political Rights. Seychelles is ruled by decree after a coup that ousted the majority government. The leader of the former main opposition party is in charge of the government. Now officially a one-party socialist state, the former ruling party is said to have "simply disappeared." There is no local government.

Civil Liberties. The press is private and governmental, and radio largely governmental. The courts apparently operate in comparative freedom. Discussion is fairly open, but there is little right of assembly and the security services have broad powers of arrest. Opposition party activities are banned. Twenty persons were arrested and held for several months because of an alleged plot in 1978. Labor and government are interconnected. Private rights, including private property, are generally respected, despite the extensive government services of a largely urban, if impoverished, welfare state.

Comparatively: Seychelles is as free as Pakistan, freer than Tanzania, less free than Maldives.

SIERRA LEONE

Economy: noninclusive capitalist
Polity: centralized one-party
Population: 3,300,000

Political Rights: 5
Civil Liberties: 5
Status of Freedom: partly free

A formally transethnic heterogeneous state

Political Rights. After progressively excluding opposition candidates from power by violence, arrest, parliamentary exclusion, or electoral malpractice, in 1978 Sierra Leone's rulers used a possibly fraudulent referendum to formally establish a one-party state. The new cabinet included, however, members of the former opposition. There is little independent local government.

Civil Liberties. The press is private and governmental. Radio is government controlled. Both are now closely controlled, but there is considerable freedom of private speech. The courts do not appear to be very powerful or independent. Special emergency powers have given the government untrammeled powers of detention, censorship, restriction of assembly, and search for the last two years. There may have been no prisoners of conscience at the end of 1978. Identity cards have recently been required of all citizens. Labor unions are relatively independent and travel is freely permitted. The largely subsistence economy has an essentially capitalist modern sector. Corruption is pervasive.

Comparatively: Sierra Leone is as free as Nicaragua, freer than Gabon, less free than Senegal.

SINGAPORE

Economy: mixed capitalist-statist
Polity: centralized dominant-party
Population: 2,325,000

Political Rights: 5
Civil Liberties: 5
Status of Freedom: partly free

An ethnically complex state

Political Rights. Singapore is a parliamentary democracy in which the ruling party has won all of the legislative seats in recent elections. Reasonable grounds exist for believing that economic and other pressures against all opposition groups (exerted in part through control of the media) make elections very unfair. After the last election three opposition leaders were sentenced to jail terms for such crimes as defaming the prime minister during the campaign. The opposition still obtains thirty percent of the votes. There is no local government.

Civil Liberties. The press is nominally private, but owners of shares with policy-making power must be officially approved; in some cases the government owns the shares. Broadcasting is largely a government monopoly. By closing papers and imprisoning editors and reporters, the press is kept under close control. University faculties are also under considerable pressure to conform. Most opposition is treated as a communist threat and, therefore, treasonable. Prisoners of conscience are held; in internal security cases the protection of the law is weak—the prosecution's main task appears to be obtaining forced confessions of communist activity. Trade union freedom is inhibited by the close association of government and union. Private rights of religion, occupation, or property are generally observed, although a large and increasing percentage of manufacturing and service companies are government owned.

Comparatively: Singapore is as free as Sierra Leone, freer than Vietnam, less free than Malaysia.

SOLOMON ISLANDS

Economy: preindustrial capitalist
Polity: centralized multiparty
Population: 200,000

Political Rights: 2
Civil Liberties: 2
Status of Freedom: free

A relatively homogeneous state

Political Rights. The Solomon Islands are a parliamentary democracy under the British monarch. There is some decentralization of power at the local level; further decentralization at the provincial level is planned.

Civil Liberties. Media are little developed. The rule of law is maintained in the British manner, alongside traditional ideas of justice. Immediately after independence, published incitement to inter-island conflict led to the banishment of several persons.

Comparatively: The Solomon Islands are as free as Tuvalu, freer than Mauritius, less free than New Zealand.

SOMALIA

Economy: noninclusive mixed socialist
Polity: socialist one-party (military dominated)
Population: 3,400,000

Political Rights: 7
Civil Liberties: 7
Status of Freedom: not free

A relatively homogeneous state

Political Rights. The Somali Republic is under one-man military rule combining glorification of the ruler with the adoption of revolutionary socialist legitimization. A one-party state was declared in 1976, but this does not essentially change the system. Ethnically the state is homogeneous, although until the military coup in 1969 the six main clan groupings and their subdivisions were the major means of organizing loyalty and power. While politics is still understood in lineage terms, in its centralizing drive the government has tried to eliminate both tribal and religious power. A coup attempt in 1978 and subsequent opposition by exiles have been based on tribal rivalries.

Civil Liberties. The media are under strict government control, private conversation is controlled, and those who do not follow the government are considered to be against it. Many political prisoners arrested in the coup have been released, some to government positions; others have received life sentences. There have been recent jailings for strikes, executions for religious propaganda against equal rights for women, and execution of rebels. Travel is restricted. Beyond the dominant subsistence economy, some individual freedoms have been curtailed by establishing state farms, state industries, and welfare programs. However, a definite private sector of the economy has also been staked out.

Comparatively: Somalia is as free as Ethiopia, less free than Kenya.

SOUTH AFRICA

Economy: capitalist-statist
Polity: centralized multiparty
Population: 24,300,000

Political Rights: 5
Civil Liberties: 6
Status of Freedom: partly free

An ethnic state with major territorial and nonterritorial subnationalities

Political Rights. South Africa is a parliamentary democracy in which over eighty percent of the people are excluded from participation in the national political process because of race. For the white population elections appear fair and open. There is, in addition, a limited scope for the nonwhites to influence affairs within their own communities. *Subnationalities:* In the several Bantustans that have not yet separated from the country, black leaders have some power and support from their people. Most black political parties are banned, but operating political parties among Indians and people of mixed blood work for the interests of their respective peoples. Regionally, government within the white community includes both central government officials and elected councils.

Civil Liberties. The white South African press is private and quite outspoken, although pressures have been increasing, especially on reporters. (1978 revealed secret government ownership of a newspaper to present its viewpoint. It is now sold.) Freedom for the nonwhite press was restricted but not eliminated in 1977. Broadcasting is under government control. The courts are independent, but do not effectively control security forces. There are political prisoners and torture—especially for black activists, who live in an atmosphere of terror. Private rights are generally respected for whites. Rights to residence of choice and occupation are quite restricted for nonwhites. **Comparatively:** South Africa is as free as Syria, freer than Tanzania, less free than Morocco.

SPAIN

Economy: capitalist
Polity: centralized multiparty
Population: 36,800,000

Political Rights: 2
Civil Liberties: 2
Status of Freedom: free

An ethnic state with major subnationalities

Political Rights. Spain has recently established a constitutional monarchy in the European manner. The current parliament has been fairly elected from a wide range of parties. Recent elections have in effect given popular approval to the monarchy and to the prime minister whose party has received a popular mandate. A 1978 referendum overwhelmingly approved the new constitution. In 1978 the prime minister remained responsible to the monarch instead of parliament. *Subnationalities*: The Basque and Catalan territorial subnationalities have had their rights greatly expanded in the last two years, and regional power is being extended to the other parts of the country.

Civil Liberties. The press is private and is now free. The television network and some radio stations are government owned. Radio is no longer a state monopoly and television is controlled by an all-party committee. There are few prisoners of conscience; imprisonment still threatens those who insult the security services. Police brutality and use of torture have been reported until very recently. The rule of law has been reestablished and private freedoms are respected. Continued terrorism and reaction to terrorism affect some areas. Union organization is quite free and independent.

Comparatively: Spain is as free as Greece, freer than Egypt, less free than France.

SRI LANKA

Economy: capitalist-statist
Polity: centralized multiparty
Population: 14,200,000

Political Rights: 2
Civil Liberties: 3
Status of Freedom: free

An ethnic state with a major subnationality

Political Rights. Sri Lanka is a parliamentary democracy in which power has alternated between the major parties. The constitution was changed in 1977–78 to a presidential system along French lines. Regional government is centrally controlled, but local government is by elected councils. A number of individuals have been barred from government for breach of trust. *Subnationalities*: Receiving a large vote in the most recent election, the Tamil minority constitutes an important secessionist tendency. Repression or private violence against the Tamils occurs; the present government is inclined to meet Tamil demands up to but not including that for independence or equal linguistic standing.

Civil Liberties. The press has been strong, both private and party. However, under the previous regime some of the largest papers were nationalized; the new government has maintained ownership; editorial policy of these papers appears to be influenced by the government in power. Broadcasting is under government control, but differing views are presented. The rule of law has often been threatened by communal violence. There are few if any prisoners of conscience, but people are sometimes still detained for vague, politically related reasons. Private rights to movement, residence, religion, and occupation are respected. There has been extensive land reform; the State has nationalized a number of enterprises in this largely plantation economy.

   Comparatively: Sri Lanka is as free as Turkey, freer than Malaysia, less free than the United Kingdom.

S U D A N

Economy: noninclusive mixed	**Political Rights:** 5
Polity: nationalist one-party	**Civil Liberties:** 5
(military dominated)	**Status of Freedom:** partly free
Population: 17,000,000	

An ethnic state with a major but highly diverse subnationality

   Political Rights. Sudan is a military dictatorship with a supportive single party and legislature. In 1977–78 there was a general reconciliation of the government and its noncommunist opposition. 1978 legislative elections allowed the participation and frequent victory of individuals from de facto opposition groups. Several cabinet and party central committee members were subsequently selected from these groups. *Subnationalities*: The Southern (Negro) region has been given a separate assembly; its former guerrillas form a part of the Southern army. A former guerrilla leader is now head of a regional government based on an assembly controlled by independents.

   Civil Liberties. The press is weak and nationalized. Radio and television are government controlled. Limited criticism is allowed, especially in private. The university campus maintains a tradition of independence, but the courts are not strong. There have been political prisoners, reports of torture, and detention without trial. All political prisoners were released in 1977–78. Religion is relatively free. Unions are government organized but nevertheless lead illegal strikes. Sudan is socialist theoretically, but in business and agriculture the private sector has recently been supported by denationalizations.

   Comparatively: Sudan is as free as Egypt, freer than Ethiopia, less free than Kenya.

S U R I N A M

Economy: capitalist
Polity: centralized multiparty
Population: 460,000

Political Rights: 2
Civil Liberties: 2
Status of Freedom: free

An ethnically complex state

Political Rights. Surinam is a parliamentary democracy with authentic elections. Its two main parties represent separate ethnic groups. Although they are not as territorially distinct, negotiation between them results in a division of communal rights analogous to that in Belgium or Canada. There are no autonomous regional governments.

Civil Liberties. The press and radio are free and varied. There is a rule of law and private rights are respected.

Comparatively: Surinam is as free as India, freer than Guyana, less free than Barbados.

S W A Z I L A N D

Economy: noninclusive capitalist
Polity: traditional nonparty
Population: 500,000

Political Rights: 5
Civil Liberties: 5
Status of Freedom: partly free

A relatively homogeneous population

Political Rights. Swaziland is ruled directly by the king with the aid of his royal advisors. The majority of the people probably support the king who is both a religious and political figure and has been king since 1900. An indirect election for an advisory legislature was held in 1978. South African political and economic influence is extensive.

Civil Liberties. Private media exist alongside governmental; there is little criticism, but South African media present available alternatives. Opposition leaders have been repeatedly detained, and partisan activity is forbidden. Public assemblies are restricted, unions limited, emigration difficult. Religious, economic, and other private rights are maintained. The traditional way of life is continued, especially on the local level. Several thousand whites in the country and in neighboring Transvaal own the most productive land and business.

Comparatively: Swaziland is as free as Lesotho, freer than South Africa, less free than Botswana.

SWEDEN

Economy: mixed capitalist
Polity: centralized multiparty
Population: 8,300,000

Political Rights: 1
Civil Liberties: 1
Status of Freedom: free

A relatively homogeneous population

Political Rights. Sweden is a parliamentary democracy in which power has recently passed to an opposition coalition. Although there are some representative institutions at regional and local levels, the system is relatively centralized. The tendency of modern bureaucracies to regard issues as technical rather than political has progressed further in Sweden than elsewhere.

Civil Liberties. The press is private or party; broadcasting is by state-licensed monopolies. Although free of censorship, the media are accused of presenting a rather narrow range of views. There is the rule of law. The defense of those accused by the government may not be as spirited as elsewhere, but, on the other hand, the ombudsman office gives special means of redress against administrative arbitrariness. Most private rights are respected. The national church has a special position. In many areas, such as housing, individual choice is restricted more than in other capitalist states—as it is of course by the very high tax load.

Comparatively: Sweden is as free as Denmark, freer than West Germany.

SWITZERLAND

Economy: capitalist
Polity: decentralized multiparty
Population: 6,200,000

Political Rights: 1
Civil Liberties: 1
Status of Freedom: free

A trinational state

Political Rights. Switzerland is a parliamentary democracy in which all major parties are given a role in government determined by the size of the vote for each party. Parties that increase their vote above a certain level are invited to join the government, although such changes in party strength rarely occur. The lack of a decisive shift in power from one party to another in the last fifty years is the major limitation on the democratic effectiveness of the Swiss system. However, its dependence on the grand coalition style of government is a partial substitute, and the Swiss grant political rights in other ways that compensate for the lack of a transfer of power. Major issues are frequently decided by the citizenry through national referendums or popular initiatives. After referendums, in keeping with the Swiss attitude, even the losing side is given part of what it wants if its vote is sufficiently large. *Subnationalities*: The three major linguistic groups have separate areas under their partial control. Their regional and local elected governments have autonomous rights and determine directly much of the country's business. National governments try to balance the representatives of the primary linguistic and religious groups; this is accomplished in another way by the upper house that directly represents the cantons (regions) on an equal basis.

Civil Rights. The high quality press is private and independent. Broadcasting is government operated, although with the considerable independence of comparable West European systems. The rule of law is strongly upheld, although as in Germany it is against the law to question the intentions of judges. Private rights are thoroughly respected.

Comparatively: Switzerland is as free as the United States, freer than Italy.

SYRIA

Economy: mixed socialist   **Political Rights:** 5
Polity: centralized dominant-party   **Civil Liberties:** 6
    (military dominated)   **Status of Freedom:** partly free
Population: 8,100,000

A relatively homogeneous population

Political Rights. Syria is a military dictatorship assisted by an elected parliament. The election of the military president is largely pro forma, but in recent assembly elections a few opposition candidates defeated candidates on the National Front, organized under the leadership of the governing party. The ruling Front includes several ideologically distinct parties, and cabinets have included representatives of a variety of such parties. Some authenticity to the election procedure is suggested by the fact that due to apathy and a boycott by dissident party factions in 1977 elections, the government had such great difficulty achieving the constitutionally required voter participation that it was forced to extend the voting period. Because of its position in the army the Alawite minority (ten percent) has a very unequal share of national power. Provinces have little separate power, but local elections are contested.

Civil Liberties. The media are in the hands of government or party, but limited freedom is allowed the press. Broadcasting services are government owned. Political parties are able to articulate a variety of viewpoints, and individuals feel free to discuss politics. The courts are neither strongly independent nor effective in political cases where long-term detention without trial occurs. Political prisoners are often arrested following violence (most in 1977 were Palestinians), and there are long-term prisoners of conscience. Torture has frequently been employed in interrogation. Private rights, such as those of religion, occupation, or residence are generally respected, but foreign travel and emigation are closely controlled. Syria's economy is a mixture of governmental and private enterprise.

Comparatively: Syria is as free as Seychelles, freer than Iraq, less free than Lebanon.

TANZANIA

Economy: noninclusive socialist
Polity: socialist one-party
Population: 16,500,000

Political Rights: 6
Civil Liberties: 6
Status of Freedom: not free

A transethnic heterogeneous nation in union with Zanzibar

Political Rights. Tanzania is a union of the paternalistic socialist mainland with the radical socialist Zanzibar. Although the governments are still not unified except in name, in late 1976 the single parties of each state were joined to form one all-Tanzanian party; it was announced that this party would have the ultimate direction of affairs in both states. Elections offer choice between individuals, but no issues are to be discussed in campaigns; all decisions come down from above, including the choice of candidates. *Subnationalities:* Ethnically, the country is divided into a large number of peoples (none larger than thirteen percent); most are not yet at the subnational level. The use of English and Swahili as national languages enhances national unity. Since the two subnations (Zanzibar and Tanganyika) are in a voluntary union at present, there is no question of dominance of one over the other.

Civil Liberties. Civil liberties are essentially subordinated to the goals of the socialist leadership. No contradiction of official policy is allowed to appear in the government-owned media. There is no right of assembly or organization. Millions of people have been forced into communal villages; people from the cities have been abruptly transported to the countryside. Thousands have been detained for political crimes, and torture has occurred. In 1978 there were fewer arrests and most prisoners of conscience were believed released. Lack of respect for the independence of the judiciary and individual rights is especially apparent in Zanzibar. Union activity is government controlled. Neither labor nor capital have legally recognized rights—strikes are illegal.

Most business and trade and much of agriculture are nationalized. Religion is free, at least on the mainland, but overseas travel is restricted.

Comparatively: Tanzania is as free as Algeria, freer than Malawi, less free than Zambia.

THAILAND

Economy: noninclusive capitalist
Polity: military nonparty
Population: 45,100,000

Political Rights: 5
Civil Liberties: 4
Status of Freedom: partly free

An ethnic state with a major territorial subnationality

Political Rights. Thailand is ruled by a military committee and a king. Political parties were officially illegal in 1978, but their leaders were well known and served on a constitutional drafting committee. By the end of the year they were beginning political activities in preparation for general elections in 1979. Government is highly centralized. *Subnationalities*: There is a Muslim Malay community in the far south, and small ethnic enclaves in the north.

Civil Liberties. The press is private, but periodic suppressions and warnings lead to self-censorship. Broadcasting is government or military controlled. There are few prisoners of conscience, but in rural areas arrest may be on vague charges and treatment brutal. Some "reeducation centers" in areas of guerrilla activity have been reported. Labor activity became relatively free in 1978, but strikes were still illegal. Private rights to property, choice of religion, travel, or residence are secure. Government enterprise is quite important in the basically capitalist modern economy.

Comparatively: Thailand is as free as Ecuador, freer than Vietnam, less free than Bangladesh.

TOGO

Economy: noninclusive mixed
Polity: nationalist one-party
Population: 2,400,000

Political Rights: 7
Civil Liberties: 6
Status of Freedom: not free

A transethnic heterogeneous state

Political Rights. Togo is a military dictatorship ruled in the name of a one-party state. In this spirit there is a deliberate denial of the rights of separate branches of government, including a separate judiciary, or even of private groups. Below the national level only the cities have a semblance of self-government. *Subnationalities*: The southern

Ewe are culturally dominant and the largest group (twenty percent), but militant northerners now rule.

Civil Liberties. Most of the news media are government owned. There is little guarantee of a rule of law: people have been imprisoned on many occasions for offenses such as the distribution of leaflets. There are, however, few if any long-term prisoners of conscience. Religious freedom exists but is threatened. There is occasional restriction of foreign travel. Union organization is closely regulated. In this largely subsistence economy the government is heavily involved in trade, government enterprise, and the provision of services. All wage earners must contribute heavily to the ruling party.

Comparatively: Togo is as free as Mali, freer than Equatorial Guinea, less free than Nigeria.

T O N G A

Economy: noninclusive capitalist **Political Rights:** 5
Polity: traditional nonparty **Civil Liberties:** 3
Population: 115,000 **Status of Freedom:** partly free

A relatively homogeneous population

Political Rights. Tonga is a constitutional monarchy in which the king and nobles retain power. Only a minority of the members of the legislative assembly are elected directly by the people; in any event the assembly has little more than veto power. Regional administration is centralized.

Civil Liberties. The main paper is a government weekly and radio is under government control. There is a rule of law, but the king's decision is still a very important part of the system. Private rights within the traditional Tonga context seem guaranteed.

Comparatively: Tonga is as free as Bolivia, freer than Seychelles, less free than Western Samoa.

T R A N S K E I

Economy: noninclusive capitalist **Political Rights:** 5
Polity: centralized dominant-party **Civil Liberties:** 5
Population: 2,200,000 **Status of Freedom:** partly free

A relatively homogeneous population

Political Rights: In form Transkei is a multiparty parliamentary democracy; in fact it is under the strong-man rule of a paramount chief supported by his party's majority. The meaning of recent elections was largely nullified by governmental interference, including the jailing of opposition leaders. In 1978 the parliamentary opposition was increased by defections from the ruling party. Chiefs remain very important in the system, but beyond that there is little decentralization of power. South Africa has a great deal of de facto power over the state, particularly because of the large number of nationals that work in South Africa. However, Transkei is more independent than the Soviet satellites; in 1978 it severed relations with South Africa.

Civil Liberties. The press is private; it supports opposition as well as government positions. Broadcasting is government controlled. Many members of the opposition have been imprisoned; new retroactive laws render it illegal to criticize Transkei or its rulers. Private rights are respected within the limits of South African and Transkei custom. Capitalist and traditional economic rights are diminished by the necessity of a large portion of the labor force to work in South Africa.

Comparatively: Transkei is as free as Panama, freer than Mozambique, less free than Botswana.

TRINIDAD AND TOBAGO

Economy: capitalist
Polity: centralized multiparty
Population: 1,100,000

Political Rights: 2
Civil Liberties: 2
Status of Freedom: free

An ethnically complex state

Political Rights. Trinidad and Tobago is a parliamentary democracy in which one party has managed to retain power since the 1950's. Elections have been boycotted in the past but now appear reasonably fair. A new opposition party has recently gained almost thirty percent of the assembly seats. There is local government.

Civil Liberties. The private or party press is generally free of restriction; broadcasting is under both government and private control. Opposition is regularly voiced. There is the full spectrum of private rights, although violence and communal feeling reduce the effectiveness of such rights for many.

Comparatively: Trinidad and Tobago is as free as Surinam, freer than Grenada, less free than Bahamas.

TUNISIA

Economy: mixed capitalist
Polity: socialist one-party
Population: 6,025,000

Political Rights: 6
Civil Liberties: 5
Status of Freedom: partly free

A relatively homogeneous population

Political Rights. Tunisia is a one-party dictatorship that preserves alongside one-man leadership the trappings of parliamentary democracy. Elections to the assembly have been pro forma, but an independent contested a seat in 1978. Opposition within the party is now muted. Regional and local government are dependent on central direction.

Civil Liberties. The private, party, or government media have been heavily controlled. Although frequently banned or fined two major opposition papers were published in 1978. Private conversation is relatively free, but there is no right of assembly. The courts demonstrate only a limited independence, but it is possible to win against the government. Unions have been relatively independent; however, a general strike called in early 1978 led to riots and subsequent large-scale imprisonments, and closer government controls followed. The unemployed young are drafted for government work. Overseas travel is occasionally blocked. Most private rights seem to be respected, including economic rights since doctrinaire socialism was abandoned.

Comparatively: Tunisia is as free as Poland, freer than Algeria, less free than Egypt.

TURKEY

Economy: capitalist-statist   **Political Rights:** 2
Polity: centralized multiparty   **Civil Liberties:** 3
Population: 42,200,000   **Status of Freedom:** free

An ethnic state with a major territorial subnationality

Political Rights. Turkey is a parliamentary democracy in which power has often shifted between the major parties or their coalitions. A marxist party has recently been legalized, but the communist party is still prohibited. The democratic system has been strongly supported by the military that has intervened against threats to the system from both the right and left. This leaves the military in a more powerful political position than is traditionally acceptable in a democracy, a position symbolized by the fact that the largely ceremonial (except in crises) position of the president has come to be occupied by a military leader. Although there are elected councils at lower levels, power is effectively centralized. *Subnationalities*: Several million Kurds are denied self-determination: it is even illegal to teach or publish in Kurdish.

Civil Liberties. The press is private and free; the government controls the broadcasting system directly or indirectly. Although public expression and assembly cover a wide spectrum, there are laws against extremist publications, assembly, and organization that are regarded as threats to the democratic order. Together with antigovernment violence this has led to frequent political imprisonment (often followed by accusations of torture). Government generally observes the law, but nongovernmental extremists have been responsible for many deaths. Martial law was imposed in some areas after extensive political violence in late 1978. Private rights are generally respected in other areas such as religion. Nearly fifty percent of the people are subsistence agriculturists. State enterprises make up more than one-half of Turkey's industry.

Comparatively: Turkey is as free as Colombia, freer than Morocco, less free than Portugal.

TUVALU

Economy: noninclusive capitalist
Polity: traditional nonparty
Population: 9,000

Political Rights: 2
Civil Liberties: 2
Status of Freedom: free

A relatively homogeneous state

Political Rights. Tuvalu is a parliamentary democracy under the British monarch. Each island is represented and seats are contested individually. An opposition bloc has been formed in the assembly.

Civil Liberties. Media are little developed. The rule of law is maintained in the British manner, alongside traditional ideas of justice.

Comparatively: Tuvalu is as free as Malta, freer than Tonga, less free than New Zealand.

UGANDA

Economy: noninclusive capitalist
Polity: military nonparty
Population: 12,500,000

Political Rights: 7
Civil Liberties: 7
Status of Freedom: not free

A formally transethnic heterogeneous state with major subnationalities

Political Rights. Uganda is ruled as a military dictatorship essentially unchecked by law or tradition. A National Consultative Forum met for the first time in 1978, with representation from districts, towns, and tribes. Its democratic significance appears slight. *Subnationalities:* The population is divided among a wide variety of peoples, some of which are subnationalities based on kingdoms that preceded the present state. The most important of these is Buganda, a kingdom with special rights within the state, that was suppressed in 1967 (sixteen percent of the people are Ganda). The president rules from a very small ethnic base in a Muslim group; his forces include many Muslim soldiers hired from across the border in the Sudan. Recent massacres have fallen especially heavily on the non-Muslim Acholi and Lango peoples.

Civil Liberties. The media are completely controlled, although some foreign publications were allowed in 1978. Thousands or hundreds of thousands have been imprisoned, executed, and tortured—both from government policy and lack of control over security forces. Essentially, there are no civil rights, with even the formerly powerful church hierarchies powerless. All small religious denominations have been banned. Avowedly the system is capitalist; yet the expropriation of Asian businesses constituted a major government intervention. Recent anarchical conditions greatly reduce the rights of both capitalists and workers in what remains a primarily subsistence economy.

Comparatively: Uganda is as free as Equatorial Guinea, less free than Sudan.

UNION OF
SOVIET SOCIALIST REPUBLICS

Economy: socialist
Polity: communist one-party
Population: 261,000,000

Political Rights: 6
Civil Liberties: 6
Status of Freedom: not free

A complex ethnic state with major territorial subnationalities

Political Rights. The Soviet Union is ruled by parallel party and governmental systems: the party system is dominant. Elections are held for both systems, but in neither is it possible for the rank and file to determine policy. Candidacy and voting are closely controlled and the resulting assemblies do not seriously question the policies developed by party leaders (varying by time or issue from one individual to twenty-five). The Soviet Union is in theory elaborately divided into subnational units, but in fact the all-embracing party structure renders local power minimal.

Subnationalities: Russians account for half of the Soviet population. The rest belong to a variety of subnational groupings ranging down in size from the forty million Ukrainians. Most groups are territorial, with a developed sense of subnational identity. The political rights of all of these to self-determination, either within the USSR or through secession, is effectively denied. In many cases Russians or other non-native peoples have been settled in a subnational territory in such numbers as to make the native people a minority in their own land (for example, Kazakhstan). Expression of opinion in favor of increased self-determination is repressed at least as much as anticommunist opinion. Most of these peoples have had independence movements or movements for enhanced self-determination in the years since the founding of the USSR. Several movements have been quite strong since World War II (for example, in the Ukraine or Lithuania); the blockage of communication by the Soviet government makes it very difficult to estimate either the overt or latent support such movements might have. In 1978 popular movements in Georgia and Armenia led to the retention of the official status of local languages in the Republics of the Caucasus.

Civil Liberties. The media are totally owned by the government or party and are, in addition, regularly censored. Elite publications occasionally present variations from the official line, but significant deviations are generally found only in underground publications. Crimes against the state, including insanity (demonstrated by perverse willingness to oppose the state), are broadly defined; as a result political prisoners are present in large numbers both in jails and insane asylums. It is important (and also frightening) that nearly all imprisonment and mistreatment of prisoners in the Soviet Union are now carried out in accordance with Soviet security laws—even though these laws conflict with other Soviet laws written to accord with international standards. Insofar as private rights, such as those to religion, education, or choice of occupation, exist, they are de facto rights that may be denied at any time. Nearly all private entrepreneurial activity is outside the law; there are rights to nonproductive personal property. Other rights such as those to organize an independent labor union are strictly denied. Literacy is high, few starve, and private oppression is no more.

Comparatively: The USSR is as free as Cuba, freer than East Germany, less free than Hungary.

UNITED ARAB EMIRATES

Economy: capitalist-statist
Polity: decentralized nonparty
Population: 750,000

Political Rights: 5
Civil Liberties: 5
Status of Freedom: partly free

A relatively homogeneous citizenry

Political Rights. The UAE is a confederation of seven shaikhdoms in which the larger are given the greater power both in the assembly and the administrative hierarchy. There is a great deal of consultation in the traditional pattern. Below the confederation level there are no electoral procedures or parties. Each shaikhdom is relatively autonomous in its internal affairs. The majority of the people are recent immigrants and noncitizens.

Civil Liberties. The press is private or governmental; self-censorship allows only limited criticism of government. Broadcasting is under UAE control. There are no large political assemblies or labor unions, but there are also few, if any, prisoners of conscience. The courts dispense a combination of British, tribal, and Islamic law. Private rights are generally respected; there is freedom of travel and some religious freedom. Many persons may still accept the feudal privileges and re-straints of their tribal position. The rights of the alien majority are less secure. Private economic activity exists alongside the dominance of government petroleum and petroleum-related activities.

Comparatively: United Arab Emirates are as free as Bahrain, freer than North Yemen, less free than Tonga.

UNITED KINGDOM

Economy: mixed capitalist   **Political Rights:** 1
Polity: centralized multiparty   **Civil Liberties:** 1
Population: 56,920,000   **Status of Freedom:** free

An ethnic state with major subnationalities

Political Rights. The United Kingdom is a parliamentary democracy with a symbolic monarch. Fair elections are open to all parties, includ-ing those advocating secession. There are elected local and regional governments, but to date these are primarily concerned with adminis-tering national laws. The devolution of more substantial powers is currently under discussion and development. *Subnationalities*: Scots, Welsh, Ulster Scots, and Ulster Irish are significant and highly self-conscious territorial minorities. In 1978 parliament approved home rule for Scotland and Wales. If approved by a subsequent 1979 refer-endum this would mark a significant increase in self-determination, although still less than an American state or a Canadian province. (In 1979 Welsh and apparently Scots voters rejected this opportunity.) Northern Ireland's home rule is in abeyance because of an ethnic impasse. Ulster Scots and Irish live in intermixed territories in Northern Ireland. Both want more self-determination—the majority Ulster Scots as an autonomous part of the United Kingdom, the minority Ulster Irish as an area within Ireland.

Civil Liberties. The press is private and powerful; broadcasting has statutory independence although it is indirectly under government control. British media are comparatively restrained because of strict libel and national security laws, and a tradition of accepting government suggestions for the handling of sensitive news. Union refusal to print what they disagree with and union demands for a closed shop have been viewed by some as threats to freedom of the press. In Northern Ireland a severe security situation has led to the curtailment of private rights, to imprisonment, and on occasion to torture and brutality. However, these conditions have been relatively limited, have been thoroughly investigated by the government, and improved as a result. Elsewhere the rule of law is entrenched, and private rights generally respected. In certain areas, such as medicine, housing, inheritance, and general disposability of income, socialist government policies have limited choice for some while expanding the access of others.

Comparatively: The United Kingdom is as free as the United States, freer than West Germany.

UNITED STATES OF AMERICA

Economy: capitalist
Polity: decentralized multiparty
Population: 218,400,000

Political Rights: 1
Civil Liberties: 1
Status of Freedom: free

An ethnically complex state with minor territorial subnationalities

Political Rights. The United States is a constitutional democracy with three strong but separate centers of power: president, congress, and judiciary. Elections are fair and competitive. Parties are remarkably weak: in some areas they are little more than temporary means of organizing primary elections. States, and to a lesser extent cities, have powers in their own rights; they often successfully oppose the desires of national administrations. Each state has equal representation in the upper house, which in the USA is the more powerful half of parliament.

Subnationalities: There are many significant ethnic groups, but the only clearly territorial subnationalities are the native peoples. The largest Indian tribes, the Navaho and Sioux, number 100,000 or more each. About 150,000 Hawaiians still reside on their native islands, intermingled with a much larger white and oriental population. Spanish-speaking Americans number in the millions; except for a few thousand residing in an area of northern New Mexico, they are mostly twentieth-century immigrants living among English-speaking Americans, particularly in the large cities. Black Americans make up over one-tentth of the U.S. population; residing primarily in large cities they have no major territorial base. Black and Spanish-speaking Americans are of special concern because of their relative poverty, but their ethnic status is quite comparable to that of many other groups in America, including Chinese, Japanese, Filipinos, Italians, or Jews.

Civil Liberties. The press is private and free; both private and public radio and television are government regulated. There are virtually no government controls on the content of the printed media (except in nonpolitical areas such as pornography) and few on broadcasting. There are no prisoners of conscience or sanctioned uses of torture; some regional miscarriages of justice and police brutality have political and social overtones. Widespread use of surveillance techniques and clandestine interference with radical groups or groups thought to be radical has occurred; as a reduction of liberties the threat has remained largely potential; in 1977–78 these security excesses were greatly attenuated if not eliminated. Wherever and whenever publicity penetrates, the rule of law is generally secure, even against the most powerful. The government often loses in the courts. Private rights in most spheres are quite secure. Although a relatively capitalistic country, the combination of tax loads with the decisive government role in agriculture, energy, defense, and other industries restricts individual choice as it increases majority power.

Comparatively: The United States is as free as Australia, freer than Italy.

UPPER VOLTA

Economy: noninclusive capitalist
Polity: centralized multiparty
Population: 6,500,000

Political Rights: 2
Civil Liberties: 3
Status of Freedom: free

A transethnic heterogeneous state

Political Rights. Upper Volta has a president and parliament on the French model. One individual, a former president, does not have political rights. Presidential and parliamentary elections held in 1978 maintained the previous ruler in power. In spite of opposition accusations, the elections appeared reasonably fair. Successful M.P.'s represented a number of parties and the presidential election was only decided after a run-off. The resulting government included all major parties. There is little official decentralization of power.

Civil Liberties. Media are both government and private. The major opposition paper is regularly critical of the government. There are no political prisoners. The rule of law seems fairly well established; within traditional limits private rights are respected. Trade unions are important. Travel is unrestricted. Essentially the economy remains dependent on subsistence agriculture, with the government playing the role of regulator and promoter of development.

Comparatively: Upper Volta is as free as Botswana, freer than Ghana, less free than Gambia.

URUGUAY

Economy: mixed capitalist
Polity: military nonparty
Population: 2,800,000

Political Rights: 6
Civil Liberties: 6
Status of Freedom: not free

A relatively homogeneous population

Political Rights. Uruguay is a military dictatorship supplemented by an appointed civilian head of state and appointed advisory council. The leading parties are inactive but still exist legally. The state is highly centralized.

Civil Liberties. The press is private, and broadcasting private and public. Both are under heavy censorship and threats of confiscation or closure, as are book and journal outlets. (Special permission is required to see old newspapers.) The right of assembly is very restricted. The independence of the judiciary and the civil service has been drastically curtailed. There are about 2,000 political prisoners, many of which are prisoners of conscience. Torture has been routinely used; convictions are generally based on written confessions. Many parties have been banned, but there is still considerable room for political discussion of alternatives beyond the limits of the present system. Although restricted, nongovernment unions continue to function. Private rights are generally respected. The tax load of an overbuilt bureaucracy and emphasis on private and government monopolies have also restricted choice in this now impoverished welfare state.

Comparatively: Uruguay is as free as Tanzania, freer than Ethiopia, less free than Bolivia.

VENEZUELA

Economy: capitalist-statist
Polity: centralized multiparty
Population: 13,100,000

Political Rights: 1
Civil Liberties: 2.
Status of Freedom: free

A relatively homogeneous population

Political Rights. Venezuela is a parliamentary democracy in which power has alternated between major parties in recent years. Campaigns and voting appear fair. The opposition presidential victory in 1978 provided a good example of the power of the average voter. Regional and local assemblies are relatively powerful, but governors are centrally appointed. Each state has equal representation in the upper house.

Civil Liberties. The press is private and free; most broadcasting is also in private hands. Censorship occurs only in emergencies. The rule of law is generally secured, but in the face of guerrilla actions the security services have on occasion imprisoned persons, used torture, and even threatened to press for its antimilitary statements. A paper may be confiscated for slandering the president. Many persons have been detained for long periods without trial, and on rare occasions members of parliament have been arrested. However, there is little evidence that those detained have been prisoners of conscience, and the government has taken steps to prevent torture. The court can rule against the government. Most private rights are respected; government involvement in the petroleum industry has given it a predominant economic role.

Comparatively: Venezuela is as free as France, freer than Italy, less free than Costa Rica.

V I E T N A M

Economy: socialist
Polity: communist one-party
Population: 49,200,000

Political Rights: 7
Civil Liberties: 7
Status of Freedom: not free

An ethnic state with subnationalities

Political Rights. Vietnam is a traditional communist dictatorship with the forms of parliamentary democracy. Actual power is in the hands of the communist party; this is in turn dominated by a small group at the top. Officially there is a ruling national front as in several other communist states, but the noncommunist parties are essentially meaningless. Administration is highly centralized, with provincial boundaries arbitrarily determined by the central government. The continued stream of refugees in 1978 provided evidence that the present regime is very unpopular, especially in the South which is treated as an occupied country. *Subnationalities:* Continued fighting has been reported in the Montagnard areas in the South. Combined with new resettlement schemes non-Vietnamese people seem under pressure in both North and South Vietnam. Many Chinese appeared to be driven out of the country in 1978.

Civil Liberties. The media are under direct government, party, or army control; only the approved line is presented. While the people do not suffer the fears and illegalities of anarchy, they have essentially no rights against the interests of the state. Severe repression of the Buddhist opposition has led to many immolations—pressure on the Hoa Hao and Catholics is comparable. In spite of superficial appearances religious freedom is generally denied. Perhaps one-half million persons have been put through reeducation camps, hundreds of thousands have been forced to move into new areas, or to change occupations. Hundreds of thousands remain political prisoners. By placing a trusted, usually Northern, leader over each group of ten families in the South, at least half of the country has been turned into a prison camp.

Comparatively: Vietnam is as free as Korea (North), less free than China (Mainland).

WESTERN SAMOA

Economy: noninclusive capitalist	**Political Rights:** 4
Polity: traditional nonparty	**Civil Liberties:** 2
Population: 171,000	**Status of Freedom:** partly free

A relatively homogeneous population

Political Rights. Western Samoa is a constitutional monarchy in which the assembly is elected by 9,500 "family heads." There have been important shifts of power within the assembly as the result of elections, although there are no political parties. Village government has preserved traditional forms and considerable autonomy; it is also based on rule by "family heads."

Civil Liberties. The press is private; radio is government owned. There is general freedom of expression and rule of law. Private rights are respected within the limits set by the traditional system.

Comparatively: Western Samoa is as free as Mauritius, freer than Malaysia, less free than Nauru.

YEMEN, NORTH

Economy: noninclusive capitalist	**Political Rights:** 6
Polity: military nonparty	**Civil Liberties:** 5
Population: 5,800,000	**Status of Freedom:** not free

A complex but relatively homogeneous population

Political Rights. North Yemen is a collective military dictatorship supplemented by an appointive People's Assembly. Leaders are frequently assassinated. The tribal and religious structures still retain considerable authority, and the government must rely on a wide variety of different groups in an essentially nonideological consensual regime. Some local elective institutions have recently been developed. Political parties are forbidden. The country is divided between city and country, a variety of tribes, and two major religious groupings.

Civil Liberties. The media are largely government owned, although there are apparently some private newspapers and limited freedom of expression. Proponents of both royalist and far left persuasions are openly accepted in a society with few known prisoners of conscience. Politically active opponents may be encouraged to go into exile. The traditional Islamic courts give some protection; private rights such as those to religion and property are respected. There is no right to strike or to engage in religious proselytizing. Economically the government has concentrated on improving the infrastructure of Yemen's still overwhelmingly traditional economy.

Comparatively: North Yemen is as free as Argentina, freer than South Yemen, less free that Syria.

YEMEN, SOUTH

Economy: noninclusive socialist **Political Rights:** 6
Polity: socialist one-party **Civil Liberties:** 7
Population: 1,900,000 **Status of Freedom:** not free

A relatively homogeneous population

Political Rights. South Yemen considers itself a communist country governed according to the communist one-party model. It is doubtful that the party retains the tight party discipline of its exemplars; it is government by coup and violence. Parliamentary elections in 1978 followed the one-party model; they allowed some choice among individuals. Soviet influence in internal and external affairs is powerful.

Civil Liberties. The media are government owned and controlled; even conversation with foreigners is highly restricted. In the political and security areas the rule of law hardly applies. Thousands of political prisoners, torture, and hundreds of "disappearances" have instilled a pervasive fear in those who would speak up. Death sentences against protesting farmers have been handed down by people's courts. Independent private rights are few, although some traditional law and institutions remain. Industry and commerce have been nationalized.

Comparatively: South Yemen is as free as Malawi, freer than Somalia, less free than Oman.

YUGOSLAVIA

Economy: mixed socialist **Political Rights:** 6
Polity: communist one-party **Civil Liberties:** 5
Population: 22,000,000 **Status of Freedom:** not free

A multinational state

Political Rights. Yugoslavia is governed on the model of the USSR, but with the addition of unique elements. These include: the greater role given the governments of the constituent republics; and the greater power given the assemblies of the self-managed communities and industrial enterprises. The Federal Assembly is elected indirectly by those successful in lower level elections. In any event, the country is directed by the communist party; evidence suggests that in spite of some earlier liberalizing tendencies to allow the more democratic formal structure to work, Yugoslavia is now no more democratic than Hungary. No opposition member is elected to state or national position, nor is there public opposition in the assemblies to government policy on the national or regional level—in spite of evidence that there is a good deal of dissatisfaction with the working of the federal system, especially in Croatia and the smaller republics.

Subnationalities: The several peoples of Yugoslavia live largely in their historical homelands. The population consists of forty percent Serbs, twenty-two percent Croats, eight percent Slovenes, eight percent Bosnian Muslims, six percent Macedonians, six percent Albanians, two percent Montenegrins, and many others.

Civil Liberties. The media in Yugoslavia are controlled directly or indirectly by the government, although there is ostensible worker control. There is no right of assembly. Hundreds have been imprisoned for ideas expressed verbally or in print that deviated from the official line (primarily through subnationalist enthusiasm, anticommunism, or communist deviationism). Some political prisoners were released in 1977–78, but political trials and imprisonments continued. As long as the issue is not political, however, the courts have some independence; there is a realm of de facto individual freedom that includes the right to seek employment outside the country. Travel outside Yugoslavia is often denied to dissidents, and religious proselytizing is forbidden. Labor is not independent but has rights through the working of the "self management" system. Although the economy is socialist or communalist in most respects, agriculture in this most agricultural of European countries remains overwhelmingly private.

Comparatively: Yugoslavia is as free as Hungary, freer than Rumania, less free than Morocco.

Z A I R E

Economy: noninclusive capitalist-statist
Polity: nationalist one-party
Population: 26,700,000

Political Rights: 6
Civil Liberties: 6
Status of Freedom: not free

A transethnic heterogeneous state with subnationalities

Political Rights. Zaire is under one-man military rule, with the ruling party essentially an extension of the ruler's personality. Elections in 1977 at both local and parliamentary levels were restricted to one party, but allowed for extensive choice among individuals. The majority of the party's ruling council was also elected in this manner. A subsequent presidential election offered no choice. The broadcasting of live parliamentary debates in 1978 revealed sharp questioning of ministers. Regions are deliberately organized to avoid ethnic identity: regional officers all are appointed from the center, generally from outside of the area, as are officers of the ruling party.

Subnationalities: There are such a variety of tribes or linguistic groups in Zaire that no one group has as many as twenty percent of the population. The fact that French remains dominant reflects the degree of this dispersion. Until recently most of the Zaire people have seen themselves only in local terms without broader ethnic identification. The revolts and wars of the early 1960's saw continually shifting patterns of affiliation, with the European provincial but not ethnic realities of Katanga and South Kasai being most important. The most self-conscious ethnic groups are the Kongo people living in the west (and Congo and Angola) and the Luba in the center of the country. In both cases ethnicity goes back to important ancient kingdoms. The Shaba "invasions" of 1977–78 showed continuing disaffection among the Lunda; other ethnic groups were also involved in revolts during the year.

Civil Liberties. Private newspaper ownership remains. There is some freedom to criticize, but censorship is pervasive. There is no right of assembly, and union organization is controlled. Government has been arbitrary and capricious. The judiciary is not independent; political arrest is common. Individual names as well as clothing style have had to be changed by government decree. All ethnic organizations are forbidden. Arrested conspirators have been forbidden their own lawyers. Major churches retain some autonomy, but independent churches have been proscribed. When founded on government power, the extravagance and business dealings of those in high places reduces economic freedom. Nationalization of land has often been a prelude to private development by powerful bureaucrats. There is also considerable government enterprise.

Comparatively: Zaire is as free as Gabon, freer than Benin, less free than Zambia.

ZAMBIA

Economy: preindustrial mixed   **Political Rights:** 5
Polity: socialist one-party   **Civil Liberties:** 5
Population: 5,500,000   **Status of Freedom:** partly free

A transethnic heterogeneous state

Political Rights. Zambia is ruled as a one-party dictatorship, although there have been considerable elements of freedom within that party. Party organs are constitutionally more important than governmental. Although elections have had some competitive meaning within this framework, recently the government has repressed opposition movements within the party. Expression of dissent is possible through abstention. A 1978 presidential election allowed no choice and little opposition campaigning, but it allowed negative votes.

Civil Liberties. All media are government controlled. A considerable variety of opinion is expressed, but it is a crime to criticize the president or his ideology, and foreign publications are censored. There is a rule of law and the courts have some independence: cases have been won against the government. Hundreds of political opponents have been detained, and occasionally tortured, yet most people talk without fear. Traditional life continues. Although the government does not fully accept private rights in property or religion and has nationalized important parts of the economy, especially copper mining, a private sector continues and is encouraged in some areas.

Comparatively: Zambia is as free as Tanzania, freer than Angola, less free than Morocco.

Index

For countries, peoples, and related territories, *see also* the Tables.

Adventists-Reformers in USSR, 121, 134
Afghanistan, 24; as failure of democratic strategy for freedom, 11-12; summary of, 205
Africa, transethnic heterogeneous states in, 203-204
Albania, summary of, 205-206
Alexander, Robert J., 157, 189, 190
Alger, Horatio, 66
Algeria, summary of, 206-207
Allende, Salvadore, 6
All-Russian Society for the Protection of Historical and Cultural Monuments, 135
"All Union Church of Time and Free Adventists of the Seventh Day," 119
All-Union Council of the Evangelical Christians-Baptists (USSR), 117
Amalrik, Andrei, x
American Civil Liberties Union, 165
American Political Science Association, 170,171
Amnesty International, 37; annual reports of, 8, 13n-14n
Angola, summary of, 207
Argentina, 25; summary of, 207-208
Aristotle, 75
Aron, Raymond, 42
Asia, self-determination of subnationalities in, 55-56
Ataturk (Turkey), 81
Australia, summary of, 208-209
Austria, summary of, 209
authoritarian Russian Empire, as type of Soviet future, 86

Bahamas, summary of, 209-10
Bahrain, summary of, 210
Bangladesh, 25; summary of, 211
Barbados, summary of, 211-12
Barghoorn, Frederick, 147, 148, 168
Basket III of Helsinki Agreement, 106
Beiliss, Mendel, 161

Belgium, summary of, 212
Belgrade Conference, 123, 124
Bell, Daniel, 166, 167
Benin, summary of, 212-13
Berbers, quest for self-determination of, 55
Berdyaev, Nikolai, 181
Berger, Peter, 78, 79
Bernstein, Edward, 163
Bhutan, summary of, 213
Biafra. *See* Nigeria
binational state, 203
blacks. *See* Southern blacks
Bociurkiw, Bohdan R., 111, 115, 133, 134, 135, 152, 153, 155, 156, 157, 182, 183, 190, 191
Bolivia, 25; summary of, 213-14
Botswana, summary of, 214-15
Bottomore, T. R., 166, 169
Bowles and Gintis, 68
Brazil, 25; summary of, 215
Brezhnev, Leonid, x, 86, 113, 152
Brezhnev Doctrine, 144
Brinton, Crane, 93, 159
Brzezinski, Zbigniew, 186
Bukharin, Nikolai, 163, 181
Bukovsky, Vladimir, 111
Bulgaria, summary of, 216
Bulletin of the Council of the ECB Prisoners' Relatives, 121
Burma, summary of, 216-17
Burundi, summary of, 217

Cambodia. *See* Kampuchea
Cameroon, summary of, 218
Canada, summary of, 218-19
Cape Verde Islands, summary of, 219
capitalism/capitalist systems: corporations in, 69-70; freedom in, 42; economics of, 43; mixed, 201; and socialist systems, 43; as statist nations, 43. *See also* political-economic systems; socialism
Captive Mind, 177

Carter, Jimmy, 15, 158, 186, 188, 190, 197
"catacomb church" (Greek Catholic Church, Ukraine), 118
Catholic Committee for the Defense of Believers' Rights (Lithuania), 124
Central African Empire, summary of, 220
Central Intelligence Agency, Muslim Brotherhood and, 135-36
centralized multiparty systems, 44
Chad, 25; self-determination in, 54; summary of, 220-21
Chalidze, Valery, 166, 179, 180
Chile, 25; during Allende's rule, 6-7; summary of, 221
China (Mainland), 29; dissidents in, support of, 58; self-determination of subnationalities in, 52; summary of, 221-22
China (Taiwan), 25; summary of, 222-23
Christian Committee for the Defense of Believers' Rights (Moscow), 123n, 135
Chronicle of the Catholic Church in Lithuania, 121, 124, 125
Chronicle of Contemporary Events, 147
Chronicle of Current Events, 121
civil freedom. *See* political freedom
civilization: as process of selection of best, 77-78; universalist, definition of, 75-76
civil liberties, 4; limitations to, in democratic society, 65-66; political rights, as necessary component of, 7; survey ratings of, 19, 21, 24; and terror, levels of, 31, 37-38. *See also* equality; freedom; political rights; USSR; *names of countries*; *names of forms of civil liberties* (*e.g.,* press; religion, *etc.*)
Colombia, summary of, 223-24
"colony," problems in defining, 7-8
"command economy," in USSR, 138-39
Committee for the Defense of Workers' Rights (USSR), 123
communism/communist states: expanding influence of, 88-89; fear of liberalization in, 7; freedom, 8-9; one-party, 44; totalitarianism and liberalization in USSR and, 88. *See also names of countries*
Comoro Islands, 24; summary of, 224

Comparative Survey of Freedom. *See* Survey of Freedom, Comparative
Congo, summary of, 224-25
"consociational democracy," 79
corporations, power of, in capitalist societies, 69-70
Costa Rica, summary of, 225
Cottam, Richard W., x, 135, 153, 156, 185, 186, 187, 188, 189, 189n, 190
Council for the Affairs of Religious Cults, 117
Council for the Affairs of the Russian Orthodox Church, 117
Council of Churches of Evangelical Christians-Baptists, 118, 120
Council of the ECB Prisoners' Relatives, 124, 212
Council for Religious Affairs (USSR), 126
criticism, political, right of, 4-5
Cuba, 30; summary of, 225-26
cultural ethnocentrism, as criticism of Survey, 6
cultures, national, universal democracy and, 75-81; Berger's hypothesis, 78-79; civilization as process of selection of best, 77-78; concept of "a culture," 76; "consociational democracy," 79-80; democratic preservation of cultural particularism, 81; ethnocentric bias of Survey, 75; historical context, necessity of understanding, 79; identity of emerging peoples and problems of modernization, 75; in India, 76-77; particularist cultures and universalist civilization, distinction between, 75-77; units of political action, 80-81; universal human rights, problem of, 78-79. *See also* self-determination and subnationalities, freedom and
Cyprus, summary of, 226-27
Czechoslovakia, summary of, 227

Daniel-Sinyavsky Trial (1966), 144
Daud, Prince, 11
decentralized multiparty systems, 44
Declaration of the Rights of Man and the Citizen, 64
de Lauwe, Chombart, 168
Demetrios, Patriarch, 122
democracy: nature of equality and freedom in, 69-70; as oligarchy, 8; preservation of group life and cultural particularism, 81; a strategy for freedoms, 11; universal ("con-

sociational democracy"), 79-80. *See also* cultures, national, universal democracy and; elections; self-determination and subnationalities, freedom and
Denmark, summary of, 227-28
despotism, 73
Detente and the Democratic Movement in the USSR (Barghoorn), 147
Deutscher, Isaac, 153
disintegrating Soviet Union, as type of alternate future, 87
dissidents, external and internal, as agents of change in USSR, 95
Djibouti, summary of, 228
dominant party systems, 44
Dominica, 29; summary of, 228-29
Dominican Republic, 25; summary of, 229
Dostoevsky, Fyodor, 146
Dudko, Dimitrii, 117
Dulles, John Foster, 186
Dunlop, John B., 135, 157, 159
Dzyuba, Ivan, 141, 168, 173, 173n, 190

economic equality and definition of freedom, 8, 10
economic inequality in American life, 67
Ecuador, 28; summary of, 229-30
egalitarian government. *See* majority rule
Egypt, 24; summary of, 230-31
elections: as characteristic of freedom, 5, 6; and referenda, 31. *See also* majority rule
elites, importance of, for freedom, 10, 13
Elizabeth Peabody's Aesthetic Papers, 175
Ellison, Herbert J., 137n, 152, 153, 156, 158, 159, 160n, 180-81, 189
Ellsberg, Daniel, 171
El Salvador, 24-25; summary of, 231
equality: absolute, as rejected by democrats, 67-68; civil and political freedom derived from concept of, 79; economic, as criteria of freedom, 8; natural law concept of, 79; of opportunity and condition, 66-67; political, power and, 72; as social equality, 68. *See also* civil liberties; freedom; political rights; self-determination and subnationalities, freedom and
Equal Rights Amendment, 170
Equatorial Guinea, summary of, 232

Erickson, John, 154
Ermogen, Archbishop (USSR), 117
Eshliman, Nikolai, 117
Ethiopia: as failure of democratic strategy for freedom, 12; self-determination in, 54; summary of, 232-33
ethnically complex states, 202; with major nonterritorial subnationalities, 202; with major territorial subnationalities, 202-203
Euro-American-type society, 42
Eurocommunism, 163, 164, 189, 196
Evangelical Christians Baptists (USSR), 124, 125, 126, 134
Executive Council of the American Federation of Labor, 164

Feuer, Lewis, 108, 111, 155, 158, 161n, 168, 178, 179, 180, 183
Fiji, summary of, 233-34
Final Act of Helsinki Conference, religious dissent in USSR and, 121-22, 123
Finland, summary of, 234
Foreign Literature, 179
France, summary of, 234-35
Fraternal Newsletter, The, 121
freedom: advance in, 25, 28-29; changes in, comments on, 29-31; Communist analysis of, errors in, 9; declines in, 24-25; definition of, 4-5, 7-8, 9; democratic strategy for, 11-12; and dilemmas for West, 11; and disaffection in 1978, ix; and economic equality, 8; and ideological success, 10-11; independence, as criteria of, 5; internal logic of development of, 7; laws, necessity of, 5; libertarian conception of, 5; map of, 26-27; and material progress, 4; and military and economic success, 10; and modernization, 4; as natural law concept, 79; political freedom, criteria of, 5; progress of, 13; in "value-free" ethos, 3-4. *See also* negative freedom; positive freedom; Survey of Freedom, Comparative; *aspects of freedom* (*e.g.*, self-determination); *names of countries*;
—, and equality, 63-73; conclusions about, 72-73; denial of equal rights through nondemocratic means, 70; as derived from concept of equality, 79; as equality to pursue goals, 66; as equivalent in terms of rights, 68-69; as human rights, 63; inalien-

ability of "life and pursuit of happiness," 66; nature of democracy, 69, 70; in one-party states, 72; opportunities and conditions in American life, 66-67, 69; political influence of individuals and classes, differences in, 71-72; political rights and civil liberties through majority rule and minority rights, 64-65, 72-73; populist tradition in America, 67-68; power, inequalities in, 69-70, 71; "public" and "private" distinction, 65-66; respect and justice, 67; as system of equal rights, 63-64
Freedom House, 165; Survey, 4. See also Survey of Freedom, Comparative
Freedom in the World, ix, x, 202
French Canada. See Quebec
French Revolution, 64
Freud, Sigmund, 168

Gabon, summary of, 235
Gambia, summary of, 236
Gamsakhurdia, Zviad, 118, 127
Gandhi, Indira, 6, 72
Gandhi, Mahatma, 78, 175, 180
Gastil, Raymond D., 156, 159, 184, 185
Georgian Orthodox Church, 118
Germany, East, 28; summary of, 236-37
Germany, West, summary of, 237
Ghana, summary of, 238
Ginsburg, Aleksandr, 119
glasnost in USSR, demand for, 120
Glauben in der Zweiten Welt, 133
Greece: democratic strategy for freedom and, 12; summary of, 239
Greek Catholic Church, 118
Grenada, summary of, 239
Grigorenko, General, 183
"Group for a Legal Struggle Against the Dictatorship of State Atheism and the Investigation of the Facts of the Persecution of Believers in the USSR," 124
Guatemala, 28; summary of, 240
Guinea, summary of, 240-41
Guinea-Bissau, summary of, 241
Guyana, 25, 28; summary of, 241-42

Haiti, 30; summary of, 242
Halest'kyi, Rostyslav, 124
Harvard Russian Research Center, 178
Helsinki Conference and Accords, 58, 121-22, 124

Helsinki Monitoring Groups, 123, 125, 135
Herald of Salvation, 121
Herzen, Aleksandr, 179
Hitler, Adolf, 81
Honduras, summary of, 243
Hospers, John, 64
human rights: Berger's hypothesis about universal, 78-79; and Carter administration, ix; as central concern of U.S. foreign policy, 185-86; compatibility of equality and freedom through, 63; policy of exception, 11-13; as universal goal, 78-79; year of (1977), ix. *See also* civil liberties; equality; freedom; political rights; self-determination and subnationalities, feedom and; *names of countries*
Hungary, summary of, 243-44

Iakunin, Gleb, 117, 122, 123
Iceland, summary of, 244
idealism: Afghanistan and, 11-12; importance of, for freedom, 9
ideology: communist, freedom and, 9; democratic, success of, 11, 12-13; importance of, 10; and liberalization in USSR, 96-97, 98-99
independence, as criteria of freedom, importance of, 7. *See also* self-determination of subnationalities, freedom and
India: economic inequality in, freedom and, 8; during Indira Gandhi's rule, 6; as multinational state and ethnic Russia, comparison between, 203; self-determination of subnationalities in, 56; summary of, 244-46
Indonesia, 30; self-determination of subnationalities in, 57; summary of, 246-47
initsiativniki of Baptists in USSR, 126
Institute for the Study of the USA, 176
International Commission of Jurists, 72
International Historical Congress (Moscow, 1970), 170
Internationalism or Russification? (Dzyuba), 141, 173-74
International Sociological Association, 116, 167, 168
Iran, 28; American role in, ix, x; as failure of democratic strategy for freedom, 12; "Case of Iran, The" (Cottam), x; liberalizing Soviet Union and example of, 185, 186-87;

"loss" of, ix; revolution of 1978, 4; summary of, 247
Iraq, summary of, 247-48
Ireland, summary of, 248-49
Iskra, 179
Israel, summary of, 249
Italy, summary of, 249-50
Ivory Coast, 30; summary of, 250-51

Jackson, Senator Henry, 188
Jackson-Vanik amendment, 107
Jamaica, summary of, 251
Japan, summary of, 251-52
Jaurès, Jean, 163
Jehovah's Witnesses in USSR, 116, 119, 121, 134
Johnson, Chalmers, 157
Jordan, summary of, 252-53
Judaism in USSR, 119

Kampuchea (Cambodia): during Sihanouk's rule, 6; summary of, 253
Kapitanchuk, Viktor, 123
Keenan, George, 184
Kennedy, John F., 189
Kenya, 28; summary of, 253-54
Keston College, 133
KGB, power of, 142, 145
Khaibulin, Hierodeacon Varsonofii, 123 123
Khan, Malkom (Iran), 76
Khan, Seyyid Ahmed (India), 76-77
Khrushchev, Nikita, x, 93, 113, 116, 134, 139, 140, 147, 152, 153, 156, 157, 160, 160n, 180, 183
Kintner, William R., 153, 184, 185, 188, 191
Klebanor (Soviet labor leader), 159
knowledge, universalist civilization and, 76
Kolkhozniki, 141
Komsomol, 135
Konstantinov, F. V., 168
Korea, North, summary of, 254-55
Korea, South, 28; summary of, 255
Kostava, Merab, 127
Kurdish nationalism, 55
Kuroedov, Vladimir, 126
Kuwait, summary of, 256

Laos, summary of, 256
Latin America: self-determination of subnationalities in, 52-53; U.S. human rights policy in, 189-90
"Law on Religious Associations" in USSR, 127

laws, necessity of, for freedom, 5
Lebanon, summary of, 257
legitimization, importance of, 10
Lenin, Vladimir, 103, 120, 163, 173, 173n, 174, 181
Leninism, 157; Soviet foreign policy and, 154
Lesotho, summary of, 257-58
Let History Judge (Medvedev), 171
Levitin-Krasnov, Anatolii, 116, 117
liberal communist union, as type of Soviet future, 86
liberal democracy. *See* democracy
liberals, as agents of change in USSR, 95
Liberia, summary of, 258
libertarian conception of freedom, 5
liberty. *See* freedom
Libya, summary of, 258-59
"life and pursuit of happiness," inalienability of, 66
lingua franca, 57
Lipset, Seymour Martin, 154, 155, 176-78, 180, 181
Listy, 167
Lithuanian Catholic Church, unusual strength of, 118, 135
Litvinov, Pavel, 166
Litvinov, Tania, 179
Lukianenko, Levko, 118
Luxembourg, summary of, 259
Luxemburg, Rosa, 153, 163
Lynd, Staughton, 71

Madagascar, 25; summary of, 259-60
Madrid Review Conference, 124
majority rule: in "consociational democracy," 80; drawbacks of, 73; as egalitarianism, 72; and freedom, 5; and minority rights, 64-65, 72-73, 80
Malawi, 28; summary of, 260-61
Malaysia, summary of, 261-62
Maldives, summary of, 262
Malenkov, Georgi, 93
Mali, 30; summary of, 262-63
Malta, summary of, 263
Mandelsstam, Nadezhda, 165
Mandelsstam, Osip, 163
Manglapus, Senator Raul (Philippines), 78-79
Mao Tse-Tung, 68, 78
Markiewicz, V., 167
Marx, Karl, 155, 163
Marxism-Leninism, 115, 123, 128, 155
Marxist "science," 8, 9
Mauritania, 30; summary of, 263-64

Mauritius, 25; summary of, 264
Medvedev, Roy, 166, 171
Medvedev, Zhores, 165, 171
Meiklejohn, Alexander, 66
Men, Aleksandr, 117, 119
Mexico, summary of, 264-65
Micronesia, self-determination in, 31
Middle East, self-determination in, 55
military nonparty systems, 44
military power, maintaining freedom
    through, 10
modernization: and freedom, 4; as
    problem for identity of emerging
    peoples, 75
Mongolia, summary of, 265-66
Montesquieu, 137
More, Thomas, 170
Morocco, summary of, 266
Moroz, Valentyn, 118
Moscow Helsinki Group, 123
Moscow Patriarchate, 117
Moslems in USSR, 119
Mozambique, summary of, 266-67
multinational states, 203
multiparty systems and freedom, 39, 42
Muslim Brotherhood (Ikhwani), 135-36
musulmanin, 119
My Country and My World (Sakha-
    rov), 148

Namibia. *See* South West Africa
nationalism. *See* self-determination
    and subnationalities, freedom and
nationalist one-party states, 44
National Security Council's Memo-
    randum Number 68, 184
natural law concept of equality and
    freedom, 79
Nauru, summary of, 267
Nazi Germany and political terrorism,
    37
Nepal, summary of, 267-68
Netherlands, summary of, 268
New Zealand, summary of, 269
Nicaragua, 30; summary of, 269-70
Niger, summary of, 270
Nigeria, 28; Ibo revolt in, 7; self-
    determination in, 54-55; summary
    of, 270-71
Nixon, Richard, 3, 72
noninclusive capitalist forms of econ-
    omy, 43
noninclusive socialist states, 43
North Africa, self-determination in, 55
Northern Ireland, problem of "colony"
    and, 7-8

Norway, summary of, 272
Notes of an Economist (Bukharin),
    181

Ogorodnikov, Aleksandr, 127
oligarchy, democracy and, 8
Oman, summary of, 272-73
one-party states, 44; freedom and
    equality in, 42, 72
opposition, as characteristic of free-
    dom, 5-6
oscillating communist tyranny, as type
    of Soviet future, 86
Osipov, Vladimir, 168

Pahlavi, Mohammed Reza (Shah of
    Iran), x, 4, 11, 12, 81, 87, 186, 187
Pailodze, Valentina, 118
Pakistan, 25; self-determination of sub-
    nationalities in, 56; summary of,
    273
Panama, 28; summary of, 274
Papua New Guinea: quest for indepen-
    dence, 57; summary of, 274-75
Paraguay, 28; summary of, 275-76
particularist cultures. *See* cultures,
    national, universal democracy and
partiinost (political partisanship) in
    USSR, 143
party systems, 39, 42, 44, 72
"people," as problematic concept, 7
Peru, 28; summary of, 276
Petkus, Viktoras, 127
Philippines: self-determination in, 57;
    summary of, 277
Pimen, Patriarch, 122
Pinochet, Augusto, 11, 189
Plato, 163
pogrom, of Ukrainian Catholic Church
    (1945-49), 124-25
Pokutnyky (Penitents), 118
Poland, 29-30; Catholic Church in,
    118; summary of, 278
Pole, J. R., 70
political-economic systems, freedom
    and, 39, 42-44; "capitalist" and
    "socialist" economics, 42-44; multi-
    party systems and, 39, 42; political
    systems, 44; in types of societies, 42
political prisoners, 24
political rights, 4; civil liberties, as
    necessary component of, 7; through
    majority rule and minority rights,
    64-65; survey ratings of, 15, 19.
    See also civil rights; equality; free-
    dom; *names of countries*

political systems, 44
population, states with relatively homogeneous, 202
Portugal, summary of, 278-79
power, types of, freedom and, 8-9. *See also* democracy
press, free, 5
private-public distinction in democratic life, 65-66
progressive income tax, 71
property, freedom and, 8
public opinion. *See* elections
public-private distinction in democratic life, 65-66
Pugachev uprising, 162

Qatar, summary of, 279
Quebec, separatism in, 51. *See also* Canada

Radio Free Europe, 184
Radio Liberty, 99, 162, 174-76, 177, 178, 179, 183-84, 188, 196
Rakowska-Harmstone, Teresa, 100n, 112, 113, 154, 156, 159, 173, 174, 189n
referenda. *See* elections
Regelson, Lev, 117, 119, 122
religion, as source of quest for self-determination, 55
Rhodesia, 28-29; summary of, 279-80
Richta, R., 169
rights. *See* civil rights; equality; freedom; human rights; political rights; self-determination of subnationalities, freedom and; *names of countries*
Rise and Fall of T. D. Lysenko (Medvedev), 171
Roman law, as basis of democracy, 79-80
Romaniuk, Vasyl, 118, 127
Rubin, Leslie, 158
Rumania, summary of, 280-81
Russell, Bertrand, 163
Russian Baptist Church, 133
Russian Orthodox Church ("True Orthodox Church"), 116, 117, 125, 133; Soviet destabilization and, 187
Rwanda, 30; summary of, 281

Sadunaite, Nijole, 127
Sakharov, Andrei, 111, 121, 123, 146, 147-48, 159, 178, 179
samizdat, 119, 121, 138, 141, 142, 147, 149, 156, 162, 173, 174-75, 176, 178, 181, 183, 191, 196

Sao Tome and Principe, summary of, 282
Sargeant, Howland H., 155, 174, 175, 176, 178, 182
Sartre, Jean-Paul, 168
Saudi Arabia, summary of, 282-83
Selassie, Haile, 3
self-determination and subnationalities, freedom and, 45, 49-57; in Arab Middle East and North Africa, 55; in Asia, 55-56; in communist world, 51-52; conclusion, 57-58; criteria for inconclusion in tables, 45; European colonialism, 45; and independence, nonnecessity of, 49; in Latin America, 52-53; in Micronesia, 31; national consciousness of large ethnic groups, 45, 54; national rights of peoples, 49; political equality of ethnic minorities in incorporating state, 45, 49; separatist expression in Western democracies, 49-51; in Southeast Asia, 56-57; in Sub-Saharan Africa, 53-55. *See also* cultures, national, universal democracy and
Senegal, 29; summary of, 283
separatist expression in Western democracies, 49-51
Sergii, Metropolitan, 116
sexual equality, as process of civilization, 78
Seychelles, summary of, 284
Shavrov, Vadim, 117
Shcharansky, Anatoly, 161
Shcheglov, Vadim, 131n
Shelkov, V. A., 119, 126-27
Sierra Leone, 30; summary of, 284-85
Signposts, The (Viekhi), 181
Sihanouk, Norodom, 6
Singapore, summary of, 285
Sino-Soviet-type society, 42
Sinyavsky, Andrei, 159, 179
Sladkevicius, Bishop, 118
slavery, rejection of, 78
Snieckus, First Secretary, 135
social democracy, as type of Soviet future, 87
social freedom, relative nature of, 63
socialism/socialist systems: forced labor in, 72; mixed socialist states, 201-202; restriction of freedom, 8, 42; socialist economies, 43-44; socialist one-party states, 44; "socialist realism" in USSR, relaxation of, 143. *See also* political-economic systems; capitalism/capitalist systems

Solomon Islands, 29; summary of, 286
Solzhenitsyn, Alexander, 112, 165, 166, 168, 178, 179
Somalia, summary of, 286-87
Somoza, General, 11
South Africa, summary of, 287
Southeast Asia, self-determination of subnationalities in, 56-57
Southern blacks, experience of, for relations of freedom and equality in American democracy, 70-71
South West Africa (Namibia), 30-31
Soviet Peace Fund, 133
Soviet Union. *See* USSR
Spain, 30; summary of, 287-88
Sri Lanka, 30; summary of, 288-89
Staatsvolk, 45, 46, 202, 203
Stalin, Joseph, 86, 116, 119, 138, 139, 140, 141, 142, 143, 144, 145, 146, 153, 155, 157, 160n, 163, 174, 185, 192; "New Religious Policy" of, 116-17; and political terrorism, 37
states: characteristics of types of freedom in various, 5-6; types of, 201-204. *See also* self-determination and subnationalities, freedom and
Steponavicius, Bishop, 118
Stevens, President (Sierra Leone), 75
strategy for freedom, democratic, 11-13
Strauss, Leo, 179
Stroessner, General, 189
subnationalism. *See* self-determination and subnationalities, freedom and
Sub-Saharan Africa, self-determination in, 53-55
Sudan, 29; self-determination in, 54; summary of, 289
Surinam, summary of, 290
Survey of Freedom, Comparative, x, 3-58; advances in freedom, 25, 28-29; changes in freedom, comments on, 29-31; civil liberties, 4, 19, 21, 24; "colony," problem in defining, 7-8; communist analysis of freedom; errors in, 8-9; criteria of country-by-country summaries, 201-204; criticism of Survey, 6-9; declines in freedom, 24-25; definition of freedom, 4-5, 7-8, 9; democratic strategy for freedom, 11-13; economic equality as condition of freedom, 8; economic and organizational perspectives, 3-4; elections, as characteristic of freedom, 5, 6, 31; elites, importance of, 10; failure of freedom by policy of exception,

11-13; free press, 5; ideology, importance of, 9, 10-11, 12-13; independence, importance of, 7; independent judiciary and freedom, 5; internal logic of freedom, 7; Iran, importance of, ix-x; laws, as guarantee of freedoms, 5; majority rule, 5; military and economic success, as basis for freedom, 10; modernization, as confused with freedom, 4; as monitor of progress of freedom, 9-10; political-economic systems, relation to freedom, 39, 42-44; political opposition, as condition of freedom, 5-6; political rights and civil liberties, 4, 7, 15, 19; political terror, 13; power, types of, freedom and, 8-9; property and freedom, 8; rankings in 1979, 5-6; rating method, 5, 24; self-determination and subnationalities, 45, 49-57; tabulated ratings (tables), 15-24; terror, levels of, 31, 37-38; tyranny, acceptance and overthrow of, 6; "value-free" ethos in assessing freedom, 3-4; voting rights, 7. *See also names of countries*
Sussman, Leonard R., 183-84
Swaziland, summary of, 290
Sweden, summary of, 291
Switzerland: democracy in, 80; summary of, 291-92
Syria, summary of, 292-93

Tadzhikistan, Soviet, and problem of "colony," 7-8
Talantov, Boris, 117
Tanzania, summary of, 293-94
terror, political, 13; levels of, 31, 37-38
Thailand, 29; summary of, 294
Third World countries, economic arrangements and freedom in, 42-43
Thoreau, Henry, 175
Togo, summary of, 294-95
Tonga, summary of, 295
torture, 24
totalitarianism. *See* communism
Touraine, A., 167
traditional nonparty systems, 44
traditional-type society, 42
transethnic heterogeneous states, 203-204
Transkei, 29; summary of, 295-96
trinational state, 203
Trinidad and Tobago, summary of, 296
"True and Free Adventists," 124, 126
Tunisia, 29; summary of, 296-97

Turkey: summary of, 297-98; voting patterns and economic equality, 8
Tuvalu, 29; summary of, 298
tyranny: acceptance and overthrow of, 6; left wing, acceptance of, 88-89; oscillating communist, 86

Uganda, summary of, 298-99
Ukraine, religious dissent in, 118-19, 120, 121
Ukrainian Autocephalous Orthodox Church, 118
Ukrainian Catholic Church (Uniate), 124-25, 134
unemployment in socialist societies, 72
United Arab Emirates, summary of, 300-301
United Kingdom, summary of, 301-302
United States of America, summary of, 302-303
U.S. State Department reports to Congress on human rights, 13n-14n
Universal Declaration of Human Rights, 197
universal democracy. See cultures, national, universal democracy and
Upper Volta, 29; summary of, 303
Uruguay, summary of, 304
USSR: Brezhnev Doctrine, 144; "command economy," 138-39; communications in, 91-92; Conference on "Supporting Liberalization in the Soviet Union," summary and conclusions about, 194-97; denial of self-determination in, 88; destabilization and nationalism, 187; de-Staliniization, effects of, 139-40; dissent in, 90, 92, 93, 95, 96, 97, 99; education and economic expectations in, 91, 92; "equal partnership" of nationalities, concept of, 102, 103; ethnic Russia and multinational India, comparison between, 203; evolution of freedom, lack of, 4; external criticism of, 92-93, 95; external governments, actions of, 95; external media, 95; external nongovernmental organizations, 95; glasnost, demand for, 120; and Helsinki Conference and Accords, 121-22, 124; information, ideology and organization, 96-97, 98-99; interest groups within, 93; interventions in Africa, 89-90; "internationalist" socialization, 102; KGB, power of, 142, 145; kolkhozniki, 141; "Law on Religious Asso-

ciations," 127; as main obstacle to world peace, 85; Marxism-Leninism, as guiding philosophy, 115, 123, 128, 155; military power of, 89; military structure of, 94; nationalism within, 87; partiinost (political partisanship), 143; pogrom and religion, 124; preeminence as world power, 89; publications of religious dissent, 121; religion in, 93-94, 196-97; repression in, 58; "revisionism," 163; revolution in Iran, impact on Soviet reform and, 156; samizdat, 119, 121, 138, 141, 142, 147, 149, 156, 162, 173, 174-75, 176, 178, 181, 182, 183, 191, 196; self-determination in, 52, 91, 100, 103, 105-109; "socialist commonwealth," 104; "socialist legality," 104; "socialist realism," relaxation of, 143; summary of, 299-300; violence in, role of, 95-96; and world war, 90-91; zakonnost (rule of law), demand for, 120
—, American activists and Soviet Power, as supporting liberalization in USSR, 161-93; attitudes and behavior of Americans to USSR, 192; attitudes and training of Soviet intellectuals, 176, 177, 178, 181-82; change, probability of, 180-182; concerns of ordinary Soviet people, 182-83; debate, acculturation of people to, 163; and destabilization of USSR, 186-87; elites, supporting liberal Soviet, 187-88, 190; elites, types of, 191-92, 195-96; emigrés, as threat to Soviet repression, 168-69, 178, 179-80; ideological conflict, U.S. unwillingness to engage aggressively in, 184-85, 192; inappropriateness of U.S. political model, 162; institutional development, emphasis on, 189; at international conferences, 166-70, 176, 192-93; language of "freedom," 170; liberalization vs. revolution, 191; liberals in USSR, advancing situation of, 161, 164; linking trade with human rights, 188; mistaken U.S. foreign policy over human rights, 185-86, 187-88, 189-90; nationalities and self-determination, supporting, 191; Olympic games in 1980, American tourists and Soviet repression, 164-65; optimism about, basis for, 173; political value of

samizdat, 178-79, 183; "principle of proximate criticism," as guide to Soviet liberalism, 162-63, 173-74, 181, 182, 196; private organizations in U.S., role of, 188-89; Radio Liberty, effectiveness of, 174-76, 177, 178, 179, 183-84, 188, 196; and Soviet foreign policy, 163-64, 187; summary and conclusions, 194-97; U.S. government's and American political parties' policies and, 172, 188; U.S. military strength and, 185; U.S. social science community, double standard of, 170-72; U.S. universities' contribution to Soviet liberalism, 166; and USSR as repressive ally, 188; weakness of Soviet liberal movement, 162, 183

—, liberalization in, supporting, x-xi, 85-99; alternate Soviet futures, types of, 85-87; change, causes of, 91-94; conclusion, 97-99; dissenters, role of, xi; liberalism vs. nationalism, 112-13; reasons for, 87-91; tools of change, 94-97; and U.S. policy toward, xi

—, national self-assertion, struggle for, and liberalization in, 100-14; Autonomous Republics, 102; autonomy in political, social and cultural spheres, struggle for, 102-103; in Central Asia, 104, 105, 113; changes in Soviet Union through ethnic nationalism, 108-109; civil and national rights, conflict between, 101, 104; communication patterns between elites and dissidents, as support for national self-determination, 106; conclusions about, 113-14, 194-97; destabilization, problem of, 111-12; education and ethnic nationalism, 104; ethnic elites, role of, 102-104, 106, 107, 109, 112-13; "ethnic key" in Politburo, 113, 110n; ethnic relations, as support for national self-determination, 105; governmental actions in support of national self-determination, 107; Great Russian ethnic group, 100; impact of foreign relations on, 104-105; international recognition of national self-determination, 106-107, 109; military manpower problem and, 113; non-governmental actions in support of national self-determination, 107-108; power structure of Soviet union, strength of nationalities within, 113;

rights of non-Russian national groups, 100-101; Soviet constitution, 109n-110n; suppressed minorities, 102; Union Republics (non-Russian), 101-102, 103; variations among nationalities, 112; world public opinion, as support for national self-determination, 105-106, 109; Yugoslavian example of decentralization, 108

—, reform and repression, Western influence and, 137-60; abuses, internal nature of, 145; agriculture, 141, 142; Brezhnev years, 152-53; communication and information, maintaining monopoly of, 142, 143-44, 145, 147-49, 156; conclusions and summary, 194-97; contradiction between Western influence and established Soviet system, 146-47; de-Stalinization, effects of, 139-40, 157, 158; dissident labor organizations, role of, 159; dynamic process of reform-repression, 137, 138; elites and continuing revolution, 141-42, 159-60; elites and repression of dissidence, 159-60; generals, role of, 159; hope for change, 156-57; ideological commitments of Soviet leaders, 152-55, 157, 158-59; intellectuals, role of, 145-47, 156, 159; Iranian revolution, impact of, 156; Khrushchev era, 139, 140, 147, 152, 153, 156, 157; means of repression, 144-45; media, impact of, 155-56; military power and aggression of Soviet Union, 154; new generation's views, 158; official reform measures, 142-43; official and unofficial spokesman for reform, 138; party policy, 141, 142; pervasive political power vs. perceived abuses in policies, 140-41; post-Khrushchev era, 157-58; post-Stalinist reform, effects of, 138, 139, 140, 141, 142, 143, 144, 145, 147, 152, 155; reimposition of controls, 144, 147; revolutionary change in society, scope and pace of, 138-40; Soviet foreign policy and ideology, 153-55; suggestions for Western policies, 147-49; tactics for, 158-59; "transfer-goal culture," USSR as, 157; unofficial reform discussion, 143–44; West's impact on, 138, 145-46

—, religious dissent, status, interrelationships and future potential of, 115-36; conclusions and summary, 194-97; current prosecutions, 134-35; estimate of Orthodox believers, 134; external support for dissenters, 133-34; future potential of, 127-28; genesis, scope and social base of, 116-19; impact of dissent on state and society, 125-27; introduction to, 115-16; movements for political and national rights and, 123-25; Muslim Brotherhood, role of, 135-36; and Russian nationalism, 135; strategies of dissent, 119-22; and unusual strength of Lithuanian Church, 135

"vanguard party," 44
Vasko, T., 169
Venezuela, summary of, 304-305
Viekhi, 181
Vietnam: aftereffects on U.S.-USSR struggle, 89-90; summary of, 305-306
Vins, Georgii, 126
Voice of America, 99, 174
voting: compulsory, as denial of freedom, 71; as process derived from natural law concept of equality, 79; right to, 7
Vynnytskyi, Mykhailo, 127

war, liberalized USSR and, 90-91
Warsaw Pact, 154

Western Civilization: Berger's hypothesis about, 78, 79; freedom and group rights in, 80
Western democracies. *See* democracy
Western Samoa, summary of, 306
Wittfogel, Karl, 154
women: relative freedom of, 204; secondary status of, 78; voting rights, gaining of, 79
Working Commission to Investigate the Abuse of Psychiatry for Political Purposes (USSR), 123
World Administrative Radio Conference (WARC), 184
World Baptist Association, 133
World Congress of the International Political Science Association (Moscow, 1979), 170, 171
World Council of Churches, 133; religious dissent in USSR and, 122
World Population Data Sheet of the Population Reference Bureau, 1978, 205n

Yemen, North, summary of, 306-307
Yemen, South, 29; summary of, 307
Yevtushenko, Y., 158
Yugoslavia: decentralization of power in, 108; summary of, 307-308

Zaire, summary of, 308-309
zakonnost (rule of law), in USSR, 120
Zambia, summary of, 310
Zheludkov, Sergii, 117
Zinoviev, Alexander, x